Arnulfo L. Oliveira Memorial Library

EVIL

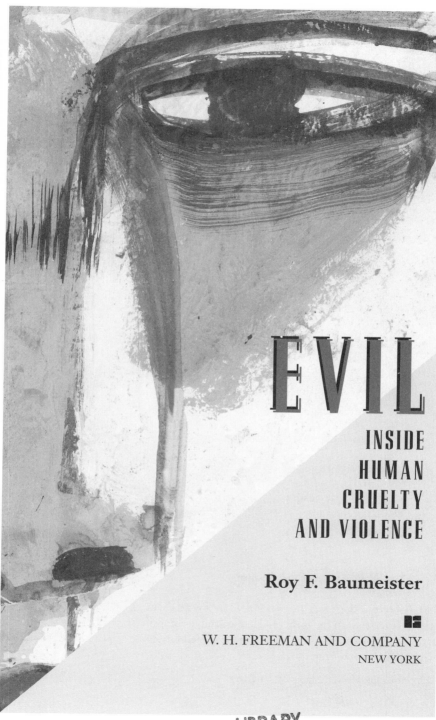

EVIL

INSIDE HUMAN CRUELTY AND VIOLENCE

Roy F. Baumeister

W. H. FREEMAN AND COMPANY

NEW YORK

COVER DESIGN: Pixel Press

INTERIOR DESIGN: Victoria Tomaselli

Library of Congress Cataloging-in-Publication Data

Baumeister, Roy F.
    Evil : inside human cruelty and violence / Roy F. Baumeister.
        p. cm.
    Includes bibliographical references and index.
    ISBN 0-7167-2902-4
    1. Good and evil--Psychological aspects. I. Title.
BF789.E94B38 1996
155.2'32--dc20   96-41940
                                                                          CIP

Printed in the United States of America

First printing 1996, RRD

Contents

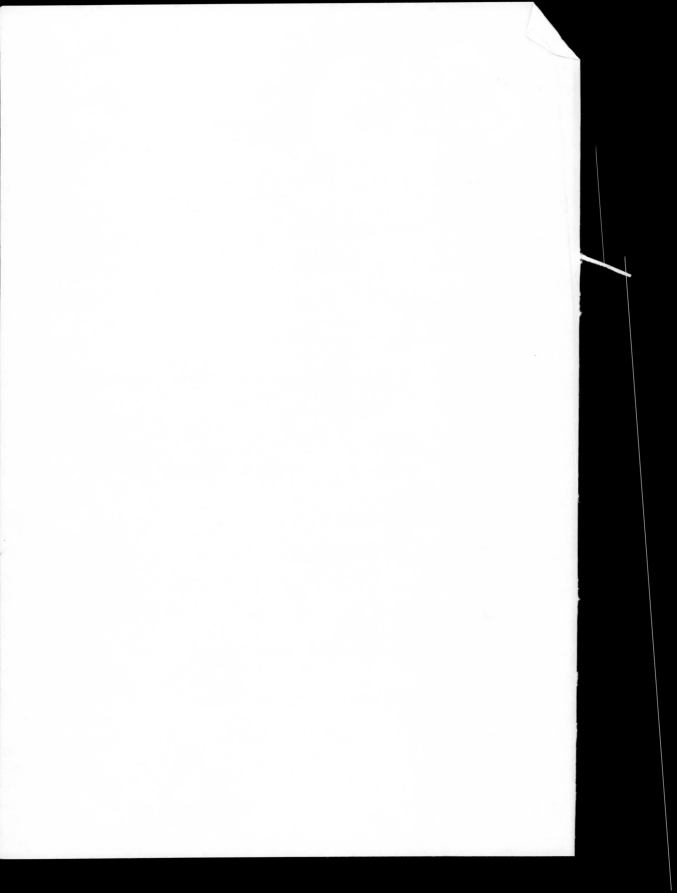

Preface

Why is there evil? What motivates those who perpetrate it? How do they manage to reconcile their actions with a self-image that does not embrace evil? This book uses the very modern methods of social science to answer these ancient questions. Our efforts to understand evil are fraught with difficulties. One prominent one is that perpetrators tend to ignore or downplay the moral dimension of their actions—a dimension that is starkly salient to victims. As a result, any sincere effort to understand perpetrators will be somewhat insensitive to the victims. The danger in this is that it might lead us to condone the perpetrators' actions. Moralistic thinking must not be canceled or forgotten but it has to be postponed for us to understand how the perpetrators view their world and their actions.

A consequence of this approach is that the considerable emotional, political, and ideological baggage that attends our cultural views of evil must be thrown overboard, at least temporarily, and the resulting analysis may offend people. This book cannot be "politically correct." One scholar who read a draft of Evil commented that by the middle of the first chapter I will have probably outraged both the far left and the far right. I have not sought to be outrageous, but if I am successful at formulating an insider's view of cruelty and violence, the results are likely to be upsetting. As you will see, our culturally-dominant view of evil is very different from the actual psychology of the perpetrators.

Evil: Inside Human Cruelty and Violence is based on an extensive survey of previous writings about the subject, but I suspect that some readers may find that their favorite theoretical works on evil have been neglected. In the social sciences, ideas are cheap but facts are precious. I sought to build a theory based on all the facts and findings I could gather, so I have not made a systematic effort to cover what theorists have had to say about evil. Some of my conclusions may have been anticipated by previous theories; others perhaps, are new. I hoped that staying scrupulously attentive and faithful to the mass of factual evidence would yield the most correct conclusions possible. Those who have addressed this topic in the past were undoubtedly able to reach some of these conclusions with less evidence; but a conclusion based on a mountain of evidence is different, and in important ways more useful, from one based on intuition, personal experience, or a small or unreliable amount of evidence.

There is another side to my emphasis on facts. I have, mostly, resisted the constant temptation to illustrate key points with episodes from literature, movies, and other fictional entertainments. Many books on evil are filled with such illustrations and some do not even seem to regard as meaningful the difference between, say, something said by Macbeth versus something said by Ted Bundy. I concluded fairly early in the project, however, that because our cultural ideas about evil are so powerful and so discrepant from the actual psychology of the perpetrators, fictional illustrations were often worse than useless. Therefore, I have used fictional examples only when discussing the constructed "myth" of evil. The rest of the book, which focuses on the actual psychology of the perpetrators, relies exclusively on true stories (and other facts) to illustrate its points. This made *Evil* considerably harder to write, because it is quite difficult to find factual examples instead of the easily available fictional ones, but it seemed essential to me.

The writing style of this book also deserves comment. Perpetrators tend to favor minimalist, distancing styles of thought. So, any effort to understand them must appreciate these linguistic tendencies, again, at the expense of downplaying the victims' suffering. Indeed, that is probably the point: In most cases, perpetrators do not wish to dwell on the victims' suffering; to do so would be disruptive to their work. At the same time, it is occasionally necessary to employ more vivid language to help one see evil where it is frequently overlooked.

My goal in writing this book was to encourage, seduce, and perhaps trick you into seeing events from the perspective of the perpetrators of evil. Of course, identifying with evil is the first step toward perpetrating it, so it is necessary to step back out of that role once one is in it! The hardest part in understanding the nature of evil is to first recognize that you or I *could*, under certain circumstances, commit many of the acts that the world has come to regard as evil. But as long as we continue to regard evildoers as a separate species, an alien category, or a wholly different type of human being, we cannot really claim to understand them. Our best hope of avoiding that fate is to learn to understand and recognize these reactions, so that we may be able to recognize them as evil before we commit them—this book is devoted to that hope.

I wish to thank the many people who have helped with this project, particularly by reading drafts and providing valuable advice and comments. These included John Darley, Richard Felson, Brad Bushman, Dianne Tice, Kristin Sommer, Donna Baumeister, and Julie Exline. The students in my Interdisciplinary Psychology class during the fall of 1995 read the full draft as well and gave valuable help and suggestions (usually egging me on to make the examples more explicit and vivid!). Laura Smart and Joe Boden worked with me on a journal manuscript that formed the basis for one of the chapters, and Lisa Macharoni provided considerable help in getting some of the scholarly chores done.

Institutional support was also quite welcome and helpful. Case Western Reserve University provided technical and library support as well as the time for scholarly work, including a sabbatical leave. The department of psychology, under the leadership of chairpersons Joe Fagan and Sandra Russ, has been supportive and helpful, and Dean John Bassett provided the funds to purchase the computer on which this book was written. The University of Virginia's psychology department was also generous in its support as host of my sabbatical. A research grant from the National Institute of Mental Health (MH 51482) provided some support during the time period I worked on this book, and a sabbatical grant from the James McKeen Cattell Fund helped me get started.

Two debts of gratitude are especially large. The first is to my editor, Susan Finnemore Brennan, and her colleagues at W. H. Freeman and Company. Working with them was a pleasure, as well as being intellectually very satisfying and stimulating. The other is to my beloved wife, Dianne Tice, who provided considerable support, intellectual and otherwise, throughout the years of work on the project.

The Question of Evil, and the Answers

Why is there evil? The question has bedeviled humanity for centuries. If there were a single, simple answer, we probably would have had it long ago. So we need not only to look for an answer but also to understand why the question has persisted despite the efforts of many wise men and women to answer it.

Evil usually enters the world unrecognized by the people who open the door and let it in. Most people who perpetrate evil do not see what they are doing as evil. Evil exists primarily in the eye of the beholder, especially in the eye of the victim. If there were no victims, there would be no evil. True, there are victimless crimes (for example, many traffic violations), and presumably victimless sins, but they exist as marginal categories of something that is defined mainly by the doing of harm. Try to imagine a society in which nobody ever did anything that had any sort of bad effect on anyone else. What would the police have to do? Would there even be police?

If victimization is the essence of evil, then the question of evil is a victim's question. Perpetrators, after all, do not need to search for explanations of what they have done. And bystanders are merely curious or sympathetic. It is the victims who are driven to ask, why did this happen? Why did those soldiers shoot my family? Why did that woman plant a bomb on that bus? Why did those boys beat me up? Why did my grandfather force me to have sex with him? As a general pattern, suffering stimulates a quest for meaningful explanation.[1] The idea that suffering is random, inevitable, and meaningless has never been satisfactory to most people, and victims desire specific explanations. Evil is a partial explanation, and many victims can be satisfied (at least for a while) by concluding that their attackers were evil. But in the long run, evil needs to be explained, too.

Evil challenges some of our most basic and important assumptions about the world, and so the question of why there is evil goes to the heart of the human being's place in the universe. The great thinker St. Thomas Aquinas wrote that the existence of evil in the world is the single greatest obstacle to Christian faith and doctrine.[2] In other words, nothing undermines the Christian belief in God more than the existence of evil. If God is all-good and all-powerful, how can God allow evil to happen?

More recently, studies by social scientists have emphasized that most people in modern Western society go through life with strong positive beliefs that the world is basically a nice place in which to live, that life is mostly fair, and that they are good people who deserve to have good things happen to them.[3] Moreover, these beliefs are a valuable aid to happy, healthy functioning. But suffering and victimization undermine these beliefs and make it hard to go on living happily or effectively in society. Indeed, the direct and practical effects of some trauma or crime are often relatively minor, whereas the psychological effects go on indefinitely. The body may recover from rape or robbery rather quickly, but the psychological scars can last for many years. A characteristic of these scars is that the victims lose faith in their basic beliefs about the world as fair and benevolent or even in themselves as good people. Thus, evil strikes at people's fundamental beliefs.

Questions beginning with "Why . . ." can be answered in several ways. One way is to describe a reasoned or intentional purpose that evil actions serve, on the assumption that the actions are taken to serve this purpose. Another is to explain them in moral terms. Yet another is to explain their causes. Many written works have dealt with the question of why evil exists in theological terms; these works tend to emphasize the possible function of evil in the cosmos and the divine reason for permitting it to exist.

This book will try to give a causal answer. The mode of explanation will not be theological or moral but scientific—more precisely, I will use the approach of social science. I will not try to defend or justify the existence of evil but merely to explain how it happens to come into the world. How evil enters the world is a question with three parts. First, how do the particular events come to happen? Second, what leads people to perceive events as evil? Third, because it will soon become apparent that people's perceptions of evil often differ greatly from the reality, what accounts for the wide gap between the perceptions and the reality of evil?

A Brush with Evil

There wasn't much time. She was hungry, but her flight would be boarding soon. Sometimes flights just worked out so that you got nothing to eat all day, and she really wanted something. As luck would have it, there was a small place open near her gate. She stood in line and bought a bag of chips and a diet cola.

But all the tables in the small airport cafeteria were full. There was not a single free table. She'd have to share with somebody who already had one.

She spotted a likely prospect: a reasonably well dressed man sitting by himself at a small table, reading a paper. Certainly he would not mind if she sat at one of the empty seats at his table and quietly ate her snack.

She sat down. They briefly made eye contact; he seemed to nod slightly and then went back to his paper. She was nervous for no apparent reason. She busied herself with her snack. She set down her diet cola, unwrapped the straw, inserted it in the slot, and had her first sip. Then another. Then she had a chip.

When her mouth crunched on the first chip, the man suddenly looked up from his newspaper. He looked angry, intent, alert, vaguely dangerous. He fixed his eyes on hers, violent, like a predator seeing prey. And then, amazingly, he slowly reached out his hand into her bag of chips, extracted one, brought it to his mouth, and ate it!

Her heart began to beat rapidly. A crazy impulse told her to flee, abandon her food to this man and save herself. She took another drink and then made herself take another chip from her bag and eat it. He glared at her, motionless. It was a hostile, evil glare. What had at first struck her as a calm, middle-aged gentleman now appeared as a dangerous individual, capable of unknown things. As she finished chewing her chip, he reached out and took another himself. Now she knew he was not just helping himself one time, as if to say she owed him a chip for sitting at his table. Now he was totally outside the bounds of normal etiquette between strangers. What sort of person was this?

They finished the bag, not speaking a single word but intently taking turns drawing chips. He looked at her the whole time; she didn't know whether to meet his gaze or to look away, so she alternated. She took big gulps of her drink. Soon it was nearly gone and the bag was nearly empty, too. She had had enough. She stood up, nodded, looked away from him, picked up her bags, and walked quickly out of the place. She got to her gate a few minutes early and sat in the waiting area, heart pounding, still unable to grasp what had just happened, what manner of creature she had just encountered. What sort of people just help themselves to a stranger's food in a restaurant?

She learned the answer sooner than she expected. They called passengers to board the plane, and she got right in line. When she came to the front of the line, she reached into her bag for her ticket. It was there, and next to it was her bag of chips. Somehow, when she paid for the snack, she had put her chips into her flight bag, and at the table she and the mysterious stranger had shared his chips, not hers. She herself was the sort of person who just helped herself to a stranger's food in a restaurant.

This minor story illustrates that evil is in the eye of the beholder. For a while, the woman saw the face of the man sitting across from her as evil. In retrospect, there was no reason to think there was anything evil about him. When she believed herself to be the victim, she saw him as evil. In this case it was a mistake, an illusion. Indeed, the man probably saw *her* as evil, at least mildly so. He was eating and reading, and a stranger sat down uninvited at his table and helped herself to his food. In any case, though, if there was evil present at that table, it was not glimpsed by the perpetrators. It was only recognized by the victims. This discrepancy is very common, even with genuine and serious evil.

The woman herself was the one who acted outrageously, yet she was horrified that anyone would do such a thing as take someone else's food in an airport. The challenge of this book is to understand how perpetrators come to do things that others see as evil. In this case, it was an honest mistake and an accident, but most of the world's evil cannot be explained away so easily.

Had you asked the woman if she would ever take a stranger's food in an airport restaurant, she probably would have said no. The same response is likely to be elicited by almost any hypothetical question about evil. Would you obey orders to kill innocent civilians? Would you help torture someone? Would you stand by passively while the secret police hauled your neighbors off to concentration camps? Most people say no.[4] But when such events actually happen, the reality is quite different.

Understanding evil begins with the realization that we ourselves are capable of doing many of these things. Ordinary, normal people have done a great many evil things, and sometimes the majority of those present have acquiesced. To understand evil, we must set aside the comfortable belief that we would never do anything wrong. Instead, we must begin to ask ourselves, what would it take for *me* to do such things? Assume that it would be possible.

The airport story hints at two core aspects of evil. The first is the infliction of harm by one person on another. In this case, of course, the harm was quite trivial—the deprivation of a few potato chips. In most cases worthy of being called evil, the victim has far more at stake. The second aspect is chaos—the violation of the friendly, orderly, comprehensible world. The woman was not upset over the loss of a few potato chips. She was upset because what was happening seemed utterly outside her conception of how decent people interact with one another. She felt that she had encountered a creature alien to her world.

Next, let us tackle the question of what is to be called evil.

What Is Evil?

At one point my wife and I discussed the possibility of adopting a child. Ever since my experience of living in a foreign country with a local family, I have been enthusiastic about diversity in families. My wife and I discovered that we both favored adopting a black child. We are both white, highly educated, and financially comfortable, and we thought we could give a child a very good head start in life. We thought that bringing up a privileged, well-educated black child might be of more value to society than rearing a privileged, well-educated white one.

Fortunately, our discussions of adoption never moved beyond vague speculation. I say "fortunately" because to many people it would have been supremely evil for us to adopt a black child. Indeed, the National

Association of Black Social Workers declared that the adoption of black babies by white parents is a form of genocide.[5] My wife and I would have been led by our seemingly innocent idealism into such an atrocity. We thought of it as lavishing love and a few advantages on a child who might turn out to help society and heal racial differences. Some people, though, would regard us as no different from the folks who stand out in the blood-stained and foul-smelling fields, holding machine guns or machetes, methodically killing long lines of people simply because of the ethnic group to which they belong.

I am not saying that I agree with the opinion that interracial adoption is a form of genocide; in fact, if national policy were up to me, I would make it the norm (in all combinations) rather than the exception. But again, evil is in the eye of the beholder. I might think of what I was doing as acceptable and even positively good, but in this I would be no different from many other agents of genocide who think they are making the world a better place. Evil is but rarely found in the perpetrator's own self-image. It is far more commonly found in the judgments of others.

The reliance on judgments by others is essential. Indeed, if we limited our examination of evil to acts that perpetrators themselves acknowledge as evil, there would be hardly any such acts to examine. For example, Frederick Treesh, a spree killer, was captured after a shoot-out with police in August 1994. During the previous two weeks, he had carried out several bank and store robberies and armed carjackings. He did not think he had done anything so bad: "Other than the two we killed, the two we wounded, the woman we pistol-whipped and the light bulbs we stuck in people's mouths, we didn't really hurt anybody."[6] Or consider the act of raping an 11-year-old girl, which most people would regard as evil. Such a rape was committed recently by a 14-year-old boy, whose lawyer saw no evil: "They were two kids with nothing better to do. They don't have cable TV, what do you do?"[7]

There is wide variation in the use and definition of the word *evil*. Even more precise terms such as *genocide* have very different meanings. For the National Association of Black Social Workers, genocide meant white parents adopting black children. The Reverend Al Page used the term to condemn the University of Virginia's plan to develop a residential neighborhood.[8] By such criteria, genocides are everywhere. In contrast, Alain Destexhe, the secretary-general of the international service organization Doctors Without Borders, wrote in 1994 that only three events in the twentieth century counted as true genocides according to the official United Nations definition: the Ottoman Turks' massacre of the Armenians in 1915–1917, the Nazi Germans' campaign against Jews during the Second World War, and the efforts by Hutu extremists to exterminate the Tutsi in Rwanda during the 1990s.[9] Destexhe specifically criticized "the growing use of the term 'genocide' without proper regard for its true meaning."

If it is that hard to agree on what genocide is, it is even harder to find a definition of evil that will satisfy everyone. Many people will see the term *evil* as too grandiose or as referring to mystical, supernatural, or otherwise esoteric phenomena. The term has an air of anachronism, especially as belief in Satan fades from our culture.[10] According to the *Oxford English Dictionary*, people hardly use the word *evil* anymore in everyday conversation.[11] When they do, they are often mocked, as happened recently when the general manager of the Montreal Expos baseball team was quoted as saying that professional baseball has come under the control of Satan. When these comments attracted broad attention and he was asked to elaborate, he said that "the forces of evil and darkness have a major influence on society—and baseball is a microcosm of society."[12] Several scholars, however, have called for more serious usage of the term and more willingness to recognize evil as such.[13]

Even less grandiose terms such as *bad* are fraught with multiple and conflicting meanings. Over the past two decades, *bad* has gradually acquired the connotation of a compliment and hence means *good* in some sense. Thus, one might describe a saxophone solo as "bad" and mean it as admiring praise. Similarly, students at the University of Arkansas like to wear T-shirts with pictures of a giant pig and the inscription "We bad." This is not a statement of low collective self-esteem or loyalty to Satan. The pig is the sports teams' mascot, and the "We bad" message is a boastful assertion of intimidating superiority over rivals.

In this book, I will use a broad, inclusive definition of evil. The one major restriction is that we are concerned here with evil acts by human beings. Some people might wish to regard such phenomena as earthquakes and epidemics as evil, but explaining how natural disasters occur is outside the purview of the social sciences. This work is concerned with human evil. It may be useful to consider occasional examples or findings that involve nonhuman perpetrators, but only insofar as they help to shed light on human ones. The most common and familiar form of human evil is violence, and that will be emphasized, although other forms of human evil such as oppression and petty cruelty will also be considered.

If I were approaching this work as a philosopher or a theologian, it would be of consummate importance to produce a very compelling and elegant definition of evil, a definition that would be sufficient to decide every possible case. Precise conceptual definitions are the stock-in-trade of philosophers. This book, however, is a work of social science, and science can work with fuzzy sets and gray areas. To explain the causes and processes of evil, it is sufficient to identify the main, prototypical cases.

The prototypes of human evil involve actions that intentionally harm other people. Those will be the focus of the book. Defining evil as intentional interpersonal harm leaves many gray areas. Some people may try but fail to inflict harm, and their would-be victims would never know to accuse them of evil. Surgeons may inflict pain to help their patients, and prostitutes may perform spankings to stimulate their clients, but neither group would be understood as evil. Accidental or unintended harm may seem evil to the victim but probably would not be judged as such by a dispassionate observer. A particular problem is that victims and perpetrators are often far apart in their judgments of what the perpetrator's intentions and motives were. Still, we will remain with the rough guideline that evil is in the eye of the beholder, and if someone believes that another person has intentionally harmed him or her, it is fair to speak of evil and to include it among the phenomena that this book must explain.

In addition to ruling out natural disasters, we will not use insanity as a satisfactory explanation of evil. Acts of intentional harm committed because of genuine insanity will not be covered. Despite the appeal of using "temporary insanity" to explain violent crimes, I share the widespread[14] opinion that insanity is in fact a relatively rare and minor cause of violence. People do become extremely upset and abandon self-control, with violent results, but this is not insanity. Loss of self-control resulting from emotional distress will be covered as an important factor in evil; psychosis will not.

The grandiosity of the term *evil* also deserves comment. I have used it because it is the traditional term and it is important to connect my analysis with the ancient and fundamental questions about human life. But the discussion will not be restricted to great crimes and horrendous acts, although plenty of them will be featured. It is also important to understand the petty cruelties and minor transgressions of everyday life, at least insofar as they involve deliberate interpersonal harm.

There is immense heuristic value in including everyday offenses in this investigation, because more is known about them. Mass murder is much more powerful than breaking a minor promise to a friend, but it is also much less common. In addition, social scientists can study broken promises much more thoroughly and easily than they can study mass murder. The crucial assumption is that the causal processes have something in common—that learning about why people break promises can tell us something about why people commit mass murder. We must watch this assumption carefully to see if evidence contradicts it, but as a working assumption it is reasonable and hence greatly increases the chances of finding reliable answers.

Once More, without Feeling

Accustomed to looking at things through the eyes of victims, we tend to assume that killings and other violent acts must be accompanied by immense emotional turmoil. Certainly, some people do commit murder in a state of extreme rage or distress. But others do not. The emotions of the victims are not a valid guide to those of the perpetrators, and indeed perpetrators may feel little or no emotions at all.

Historian David Stannard quoted the following story told by a cavalry major who was reporting to Congress on the Indian wars in Colorado in 1864. One fine morning the soldiers came upon an Indian village and attacked it. Actually, the braves were mostly gone; it was just old folks and women and children. The officer recalled seeing a particular child, "about three years old, just big enough to walk through the sand," running along after some of the Indians who were fleeing the massacre. The major watched one cavalryman get down off his horse, aim his rifle, and shoot, but he missed the child, who was toddling along the sand about 75 yards away. Another man rode up and said, "Let me try the son of a bitch; I can hit him." He dismounted and fired from a kneeling position, but despite his boast he too missed the small moving target. A third man came up and expressed confidence that he could be more accurate. He took careful aim and fired, "and the little fellow dropped."[15]

It is natural to react with sadness and disapproval to this story. Stannard invites the reader to think about the now long forgotten little boy who probably liked to run and play by the stream, whose life with his parents and neighbors may have been full of excitement and promise until American soldiers came by and shot him dead, along with everyone he knew. One is especially shocked at the attitude of the soldiers. They are engaged in an egotistical discussion about their respective rifle skills, and their conversation treats shooting a little boy as a form of macho competition instead of a horrific act of genocidal cruelty.

I don't wish to discourage moral outrage; such acts must be recognized and condemned as evil. But that is not the focus of this book. Instead, we want to understand how ordinary people can do such things. There is no reason to think that the soldier who shot the little boy was a deranged psychopath or criminal. Indeed, three soldiers took shots at the boy before bringing him down. The apparent sense of ordinariness with which the soldiers acted is an important clue to the mental state of people who commit such acts. We have to assume that they were ordinary young American males, not unlike boys who might grow up in a nearby suburb today, playing ball for their school team. Two key themes are suggested in the soldiers' attitude.

First, they seem to have regarded shooting that child as an ordinary and unremarkable action. The one man's reference to the boy as a "son of a bitch" did not seem to reflect any rage toward the child but rather was a remark sympathetic to the other soldier's frustration at having missed, an acknowledgement of the difficulty of hitting a small moving target at that distance. The men were not talking about how awful it was to kill children, nor were they acting with demented glee or sadistic pleasure at the killings. It is an attitude devoid of moral reflection or profound emotion: a matter-of-fact attitude. It is an attitude a group of men might have while trying to tighten a plumbing fixture so it will stop leaking. Indeed, the soldiers seemed to be preoccupied with the marksmanship competition, which suggests an effort to liven up a dull and routine task. As we will see, this is an attitude more common of experienced killers than of novices. Typically, a first killing is psychologically difficult and upsetting, even traumatic. Somehow, though, people can get used to killing, so that it produces less and less reaction.

The marksmanship competition brings up the second key point, which is egotism. Each man arrived with a boast. Each was focused on impressing and outdoing his fellows. The boy's survival was a blow to each shooter's ego. Take the scene out of context: There were three men standing together, and one of them shot a three-year-old boy to death, and he was the winner. The others would have to concede his superior performance. They had fired and missed, whereas he had scored. We will see that egotism is an important and pervasive cause of evil. Unlike this case, though, egotism usually causes evil because people strike out at those who insult, criticize, or humiliate them.

In the midst of moral outrage, we can be further shocked that the soldiers would be preoccupied with winning a little informal competition among themselves. But I propose that such an attitude is actually quite an important way that people cope with performing such actions. For soldiers to dwell on moral issues and human sympathy would make it very stressful for them to carry out these duties. If we want to understand how evil happens, it will be necessary to recognize that these unemotional, problem-solving attitudes and petty egotistical games may be important. We will see that sensitive perpetrators often suffer nightmares, anxiety attacks, debilitating guilt, gastrointestinal problems, and many other signs of stress. Hence perpetrators are better off if they are not sensitive. To focus on playing such games is one way to make the job easier and less upsetting.

Impulse and Commitment

One day in Los Angeles, young Kody Scott was informed by his girlfriend Tamu that she was pregnant. He wasn't at all ready to face this fact. He did like her very much, but he didn't want to settle down and have obligations. He felt like he was just a kid himself.[16]

Kody had joined a street gang the same day he graduated from elementary school. The gang initiation meant a lot more to him than the grade school ceremony. His gang nickname was Monster. He was doing well in the gang and didn't want to sacrifice that career to raise a child. This sense of conflicting obligations ate away at him for several months. He was needed to protect the neighborhood from its enemies; but he also shouldn't desert his girl, not to mention the baby who "would be a totally innocent party in this matter and deserved a fair chance," as he said thoughtfully. He felt the pull of both calls to duty.

Summer came, and one day he got a call from Tamu: "I'm in labor," she said. Then she asked in a scared voice whether he was coming. "Yeah", he said, feeling the conflicting pulls on him reaching a crisis. By now he was a big man, with other gangs' death threats against him spray-painted on various nearby walls. So he took his gun along.

There was no convenient way to get to the hospital; the best way was to walk down to the main street and take a car from there. He made the walk, full of his confused thoughts. Having a baby? When a car stopped at the light, he stuck his pistol in the driver's chest and told him to get out of the car. The driver obeyed, and young Kody drove off toward the hospital.

But he didn't want to get there too soon; he wanted to delay the moment of commitment a little bit longer. He took a detour through the neighborhood of one of the enemy gangs. There he saw one of his main enemies, a teenager nicknamed Bank Robber, walking along by himself. Thinking he was safe in his own neighborhood, Bank Robber was not on guard, not watching out.

Kody drove around the corner and parked. The other young man was walking right toward him without realizing it. Now it was really time to decide. Young Kody thought very hard for several minutes, about his place in the world, about what life meant to him, about who mattered most to him, about birth and death. These thoughts bounced through his head in an intense moment while his girlfriend was giving birth to his child and while an enemy walked directly toward him. He recalled feeling his mind stretch to encompass the full situation, and he felt true freedom for the first time.

The other fellow was walking right by the car. Kody called out to him to ask for a light. When Bank Robber reached into his pocket for matches, Kody told him to say his prayers and shot him twice in the chest. Bank Robber's corpse lay warm and bleeding on the street while Kody sped off in his stolen car. He drove home, went to his room, and turned on the TV. He watched "The Benny Hill Show" to wind down the evening before turning in. He had made his decision.

Kody's story differs in several respects from that of the cavalry soldiers in the Indian massacre. They seemed simply to be doing a job, whereas he was engrossed in broad, heavy thoughts before this murder. His story reveals the shift in level of thinking that often accompanies violence. He had been debating broad issues of commitment, love, obligation, and his place in the world. After the killing, however, his thoughts did not return to that level. Indeed, he went home and watched a low-budget rerun of comedy skits on television. The girlfriend giving birth to his son did not even get a phone call to say he would not be coming after all. After the crime, he left off the meaningful, reflective thinking and instead focused on mundane, trivial distractions.

The broad choice Kody was debating is a prototype of the choice between good and evil. On the one hand, he felt pulled toward settling down with a woman and child to live an orderly life and take care of his family. On the other, he was drawn toward a violent, dangerous life outside the law. As I have stated, the two core elements of evil are intentional violence and chaos, and the gang life meant both. It meant lethal fighting, and it meant rejecting the orderly, rational life that society offered.

It is also noteworthy that Kody knew his victim. The stereotype of evil, nurtured by crime stories in the modern mass media, depicts malicious intruders seeking innocent strangers almost at random. Such crimes do occur, but in the United States today, people are far more commonly victimized by people who know them than by strangers. This is particularly true for women, but it is also true for men. Despite the recent surge in stranger violence, people are most likely to suffer murder, beatings, and rape at the hands of acquaintances, relatives, and even family members.

This episode from Kody Scott's life also raises the question of choice and the related issues of self-control. One theme of this book, which will be considered carefully in Chapters 8 and 9, is that violence is often an impulsive action representing a failure of self-control—but a failure in which the person often acquiesces. Scott's killing of the other young man was neither a premeditated action nor an irresistible impulse. Rather, it was an impulsive crime that he allowed to happen, and indeed it is apparent that he helped it happen. He did not intend to go looking for trouble when he set out that evening, and he did not even think of Bank Robber until very shortly before he killed him. When he left his home and stole a car, he was intending to go to the hospital, and only an impulse and an accidental encounter gave him the opportunity to kill someone. In that sense it was an impulsive crime.

On the other hand, his detour through the enemy neighborhood was not a pure accident. To use the familiar phrase, Scott "accidentally on purpose" put himself in the position where he was confronted by a personal enemy, and then once he found himself in that situation he responded in standard fashion. The episode was neither planned nor accidental. To ask whether violent perpetrators intended to be violent is a question that often cannot be answered with a simple yes or no. In many cases, they choose or arrange situations in which they will feel that they have no choice. Self-control is thus thwarted.

Self-control will play an important role in my analysis of evil. One starts a work like this wondering "Why is there evil?" But after reviewing what is known about the causes of aggression, violence, oppression, and other forms of evil, one is led to the opposite question: Why isn't there more evil than there is? Suppose it were true that frustration, violent movies, poverty, hot weather, alcohol, and unfair treatment all cause aggression, as prominent theories have claimed. Then why wouldn't almost every adult in America have committed several murders and dozens of assaults by now? After all, how many adult Americans have not been frustrated? Have not seen violent films? Have not felt poor or suffered from hot weather or so forth?

The answer is that most violent impulses are held back by forces inside the person. In a word, self-control prevents a great deal of potential violence. Therefore, regardless of the *root* causes of violence, the *immediate* cause is often a breakdown of self-control.

This fact has important implications for understanding the spread of violence in the world. When evil increases, it does not necessarily mean that the causes of evil have become more powerful or important. Rather, it may mean that the inner controls have become weakened. Or, to put it another way: You do not have to give people reasons to be violent, because they already have plenty of reasons. All you have to do is take away their reasons to restrain themselves. Even a small weakening of self-control might be enough to produce a rise in violence. Evil is always ready and waiting to burst into the world.

The violence of inner-city residents, especially of poor young black men, has prompted various controversial theories about whether the particular social environment or the inborn genetic nature produces violence. The question of nature versus nurture is an important one in any effort to understand evil. Scott's memoir illustrates some valuable relevant points that lend support to opposite sides of the debate and suggest that any final theory may have to invoke both nature and culture.

The role of the social environment is clear, particularly from an important change in Scott's life that took place some years after the killing of Bank Robber. Scott spent some years in prison (although not for killing Bank Robber), and when he got out he was ready to resume the bitter and deadly rivalries with nearby neighborhoods. He discovered, however, that everything had changed and that former enemies were now often on friendly and casual terms. The reason for the change was that crack cocaine had appeared on the scene, and the young men were mostly busy selling it instead of shooting at one another. Now, it is ironic to think that the drug trade would reduce violence, because certainly drugs have been implicated in increasing violence in some circumstances, but in this case (and apparently many others), drugs simply meant a very profitable business opportunity, and violent shoot-outs were discouraged as being bad for business.[17]

Thus, a small change in the structure of economic opportunity led to a substantial reduction in violent incidents. Indeed, although the American mainstream regards drugs as a foreign and evil force intruding into our nation, it does not take much thought to realize that to these young black men, selling drugs is simply the latest form of American bootstrap capitalism. Scott is quite vehement in his book that young black people feel excluded from the American dream, that the so-called land of opportunity offers no opportunities for them—and that the option of selling drugs offers a way to make very good money by marketing a product that is much in demand. For decades, such young men devoted their lives to their violent, deadly rivalries, but when an opportunity to make money appeared, many of them abandoned the violence. Thus, patterns of violence do change in major ways due to relatively small changes in the social environment.

Still, it would be premature to exclude nature from any theory about violence. Scott's memoir describes plenty of violent activity by himself and his friends—but mainly his male friends. Given the present state of knowledge, there is plenty of room to debate whether the races differ in violent tendencies, but there is much less latitude for arguing about sex differences. All over the world, and throughout history, by far the vast majority of violent acts have been committed by young males. If male aggression were simply a product of culture and socialization, as many theorists believed in the 1960s and 1970s, one would expect to find some cultures in which females are more aggressive, just by chance variation. Moreover, one would expect changes in socialization (such as the increase in mother-only households, which give women increased control over the socialization of children) to have reduced or eliminated male aggressiveness. But the facts do not fit such theories. There is no culture in which the most aggressive trouble-prone group is, say, middle-aged women. As the evidence about male aggression continues to accumulate, it is increasingly difficult to deny that some natural or genetic component plays a role.[18]

Aggression is probably a product of the interaction of nature and nurture. The universality of some patterns, such as young male aggressiveness, suggests that nature has programmed aggression to be more pronounced in some groups than in others. Yet aggression and violence seem to be quite sensitive to many factors in the social environment. Changing the environment will probably not be enough to eliminate violence completely, but it can increase or decrease it and can channel it into particular patterns. The net effect on local mayhem could be substantial. By the same token, aggression does not erupt randomly as a product of inner forces and processes but occurs in certain situations and is a meaningful response to them.

True Crime and False

Small towns in South Carolina are not accustomed to receiving national media attention, but one of them abruptly became the center of such attention on an autumn day in 1994 when a distraught, pretty, 23-year-old blonde woman told police that her car had been stolen at gunpoint by a black man—with her two little sons strapped in the back seat. As Susan told the authorities and reporters, she had been stopped at a traffic light when the man pulled a gun and ordered her out of the car. She asked him to wait long enough to get her children out of the back seat, but he said he did not have time, pushed her out of the car, and drove off.[19]

A massive hunt began for the car, the little boys, and the black man, with national media coverage and tips coming in even from the other side of the continent. Sympathy poured in as people felt for the young mother's pain and were appalled by the sensational nature of the crime. Car theft is a familiar offense, but the random and threatening way it was done alarmed people, and kidnapping two little boys seemed so needless and senseless. Parents all over the country worried at the thought of anonymous gunmen, especially gunmen of another race, speeding away in stolen cars with the owners' children strapped into the back seat. These facts held people's interest for the tense days during which the leads and tips led nowhere and the hope of finding the boys alive dwindled.

This titillating crime then turned out to have been a mirage. A week later, Susan Smith confessed that there had been no black man, no gun, no kidnapping. She herself had pushed the car into a small lake, where it slowly sank and drowned her sons who were sleeping in the back seat. The authorities had in fact checked the lake earlier, but only near the shoreline, and now they found the car out in the center of the lake, where it had drifted before sinking. Everyone was stunned by Susan's confession, and after a quick trial she was sentenced to life in prison.

One danger of relying on the news media to learn about crime and violence is that the major, featured stories do not generally depict the statistically most common crimes. Instead, they emphasize unusual crimes that capture the imagination or move the emotions of the public. And a major reason for those reactions is that the crime may correspond to common beliefs, including false beliefs, about evil. This book will explain the main actual causes of violent and oppressive acts, but it is also necessary to understand people's beliefs about evil and how they differ from reality.

The Susan Smith story illustrates several key features of these beliefs. The two main components of evil, the infliction of harm and the unleashing of chaos, were both involved in the kidnapping story. Abducting two little boys from their mother at gunpoint is certainly harmful. As for chaos, her story caught the public's interest because it seemed to show that the apparent safety and peace of small-town America are illusory, because gun-wielding strangers can victimize unsuspecting young mothers who stop at traffic lights.

The kidnapping story included several additional features that fit the broad stereotypes about evil, which I will call the *myth of pure evil*. The victim was wholly innocent, according to her story. Popular images of evil feature wicked, malicious, sadistic perpetrators inflicting senseless harm on innocent, well-meaning victims, and the kidnapping story exemplified this image.

The perpetrator, meanwhile, was not depicted as sadistic (contrary to a common feature of the myth of pure evil), but the abduction of the boys was senseless. He was not kidnapping them for ransom, for clearly the young mother had no money, and of course no ransom note or demand appeared. If he had wanted to steal the car, he would almost certainly have wished to be rid of the two boys as quickly as possible. For a car thief to bring along two children would be foolish.

The race difference is also important, despite how the inhabitants of the town tried to downplay it afterward. All over the world, people generally think of evil as a force that comes from outside their own sphere. People much more readily see foreigners or people who are different from themselves as evil, as compared to their relatively slow acknowledgment of evil among their own group. Susan Smith's story attracted attention in part because of its interracial aspect, even though statistically it is far more common for the victim and perpetrator of a crime to belong to the same race or ethnic group. Her story would have been more plausible on a statistical basis if she had invented a white perpetrator instead of a black one. That is, a white perpetrator might have had more resemblance to *actual* crime. But having a perpetrator from a different race increased the resemblance to the popular, deeply rooted *myth* of evil.

Wherever we look to try to understand perpetrators, we will find that clear insight is rendered difficult by the myth of pure evil—that is, by a certain stereotype of cruelty and violence. People are strongly attached to these particular ways of thinking about evil, and news stories or victim accounts about violence are often chosen, distorted, and adapted to correspond more closely to this myth.

The distorting effect of the myth of pure evil is responsible for another unusual feature of this book. I have mostly resisted the frequent temptation to illustrate points with episodes from popular movies or famous literature. Using such stories would have made the writing of the book much easier, because they are widely available to suit almost any given point that needs an example, and many books on evil have scarcely bothered to keep a distinction between genuine and fictional misdeeds. But it is easy to be misled by fictional examples because of the distorting power of the myth of evil. Therefore, in this book, fictional stories will be used only for illuminating the myth of evil, not its reality. The rest of the stories throughout this book, from appalling atrocities to petty everyday hurts, are true.

The Magnitude of Evil

A central fact about evil is the discrepancy between the importance of the act to the perpetrator and to the victim. This can be called the *magnitude gap*. The importance of what takes place is almost always much greater for the victim than for the perpetrator. When trying to understand evil, one is always asking, "How could they do such a horrible thing?" But the horror is usually being measured in the victim's terms. To the perpetrator, it is often a very small thing. As we saw earlier, perpetrators generally have less emotion about their acts than do victims. It is almost impossible to submit to rape, pillage, impoverishment, or possible murder without strong emotional reactions, but it is quite possible to perform those crimes without emotion. In fact, it makes it easier in many ways.

On the news last night, there was a case of a convicted child molester, a plump white man with short hair and a sad expression. He had been a gym teacher and wrestling coach at a school, and he had sexually molested about two dozen children, perhaps more. He was sorry; he apologized to his victims in an open statement in court, with the television cameras rolling. He had spent a couple months in jail and was ready to get on with his life, including therapy for his "problem," as he saw it. His victims were testifying about their continuing problems stemming from being raped and molested. They suffered from eating disorders, nightmares, panic attacks, problems in school.

One can understand why he might feel that it was time to put the crimes behind him and move on, while the victims remained adamant that he should stay in prison. The molester had undoubtedly gotten some pleasure from his acts, but not a great deal, and in any case those benefits were long gone and dissipated. The illicit pleasure was over, and he was perhaps truly sorry for the harm he had caused. But the suffering of his victims continued. They had lost a great deal more than he had gained.

As we will see, this is a typical difference between victims and perpetrators. Even crimes of lesser violence are marked by the magnitude gap. In robbery or burglary, for example, the value of the stolen goods is generally less to the thief than to the victim (unless cash itself is stolen). The victim loses the full value of the jewelry or a stereo, but the thief can only sell those items for a fraction of their worth. The magnitude gap is also reflected in different time perspectives. Oppression, violence, and cruelty fade much faster into the distant past for the perpetrator than for the victim.

The magnitude gap creates a moral dilemma for the social scientist and the reader. To understand perpetrators, it will be necessary to grasp what these crimes and other acts mean to them—which often entails seeing the acts as relatively minor, meaningless, or trivial. If this book tries to do its job of understanding the perpetrators, it will inevitably seem insensitive to the sufferings of victims, at least at times. Indeed, many works on evil use a vivid, passionate prose style to drive home the enormity of the crimes. But the very enormity of the crime is itself a victim's appraisal, not a perpetrator's. Perpetrators favor a detached, minimalist style, and to understand their mental processes it is essential to lean toward that style, too.

This discrepancy compounded my own personal struggle to write this book. I am a research psychologist and a university professor, and so my main task in this book is to understand the causal processes that produce evil actions. I am also a human being, however, and it is difficult to avoid reactions of shock, outrage, and repugnance at many of the heinous acts that I had to study. As a moral being, I want to protest and condemn these crimes in their full horror, but as a research scientist I often felt it necessary to try to understand how small and casual these acts were to the perpetrators.

Eventually, I concluded that appreciating the victim's perspective is essential for a moral evaluation of such acts—but it is ruinous for a causal understanding of them. The main goal of this book is psychological understanding, not moral analysis. It will be necessary for me to tune out the overwhelmingly powerful victim's perspective to understand the perpetrators, and it will be necessary for you, the reader, as well. This is a technique to aid understanding, and we must not allow it to lead to a moral insensitivity. I do not want to make apologies or offer excuses for people who commit terrible actions. I do want to understand them, however, and so it is necessary to understand the excuses, rationalizations, minimizations, and ambiguities that mark their state of mind.

A Pair of Hate Crimes

Let us contrast two hate crimes. The first was featured in a recent documentary on Home Box Office, the leading cable television channel. It occurred in Omaha, Nebraska, in 1919 and was exceptionally well documented. The city had been suffering through a series of rapes of white women by a black man or men. The idea of black men raping white women is important. Although such crimes have increased significantly in recent decades,[20] they were quite unusual at that time—but interracial rape was often discussed back then, and false accusations were commonly used by white mobs to justify lynching black men. In any case, it was an issue about which white men felt very strongly, partly because they believed themselves responsible for the protection of white women. Racial tensions in Omaha were high that summer.

A 19-year-old white woman claimed that she had been raped by a black man while she was walking home from the movies one Thursday night in September. Will Brown, a black man who worked in a packing house, was arrested. The woman made a positive identification with high confidence. He was held in the county courthouse to await trial, but the trial never happened. On Sunday, a mob formed outside the courthouse and jail. By late afternoon, it was estimated that around 15,000 people were there, nearly all of them angry white men, many of whom had been drinking.

Around 5 P.M., the mob began to try to force its way into the courthouse building. Newspaper photos show them climbing the outer walls and breaking windows. Around 8, fires were started. Members of the mob said that someone in a blue police uniform threw a note down to them saying, "Come up, and you'll get the Negro." They did. Mr. Brown was handed over to the mob. They stripped his clothes off and beat him unconscious while dragging him down the stairs and out to the street.

He was shot more than a thousand times, and his corpse was burned. These facts are important, because they show that the mob was not satisfied with his death alone. A man can often be killed with one bullet, and a couple dozen are sufficient to make the outcome certain. To go on shooting many hundreds of times beyond this is a sign that the perpetrators were driven by something more than a desire for the victim's death. And then building a fire to burn a corpse that has already taken enough bullets to wipe out a regiment is wholly unnecessary in practical terms. The violence simply went far beyond any practical need that one could imagine. This was not a pragmatic policy, like that of the ancient Mongols, who destroyed entire cities that resisted them. To be sure, one might suggest that these white Americans wanted, like the Mongols, to intimidate potential resistance among their opponents, but a beating and perhaps a few bullets would suffice for that.

The newspaper photo was shown on television. Lines of well-dressed white men stood in front of the bonfire with Mr. Brown's visible remains. The HBO announcer made a telling point about the photo: "Almost everyone was smiling." Smiles mean happiness, pleasure, satisfaction. Such emotions suggest one reason for the thousand bullets and the bonfire: It was fun.

The problem with this explanation is that the announcer was wrong. The faces that shone out over HBO from the Omaha newspaper photo were not smiling, with one possible exception. Most showed no emotion. To me this seemed obvious, but as a way of checking I showed the tape with no explanation and no sound to several other social scientists and asked them how many were smiling. They too saw only one smile, and a questionable one at that.[21]

Whether those men were smiling or not may seem trivial. It might matter little to the victim or his family, and there is no legal or moral relevance to whether the faces of the killers showed smiles or not. But it does serve to highlight several issues that are central to this book.

One is the hard but crucial question of whether the perpetrators of violence enjoy their actions. In a word, is *sadism* a major cause of evil? Sadism means receiving direct pleasure from hurting others. In this case, it is important for any theory of evil to know whether those men derived pleasure and enjoyment from killing that man, or, as an alternative and lesser possibility, did they get pleasure from normal sources (for example, camaraderie, good jokes) while they were killing that man?

Then we must consider the fact that the announcer was wrong. Why? How did that mistake happen? The announcer's mistake corresponded to a stereotype of evil: Perpetrators get pleasure out of inflicting harm. This brings up the issue of appearance (or myth) and reality. Whether sadism actually creates evil will be an important question in this book, but there is no debate about the role of sadistic pleasure in the common stereotype of evil. From medieval images of Satan to bad guys in today's low-budget action films, one repeatedly notes the theme that perpetrators of evil enjoy their violent and cruel actions. They laugh and congratulate each other while harming and killing victims. This is obvious even in children's cartoons.[22] The announcer's comment about the bogus smiles is important as a mistake because it embodies a popular image of evil as based on sadistic pleasure. The men who lynched young Mr. Brown were clearly breaking multiple laws and violating his rights, but perhaps they only appear as *fully* evil if they are also depicted as having fun doing it.

Instead of being swept along by preconceptions, it is necessary to ask, in simple curiosity and with genuine open-mindedness: How were those men actually feeling? It is difficult to be certain, but one can make a fair guess based on what they said. Several made comments about "teaching these fiends a lesson," which can be understood at two levels.

At one level, the lynch mob presumably believed that Mr. Brown had in fact raped the young woman who identified him, and they probably suspected him of the other rapes that had been occurring. Of course they should have allowed the authorities to handle the manner legally, and their opinions about his guilt or innocence did not in any way justify what they did, except to themselves. But to understand their mental state, it is probably essential to appreciate that they thought they were punishing a man who had committed terrible crimes against the innocent women they were supposed to protect.

The other level involves attitudes toward black people in general. Lynchings and other violence by whites against blacks have long been motivated by resentment at the upward mobility of ambitious black people. Many white people had campaigned, fought, and even died to free America's black people from slavery, but when the descendants of slaves began to want to share the jobs, neighborhoods, and other opportunities that the whites enjoyed, many whites discovered that this was not the outcome they had been seeking. The image of a black man raping a white woman was a symbol (again, one that usually lacked substantive reality) of black people intruding on white privileges and displacing them. Thus, at this second level, killings like the one in Omaha may have been meant to teach black people in general the lesson that they should stay in their place and give white people the respect that white people deserve.

The role of economic competition was shown in a classic research finding by Hovland and Sears.[23] They examined the relationship between cotton prices and lynch mob violence in the Old South. A significant negative correlation was found, and subsequent work with more sophisticated statistics[24] has upheld that conclusion: When prices went down, lynchings went up. The mobs probably consisted of men who made their living growing and selling cotton, and a drop in prices meant that business was bad. Financial hardship made people more willing to countenance and even to perpetrate violence against people they disliked. In contrast, in times of relative prosperity, white people were more tolerant toward black citizens, at least in the sense of being less prone to kill them illegally over suspected or trumped-up crimes.

The lynch mob is still the most vivid symbol of hate crimes in America, but lynchings are largely a thing of the past. There are still plenty of hate crimes today, but they take a different form. Indeed, the very racial direction of hate crimes has seen a fundamental reversal. According to an FBI report on violence during 1993, black people were four times more likely than white people to commit hate crimes.[25]

A rare perpetrator's memoir described one such recent crime in Virginia. The author, at the time a teenager, was hanging out on his neighborhood corner with his friends one afternoon when they saw "a white boy, who appeared to be about eighteen or nineteen years old . . . pedaling a bicycle casually through the neighborhood."[26] One of the black fellows pointed him out to the others, called him a derogatory name, and suggested that he must be crazy to have come there. The group's response "was automatic." They ran after the white boy, knocked him down, and beat him unconscious while cars drove past. They kicked his head until blood gushed from his mouth, and they tried to damage his sex organs. The author said that when he realized how badly the victim was injured, he backed away, as did several others, but one of his comrades continued "like he'd gone berserk" and even topped off the episode by picking up the bicycle and smashing it down on the victim as hard as he could.[27] The boy on the ground did not even flinch with the impact, apparently being out cold at that moment.

As I have already suggested, one must generally remain skeptical when victims or moralistic bystanders claim that perpetrators get pleasure out of inflicting harm. In this case, however, the perpetrator's own memoirs claim that he enjoyed such crimes. "Fucking up white boys like that made us feel good inside," he wrote, adding that as they walked away they laughed and compared boasts about who had done the most damage.[28] He recalled that during the assault, "Every time I drove my foot into his balls, I felt better."[29] He said that when his older brother got his driver's license, the gang would cruise around nearby white neighborhoods, picking out vulnerable targets and beating them close to death.

Yet even these remarks do not indicate that the motive was the sheer enjoyment of inflicting harm. The satisfaction described by the black perpetrator was one of revenge, and indeed he gave his story on the crime the title "Get-back," a slang term for revenge. He said that white people had oppressed black people for a long time, and so he and his friends felt entitled to take revenge on whoever fell into their clutches. As he wrote, in retrospect "our random rage in the old days makes perfect sense to me,"[30] and he said that while beating the teenage cyclist he thought back over past racial slights and injustices.

The role of simple racial antagonism is not to be denied. As the violent young black man put it, he felt that some of the blows were directed at the boy on "General Principle—just 'cause you white."[31] Obviously, this particular boy had never done anything to him or his friends, and in fact they did not know who he was. They had no grievance toward him in particular, but they claimed two reasons for attacking him. One was that people who shared his skin color had mistreated people who shared their skin color. The other was simply that they did not like his skin color.

Central to this young man's grievances—and the same theme is found in most works about the young black outlaw today—was that white people in general had humiliated his people, including his parents and possibly himself. The brutal assault on the boy, and the later similar crimes he mentioned, were partly meant to carry a message to white people: They should stay in their place and give black people the respect that black people deserve.

What other common features do the Omaha and Virginia hate crimes have? Both mobs thought their acts were justified. Moreover, in both cases there seemed to be a sense that the victim should bear the guilt for misdeeds by others of his race. There were some differences, to be sure. The white mob had perhaps more reason to blame this individual victim and less reason to blame the racial group in general; the reverse was true for the black mob. Still, the hate crime was felt to be a response to bad actions on the victim's side and probably on more than one level. The pretext for both attacks was ultimately weak, which indicates that deeper antagonisms lay behind the crimes. These violent acts were both ready to happen before the circumstance presented itself.

We will see that perpetrators often believe themselves to be totally justified in responding to perceived attacks by their victims. Or almost totally justified. There are important elements of truth in these beliefs more often than we would like to think. The popular myth of evil depicts malicious, sadistic perpetrators and innocent victims. Some incidents do actually conform to that stereotype, but more often violence is a result of mutual, escalating provocations and grievances. From the perpetrators' perspective, they could fairly point to provocations that had some basis in reality. Will Brown had been positively identified as having raped a teenage white woman that week. White people had oppressed and discriminated against black people for a long time.

Another feature of these two crimes concerns how people think of themselves—whether one uses the term pride, self-esteem, narcissism, or another. I prefer the neutral term *egotism*, which means both the good kind, as in healthy high self-esteem, and the bad kind, as in being conceited or arrogant. Egotism simply means thinking well of yourself (regardless of whether those thoughts are justified or not).

Today, it is common to propose that low self-esteem causes violence, but the evidence shows plainly that this idea is false. Violent acts follow from high self-esteem, not from low self-esteem. This is true across a broad spectrum of violence, from playground bullying to national tyranny, from domestic abuse to genocide, from warfare to murder and rape. Perpetrators of violence are typically people who think very highly of themselves.[32] This phenomenon will be explained at greater length in Chapter 5. In this chapter, though, it has already come up several times. The soldiers who shot the Indian child, for example, were competing to prove their superiority.

Actually, it is more precise to say that violence ensues when people feel that their favorable views of themselves are threatened or disputed by others. As a result, people whose self-esteem is high but lacks a firm basis in genuine accomplishment are especially prone to be violent, because they are most likely to have their narcissistic bubble burst. If you think you are a great success and you really are, most people you meet are likely to confirm that reality, and you may even be able to ignore the ignorant few who fail to recognize it. On the other hand, if you are not a success but merely think you are, you may frequently encounter other people whose opinion of you is less flattering than your self-image. That is a common recipe for violence. If you are like most people, you will feel like lashing out at anyone who says you are not as great as you thought. The more inflated your self-esteem is, the more common such encounters are.

The role of such vulnerable egotism is apparent in both these hate crimes. As we saw, white people became violent against blacks when they felt that blacks were threatening to become equals and take away their special privileges. The mob wanted to teach black people a lesson about staying in their place. In a similar fashion, the black mob wanted to teach white people a lesson about staying in their place and to punish them for having treated black people with disrespect. Both mobs saw their victims as having made claims on status that were not permitted to them—as having been unfairly egotistical. The violence was meant partly as a way of putting the victim's fellows down, of teaching an apparently overdue lesson in humility.

Because statements about race are easily misinterpreted, it is important that I make myself clear on this point. The history of hate crimes does not offer either whites or blacks much basis for claiming moral superiority. In fact, this history suggests that black and white people are all too similar. Both turn violent when they feel that others are not giving them the respect they deserve. Both have proved the fallacy of thinking that you are entitled to special respect on the basis of your race; society may work better if people try to earn respect as individuals, by their virtuous acts and achievements. More important, low self-esteem does not explain or cause violence. Rather, unsatisfied egotism—one form of high self-esteem—is what makes people lash out at others.

Both of these hate crimes went far beyond what had any practical value or was warranted by the circumstances. Thus, both suggest the existence of latent racial animosity waiting for an occasion to break out. As we will see, people almost universally form into groups and hold negative attitudes toward other, competing groups. When people believe that their rights and their group pride have been injured by someone from another group, they are all too often ready to respond in a violent fashion that goes beyond any practical or instrumental use. Groups are a vital part of human social life and are necessary for survival, but they also reflect a built-in predisposition toward a certain pattern of antagonism.

A Young Woman's Faith

The little family was disappointed on that January morning in 1962 when the new baby turned out to be a girl instead of the hoped-for boy, but soon they forgot their dismay and loved the precious child. Like most babies in North Korea, the first words little Hyun Hee learned were "Thank you, Kim Il Sun, Our Great Leader." She was taught about the distant enemy, America, which her father told her was "the worst place in the world."[33]

The collective egotism, the high self-esteem, of North Korea fits very well with the standard recipe for violence. North Korea regards itself as the best and greatest land in the world, but it is constantly presented with reminders that other countries have somehow become richer, more powerful, and more successful. Hence, its sense of superiority is fragile and vulnerable to being questioned.

Between her father's connections and her own talents and hard work, the girl grew up to be a success. She got into the only decent university in the land, named of course after the great leader himself. It was difficult to keep up with her studies while making time for the mandatory farmwork in the countryside and the mandatory military training. Consistent with Communist beliefs, women were treated exactly the same as men, including the same athletic tests and hand-to-hand unarmed fights against black belt (male) instructors. (She saw other women get broken noses or ribs, but she won her bouts.) The only noticeable difference was that the women's training included gynecological examinations to ensure that they kept their virginity. After doing well on many tests, she was chosen to become a special agent for the foreign intelligence service.

One of the biggest days of her life came when she was summoned to the service's national headquarters. The director gave her a mission that he said had come from specific orders handwritten by the Dear Leader himself, indicating supreme importance. In fact, the director said that this was probably the most important mission ever attempted by the foreign intelligence department and that it would decide "our entire national destiny." She and her male comrade were to destroy a South Korean airplane. The director explained that the airplane's destruction would create a broad sense of chaos and uncertainty that would prevent South Korea from hosting the upcoming 1988 Olympic Games as scheduled. This in turn would lead to the reunification of Korea, and that was "the great goal of our generation."[34] If she succeeded, she would be a national hero. She would be permitted to return to her family and retire from active duty "with every luxury the Party can provide."[35] She wrote later that she never understood precisely how blowing up an airplane full of tourists would lead to reunification, but she did not question the director, even in her own mind. She knew that there was much about politics that she did not understand, and she had faith in her national leaders and superiors.

The young woman was overcome with feelings: awe, dread, gratitude, responsibility, patriotism. She did not, however, think or feel anything about the moral questions, "not for a moment," even though the mission would mean killing more than a hundred people. "The act of sabotage was a purely technical operation,"[36] she thought. In fact, she wrote that it was not until after the mission succeeded and she had been captured, not until she walked into the South Korean courtroom and faced the families of her victims, that the real meaning of her violent act hit home.[37]

The mission itself encountered only minor hitches. Their contacts met them at the Baghdad airport and gave them the bomb. She went into the ladies' room and set the timer while sitting in a toilet stall, working methodically and with no thoughts to spare for guilt or remorse. They smuggled the bomb aboard KAL flight 858 in a briefcase and put it in the overhead compartment. At the stopover in Abu Dhabi, they got off but left the bomb. As the plane took off, she had her first disturbing thoughts: She recalled the South Korean people on the plane and how they had been laughing, all on their way home from a long journey. The next day, when she heard about the plane crash, her feelings were mainly just relief at the success of her mission and pride at having contributed to the imminent reunification of her country.

She was captured, and only at this point did she begin to suffer inwardly over what she had done. She began to have nightmares, such as that her family was on board that flight, that she was shouting at them to deplane but they weren't listening. The extremely intense misery and anxiety of these dreams would linger even after she woke up. Gradually, she came to feel terrible guilt much of the time. She confessed her crime, pleaded guilty, was sentenced to death, and then was pardoned by the South Korean government.

Three important points are illustrated by this story. First, during the act, her focus was on here-and-now details, and she was untroubled by guilty thoughts about the innocent people she would be killing. Still, after she went through with it, she was surprised to find how disturbed she was. The constant nightmares, from which she often awoke screaming, are one fairly common result of committing such violent actions, and they are a major source of stress even for policemen and soldiers who shoot someone in the line of duty. I have said that the mythical image of evil involves getting pleasure and enjoyment out of killing. In reality, however, most people have very unpleasant reactions to killing, at least at first.

Second, her act of vicious terrorism was motivated by the highest ideals and principles. It was not a spontaneous act of hatred toward her victims, although she had dutifully learned to regard people from non-Communist countries as enemies. She was not seeking personal gain, although rewards had been promised. Her main reason was to serve her country. She loved her country, she trusted her leaders and superiors, and she honestly believed that her mission would help lead to the triumphant reunification of Korea, in some way that she could not precisely understand. In retrospect, she was committing a horrible, pointless atrocity, but during the episode she thought she was doing something good: not just acceptable or justifiable, but something strongly and positively good. As we will see, many especially evil acts are performed by people who believe they are doing something supremely good.

Third, her action did not lead to the desired goal. She succeeded in blowing up the airplane, but the expected consequences did not materialize. The 1988 Olympics were held in Seoul anyway, despite the director's assurances that the airplane bombing would prevent them. Even more important, the reunification of Korea under North Korean leadership not only did not happen but was in no way furthered by the bombing. That reunification looks less likely than ever. In operational terms, the mission succeeded; in terms of its basic, political purpose, it was a complete failure.

This pattern of long-term pragmatic failure will be found repeatedly. Most robberies bring only a few dollars in income. Rapes typically bring only minimal sexual pleasure. Torture almost never elicits useful, accurate information. Terrorism and assassination do not bring about the political goals they were meant to promote. Most murderers soon regret what they did as a pointless, self-defeating act emerging from a trivial dispute. Governments that use repressive violence to silence dissent do not end up with the popular support they envisioned. People who beat up their loved ones do not achieve the family relationships they want. Violence is a relatively common means but not a very effective one, especially when judged by its long-range consequences. Evil cannot be satisfactorily understood in terms of rational efforts to solve problems and pursue goals.

PART 1

Image and Reality

CHAPTER 2

Victims and Perpetrators

The problem of evil can be approached in two completely different ways. One is to understand the image of evil, that is, the way evil is imagined and portrayed—the way it exists in people's understanding. The other is to understand the causes of behavior that is seen as evil.

Because the reality of evil is sometimes shaped and altered by the image, it is sensible to begin with the image. This chapter and the next will undertake to distinguish image from reality and construct a basic understanding of the image. This chapter addresses the different perspectives of victims and perpetrators. To pursue our task of understanding the perpetrator, it will be necessary to see the limitations of the victim's view and be able to step outside them. This is especially important because the habitual ways of looking at evil generally start from the victim's viewpoint. Chapter 3 will discuss the image of evil. In Chapter 4, we will begin to look at the causes of evil.

As I said in Chapter 1, evil exists primarily in the eye of the beholder, especially in the eye of the victim. Most people do not think of their own actions as evil, even if others regard what they are doing as supremely evil. But if no one deliberately does evil, how do so many evil things get done? In this chapter, we will look at how the people who perform evil acts think and feel about them. If they don't see their own actions as evil, how *do* they see them?

Killers Dressed in Black

In the twentieth century, the most compelling and enduring image of evil is the Nazis. The Nazis have replaced the red-skinned, pointy-tailed Satan as the prototype of evil. Men dressed in black, with leather boots and skull insignias, carrying out the large-scale and systematic murder of millions of innocent, unarmed, naked citizens: What could be more evil? And so the question can be asked: Did they regard what they did as evil?

The answer appears to be no. Perhaps it should be a qualified no, for many of them had serious doubts and misgivings, and some objected strongly to the Nazi regime's actions as morally wrong. But these people, who saw or suspected evil, were not the ones most involved; indeed, many of them ended up withdrawing from active participation in the killings. The people who carried out the worst acts did not believe they were doing evil, or at most they struggled between doubts and conflicting obligations. There is nothing to suggest that large numbers of people came to adopt a positive attitude toward doing things they saw as evil.

Then how *did* the Nazis regard their actions?

Nazi Idealists

First, they seem to have thought they were making the world a better place. The Nazis were idealists and utopians. It is paradoxical to suggest that many of the men who performed the greatest evil regarded themselves as doing good. But that is how they saw it.

The Nazis were guided by a strong utopian vision: They wanted to build the perfect society. In order to transform an overpopulated country into a Jeffersonian rural democracy (their particular idea of the perfect society) they required more land. They saw some very suitable land to the east. Unfortunately (in their view), that land was already occupied by all those Polish people. Those people were in the way, and the logical plan was to move them out somehow. Concentration camps were initially for relocating people, not for killing them. The systematic killings seem to have started only after alternative options for relocation became impractical.[1] The original plan was just to get certain people out of the way in order to carry out the start of the perfect society.

Indeed, the Nazis felt that they were falling behind other nations in their efforts to create an ideal society based on modern science.[2] They pointed in particular to the United States, where compulsory sterilization was practiced and euthanasia was being debated, and where the Indians who had occupied the desirable land had been herded off onto reservations. Moreover, it was not a matter of the Nazis saying, "Look, the Americans are doing these things, even though they might seem bad, so we should be allowed to do them, too." Rather, the Nazis used the American example to persuade reluctant Germans that their country was falling behind in the great march of historical and scientific progress. Their argument was along these lines: "Look, the Americans have applied modern ideas to build a better society, and if we do not do the same we will be left behind as a foolish, doddering, obsolete form of society. Instead, we must rush to the forefront of historical and scientific progress. We must do as well as the Americans, and even better." Very likely, and not entirely without evidence,[3] the Germans probably thought they were smarter than Americans, and so they could use that advantage to surpass us. They wanted to build the perfect society, but we Americans were clearly racing ahead.

Many Germans may have had some resentment and dislike of the Jews, but these were not the main factors. As Zygmunt Bauman has pointed out in his important book on the Holocaust, it would have taken the Nazis centuries to carry out the Holocaust if they had relied on making ordinary German citizens angry enough to kill Jews.[4] Inciting crimes of passion is a very inefficient and unreliable way to conduct a genocide. The Rwanda holocaust of the 1990s, which in several respects surpassed the Nazi system in efficiency of killing, seems to have been carried out amid a deliberate silence of emotion.[5] Apparently, passion is disruptive.

Rather, Bauman says, the mentality that directed the Holocaust was a gardener's mentality. A gardener is raising flowers and other plants in accordance with a particular plan for a beautiful, fine place. The weeds must be removed to make this vision reality. Some gardeners may hate the weeds, while others may regard them merely as an inconvenience. In the end, however, it doesn't matter much what the gardeners' feelings are: Both types of gardeners end up killing the weeds. All that really matters is that the envisioned perfection of the promised garden requires getting rid of the weeds. The great society imagined by the Nazi leaders required getting rid of Jews, Slavs, Gypsies, and others who were in the way and who could by their mere presence spoil the perfection of the society the Nazis wanted to create. Killing all those people, like weeding a garden, boiled down to a fairly unpleasant chore that had to be done to achieve an envisioned wonderful outcome—one that would be a positive good for everyone. At least, everyone who mattered to them.

Righting Past Wrongs

Many Nazis regarded their actions as getting even for past wrongs and injustices. In their view, they had been mistreated and they were setting things right. To be sure, they were overdoing things; the retaliation far exceeded the scale on which they thought they had been wronged, with a few possible individual exceptions (such as those who believed that their family members who had died in the First World War were victims of conspiracies, machinations, and betrayals perpetrated by the Jews).

Still, many Germans believed they had suffered substantial injustices. They felt their country deserved a leading position in Europe, but instead it had been treated with disrespect; conspired against by the older powers; tricked into losing the war; and then utterly exploited, humiliated, emasculated, and looted by the outrageous Versailles treaty and postwar settlements. It defied their common sense to see how their proud and mighty country had become a military, economic, and political basket case. The Jews had undermined the war effort and stabbed their country in the back (or so many Germans came to believe), and the Allied enemy powers, unable to win on the battlefield, had cheated and then exploited Germany.

From an objective viewpoint, there were some kernels of truth in their complaints. The Versailles treaty was unfair, and they had been badly used. Very clearly, though, the Jews had not stabbed the Germans in the back. But the Germans' perception was what mattered in terms of the actual flow of events.

Given the realities of the battlefield and the flattering distortions of official propaganda, the Germans had believed they were doing extremely well in World War I. They had won the eastern war, decisively defeating the Russians (who had surrendered on terms highly favorable to the Germans). They had fought to a standoff in the west, their boys and generals producing an even draw against the combined rest of the civilized world. It was almost the miracle of Frederick the Great[6] all over again. Abruptly, the Germans learned that they had lost the Great War, that the Kaiser was abdicating, and that they were being stripped of conquered lands and forced to pay ruinously large reparations. Even their victory in the east was being nullified, and they were being treated as losers there, too, having to give back all the new territory that had been surrendered to them in the 1917 victory treaty with Russia. And on top of everything else, their money had become worthless and the social order was crumbling. Conspiracy theories, such as that the Jews had stabbed them in the back, were not merely plausible; they were almost the only way such a stunning turnabout could be understood.

A full appreciation of the German mental state must also incorporate the shock of the war itself, win or lose, which is now rather difficult for people to imagine. Before World War I, Europe in general had almost forgotten how bad war could be. They had not had any mid-nineteenth-century bloodbath comparable to the American Civil War; it was not since the Napoleonic wars a century earlier that Europe had been laid waste, and the memory of those horrors had faded substantially.[7]

Moreover, even if those memories had been fresh, they would not have prepared Europeans for World War I. A century's worth of rapid technological innovation had made the weapons far more cruel and deadly than had been imagined. The guns used in the Napoleonic wars, for example, were so inaccurate that soldiers who were the targets did not even hide behind trees or dig holes in the ground. World War I shocked Europe with its brutality: guns that could kill at several miles' distance, heavy artillery, poison gas. A second shock was that the war lasted much longer than anyone anticipated. It gradually killed so many young men that the grinding losses affected nearly every family.

Of all the summaries of the causes of World War II, the best brief one I have found is that of John Keegan.[8] The First World War had been so much more horrible than anything Europeans had remembered or even imagined that it produced a lasting and profound psychological impact. The winners concluded that there must be no more wars. The losers concluded that there had to be another war to set things right: So much sacrifice could not be allowed to be in vain. And so Germany rearmed while England and France made concessions ("appeasement") and hoped for peace. The Germans saw embarking on the conflicts and policies that led to the Second World War as a way of getting back what was rightfully owed them and getting even with some of the enemies who had robbed them.

Cruelty as an Unfortunate By-Product

Some Nazis felt that the cruelties were a relatively small part of a positive, admirable program. After all, no one is perfect, and considering the radical social changes that were taking place, some problems and missteps were to be expected. Indeed, after the war, some older Germans would try to say that Hitler was not all bad, that he had done many good things.[9] They tended to find that no one would listen and that the rest of the world objected strongly. But to them, the bad parts were unfortunate by-products of something that had had much to recommend it. The country had really gotten back on its feet, and there was a strong public morality with "family values" heavily and consensually emphasized. After collapse and depression, the return to normality seemed a miracle.

A variation on this view was that the mistreatment and killing of unfortunate victims was a regrettable but necessary part of what had to be done. No utopia has been built without pain, and no war has been won without loss. Many individuals probably regretted seeing their Jewish friends deported and otherwise mistreated, but perhaps they thought such actions were a sad part of a desirable process: bad means toward a good end.

The men and women who carried out some of history's most evil acts did not generally regard their own actions as evil. Some felt they were getting revenge for past injustices they had suffered. Others felt they were simply helping to make their world a better place. Still others felt they were carrying out their duty. Among these, there were many who disliked the mistreatment and killing of other human beings, but most were able to see their objections as merely a personal reluctance to carry out an unpleasant duty—and as a sad or dirty part of a great, noble enterprise. We should not condone or forgive the catastrophically cruel wrongness of some of the Nazis' ideas. But we must understand those ideas if we are to understand the extraordinary evil that was enacted.

How Perpetrators Think

Although evil may exist most palpably in the minds of victims, one cannot rely on victims' accounts alone to explain or understand evil. The perpetrators of evil are often ordinary, well-meaning human beings with their own motives, reasons, and rationalizations for what they are doing. Although victims deserve to be heard, their views cannot be taken as the definitive account of why the perpetrators acted as they did. To reach an understanding, it is necessary to hear what the perpetrators have to say.

Unfortunately, perpetrators of crimes and atrocities tend to say rather little. They tend not to write their memoirs or furnish interviews to social scientists. Histories of major episodes of oppression, terror, and genocide tend to be based heavily on victims' stories, because those are mainly what's available. This imbalance is compounded by the recognition that perpetrators have ample reason to lie or distort the truth to reduce their guilt, and so whatever they do say is met with suspicion. Only recently have researchers begun to realize that victims also have an agenda and that their accounts may be biased. Still, even if the victims distort, it is quite clear that the perpetrators do too.

One way to work around the practical and legal obstacles to understanding heinous criminals is to look at how people explain the relatively minor and common misdeeds of everyday life. Accordingly, we will now turn our attention away from large-scale, systematic mass murder and examine ordinary interpersonal conflicts. Using modern research techniques, it is possible to gain a fairly thorough understanding of how people recall and perhaps rationalize the things they have done wrong.

These everyday sins may fall far short of what one would call "evil," but it is likely that learning how everyday perpetrators think about their offenses will provide valuable clues to how the perpetrators of major violence and other crimes think. The very fact that these phenomena are so common makes them important and interesting. After all, a theory that applies only to serial killers is not very useful for understanding people in general, because less than 1 percent of 1 percent of the population are serial killers. Also, because everyday events are relatively easy to study, one can study them very carefully and thoroughly and reach solid conclusions. In contrast, the perpetrators of exceptional crimes are difficult to study: They are often in prison or in hiding; there are not usually enough of them available to make a statistically "robust" sample; and there are numerous technical, legal, and other difficulties for the researcher.

To learn how perpetrators think, two graduate students and I collaborated on a research project designed to see how people would talk about something they had done that at least someone else thought was wrong.[10] We asked people to write an account of a recent incident in which they had done something that made someone else very angry. For comparison, we also asked them to write an account of an event in which someone else made them angry. Thus, each person wrote one "perpetrator" story and one "victim" story. This procedure yielded insight into how *ordinary* people commit such acts, as opposed to how semihuman monsters or deranged sociopaths might think. We then spent several months carefully coding the collection of accounts to see what patterns were statistically more frequent among the perpetrator accounts than the victim accounts, and vice versa. What follows is a quick tour through the aspects of the perpetrator's mentality that can be gleaned from those findings. These are key differences to be kept in mind as we shift from the victim's perspective to the perpetrator's.

How Bad Was It?

A first conclusion was that the actions seemed much less evil—less *wrong*—to the perpetrators than to the victims. Victims tend to see things in stark, absolute categories of right and wrong; perpetrators see a large gray area. Many perpetrators admitted that they had done something that was partly wrong, but they also thought that they were not fully to blame and that it was not as bad as others (especially the victims) had claimed. Even while blaming themselves, these perpetrators still thought the victims had overreacted and blown things out of proportion.

If the perpetrator's first slogan is "It wasn't so bad," the second is "I couldn't help it." From the perspective of people who have done something wrong, it is often quite obvious that factors beyond their control played a large part. These external causes diminish their responsibility, according to them. This is indeed what perpetrators of major crimes have been saying for a long time: for example, the Nazi functionaries' postwar defense of "I was only following orders." The same excuse is alive and well today. It is found in the legal and personal claims of members of violent youth gangs.[11] Likewise, Argentina just granted a blanket amnesty to all soldiers and lower officers who were involved in the repressive terror perpetrated by the military state (mainly in the late 1970s). The pointing to external factors is equally implicit in the modern American legal defense that an externally induced "irresistible impulse" or "temporary insanity" had caused one to kill. Once again, this is something people say even while admitting that they did something wrong. They do not deny what they did, but in their eyes they are not fully responsible for acting maliciously or wickedly.

A minority of perpetrators claimed that their actions were fully justified. In their view, they had a legitimate reason and even a full right to do what they did, and the victim was unreasonable in objecting to it. A person might be angry, for example, that a friend (who is the perpetrator in this case) had insisted on dictating where and when they would go out, being unwilling to compromise, but the friend might well say that she had paid for the car and so had a right to make such decisions unilaterally. Lest we regard these as trivial patterns, we should take note that many wars seem to fall into this pattern. War-making nations rarely admit that their cause is unjust or self-serving, nor do they claim they were prompted to attack by an irresistible impulse. Rather, they cite the need to defend their own legitimate (in their view) rights.

Again, these research findings are based on minor transgressions, typically among friends and relatives. But one does not have to look far to find similar patterns among people who commit serious crimes. Diane Scully's[12] interviews with convicted rapists found them using similar arguments to reduce the severity of their offenses. They blamed alcohol or other factors, and some even claimed that rape became an addiction so that they could not stop themselves from raping women once they had tasted this forbidden pleasure.

The prize for minimizing one's crime must go to one serial murderer and rapist whom Scully interviewed in prison. His account would be almost humorous if it were not for his shocking actions and his appalling insensitivity to the victims' suffering. This young man had captured five different women at gunpoint and raped them, after which he stabbed them to death. It is difficult to imagine how anyone could regard such acts as anything but brutal, cruel, and evil. Yet the man described them in quite different terms. He said he had always made sure to be "kind and gentle" with them, at least "until I started to kill them." He claimed they enjoyed having sex with him (which is almost certainly false, because surveys of rape victims have found that approximately zero percent of them report any enjoyment or pleasure).[13] And even the murders seemed less heinous in his retelling: "The killing was always sudden, so they wouldn't know it was coming."[14]

Deliberate and Intentional?

One of the most important discrepancies between the accounts of victims and those of perpetrators involves the crucial question of why the perpetrator acted as he did—in other words, his motives and intentions. Two versions prevail in the victims' accounts,[15] and in fact the two are probably. In one, the victim emphasizes that the perpetrator had no reason at all related for what he did. Victim stories do not merely tell what the perpetrator did; they imply or even point out that there was no reason for acting that way. The utter outrageousness, the sheer incomprehensibility of the perpetrator's action is emphasized. The act seems arbitrary, random, gratuitous. When people describe such events in everyday conversation, they use such phrases as "Can you believe it—what so-and-so did?" or "There was no reason for X to say that." The perpetrator appears to have acted on a capricious whim.

The other version found in victims' accounts presents the perpetrator as deliberately malicious. The perpetrator seems to be acting out of a focused, sadistic desire to do harm, as an end in itself. The attitude of the perpetrator, as portrayed by victims in such stories, ranges from moral indifference to sheer meanness. This is a very important aspect of victims' perceptions, and there will be much more to say about it in the next chapter.

For now, though, the crucial point is simply that perpetrators' stories about what they have done very rarely exhibit plain meanness. Occasionally, a perpetrator will say something to the effect of, "I don't know why I did it," but the vast majority present comprehensible reasons for the way they acted. Likewise, they may admit that what they did was wrong, but they almost never say they were motivated by sheer meanness or out of a desire to inflict harm as an end in itself.

Thus, the view of perpetrators as casual, arbitrary, or sadistic is predominantly a victim's view. Perpetrators rarely portray themselves that way. The contrast is especially surprising in the context of this particular study, because the same people wrote both perpetrator and victim stories. Each person seemed to change his or her style of thinking when moving from the victim to the perpetrator role.

What to Do with Bygones: The Elastic Time Frame

Another important difference between victims and perpetrators is the time span of their stories. In this, our data corresponded very well with other data the world over. Victims use a very long time span. When describing what happened to them long ago, they will often provide background leading up to the incident, describe consequences, and even relate their story to the present. Individual victims may continue to ruminate about their traumas and suffer over them for decades. Whole societies and cultures may nurse one grievance for centuries. The victim's motto is "Never forget."

In contrast, the perpetrator's motto is "Let bygones be bygones." Perpetrators can furnish a clear and detailed memory of something that happened long ago, but it seems to be bracketed in time. They do not usually give background events leading up to the act, nor do they describe lasting consequences. If they refer to the present at all, it is usually to say how different the present is from the episode in the past or that what they did wrong long ago has no bearing on the present.

And so a violent or oppressive event recedes into the past much faster for the perpetrators than for the victims. For the perpetrators, it soon becomes ancient history, whereas the victims may see it as crucial to understanding the present. This difference in time span can be seen in many places and conflicts. It is apparent in the difference between white and black American attitudes about slavery, between Jewish and German attitudes about the Holocaust, and between Northern and Southern views about the American Civil War and Reconstruction. The injustices that remain fresh in the victims' minds fade rapidly into long-ago, irrelevant history for the perpetrators.

One important reason for the time span difference is probably the magnitude gap. What the perpetrator gained was generally smaller than what the victim lost, and so the perpetrator has less reason to replay that memory. The event affected the victim much more than the perpetrator, and so it would almost inevitably tend to linger in memory and come up more often.

Seeing Oneself under Attack

Our research was not the only project to tackle the perpetrator's mentality. Several other studies have made similar attempts, and an important finding is the tendency of perpetrators to view others' actions as attacks on them. Bullies, wife-beaters, tyrants, and other violent people tend to think that other people are attacking or belittling them, even when others would not have the same interpretation.

In one study of emotionally disturbed boys at a residential treatment center,[16] researchers classified the boys along a continuum based on how much they tended to display behavior problems involving inappropriate aggression, such as arbitrarily hitting another boy who was just sitting there. Then the researchers showed the boys a series of photos of people engaging in various social interactions. They boys were supposed to say what they thought was going on in the pictures. The most aggressive boys tended to see hostility and aggression when it wasn't really there. They interpreted relatively innocuous and agreeable interactions as attempts to dominate others aggressively.

The same conclusion has emerged from studies on family violence.[17] Men who beat their wives differ in many respects from other men—and one important difference is their tendency to construe seemingly innocuous or ambiguous acts by the wife as deliberate personal attacks.

Suppose, for example, that two couples are talking one evening, and one couple mentions that they recently enjoyed a great meal at a very expensive restaurant. They describe the excellence of the food and the shocking size of the bill. The other husband turns to his wife and says casually that the two of them "ought to try that place some time." The wife responds, "I don't know, dear, it sounds awfully expensive."

A typical husband might simply agree and forget about it, and many husbands would have a feeling of appreciation and gratitude at having a sensible, frugal wife. But a few husbands might take that remark as a criticism: She is implying that he doesn't earn enough money. She is saying he's a failure as a provider, as a man. She thinks he's not as good as other men who can afford such fancy meals. And she's saying this right in front of their friends, to humiliate him publicly. She's being really mean to him and making him feel and look terrible. He'd better teach her a lesson.

This is the style of thinking that is more common among abusive husbands. Compared to happily married men, and even compared to most unhappily married men, abusive husbands tend to think that their pride and dignity are being attacked whenever there is any disagreement or conflict. One research project asked men to evaluate a series of scenarios in terms of whether they thought the wife's actions damaged the esteem of the husband. The scenarios included various disagreements between husbands and wives. In some, the wife deliberately opposed her husband; in others, the opposition was presented as accidental; in yet others, it was a mere difference of opinion. The abusive husbands saw more than twice as many of these common scenes as damaging to the husband's dignity as did men who were satisfied with their marriages.[18] The implication was clear: Abusive husbands tend to interpret many of their wives' behaviors as assaults on the husband's self-esteem.

Similar observations have been made about street violence.[19] A man receives seemingly minor signs of disrespect as if they were major blows to his pride, and he responds with violence. From the perspective of the victim, and often from the perspective of bystanders as well, the provocation seems minor and the response excessive. Indeed, try asking a middle-aged suburban mother of three, "What might someone say to you in a bar that would cause you to kill that person, assuming a weapon were available?" Her answer is likely to be that nothing or almost nothing anyone could say would elicit such an extreme response. Yet we know that in many cases relatively minor or casual insults elicit just such severely violent reactions. The apparent conclusion is that the people who respond violently are prone to overestimate the degree to which comments by others are meant as powerfully insulting attacks on them.

Several important implications follow from this finding. For one thing, it becomes possible to begin to predict who is likely to be dangerous or violent. Hypersensitive people who often think their pride is being assaulted are potentially dangerous.

This hypersensitivity to insults also makes it possible to understand what might otherwise appear to be senseless violence. A man who beats up his girlfriend or stabs a stranger in a bar might seem a malicious villain to observers. In his own eyes, however, he is merely defending himself against an attack. Many violent people believe that their actions were justified by the offensive acts of the person who became their victim.[20]

Even when a neutral observer would conclude that no serious provocation occurred, it is still important to recognize that, in the perpetrator's own view, he or she was merely responding to an attack. In the example of the couple talking about the expensive restaurant, maybe the woman was merely trying to be sensible and frugal, and maybe the other couple saw no harm in her remark, but to her angry husband, his manhood had been publicly trashed. Of course, nearly everyone would condemn him for beating her up later that evening, regardless of what he thought she said or meant. Nonetheless, from his point of view, he was merely making a somewhat justified and understandable response to a vicious assault on his identity.

The driving force was his own pride, his high self-esteem, his male ego. He was so intent on being superior to her that he watched for any little episode or remark that could possibly be interpreted as reflecting badly on him, and whenever he found one he turned violent against her in response. But if you accept his need for high self-esteem as a given, then on his terms he was at least partly justified in beating up his wife later on after she had belittled and humiliated him in front of their friends.

Who Is Correct?

There is one more crucial question that arises once these differences between perpetrator and victim stories are understood: Who's telling the truth? One assumes that both versions cannot be correct. The traditional answer has been to assume that victims are telling the truth and perpetrators are lying or distorting the facts to reduce their guilt. That certainly seems plausible. Still, one cannot accept this assumption without question and without evidence. Victims do have their own reasons to see things in a certain way, and it could be that they distort, too.

The question of who's telling the truth is very difficult to answer, especially because both perpetrators and victims may sincerely believe what they are saying. One would need objective evidence against which to compare the stories of victims and perpetrators, and such objective evidence is not often available.

Although researchers have not yet found a reliable way to compare victim and perpetrator stories to the objective truth in some real episode, a simulation was recently conducted in a laboratory study. Psychologist Arlene Stillwell assigned ordinary college students at random to play the role of either the victim or the perpetrator in a small incident.[21] They were given a description of what happened and then asked to tell the story in their own words, as if they had been the person involved in it. Thus, they had to recite the story from memory as if it had happened to them—as either the victim or the perpetrator, decided by the flip of a coin. By using this method, Stillwell could compare the victim and the perpetrator stories to the objective information she had initially supplied them, which was exactly identical for everyone.

The results of this experiment surprised everyone: Victims and perpetrators distorted the facts to an equal degree. The distortions were systematically different, of course. The victim stories generally reshuffled and twisted the facts to make the offense seem worse than it was, whereas the perpetrators reshuffled and twisted things to make it seem less bad. For example, a mitigating circumstance such as being under severe stress at the time might be played up by the perpetrator as an important part of understanding why he acted the way he did; meanwhile, the fact that the perpetrator was under stress might be entirely omitted from the victim's story. Along the same lines, the victim might dwell on the lasting bad consequences of what the perpetrator did, whereas those consequences would probably be downplayed or even missing in the perpetrator's story.

The implications of these findings are important. Consistent with the view that evil exists in the mind of the beholder, it is clear that victims see things much differently, and much worse, than perpetrators see them. Moreover, it is not safe to take the victim's story as objective truth. It is true that perpetrators have reasons for shading and altering the truth, but victims appear to have their own wants and needs that alter the way they describe what happened. One cannot rely on either the victim's story or the perpetrator's; the reality may lie somewhere in between. No one's story can be fully trusted in a scientific sense, although most stories do contain some significant elements of truth.

What, then, can be concluded about how perpetrators think? They do not see things in the simple, black-and-white absolutes that victims and lawmakers are fond of. To them, events are complex and morally ambiguous. They may see something wrong in what they did, but they also see how they were affected by external factors, including some that were beyond their control. In other cases, perpetrators see themselves as having acted in a way that was fully appropriate and justified. In addition, to the perpetrators, a misdeed may seem like an isolated event in the distant past that has no relation to the way they live their lives in the present.

Perhaps most important, perpetrators typically do have reasons and motives that make some sense to them. Victims may see random, gratuitous acts of cruelty, but perpetrators rarely see their own acts that way. We cannot rely on victims to tell us why the perpetrators did what they did.

Mixing and Blurring the Roles

When Perpetrators Become Victims

So far, we have seen that the perpetrators of evil generally do not regard themselves as evildoers. Their actions become evil when viewed by their victims or, sometimes, by other people. In most cases, then, evil comes into being only through a combination of two different roles: One person performs the actions, and the other sees them as evil. The roles of victim and perpetrator are interlocked.

There is a further, ironic twist to the interrelationship between victim and perpetrator roles: Many perpetrators regard themselves as victims. In their accounts, in their recollections, and probably even in their most sincere gut feelings, many perpetrators see themselves as people who have been unjustly treated and hence deserve sympathy, support, and extra tolerance for any wrongs they have committed.

Perpetrators of minor transgressions often see themselves as having been provoked by the victim. They see the victim's anger as an unjustified overreaction (even if they do admit that what they did was wrong). In a recent study in which people were asked to describe something they did that hurt somebody, many people added information about how they had suffered or been mistreated, so that their stories effectively cast them as victims, too (even though they were supposed to be the perpetrators).[22]

The metamorphosis of perpetrator into victim can also be seen outside the laboratory. In a noted book, Peter Sichrovsky described his interviews with the children of Nazi war criminals.[23] Many had grown up thinking that their parents were victims of the war rather than perpetrators. They had been led to believe that their parents had been forced to do undesirable things and were the targets of unfair persecutions. He quoted one woman who recalled her father after the war as a "nervous, trembling man, in constant fear that the police would get him. Four of us were living in a single room, my father had no work, and was afraid to go out in daytime." She went on to say how that memory of him as victim precluded seeing him as a criminal perpetrator: "Is that what power-hungry monsters responsible for the deaths of millions look like? I could never see my father in that role."[24] Sichrovsky adds that these impressions were not simply the result of the parents misleading their children. Rather, the parents saw themselves as victims (of a lost war, of a totalitarian system, and of vindictive, mean-spirited persecution), and the children came to share that view through daily contact.

Indeed, the efforts of the Third Reich's children to distance themselves from their guilty families have often involved remarkable pursuits of the victim role for themselves. As documented in Sichrovksy's book and in a similar work by Dan Bar-On,[25] many of these children sought out Jewish friends, married Jews, or converted to Judaism themselves. Others chose careers as public defenders or Amnesty International functionaries where they could work on behalf of political prisoners and other victims of oppression. Others sought out desperate causes that promoted the welfare of various oppressed groups, and some committed suicide, which is an effective way of claiming a permanent role of victim for oneself.[26] In one case, the daughter of a prominent Nazi had carried on a long love affair with a Jewish man. She wanted to marry him but found herself unable to return to his home with him—because in his home in South Africa he, as a white man, belonged to the class of oppressors. Apparently, she wanted to link herself to a victim, and although he qualified very well as a Jew, he became disqualified as a white man in the land of apartheid. In his home country he was not a victim, and so she couldn't marry him.[27]

At the extreme of modern violence is the serial murderer. J. Norris's book on these individuals shows that many of them suffered prolonged abuse and mistreatment early in their lives and considered themselves to be victims. Arthur Shawcross, for example, was a victim of homosexual rape. During his childhood, he suffered rejection and other mistreatment by his mother. He also claimed that he had been exploited by several women in the neighborhood, who induced him to perform oral sex on them. His sense of victimization did not desert him even when he began to kill people. "He perceived himself to be the victim even as he was becoming the aggressor," a pattern that Norris regards as common among violent sex offenders.[28]

John Wayne Gacy seems to have felt the same way. He kidnapped boys and young men. He would torture them, abuse them sexually, and then kill them. Serial killers often face difficulties in disposing of the corpses, but Gacy's solution was to bury them underneath his house, where there was a crawl space. At night, after a killing, he would take the body down under the house, dig a hole for it, put it in, and cover it over. One wonders what his thoughts were in the mornings, getting up for breakfast while the mutilated bodies of his victims decomposed underneath his feet. Gacy is known to have murdered 33 people this way, mostly children. Possibly there were many additional victims. In any case, Gacy would have to make any list of the most vicious and evil perpetrators in recent decades in the United States.

Yet he did not see himself that way. "I see myself more as a victim than a perpetrator," said Gacy.[29] His victimization proceeded along multiple lines, at least as he saw it. His early life had not been satisfactory: "I was the victim, I was cheated out of my childhood," he complained, although it might be pointed out that at least he was able to live through his childhood, unlike the lads he killed. His victimization continued in adulthood. He felt that the media presented an unfairly negative portrayal of him to the public: "I was made an asshole and a scapegoat." Thus, he saw himself as the victim of misunderstanding and lack of sympathy, causing him to wonder whether anyone could "understand how badly it had hurt to be John Wayne Gacy."[30]

Studies of ordinary street crime in the United States show a similar blurring of victim and perpetrator roles. Sociologist Jack Katz, referring to "a long line of studies that have provided evidence . . . of precipitation by the victims,"[31] says that the roles of perpetrator and victim are often exchanged during an incident. One person may behave aggressively by attacking or insulting another. The person who is attacked regards himself (or, far less often, herself) as a victim with a righteous cause to defend and strikes back, often with dangerous or lethal levels of violence. Thus, the outcome is tragically ironic to many a killer: He meant well, he was attacked, and he acted only in well-justified (in his view) defense of the Good, yet he ends up being cast as the villain and perhaps convicted of murder. His sense of being unfairly treated is likely to continue into prison.

And sure enough, prisoners often feel more like victims than like perpetrators. Jan Arriens has compiled a set of letters and other writings by prisoners on Death Row in the United States, and these killers do not see themselves as evildoers. "I am the hunted, the caught, the prey, the victim of the crafty, the cunning, and powerful," as one wrote.[32] Others compare themselves to victims of the Holocaust, slavery, and other evils. They commonly refer to the execution of convicted prisoners as "legalized murder," thereby implicitly comparing themselves to their victims. Indeed, a number of them contend that their own execution is a greater crime than the one they committed. In their view, they killed someone during a spur-of-the-moment loss of control, whereas the state's execution of them is fully premeditated, which makes it all the more heinous. The legal system itself says that premeditated murder is worse than a crime of passion; so, these convicted men reason, what the state does to me is far worse than what I may have done to my victim. "I may have committed a crime, but all in all I am a bigger victim than a perpetrator:" Thus speaks Death Row.

These same patterns of distortion can be seen in the thinking of the perpetrators of brutal ethnic violence in what was once Yugoslavia. For several years, the world has been fascinated and horrified by the reports of mass murder, wanton destruction of property, systematic rape, killing of prisoners, and similar atrocities that seem to go on and on there. A recent news report focused on the irony that the Serbs, who are generally regarded as the perpetrators of the worst atrocities, regard themselves as the victims in Bosnia. "Far from being weighted down by guilt, they consider themselves, if anything, the most aggrieved party in the Bosnian nightmare—indeed, one of the most aggrieved peoples in the entire world."[33] The reporter noted that the Serbs used the expanded time frame common to victims: "Visitors are lectured about Turkish atrocities against the Serb people going back to 1389."[34] Similar patterns can be seen among the perpetrators of horrors and atrocities throughout history. The ones who carry out the massacres perceive themselves as victims of mistreatment and injustice.

Why do perpetrators often claim the victim role for themselves? There are multiple advantages to the victim role after the fact. During the crime, of course, the victim gets the worst of it, and there is no rush to claim the victim role before or during the crime. It is only in retrospect that people want to be victims.

Before considering why the victim role might appeal to the perpetrators, it is necessary to clarify one point: Do perpetrators really regard themselves as victims, or do they simply pretend to claim that role? It is almost certain that there are some perpetrators at each extreme, that is, some who sincerely see themselves as victims and others who are completely disingenuous in their self-serving claims. Moreover, many perpetrators do see themselves as under attack by someone else, and hence their claim to the victim role may start well before their own violent act. In any case, most perpetrators probably fall somewhere between total sincerity and total hypocrisy. They tend to look for whatever will help them believe what they want to believe: namely, that they should be regarded as victims rather than as evildoers.

The first advantage of the victim's role is that victims have a legitimate claim on the sympathy of others. Victims have already suffered, and everything from moral calculation to simple human decency makes us want to extend a helpful hand to them. Most people feel some obligation to try to bring a victim's suffering to an end, not make it worse. To a perpetrator who is looking for ways to avoid punishment, victim status seems very promising. Having some claim on the sympathy of others would help to reduce one's own vulnerability.

Moreover, victimization is often seen as an acceptable explanation for one's own misdeeds. The simplest and most familiar form of this argument is the traditional belief that killing in self-defense is acceptable. If you are the victim of another's attack, you are allowed to defend yourself.

In a more recent form of this argument, the claiming of victim status by alcoholics, drug addicts, and similar others is often an effective way to get themselves off the hook for their actions. The stern morality of personal responsibility holds people accountable for their actions and punishes their misbehavior, including drinking or taking drugs. In recent decades, a rival view has portrayed these individuals as victims of urges they cannot control.[35] In this view, one should not blame these people for what they have done, because it was not by their choice. They are victims who need help, and clearly this is a better position than being a self-indulgent pleasure-seeker who deserves to be punished.

The victim holds a moral high ground that starts to look mighty good to the perpetrator. This is especially true if the victim's side comes to win the war or gain power in some other way. Perpetrators may be troubled by guilt and may feel worried about what society will do to them if they are caught. Thus, they may envy the former victims: Society views them with compassion and solicitude, and they are often treated as immune from normal criticism. If only I could claim those advantages, thinks the former war criminal, I'd be home free.

Mutual Fault and Shared Blame

There is one more crucial feature of the blurring of victim and perpetrator roles. The violent incident may emerge from a cycle of events in which victim and perpetrator both acted dangerously or aggressively. The causes of violence often involve reciprocal actions by the victim and perpetrator. Both may be to blame.

Several strangers are drinking in a bar. One man makes a joke at another's expense. The second man responds with a direct insult, with no pretense at humor. The first responds with an explicit insult of his own. The second man shoves the first, spilling a little of his drink, and the first man angrily throws the rest of the drink in the second man's face. The second man lunges at the first, swinging his fist but missing. The first man dodges the blow and then hits the second man in the stomach twice, hard. The second man hits back several times, knocking the first man down and giving him a painful bloody nose. The first man gets up and draws his knife. He stabs the second man fatally. Who started this? Who was the aggressor? Who acted in self-defense?

Such cases of mutual provocation and aggression appear to be more the norm than the exception. To be sure, there are some cases in which wholly innocent victims are attacked by predatory individuals, but these are relatively rare. One study by David Luckenbill found, for example, that the majority of cases of criminal homicide involved reciprocal provocations in which mutual hostility escalated until one person killed the other.[36] Often there were other people present when the argument started, and the audience would take sides and egg the two on. In any case, the norm is for both people to be involved. Let us consider some of the evidence.

We have already seen that street crimes often arise from mutual antagonism and spiraling provocations. It is no accident that victims and perpetrators tend to be the same kind of people.[37] People spend much of their time with others who are like them, and they tend to commit crimes against the people with whom they come into contact. Many killers see themselves as having been attacked or victimized by others, and in their eyes they were defending themselves or striking back.

A study of men imprisoned for violent (but not deadly) assault revealed the same pattern of provocation and reciprocal aggression. According to researcher Leonard Berkowitz, hardly any of the men thought they had even landed the first blow during the fight. Berkowitz thought it was difficult to ascertain who was the original aggressor. Most often, a quarrel simply escalated until it became violent.[38]

Turning from crimes among strangers to violence in the intimate world of love and family, one finds similar patterns of mutual, reciprocal causation. This is an unpopular view nowadays, and the general public prefers to think of family violence as a matter of evil or sick individuals who lash out against totally innocent, helpless family members. And there are undoubtedly many cases in which that picture is accurate. More often, however, and especially among adults, there is evidence that both parties are aggressive and that violence is the end point of an escalating quarrel.

In the landmark studies of marital violence conducted by Murray Straus, mutual aggression was the norm.[39] In fully half the cases where any domestic violence was reported, both spouses were violent. Moreover, even if only one spouse was violent, that person tended to believe that he or she was responding to some injustice by the other.

Recent work has also revealed that a surprising amount of violent behavior occurs in dating relationships. There, too, the pattern seems to be mutual. Most high school and college students who report hitting or otherwise physically attacking a dating partner say that they have been victims of such aggression, too.[40]

Moreover, about half the couples who experience any sort of violence tend to say that both parties were responsible for initiating it. This seems to mean that they recognize that the victim of violence may have done something to provoke it. Thus, if a girl slaps her date in the face, the couple may later agree that he had done something to provoke her, such as insult her. They don't just blame everything on her.

Researchers who study marital violence are quite familiar with these cycles of mutual, escalating violence.[41] A common pattern is for the argument to start when one spouse criticizes the other for some perceived inadequacy, failure, or misdeed. The other may respond angrily, and the exchange of critical views degenerates into name-calling and similar insults designed to offend and hurt the other person. At some point, one may push or shove the other angrily. Genuine physical violence, such as hitting or slapping the partner, may come only after these initial steps.

These patterns suggest that there may be some truth to the common claim by perpetrators that they are the victims. A recent work on domestic violence approvingly quoted the following (slightly overstated) conclusion from an earlier study: "Batterers always see themselves as the victim of the battered woman."[42]

A dramatic example was provided on national television recently. Former football star and sports commentator O.J. Simpson was arrested following the brutal murder of his ex-wife and her male friend. Police records confirmed that there had been many complaints of domestic violence in their household, including cases in which he had struck her, destroyed property, and threatened her with severe injury. Yet before his flight to avoid arrest, he left a note saying that he felt he was the victim. On the face of it, this seemed absurd: His wife had been beaten and now lay dead, so surely one ought to regard her as the victim. He did not deny her status as victim, but he did claim that he should also be considered a victim. One can only assume that he felt he had been mistreated by her in some cruel fashion, which made his violence against her a retaliation rather than a spontaneous outburst.

It is worth considering that this mutuality is the most plausible view. Most people wish to see violence in morally clear terms with innocent, virtuous victims and evil, malicious perpetrators. In fact, however, most people become violent only when they think they have been attacked in some way. The idea that some people simply start beating up their spouses out of the blue, for no apparent reason, does not fit well with what is known about human nature. It is far more likely that in a marriage full of mutual resentment, hostility, power struggles, and occasional exchanges of ugly and cruel remarks, one person may cross the line into physical violence when he or she feels that the spouse's actions were unfair and unacceptable. This is not to defend the perpetrators of family violence—in fact, as we have seen, the tendency to misread innocuous comments as attacks on one's esteem or rights lies at the root of a great deal of seemingly avoidable violence. But it does render the perpetrators' actions more understandable.

Large-scale aggression often shows similar patterns of mutual, escalating provocations. In war, for example, it is common for neither side to regard itself as the aggressor. To be sure, it does occasionally happen that one country unilaterally decides to invade or attack another for its own potential gain. More often, however, history records that the outbreak of war followed an exchange of ultimatums, threats, warnings, and other provocations. On a smaller scale, terrorists see themselves as victims fighting back against an oppressive, intrusive, unjust state. In their view, they have been mistreated and denied legitimate means of expressing their views for so long that they have no recourse but to strike back violently.[43]

Let us now take a close look at one case of mutual violence, to see how it was experienced and perceived by both sets of perpetrators. Neither side saw itself as evil. But both sides were sure they were in a battle against evil.

I have chosen the famous story of Masada because it does have several sides and can be viewed in more than one way. Although a recent, somewhat fatuous television movie depicted the incident as a simple matter of heroic resistance against overwhelming numbers of wicked, decadent conquerors, the facts of the matter make it much harder to draw a simple conclusion about who was the aggressor and who, if anyone, was evil.[44] The prevailing and simplistic view of an evil army destroying an innocent community of religious patriots and their families is not the full story.

The basic historical facts are well known and straightforward. Jews rebelled against their Roman conquerors. After several defeats, a large number retreated to a mountain fortress (Masada) where the Romans besieged them. The defenders resisted for a while, until the Romans undermined their defenses and made defeat a certainty. At this point, the Jews made a suicide pact. The men killed their wives and children and then began to kill one another and themselves. The Roman assault in the morning met no resistance, because all the Jews were already dead.

Consider this episode first from the view of the resisting Jews. Their country had been conquered, and they were fighting for their freedom. At first they had resisted in covert ways, as best they could, and finally they had accumulated enough popular support for a military insurrection. They led a major uprising all over Israel.

Unfortunately, they turned out to be no match for the Roman legions, who followed up their victories in the field by destroying the holy city of Jerusalem and demolishing the sacred temple, as well as carrying out occasional massacres of innocent civilians. Thus, not only the Jews' national freedom but also their religion and their lives were threatened.

Finally the Romans were pursuing the last of the freedom fighters. The fierce defense of the mountain citadel had been able to resist Roman efforts to take it by storm, but the Roman engineers had finally undermined the walls, and the next day's assault was bound to succeed. Rather than be defeated and either massacred or enslaved, the defenders chose death by their own hands.

Now consider the Roman side of the story. They generally treated their conquered peoples with tolerance and good sense, and the empire was mostly peaceful. Most Jews favored cooperation or peaceful co-existence of some sort, except for a small group of fanatics who began a campaign of terror, assassination, and murder. During peacetime, many Roman administrators as well as a great many Jews who cooperated with the Roman authorities were killed by the daggers of these Zealots.

Efforts to compromise and to keep the peace failed. When the terrorist campaign evolved into a full-scale revolt, it was necessary to call in the troops. Rome's policies were to tolerate indigenous religions and safeguard the conquered peoples, but the brutal treacheries of the terrorist and military resistance made it necessary to crack down on the Jews and even to carry out some reprisal killings in the hope of discouraging further resistance. The Romans also destroyed the Temple in Jerusalem, but this was after the Zealots had used it as a fortress during the fierce battle and many Roman lives had been lost in an effort to capture it. Even after the cause was lost, though, the Zealots exasperated the Romans by continuing to resist. They fled to their mountain fortress and put up a further resistance, which necessitated a costly and dangerous siege. Even when their defense became hopeless, they continued to create trouble and expense, which would have to be paid somehow, quite possibly by taxes on their fellow Jews who had never supported them anyway. Not to mention more deaths of Roman soldiers.

And what about the mass suicide? According to historian Franklin Ford, the Zealots were probably right to expect little mercy from the Romans after all they had put them through. There might well have been a massacre of the Jewish soldiers. On the other hand, the Romans almost certainly would not have massacred the noncombatants, especially the women and children. Probably, most of them would have ended up as domestic servants in Roman households, which is not the best situation in the world, but not the worst either, and in any case individuals have nearly always chosen slavery over death. For the Zealots to kill their women and children thus shed a great deal of blood that need not have been shed. From the perspective of the Romans, it may have seemed quite appropriate for them to use whatever force was necessary to put down what was to them a disruptive and bloodthirsty group of traitors.

Thus, violence often emerges from a pattern in which both sides perform hostile or provoking acts. In retrospect, this should not surprise us: People do not typically beat their loved ones or attack strangers for no reason. One may dispute whether these reasons are sufficient to justify the violent response. But it is rather clear that people who act violently often think that they are responding to an intolerable and often aggressive set of acts by someone else.

Is No One to Blame, Then?

I have already said that many of these conclusions are unfashionable. Should we blame the woman whose husband beats her, simply because she criticized him beforehand? Are terrorists to be forgiven simply because they claim to have legitimate grievances? Should a knifing in a bar be dismissed as an unavoidable result of escalating provocations rather than an illegal and immoral taking of a human life? Aren't we committing the cardinal error of blaming the victim?

In my view, these moral dilemmas arise from a common, deeply rooted, but fallacious tendency to confuse causation and responsibility— or, to put it another way, the mistake of wanting to find a single person who is to blame. What is needed is a much broader sense that being victimized does not justify a violent response. Yes, victims do sometimes need to be blamed; but this should not exonerate the perpetrators. We should be willing to blame both the victim and the perpetrator, if necessary. In fact, in the majority of cases where aggression was mutual, we *should* blame both sides.

There seems to be little doubt that many assaults and murders begin with an exchange of angry words. In an important sense, the insulting remarks cause the subsequent killing. They cause it, but they do not excuse it. It was wrong of the first person to insult the second, but this does not make it less wrong for the second person to hit or kill the first.

Unfortunately, America's legal system and therapeutic culture often seem to support the view that perpetrators should be forgiven if they were victims. A case of child abuse is discovered and the community is outraged; then the lawyer demonstrates that the abuser was herself abused as a child, and the social scientists confirm that being a victim of abuse is a significant cause of becoming abusive oneself. She should not be blamed for what she did to her little girls, because her father was the truly evil one. Sympathy is garnered, and the defendant is given a lighter sentence or even acquitted. A more appropriate response would be to pity the abuser for what she suffered during her own childhood—but condemn her own abusive actions nonetheless.

During the years I have spent working on this book, one of the most dramatic news events involved the marital catastrophe of John and Lorena Bobbitt. The couple came to national attention when Lorena was arrested for cutting off her husband's penis with a kitchen knife while he lay in bed one night. She admitted that she did mutilate him in this way, but she accused him of having mistreated and raped her on multiple occasions, which he denied. He too was indicted, and both cases went to trial.

There are only four logically possible conclusions about the Bobbitts' case: that he was the guilty party; that she was the guilty party; that both were guilty; or that neither was guilty. In the national debate carried on in the mass media over several months, three of these four conclusions were extensively discussed. The first two—whether he or she was the guilty one—were featured in the debate in the early months. At the end, the fourth was officially adopted and both John and Lorena were acquitted of all crimes. Apparently, no one had done anything wrong.

The one conclusion that was almost never considered was that both of them had committed crimes and should have been found guilty. Quite possibly, John had abused his wife, and if so he ought to have been punished to the full extent of the law. Still, whatever he did, it was not acceptableto go to the kitchen, return with a knife, and mutilate him in his sleep. Whatever her grudge against him was, it is hard to regard her actions as legal.

My point is that our cultural tendency to see good guys and bad guys, or bad guys and innocent victims, may make us unable to see the common reality in which both sides are in the wrong. What one has suffered as a victim does not excuse one's subsequent violent action. This is the crucial blind spot in the way Americans assign blame today. And it is probably no accident that our being so reluctant to blame anybody coincides with our being an exceptionally violent society.

Regardless of what one thinks of the details of the Bobbitts' case, it is clear that the cause of controlling domestic violence in the United States would have been much better served by a pair of convictions than by the pair of acquittals. Police are often reluctant to intervene in marital fights, partly because they think it is a waste of time. Even if they arrest one partner, the other is likely to drop the charges in a few days. Finally, here was a case in which no one dismissed the charges and both cases went all the way through trial; yet the juries let both of them go. It would be hard to imagine a more discouraging message to send to police officers across the country.

CHAPTER 3

The Myth of Pure Evil

Where does one look for the face of evil? One can search with some success in the writings of theologians, in the scripts and images of low-budget horror movies, in wartime propaganda, and in similar sources. When I was a boy, though, my most vivid and detailed lessons about evil came from comic books. Among the most durably successful comic books are those produced by the Marvel group, and one of their most popular titles is *X-Men*. This series is about a band of mutants with unique superpowers who fight more or less in secret to defend the human race from various threats, including the evil workings of other mutants who are less noble and altruistic than the X-Men. I followed the X-Men for years. One of the perennial adversaries of the X-Men, starting from the very first issue, was a group called the Brotherhood of Evil Mutants. They had vague plans of conquering the world, but they were also motivated by an apparently thoroughgoing hatred of ordinary people. They were in many respects the consummate, archetypal bad guys.

In retrospect, what is especially striking about the Brotherhood of Evil Mutants is their name. It seemed quite appropriate and natural to me at the time, and I never questioned it. But during the research for this book, I have gradually come to realize how extremely rare it is to find an organization that names itself as dedicated to evil.

Indeed, the positive affirmation of evil is almost entirely lacking in the real world. At most, some few organizations (usually those involved in physically competitive undertakings, such as teen delinquent gangs or sports teams) give themselves names that will presumably strike fear into the hearts of opponents: Raiders, Pirates, Demons. The Hell's Angels motorcycle gang was like that, although they were hardly dedicated to evil.[1] There are also musical groups such as Public Enemy or Black Sabbath who adopt titles connoting enmity to virtuous life, but even these usually imply rebellion against conventional standards rather than outright evil. Some sports teams call themselves devils, but usually there is a modifier to soften the evilness of the name: the Blue Devils, the Sun Devils. Moreover, the images and pictures these teams use are often manifestly nonevil. They tend to depict an amusing devil with a funny costume and a cartoon face, as opposed to something more obviously sinister. The categories that our modern culture perceives as seriously evil are never used as group names. No sports teams call themselves the Child Abusers or the Bigots.

Indeed, many groups that are known under evil-sounding names prefer more positive, favorable names for themselves. Researchers have noted, for example, how unsuccessful most terrorist groups are at getting the public to use the names they choose for themselves.[2] They usually want to be known as "freedom fighters" or as such-and-such a liberation army.

Occasionally, an individual wants to adopt an explicitly evil name, but such people tend to encounter severe resistance. A recent Associated Press news story reported the case of a Japanese businessman who wanted to name his son Akuma, which means "Devil." The man explained that his surname (Sato) was so common in Japan that he wanted to give his son a name that would stand out. But the local authorities refused to accept the name. After a six-month legal dispute, the man gave in and named his son more conventionally.[3] Members of violent gangs occasionally choose names connoting evil, such as the sobriquet Monster used by the Los Angeles gangland murderer Kody Scott. Yet even he did not see himself as evil. He regarded himself as defending his neighborhood and the honor of self and friends against the forces of evil, embodied principally in the members of rival gangs (and to a lesser extent in the police forces who sought to prevent and punish the lethal street battles). He seems to have chosen the name Monster more to boast about his martial prowess than to celebrate evil, and in his memoir he seeks to portray himself as mostly on the side of the good guys.[4]

Given that there is so much evil in the world, why do so few groups or individuals name themselves in positive affirmation of evil? As we saw in the last chapter, most people who do evil do not think of themselves as doing evil. Like "Monster" Kody Scott, most of them regard themselves as good people who are trying to defend themselves and their group against the forces of evil. If we talk to their enemies, however, we soon learn that the enemies also see themselves as the good guys fighting against evil. The world often breaks down into us against them, and it almost invariably turns out that evil lies on the side of "them."

In one sense, then, the face of evil is no one's real face—it is always a false image that is imposed or projected on the opponent. But the image of evil is familiar to everyone today, just as it has been familiar to everyone for thousands of years. How can we be so familiar with something that doesn't exist? How can so many different cultures and peoples all over the world come up with roughly the same image of evil, if it is not founded in reality? Or, to turn the question around, how can the image of evil survive so well if it is a mistake?

This chapter will explain the perennial image of evil. I will argue that the image of evil is not confined to archaic superstitions and quaint religious theories—indeed, it has been an important force in the twentieth century. The purpose of this chapter is to understand what psychological needs or forces sustain this image despite its weak relationship to empirical reality.

The most pervasive and compelling image of evil has pretty much the same characteristics wherever it appears. Actual events are then often distorted, misperceived, or otherwise twisted to fit this image. The image survives in the eyes of beholders everywhere because it satisfies several important needs and reassures people about their own goodness and innocence.

This image requires a name, because it will come up repeatedly. For convenience, the *myth of pure evil* approximately captures the main implications.

Images of Evil

Let us take a close look at how evil has been depicted in several major sources. An accurate appreciation of how evil is usually portrayed provides keys to understanding the psychological forces that sustain the myth of pure evil. To draw valid conclusions, one wants to have converging evidence from widely different sources, and so religious theology and popular modern films are a valuable pair of sources in which to look for parallels. Because the effects of culture often operate mainly in the socialization of children, it is desirable to consider some of the messages aimed directly at children; I will include some research on depictions of evil in children's cartoons. Last, because Christian thought, movies, and children's cartoons all reflect the cultural mainstream, it seems desirable to add a source of evidence outside the mainstream. I will briefly examine the modern paramilitary cult in the United States, which has attracted notoriety through its links to home-grown American terrorism and other antiestablishment violence.

We should pay special attention to the motives of evildoers and to the relationship between them and their victims. What drives them to do wicked, hurtful things? And how do they come into contact with their victims?

Evil at the Movies

Undoubtedly, today's Americans gain more frequent and vivid glimpses of the face of evil from movies than from religious writings. The enduring popularity of horror films is quite surprising; indeed, several scholars have concluded that horror films are the most reliably popular movie genre.[5] This is no doubt partly due to two advantages of horror movies over other movies: They can be made relatively cheaply, and they are less likely to fail at their assigned task. (Humor, for example, is delicate and difficult, but fright is easily achieved.) Yet the public's enduring fascination with being frightened by evil figures is also a main reason that horror films make money.

Admittedly, not all movies have villains. It could be argued that the movies that do have villains are somehow less realistic or of lower quality. There is some merit to that argument. Lionel Trilling, in his overview of the evolution of Western literature, concluded that villains vanished from serious literature around the start of the twentieth century because they were insufficiently realistic.[6] Just as serious modern literature does not have plain old bad guys, sophisticated movies may also avoid such stock figures.

Yet this is beside the point. Villains survive in popular entertainments because people still like to see them—in some important way, they do correspond to how people see the world. Indeed, the very fact that villains endure in popular entertainments despite being discredited by high literature, theology, and psychology is a testimony to how strong the appetite for them is. After all, if they were merely realistic, it might be difficult to draw psychological conclusions about their presence in movies, just as the appearance of computers in modern movies probably means nothing more than that they have become a fact of life. But to the extent that movie villains depart from reality, we can safely conclude that they speak to a deeply rooted preference for understanding evil in certain ways.

The theme of chaos is a perennial aspect of evil in movies. According to one authoritative book on horror movies, a common theme is the creation of fear through "the invasion of the abnormal into the world of the normal."[7] A horror movie starts with a vision of a happy, peaceful, ordinary life, and such visions have been an important and desirable element of the *good* throughout history. Horror movies like to start with this stable, happy setting and then show how it gets turned upside down by the invasion of evil. The loving family that is laughing and smiling at its picnic in the opening scene will undoubtedly be screaming and weeping before long. They will find themselves in the grip of hostile powers that they cannot understand, and they won't even know why these terrible things are happening to them. That is how evil works, in the movies.

There was a major change in the history of horror movies, and it separates two eras of this kind of filmmaking. The first emphasized supernatural villains such as vampires, werewolves, mummies, witches, and evil invaders from outer space. The second era began with Alfred Hitchcock's *Psycho* (1960), which featured a *human* villain. The Hitchcock approach has been refined (or has deteriorated, depending on your point of view) into the "slasher" films in which a vaguely defined human character murders victims seemingly at random until he is finally thwarted. According to Carol J. Clover's thoughtful book *Men, Women, and Chainsaws*,[8] the landmarks of this subgenre included *The Texas Chainsaw Massacre*, *Carrie*, and *Halloween*, all of which came out during the 1970s. A variation on this theme, starting with *I Spit on Your Grave*, consists of films in which a woman is raped by a group of men and takes revenge by murdering them one by one. This genre likewise began in the 1970s.

Films of this type gradually clustered around a fairly standard plot, according to Clover. A demented killer more or less inexplicably inflicts brutal, painful death on young couples who are engaging in illicit sex. Traditionally masculine responses such as fighting back, taking charge, or reporting to the authorities are fruitless, and the men who try these lines of action are quickly killed. Meanwhile, helpless young females die lingering, bloody deaths. Eventually, a tomboyish female figure (and usually one who has resisted the temptations of illicit sex) resists the killer, escapes, fights back, and ultimately succeeds, often by killing the killer. Clover says the audience (made up largely of young males) typically cheers for the madman's murders, especially as disliked or envied characters are killed, but they also cheer the young woman's victory over the madman.

The subthemes of punishment for illicit sex and reward for adolescent self-control are apparent. Still, these themes of controlling adolescent sexuality are subtle and seem almost tangential to the plot. In the story itself, the killer's motives are not explained at all or, at best, are presented as some vague desire for revenge. A good example is provided by the popular series of films that began with *Nightmare on Elm Street* and for a time made Freddy Krueger one of the most famous villains in American pop culture. The basic story of this series was that a group of neighbors had banded together to kill Freddy (by trapping him in a building and burning it down) because he was molesting and killing children. Freddy then began to strike back from beyond death. His method was to come into children's dreams and murder them there, with the twist that when they were killed in their dreams, they died in reality. In one sense, then, Freddy's motive was a simple wish to avenge his own death. Yet that explanation is patently inadequate, because he was a child molester and murderer before he was killed. It appears, then, that he was evil all along, maliciously and inexplicably, and revenge was merely a secondary motive that spurred him on to extra efforts (and required a change in strategy because of the practical drawback of being physically dead). In the story, Freddy was evil from the start and was merely forced to change his venue from waking life to dream life.

Villains are not confined to horror movies, of course. Action movies are full of bad guys. These movies also seem to conform to a fairly standard pattern. Usually, the villains are motivated by greed for either money or power. These motives tend to be presented without much elaboration. Two additional features are common: sadism and egotism. Many of the movie villains seem to enjoy hurting their victims simply for the sake of doing so, and they tend to have very exalted opinions of themselves. Indeed, their pride often proves to be a fatal flaw, because their overconfidence gives the hero a chance to escape from their clutches and defeat them. The sadism is part of the essence of the villain. In a recent television special on villains in movies, the nationally prominent movie critics Siskel and Ebert emphasized this general point: "Enjoying being evil is the key to any successful villain."[9] They added that this is the "most important feature." Thus, it is not enough to perform harmful acts. The truly evil villains derive pleasure from inflicting harm.

Not all these traits are necessarily combined in the same person. In recent years, the most popular movie villain is a group of drug dealers.[10] The leader is usually motivated by greed and egotism, but he typically employs some henchmen who are often merely sadistic (and usually egotistical, too—especially with regard to assessing their ability to defeat the hero in individual combat). They enjoy hurting people, and they go away feeling superior. They are sometimes also portrayed as motivated by drug addiction, an issue to which we will return because of the prominence of the drug menace as a favorite image of evil in American society today. First, however, let us examine another important and quite different source of information about the face of evil.

Religion and the Devil

Probably the best place to learn how people think of evil is in religion, which often provides explicit, vivid explanations of evil. The noted scholar Jeffrey Burton Russell has written extensively about the images of evil in Christian thought. As he points out, cultures all over the world have arrived at "remarkably similar" versions of evil figures and forces.[11] The idea that these similarities are the result of the spread of certain concepts from the same original place to cover the entire world is not plausible. Instead, Russell says, one must conclude that some common psychological process is responsible: The same version of evil was invented several different times, in different parts of the world, independently. Religious ideas of evil thus spring from the way people see the world.[12]

Russell notes that the word *devil* comes from words meaning "adversary." Essentially, evil is seen as the adversary of the good.[13] Evil is defined in relation to good, as its opposite. Evil does not exist by itself—there must be some positive forces of good, some conceptions of what is right and desirable, so that evil can emerge as the opposite.

There are two important implications of the idea that evil originates as the opposite of the good. The first has to do with the prospect of eventual victory. If evil is dependent on good (as a reaction against it), then there is hope of eventual victory. In past eras, this issue was debated in theological terms: Was God responsible for creating Satan? If so, is it likely that Satan will eventually be defeated and perhaps even saved? Christian views of the supremacy and omnipotence of God have grappled with how to understand the notion of Satan as God's intentional creation, because it seems to suggest that God created evil. In Russell's terms, the theological dilemma is as follows: You assume either that God chose to permit evil (in which case God seemingly shares the blame) or that God was unable to prevent it (in which case God is revealed to be something less than all-powerful). Neither of those views is acceptable to the faithful, because the first implies that God's goodness is limited and the second that God's power is limited. Generation after generation of Christian theologians have searched for a way to explain evil without accepting either of those options.

Other religions have frankly acknowledged Satan as the equal of God. For example, in Iranian religions, Ohrmazd and Ahriman were twins, one good and one evil, and they competed on a fairly equal basis in the divine tasks of creation and rule.[14] Such dualistic views see the universe as a permanent struggle between ineradicable principles of good and evil, and it is not likely that either will ever fully destroy the other.

In our own time, the issue of the relationship between good and evil is usually phrased in terms of human nature: Are people fundamentally good, or is there a side of everyone (or of some people) that is fundamentally bad? The utopian idealisms that flourished in recent centuries blamed society for making people bad, and there was sincere hope that by reforming society—whether through a Rousseauian return to nature, sharing the benefits of liberty and equality, or helping society to evolve into a socialist paradise where everyone would share things equally and work for the betterment of all—human evil could be obliterated. The perennial disappointment of these idealistic visions has discouraged most modern thinkers from advocating them seriously. In particular, the twentieth century's love affair with communism, which at first brought hope and faith to millions of people all over the world, led to shocking disillusionment when communist regimes repeatedly degenerated into tyranny, police repression, internal and external oppression, lack of freedom, and other abuses. In the 1930s, one prominent Western idealist after another turned away from communism and described the bitter disappointment he or she felt about Soviet Russia. What had seemed to be the last, best hope of humanity was now a terrorist police state, arresting and killing innocent citizens, making deals with the Nazis, and exploiting the masses while providing lavish special privileges for its gangster-style leaders.[15]

My point is that these utopian flops, from Communist Russia to the short-lived hippie communes of the 1960s, have prompted a reconsideration of human nature. It will not be nearly as easy as everybody once thought to produce an ideal society, because human nature is not as malleable or as benevolent as the idealists had naively hoped. The forces that create evil are very deeply rooted in human nature. Even radical overhauls of society are far from sufficient to remove them. People may think that if only everyone had enough to eat, or a little freedom, or a little land, or a little more self-esteem, then hatred and violence would cease. Perhaps hatred and violence do subside for a little while when people first get these things, but in the long run hatred and violence have proved far more pervasive and durable than any of the social conditions on which they have been blamed. As far as we can foresee, evil will continue to be the opponent of the good. The final victory of the good is not in sight. Not by a long shot.

The second important implication of the view of evil as the adversary of the good is that it seems tailor-made to increase hostilities between rival nations, ethnic groups, and other social units. One of the most powerful and universal human tendencies is to identify with a group of people similar to oneself, and to square off against rival groups. Moreover, people automatically and inevitably begin to think that their group is good. But if *we* are good, and *you* are our opponents, and evil is the opponent of the good, then *you* must be evil. Groups of people everywhere will come to that same conclusion, even groups on opposite sides of the same conflict. The stronger the tendency to see one's own group as good—and this tendency is often surprisingly strong—the more likely one is to regard one's rivals and enemies as evil. Such views may then be used to provide easy justification for treating one's enemies harshly, because there is no point in being patient, tolerant, and understanding when one is dealing with evil.

Throughout history, people have asserted that their rivals or enemies were in league with the Devil. Popular mythology has often invoked the theme of someone voluntarily making a pact with the Devil. Russell concluded that this theme has been especially common when applied to minority groups who are different in some way from the dominant group in the culture, such as Jews in Europe.

What drives Satan and other evil figures? Apart from some vague ambition to gain power, the answer appears to be: nothing. Or, rather, nothing beyond the sheer satisfaction of doing evil. In Russell's words, the Devil is a figure who is bent on "inflicting suffering for the sake of suffering."[16] In this book, I will use the term *sadism* to refer to a tendency to enjoy harming or hurting other people (along with going out of one's way to find opportunities for that pleasure). As we will see, sadism is an elusive, controversial, and complex phenomenon in terms of the psychology of actual perpetrators of evil. But it is not elusive, controversial, or complex in the image of evil. It is central. Pure and simple, the Devil is sadistic.

Not all religious views of evil focus on malice, however. Another trend emphasizes evil as chaos. Evil is disorder, unreason, and generally the disruption of the rational, stable, predictable, ordinary patterns of life. This was not just a device invented by the moviemakers; it has marked religious ideas about evil for many centuries.

There is one additional religious trend that does not receive much attention these days but has long been prominent: pride. Indeed, Satan's first sin was pride. He wanted to be God's equal; in some versions, he even wanted to replace God as ruler of the universe. In modern life, given the apotheosis of self-esteem, religious figures have backed away from condemning the sin of pride, but through most of history, pride was a central aspect of badness. The great evil figures of religion and mythology do not have low self-esteem—on the contrary, they have always been inordinately proud, confident, and even arrogant. Satan had high self-esteem, very high. His high self-esteem is central to his evilness.

Bad Guys for Kids

Another important place to look for depictions of evil is in material created especially for children. It is through such material that a culture teaches its basic values and beliefs to the next generation. Nowadays, children probably learn less from books of fairy tales than from cartoon shows on television, and so I will examine a study of these shows. As one might expect, many of them present stark and simple battles between the forces of good and the forces of evil.

Two psychologists, Petra Hesse and John Mack, made a detailed study of taped versions of children's cartoons in the late 1980s. Specifically, they identified the eight most highly rated cartoon shows at the time, taped 20 episodes of each, and then spent a long time carefully analyzing their content to understand how they presented images of evil, enemy figures.

Their conclusions are consistent with what we have already seen in movies and religious depictions. The villains have no clear reason for their attacks. They seem to be evil for evil's sake, and they have been so all along. They are sadistic: They derive pleasure from hurting others, and they celebrate, rejoice, or laugh with pleasure when they hurt or kill someone, especially if the victim is a good person. The mere wish to inflict pain for the sake of doing so was aptly captured by a phrase repeatedly uttered by the evil villain Cobra Commander: "Let's reach out and crush someone." The nonspecific "someone" suggests that the main point is just to inflict hurt, almost regardless of who is hurt.

Apart from the joy of creating harm and chaos, these villains seem to have little motive. Even when they are depicted as wishing for money, power, and war, these wishes are not explained. They already have plenty of money, and it's not clear what use they would have for more. Likewise, they often seem driven by a fierce and implacable hatred of the good guys, which is also not explained.

Evil is presented as being inherently the enemy of peace and order, as well as of beauty. "If it were not for the enemies, the world would be at peace,"[17] as the researchers concluded. The protagonists and heroes want to live in peace, and they only become violent in self-defense against the attacks of the bad guys. The villains want war for the sake of war, and they claim to enjoy destruction and chaos. In some cases, they find beauty threatening and make a point of trying to destroy beautiful things.

A few additional observations by these researchers are worth mentioning. First, the evil figures tend to speak with foreign accents, unlike the heroes, whose speech is nearly always perfect American English. The foreignness of the villains is often underscored by depicting them as nationalities who have been enemies of Americans, such as Germans,

Eastern Europeans, Asians, or Arabs. Second, they tend to use oppressive techniques to enforce their power, such as torture, mind control, and arbitrary dictatorship. Third, they tend to lose emotional control from time to time. In some cases, the loss of self-control contributes to their undoing, because they make errors that allow the heroes to defeat them. Their anger, in particular, escalates until they lash out blindly and thereby perform self-defeating or self-destructive acts (such as destroying their own resources, weapons, or allies).

The New War

One more useful source of images is the popular paramilitary culture that has emerged over the last couple of decades to idolize and idealize the violent pursuit of traditional American ideals. Sociologist James William Gibson spent many years immersing himself in this subculture, from *Soldier of Fortune* conventions to "Paintball" mock battles, and he has furnished a thoughtful and fascinating description of it in his book *Warrior Dreams*.[18] In many ways, the paramilitary culture is just the latest version of the traditional American theme of regeneration through violence, but there are some new twists. The technological fascination with powerful weapons is a central aspect, and it can be dated back to the famous Clint Eastwood detective movie *Dirty Harry*, in which the hero carried an immensely powerful handgun. The gun was a running theme in the movie's dialogue and stimulated a huge demand among private owners, even though knowledgeable sources regarded the gun as completely unsuitable for actual urban violence. Also, Gibson emphasizes that the novels and movies that constitute the "New War" subculture show the act of killing with a loving emphasis on detail that was largely missing from the classic shoot-'em-up Westerns and war films of past decades.

For our purposes, the most relevant part of Gibson's work is his analysis of the enemy as depicted in these novels (such as William Pierce's *The Turner Diaries* or Jack Hild's *SOBs: Soldiers of Barrabas* series), magazine features (most notably in *Soldier of Fortune*), and films. These enemies live in dark, chaotic regions outside the civilized world, and they are "deeply savage animals [and] perverts who commit crimes for pleasure."[19] On one level, they are driven simply by the standard material motives of greed and lust, even though these go beyond normal desires: They scheme to get endless millions of dollars, and they somehow manage to have harems of attractive females at their service. On another level, though, they are driven not by pragmatic wants but by sadism.

They get a sort of sexual joy from violent acts of torture, rape, and murder. Often they are sadistic to the point of refusing to let their victims die a quick death, wanting instead to prolong the death agony for their enjoyment.

Another main goal of the enemy groups is the destruction of the American social order, along with its moral values. Gibson says: "Creating chaos is the objective of the evil ones in the New War, just as it was at the beginning of time."[20] The evildoers (as perceived by the paramilitary subculture) hate the vision of peace, harmony, and order that traditional American society represents.

The enemy villains of modern paramilitary culture are outsiders, many of whom resemble enemies of past wars. Often they resemble Indians (although usually they are merely street punks or gangsters who have adopted Indian motifs of warpaint and costumes). Others resemble the Nazi German or Japanese enemies of World War II. Many are nonwhite, although the protagonist group is usually racially integrated so that any implication of racial antagonism is muted.

Last, Gibson notes that the enemies are often so overwhelmed by their rage and wicked desires that they are unable to control themselves. The heroes and protagonists, in contrast, "are men of nearly impeccable self-control."[21] Thus, many New War novels can be read as simple allegories of battle between those who have self-control and those who lack it, with the latter seeming to gain the upper hand in this modern era of American decadence.

Pure Evil

What can we conclude from this survey of depictions of evil? The myth of pure evil can be seen as a composite of these images. The myth defines the way people think of evil—which is in some crucial respects quite different from the real, actual causes of violence and oppression.

First, *evil involves the intentional infliction of harm on people.* I began this book by noting that evil is in the eye of the beholder; now we can add that these beholders are generally people who suffer harm. They see the agent of evil as someone who harmed them. Moreover, the harm is intentional. Evil seeks to do harm and does it deliberately. At least, that is how people think of it.

Second, and of crucial importance, *evil is driven primarily by the wish to inflict harm merely for the pleasure of doing so.* By and large, evil is not understood as something that *reluctantly* uses violence as a means to an end. Rather, the harm inflicted by evil forces is *gratuitous.*[22] Evil is sadistic: Evil people enjoy the suffering they cause, and they inflict harm to get this enjoyment. Sometimes evil is seen as driven by cravings for power or money, but these are not well-articulated motives, and such desires are certainly not part of some positive scheme (such as the wish to gain power in order to make the world a better place). If evil wants money and power, the money and power are often seen merely as means toward further evil.

This lack of a comprehensible motive behind evil is strikingly similar to the research findings about ordinary interpersonal conflicts that I discussed in the last chapter. When people have been angered or victimized by someone else, they tend to describe that person's actions as having no coherent or apparent reason. Sometimes, they simply present the actions as arbitrary and almost incomprehensible. At other times, they depict them as motivated by sheer malice. But perpetrators almost never describe themselves and their own actions in either of those ways.

Thus, ordinary interpersonal conflicts seem to become assimilated in the myth of pure evil. People are unable or unwilling to see that someone who hurt them had an understandable reason. They distort the other's actions to fit the myth of pure evil.

Third, *the victim is innocent and good.* The forces of evil may occasionally turn on one another, but for the most part they try to attack good people. Victims are usually good people who are going about their business decently and appropriately. They are set upon out of the blue and for no reason by evildoers. Such victims deserve the utmost sympathy and support from all decent people, because what happened to them could happen to anyone. The evil one bears all the blame—in sharp contrast to the patterns of mutual, shared responsibility that are often found behind actual violent events.

Fourth, *evil is the other, the enemy, the outsider, the out-group.* Evil does not exist by itself but only in relation to the good. And what usually happens is that the conflict of good versus evil is often superimposed on the conflict of *us* against *them.* The pattern of having cartoon bad guys speak English with foreign accents, even among themselves—which is absurdly unrealistic on the face of it—reflects this underlying assumption that evil attaches mainly to people outside our own group.

Fifth, *evil has been that way since time immemorial.* Evil is not a matter of well-meaning, decent people turning bad in response to traumatic, difficult, or otherwise unpleasant experiences. Evil is steady and relentless and, for the most part, unchanging. Maybe once long ago there was a turning to bad, a fall from grace, an evil awakening, a new recognition, but throughout all of recent history, evil has been just that: evil. With individual people, the same is true: They were always evil, at least since childhood. Generally, they are born to be bad, as opposed to starting off good and turning bad in response to some decisively influential experience.

Sixth, *evil represents the antithesis of order, peace, and stability.* The normal world, the good and peaceful world, is stable and predictable. The intrusion of evil is essentially a disruption of the normal pattern of things. Evil is not just harm; it is also chaos and irrationality. Hence the common tendency, especially in a slightly more superstitious past, to think that earthquakes and other natural disasters are evil, because they bring both harm and chaos.

Seventh, *evil characters are often marked by egotism.* They do not lack for self-esteem. If anything, they have too much self-esteem, because they overestimate themselves. They are wildly ambitious and supremely confident, and they look down on everyone else. From Dracula and the Sheriff of Nottingham to the latest action movie's drug lord villain, evil characters are arrogant and self-assertive. Satan himself became bad through pride, back at the dawn of time.

Last, *evil figures have difficulty maintaining control over their feelings, especially rage and anger.* This characteristic is not as well established as some of the others, and there may be many exceptions. Indeed, some depictions of evil characterize it as coldly calculating, driven by an implacable hostility toward the good and normal, as opposed to being out of control. Still, there is some tendency to depict evil as given to impulse and wild actions, and indeed this wildness is sometimes seen as the vulnerable spot or fatal flaw that allows good to triumph.

The last two features, high self-esteem and poor self-control, are less central to the myth. (Ironically, we will also see that they conform to reality more than the other features. These features of the myth may reflect the intrusion of reality into a psychological fabrication.) Taken together, then, the other features constitute the myth of pure evil. A force, or person, that seeks relentlessly to inflict harm, with no positive or comprehensible motive, deriving enjoyment from the suffering of others, is evil. It maliciously and gratuitously seeks out unsuspecting, innocent victims from among the good people of the world. It is the eternal other, the enemy, the outsider who despises the orderly and peaceful world of the good and seeks to throw it into chaos.

Pure Evil in Modern Life

Let us now examine how the myth of pure evil is used outside the realms of fiction and theological theory. In the everyday affairs of ordinary men and women, how is the myth active? This examination will help shed light on why people favor such depictions of evil, because it will show what kinds of functions the image serves.

Crime and Evil in the News

Here is a story from the newspaper. A young couple was watching television in the living room of their nice suburban home one evening. Suddenly men broke in and attacked them. They beat the husband and wife brutally. The husband had to be put in the hospital, and the medical experts said his condition was serious. Nothing was stolen from the home; the men who broke in were not there for the purpose of robbery. No one knows who did this. The perpetrators are at large now (when the story appeared).

Several newspapers left the story at that, but others added another fact: The male victim was currently under indictment for involvement with juvenile prostitution.[23] Not surprisingly, people who read this second version of the story were less shocked and frightened, because it made the crime seem less random. It starts to seem plausible that someone might want to punish a man who was seeking illegal profit by exploiting and ruining the sexual innocence of children, and one can even imagine that perhaps some distraught relatives of one of his child prostitute victims inflicted the beating. In contrast, without that information, the story seems to show that ordinary, well-meaning suburbanites are vulnerable to being attacked for no reason in the false security of their own living rooms.

Thus, the news media sometimes have considerable latitude in how they portray a crime. In this case, providing all the facts made it seem (perhaps unfairly) as if a wicked person brought misfortune upon himself. But by omitting the victim's indictment, the story is easily made to resemble the myth of pure evil: Innocent victims are attacked for no apparent reason by vicious, alien forces. The forces of chaos and suffering are poised to intrude into our suburban homes—that is the implicit message in the shorter version of the story that many newspapers ran.

The focus of this section is crime, more precisely, the *perception* of crime. To be sure, the actual causes of crime are important for any understanding of evil; but the next few chapters will examine those causes in detail. To understand how the myth of pure evil operates today, it is essential to look at how crime is perceived, especially insofar as its perception differs from its reality. For this task, it is useful to look at how the news media deal with crime.

As we will see later on, most crimes follow fairly standard and predictable patterns.[24] In particular, murders tend to be the result of escalating arguments between relatives, neighbors, or other acquaintances, in which one person deeply offends or insults another, who responds by resorting to violence instead of pursuing the debate verbally. The victims of crime tend to be quite similar to the perpetrators in many superficial respects. Young, poor, urban black males tend to be the victims of crime, just as they make up a disproportionate share of the perpetrators. In many cases, the eventual perpetrators and victims know each other and are in intermittent conflict, and assault, robbery, and murder tend to be committed between them as a product of their conflicts.

Although such crimes may be the norm, they are not the ones to gain top billing in the nightly news. Instead, acts of random violence are featured, especially ones that seem to lack comprehensible motives. Consider some examples of the most talked about crime news stories of recent years, ones that ran for more than one day and that made weekly magazine covers—the most prominent news events.

In one, a woman was jogging in New York's Central Park. A gang of young men reportedly just out looking for some excitement found her, ambushed her, beat her up, and raped her. They smashed her head with big stones and left her in a coma. She survived the attack, although she was badly injured and disfigured. The news reports emphasized her unsuspecting innocence and the apparent capriciousness of the brutal attack on her. The attackers were presented as casual and unrepentant. The term *wilding* was adopted from the young men's discourse and passed briefly into national usage. It meant performing wild, aggressive actions merely for kicks.

In another story, two young women were passing through a park in Houston. Several young men had just completed a gang initiation that involved ritual fisticuffs. They were feeling both proud and flushed with aggressive arousal when the young women came upon them. They killed the young women. The media emphasized how one of the boys had placed his foot on the neck of the dead girl, seemingly proud of his putative victory.

The media also described how the young men had congratulated one another during their arraignment as having "made the big time," that is, attracted attention from the news media and the establishment. The remark was understood to mean that the young men were unrepentant and were actually enjoying the media coverage as a kind of recognition of their success. Quite possibly, of course, it meant no such thing. The young men may have had little chance to talk, and when they happened to meet in the midst of the dramatic proceedings, one might have tried to make a small joke about how all this attention contrasted with how society seemingly had ignored them through most of their lives. But it was reported in a way that made it seem that they were enjoying the fruits of their malicious and deadly acts.

Both of these crimes bear a clear resemblance to the myth of pure evil. The innocent victims were going about their legitimate business when they were attacked by wicked young men for no reason. The bad men sought to do harm just for the sheer pleasure or sadistic enjoyment of hurting someone (and possibly for the perversely egotistical satisfaction of being recognized on television). They represented the horrific intrusion of chaos and lawlessness into the peaceful, civilized world in which young women can walk or jog without fear.

The reason these stories were featured on the news was not that they were typical of crime in general. If anything, they were featured because they were atypical. But a crucial aspect of their appeal—the part that probably boosted the sales of newspapers and magazines and commercial advertisements during televised news—was that they conformed to the myth of pure evil. Random crimes are unusual and exceptional, but random crime is what epitomizes evil to many magazine subscribers.

In another famous recent crime, a man was severely beaten by a group of policemen. By coincidence, most of the beating was captured on videotape by a citizen witness, and the films were on the news. The media played the story as racial violence, emphasizing that the victim was black and his attackers were white, suggesting that the white police were simply out to inflict harm on minority citizens. The victim was described as a "black motorist," which thus invoked the theme of racial victimization while presenting him as an innocent person driving a car. This depiction helped the story conform more to the myth of pure evil than certain of the omitted facts would permit. For example, it turned out that the victim had a criminal record, was currently violating his parole, and had resisted arrest during a high-speed car chase. Yet such facts were downplayed in most stories, because they make the policemen's action seem more understandable and hence less evil. The depiction of him as an innocent motorist helped place the policemen (who were certainly far from innocent, regardless) into the role of pure evil.

There was an interesting sequel to this episode. When a jury acquitted the police officers, the public was outraged, and many black neighborhoods in that city (Los Angeles) rioted. It seems likely that the media's portrayal of the offending policemen along the lines of the myth of pure evil helped fuel the outrage; after all, had the victim been depicted as a criminal, fewer law-abiding citizens would have been prone to riot in protest of his mistreatment. Out of the many crimes occurring during the riots, one in particular was selected for maximum attention, and this also invoked the myth of pure evil. A white truck driver was dragged from his vehicle by black rioters and severely beaten, including being bashed in the head with a brick. His innocence was emphasized—he had certainly had nothing to do with acquitting those policemen over the earlier beating of the motorist. He was turned into a symbol for black rage directed randomly against white people in general. Meanwhile, the fact that other black people had found him and taken him to a hospital received considerably less attention in the news. Black people threatening the life of a white person was apparently a highly newsworthy item, but other black people saving the life of that same person was less so.

The interracial aspect of these crimes is significant because it too plays on the myth of pure evil. The evidence is overwhelming that the majority of crimes are committed between members of the same racial and ethnic groups. That is, whites kill whites, and blacks kill blacks. The media, however, prefer to feature stories about interracial crimes. They assume, quite plausibly, that America's sensitivity about racism generates a special interest in such crimes. Such crimes presumably sell more papers and magazines.

And why is that? One reason is that racism lends itself to being understood in terms of the myth of pure evil. When antagonism develops between blacks and whites, each will quickly tend to see the other as being motivated by sheer unreasonable malice. The myth of pure evil emphasizes the otherness of evil, and someone from a different race is easier to see as different from oneself and more fundamentally "other" than is someone of one's own race.

The incorporation of racial conflict into the myth of pure evil suggests one risk in the current American rush to categorize everyone by race and gender. The more people become sensitive to these differences, the more easily they will fall into the us-against-them mentality, and the more readily the myth of pure evil will be pasted onto the other side. The more people are pushed to be constantly aware of differences, the harder it may be for them to get along. In the history of the world, increased recognition of differences between groups has led more often to conflict and violence than to peaceful cooperation and sharing. America is now making a dangerous gamble on the opposite result.

Drugs and Alcohol: The Chemical Demons

What is fueling the current epidemic of violence in the United States? Many citizens will offer a fairly simple answer: drugs. The mass media reinforce this view by depicting crime and violence as stimulated by the ingestion of drugs. In another variation, they emphasize that gangs sell drugs and rival gangs kill each other (and anyone else who happens to get in the way) in battles over the right to sell drugs in certain areas or over ownership of particular shipments of drugs. The media cater to the belief that many people who take drugs are addicted and that these desperate, brain-fogged people will rob and kill innocent victims to get money for drugs.

Occasionally, events do conform to such beliefs. Certainly gangs fight over drugs and over specific opportunities to distribute and sell them. Certainly addicts have been known to commit robbery and burglary to get money to buy drugs.

Still, it is inaccurate to take these events as the norm. A close look at the evidence suggests that the impact of drugs on gang violence is uncertain and inconsistent. A report by *The Economist*[25] concluded that the drug business in general makes American gangs less violent, for several reasons. Foremost is that violence is bad for business: It scares customers away. Many people might like to buy drugs but are reluctant to drive their nice cars down inner-city alleys full of young men who carry Uzi machine guns and periodically shoot at one another.

Indeed, as some gang memoirs indicate, American youth gangs were violent long before drugs appeared.[26] The violence was often linked to neighborhood rivalries, grievances, feuds, and the exchange of insults and humiliations. In the 1970s and early 1980s, many young men devoted much of their lives to these violent contests over reputation and pride. When it became possible to sell drugs, however, many of them abandoned old grievances and turned their attention to making money. Getting rich is much more appealing, and more compelling, than shooting up your neighbors. As mentioned in Chapter 1, "Monster" Kody Scott describes in his autobiography his shock at getting out of prison and returning to his old neighborhood where long-standing hatreds and grievances had been forgotten by gang members who now all just wanted to enjoy the easy profits of selling drugs. He was ready to resume the war, but everyone else seemed to have lost interest in those ancient vendettas.

Yet the media continue to present drugs as the cause of gang violence. In a revealing incident, a Chicago police investigation developed two theories about a three-day gang battle that killed 13 people. One theory was that the two gangs were fighting over who held the unwritten right to sell drugs in a particular area. The other was that two men, one from each gang, had gotten into a deadly argument over a woman, and their argument escalated into the shoot-out between their groups, which had long been enemies anyway. The local news media reported only the drug turf theory, ignoring the equally plausible theory about the dispute over the woman.[27] Men have been fighting over women for thousands of years (remember Helen of Troy?), but the current preference is to blame violence on drugs. Appallingly, the media reported only the theory that fit popular stereotypes and ignored the other one.

Why would the media present a misleading picture? One might accuse reporters of bias or incompetence, but this is not entirely fair. The news media are involved in a highly competitive business of their own, and for them the need to make money is a matter of inducing citizens to consult a particular newspaper, radio station, or television program for their news. Ideally, one might hope that competition would raise standards for accurate, intelligent, thoughtful coverage. It has become clear to nearly everyone in journalism, however, that the entertainment value of news coverage is more effective in attracting an audience. One has to tell the public what it is interested in hearing, and often this means presenting simplistic explanations that conform to the expectations, beliefs, and prejudices of the public. Journalists do not see themselves as in the business of educating the public so much as of informing it of what it is interested in hearing about. They do try to get the facts right, but the world is full of facts, and they can present only a very few. So they choose the hot ones, the ones that seem to fit the public's appetites. Drug-related crime sells papers.

Coupled with this need to cater to the audience is the pressure to provide simple explanations. In the 1980s, the news world had to confront the fact that more people now learned about the news from television than from newspapers and other printed media. The informational implication was widely noted: An article in the daily newspaper contains a great deal more information than an evening television broadcast. The pressure to provide brief sound bites and quick, flashy presentations has increased. "Gang war over drug turf; film at 11" might fit into the 10-second promotional time slot and attract viewers for the local news that night. "Police speculate that gang war may be either a dispute over a woman or a feud over drug turf; film at 11" is too long and complicated. Besides, people are impatient with multiple explanations, which always give the impression of uncertainty and lack of closure. One theory is always better than two, where the public is concerned.[28] In contrast, in the academic disputes of experts, there are nearly always multiple theories.

So the question becomes: Why does the public prefer to hear that drugs are the source of most violence, even if this is not really true?

The answer is that drugs support people's beliefs in the myth of pure evil. Drugs are an alien force, an other, an outside entity that forces itself into our world of normality and brings chaos and destruction. People who are under the influence of drugs are different, incomprehensible, unpredictable. Moreover, the public persists in believing that drugs create intentions, such as the intention to commit violent acts. In fact, of course, the drug is merely a chemical substance and has no such power to create intentions. Violent impulses exist in people; at most, drugs may bring them to the surface and impair people's ability, or willingness, to stifle them.

Drug-induced violence sustains an important feature of the myth of pure evil—the innocence of the victim. There is no reason to worry about reciprocal causation or victim provocation if one invokes drugs. *"He took drugs, and the drugs made him kill people."* Enough said: One doesn't ask whether the victims had started a fight or offended him, or whether he had been nourishing a grudge for years, or whether he in fact was mentally ill and drug use was merely an irrelevant symptom of what was causing the violence. Such is the simplistic form of explanation that many people prefer, and the presentation of information about drugs in the mass media caters to this prejudice and sustains it.

In an important sense, the popular mythology of drug use is the modern version of possession by demons. Superstitious medieval citizens believed that demons from the underworld took possession of people and forced them to do evil things. Modern citizens no longer believe in demons, for the most part, but many do believe that drugs operate in roughly the same way. The drug is seen as an alien, evil force, coming from outside our land, brought by dangerous, wicked people with foreign accents. The drugs operate just like the demon, who takes control of a human being and causes him to perpetrate wicked, malicious crimes.

The popularity of this "demon possession" image of drugs is boosted by the fact that many drug users find this myth somewhat appealing and useful. It reduces their guilt to claim that an alien force (drugs) took possession of them and forced them to do bad things. This is much better than saying that they simply took drugs because they liked the feeling of being high, and they didn't mind doing other nasty things as well. People are not sympathetic to somebody who is responsible for self-indulgent crimes such as taking drugs and hurting others. But they are sympathetic to "victims" of drugs who can say with a straight face that they found themselves in the power of an external, evil force that made them perform heinous acts against their will.

The tendency to think about drugs in terms of the myth of pure evil is not confined to modern America or to crack cocaine. Similar arguments have been made about LSD, PCP, heroin, and others.[29] The strangeness of illegal drugs contributes to the image of them as an alien force bringing chaos into our rational world. Yet even the most familiar of drugs, alcohol, has been assimilated into the myth from time to time. The phrase "demon rum" from the nineteenth century is only the most obvious indication that alcoholic intoxication has been regarded as a modern version of demonic possession. The modern beliefs that most alcoholics cannot control their drinking (such as the theories promoted by Alcoholics Anonymous) imply as much: Alcohol is a dangerous substance that overwhelms helpless individuals and forces them to engage in acts against their will. Stanton Peele and other thinkers have criticized the lack of individual responsibility implicit in some of these doctrines, and there is little doubt that some addicts and alcoholics like to excuse their misbehavior by blaming it on the external force of drugs or alcohol. To thwart such easy escapes, AA insists that its members take responsibility for their actions, including things they have done while under the influence of drink.

In particular, alcohol is often used to explain violent behavior. When someone abuses a spouse or child, gets into fights with strangers, or murders an innocent bystander or romantic rival, the people involved often blame alcohol. Crime statistics, it is true, show that alcohol is involved in over half of violent crimes.[30] Yet the evidence does not support the easy explanation that alcohol "caused" the violence. Alcohol is neither necessary nor sufficient to cause aggression, and the vast majority of drinkers do not hurt anybody. A glass of sherry will not turn a little old lady into a dangerous bully, nor will a couple of beers set a mild-mannered schoolteacher off on a killing spree.

Apparently, alcohol merely reduces the inner restraints against violent impulses; it does not create those impulses. Peaceful, friendly people will remain so under the influence of alcohol. Alcohol increases aggression only if the person has hostile, aggressive tendencies caused by other factors. In a well-known experiment, for example, college students who had consumed alcohol were no more aggressive (as measured by how severely they decided to zap a rival student with electric shocks) than students who had not had alcohol—except if the other person had provoked and angered them. The person who had had alcohol and then was provoked was exceptionally aggressive—more aggressive than the person who was provoked but had not had alcohol. Thus, alcohol increased aggression only when there was already some angry impulse present.[31]

So alcohol alone is never an adequate explanation for violence. It can increase the degree of aggression, but it does not by itself cause it. The same is true of certain other drugs Why, then, do people persist in speaking as if drugs and alcohol were the full explanation?

Part of the answer no doubt has to do with people's tendency to simplify matters and invoke the most obvious cause. But another part is that in some ways the alcohol/drug explanation is preferable. It satisfies people in a way that a more complex, integrative explanation would not. Blaming violence on alcohol or drugs is appealing for the same reasons that the myth of pure evil is appealing.

The appeal can be appreciated by considering domestic violence. Too often, we forget how much ambivalence is involved in domestic violence, especially on the side of the victims. They hate being attacked and hurt, but usually they also love the perpetrator for many positive things that are unrelated to the abuse. How can they explain the fact that someone who loves them and whom they love will hurt them? To acknowledge that the abuser feels some implacable hostility toward the victim would be very upsetting, because it would force the victim to face unresolved conflicts and possibly fundamental incompatibilities in the relationship. In contrast, blaming the violence on alcohol allows the victim to go on loving the abuser apart from the abuse. The alcohol is the alien, evil force that takes over the beloved partner and forces him (or her) to commit these terrible, hurtful actions. The abusers encourage these views, because for them alcohol is an excuse that is less damaging than any of the other likely explanations for their acts.[32]

The Hated Face: Enemies in War

Turning from the bedroom to the battlefield will offer another valuable perspective that can shed light on the appeal of the myth of the pure evil. As Carl von Clausewitz (the Prussian veteran whose *On War* became the most famous book ever written on the topic) once said, "War is inconceivable without a clearly defined image of the enemy."[33] And opposing sides in war have often gone to remarkable lengths to depict each other in terms of the myth of pure evil.

One reason to depict the enemy as purely evil is that such an image helps create an obligation and an incentive to fight. If the enemy is clearly evil, then it is right to hate him and it is appropriate to do one's part to defeat and destroy him. Most wars—whether major international conflicts or brutal series of battles between street gangs—require popular support. To marshal such support, it is necessary to justify one's own violent actions. Indeed, if the combatants in a war were limited to the people who would directly benefit from victory, there would be too few participants. Hence, leaders who want to make war need to find a way to get people who have little or no personal stake in the matter to risk their lives to kill and maim other people whom they have never even met.

For example, in the American Civil War, the ruling class in the South needed some way to enlist the support of poor white Southerners, who did not benefit from slavery and had little interest in broad Constitutional issues such as states' rights. There were not enough sons of plantation owners to make up an army, and no one else had that much at stake. Likewise, in the Vietnam War, young men who had never heard of obscure places in Southeast Asia were asked to travel there and fight over them. Closer to home, researchers who have observed gang wars have noted that gangs sometimes need to draft nonmembers into their ranks when a major conflict with an enemy gang is brewing. In some cases, these gangs force reluctant teenagers to join them during the dangerous, violent conflict and then kick the survivors out of the gang once the war is over.[34]

The need to justify one's own aggressive actions is one of the perennial problems of war. Just as warring armies need food, ammunition, and medical supplies, they and their civilian supporters need justifications for why they are fighting. Otherwise, they lose the will to fight. The Vietnam War was not lost on the battlefield, where there were something close to 10 enemy casualties for every American death. It was lost because the population at home could no longer find justifications for the sacrifices that were involved. In that same war, the North Vietnamese had to make much greater sacrifices, partly because their armies were less well equipped with the most deadly weapons. But they were far better equipped with justifications than the Americans. They were fighting for their national survival, their right to govern themselves, and for freedom. Nothing on the American side came close to matching those reasons.

A common solution to the problem of justifying one's aggression is to depict the enemy as evil. If your enemies are pure evil, there is little need for additional explanations of why you want to fight against them. Hence, the more thoroughly one can assimilate the enemy into the myth of pure evil, the less one needs to provide valid reasons for one's aggression.

In addition, people who are reluctant to enter a conflict or are undecided about their loyalties and interests can be effectively won over if they can be persuaded that the adversary is evil. Perhaps the most famous example of this in the twentieth century was the British propaganda early in World War I, which depicted the German troops as savage, cruel Huns. Many of the atrocity stories were later revealed to be extreme exaggerations or outright falsehoods, but they played an important role in convincing an ambivalent American public—which included many people of German descent—to support the Allied cause and eventually to enter the war, decisively, on the Allied side. After all, how could one support a country whose soldiers were reported to kill innocent babies with bayonets? Indeed, how could one even fail to be firmly and actively opposed to them?

A second, related benefit of construing the enemy in terms of the myth of pure evil is that there is no need to feel bad about killing the enemy, or indeed about any sort of abusive or atrocious treatment of the enemy. This is an important theme of *War Without Mercy*, John Dower's book on the Pacific theatre of World War II.[35] Hatred and demonization of the enemy were much greater in the Pacific than in the European side of that war, partly because of racial antagonism between Americans and Japanese. Dower showed that violent acts by American boys fighting in the Pacific far exceeded those reported from Europe. They killed Japanese prisoners, urinated in the mouths of corpses, fired upon lifeboats carrying survivors of sunk Japanese ships, and collected "grisly battlefield trophies"[36] such as gold teeth, ears, bones, scalps, and skulls, some of which were sent home as gifts to their American sweethearts. This is not the way American boys usually act in war, but when their perceptions of the Japanese enemy were sufficiently colored by the myth of pure evil, they were capable of remarkable excesses of brutality.

A less obvious but still very powerful benefit of demonizing the enemy is that all the misfortunes and suffering on both sides can be blamed on the enemy. If there is conflict, then of course it must be blamed on evil, for the good side would never seek out or desire conflict. What the good side suffers is the fault of the evil side. By the same token, whatever the evil side suffers is also its own fault, because it brought it on itself by means of its evil activities.

The clearest examples do not involve explicit warfare, because such examples are generally ambiguous. An example in which an essentially innocent party is blamed for both sides' suffering, however, can be found in the antagonistic relations between the Christians and the Jews. When the Black Death was decimating central Europe, many Christians came to the conclusion that the Jews must be responsible (it was rumored that the Jews were poisoning the water supply). It is well known now that the Black Death does not result from any such poisoning, but at the time it seemed plausible, especially because people thought that the plague seemed to spare the Jews, which of course it would do if they were causing it. (At the time, Christianity was strongly opposed to bathing, whereas Judaism promoted cleanliness, and so illnesses that flourished because of poor hygiene practices preyed more on Christians. Hence the observation that the plague seemed to spare Jews.) The Jews were regarded as evil, and so it made sense that they would have perpetrated such a dastardly action as poisoning the water supply to spread a fatal plague. These beliefs prompted a number of riots and massacres of Jews. The Jews' suffering was regarded as their just deserts for their wicked acts.[37]

Hope and confidence constitute a final benefit of demonizing the enemy. If the enemy is bad, then God must be on our side, and so it seems certain that we will win in the end. To be sure, there are dangers of overconfidence, but it is much easier to enlist people in a cause if ultimate success seems ensured. Consider the Crusades, as a dramatic example. Militarily, the Crusades were clearly a very risky venture, as the events proved over and over. The majority of knights and soldiers who departed for the Holy Land never came back. Usually they died from disease and the other dangers that attended the journey. Many were killed in military combat with the enemy, who uncannily seemed able to win battles, despite having to fight without the support of the Christian God.

The Children's Crusade[38] is one of the most tragically absurd examples of overconfidence springing from belief that God would join the side of the just and faithful and would guarantee victory over the heathen enemy. In 1212, two boys reported visions in which God told them to lead an army of innocent children to liberate the Holy Land. Children from the tjwns and villages of central Europe came and followed the boys. The large groups of chanting children walked to Italy. The Pope sent some of them home; many died of disease or starvation along the way. Many others were reportedly sold into slavery by the Italian merchants who disingenuously offered to ferry them across the Mediterranean.

The notion that a motley gang of children could walk more than a thousand miles without logistical support, cross the Mediterranean Sea along the way (supposedly by means of a dry passageway that would suddenly appear for the young Crusaders, just as the Red Sea had opened for Moses and his flock in the Bible), and then inflict a battlefield defeat on a well-equipped army of adult soldiers who lived there is preposterous by military standards; but religious faith made the idea seem plausible back then. The important point is the appeal of the belief that victory is ensured because divine powers will intervene on one's side.

Viewing the enemy as evil was extremely helpful in getting people to participate in the Crusades.

Innocent Victims

Why does the myth of pure evil continue to exert such a hold over the way people think, when it so rarely corresponds to the reality of events? With any phenomenon that is so broad and common, there are likely to be multiple explanations, and no single or easy answer will be enough. One important factor in the myth's appeal is that it portrays the victims as wholly innocent. The victims, and the many people who identify with victims, will clearly find such a portrayal very agreeable.

The broader context of this argument is that people favor certain explanations over others because the preferred ones appeal to their psychological wants and needs. People are not relentlessly driven to find the truth; often they want to reach a particular conclusion. To be sure, there are severe limits on what people can convince themselves of, and the human capacity for self-deception (contrary to some stereotypes) is constrained by many factors. Still, many events involve ambiguous circumstances with several possible explanations that are all somewhat plausible and that roughly fit most of the facts. It is in precisely such situations, where a person can see several possible explanations but is not compelled by powerful evidence to settle on a particular one, that people are most able to find ways to draw the conclusion that they personally prefer.[39] In such circumstances, people will tend to rely on the myth of pure evil to explain events—as long as that myth makes them feel better, comforts them, or offers them an explanation that they find congenial.

With almost any form of misfortune, the people who suffer immediately begin to ask themselves whether they were at fault. One study of victims of severe accidents, for example, found that all of them had asked, "Why me?" and found some sort of answer.[40] Some of them blamed themselves; others blamed an assortment of other factors. It seems to be a very deeply rooted pattern in human nature to respond to disaster by wondering whether it was your own fault.[41] People look for explanations for their suffering, whether religious, scientific, or causal, and one perennial dimension of these explanations is whether people blame themselves or not. But people want to think that the bad things that happen to them are not caused by their own actions. This preference has been well documented in many contexts, ranging from the reactions of corporate managers and executives at "blame time"[42] to the responses of college students who are led to believe during a psychology experiment that they have just done quite poorly on some test.[43]

The myth of pure evil depicts malicious, alien forces intruding on the world of well-meaning, unsuspecting, virtuous people. The victims are thus freed from any blame or responsibility for their own misfortune. Their problems are not entirely solved by such an explanation, of course, but it is comforting in at least one respect: They do not have to feel guilty, stupid, or otherwise responsible.

An explanation that frees the self from all blame is likely to have strong appeal to victims, for several reasons. One is that people simply like to see themselves in a favorable light.[44] They may be suffering, but at least their self-esteem can survive intact. Another reason is more practical and interpersonal. As long as you are an innocent victim, you have a legitimate claim on the help, sympathy, and support of others, which may extend to financial or material aid. In contrast, if you are the author of your own misfortune, people are less willing to help you. When people's capacity for helping is limited—as it often is in times of crisis or misfortune—they tend to give priority to innocent victims, while those who brought their own suffering on themselves are the first to be cut off.[45]

A good way to appreciate this process is to imagine the choice you face when you have been injured by another person. One possibility is to blame yourself: I started this, so I deserved whatever happened to me. Clearly this is not a very pleasant or comforting explanation. In fact, if you decide that you deserved this misfortune, then perhaps you will deserve others, and the future can start to look rather bleak and depressing.[46]

Another possibility is to decide that the problem was simply a difference of opinion or a problem of communication: You decide that no one is to blame. When you are suffering or in trouble, however, it is unsatisfying to decide that your problems are no one's fault. Presumably, such accidents can occur at any time, and so your troubles could arise again.

Not surprisingly, then, people prefer to blame their problems on someone else's actions. There are two ways to do this. One is to see the other's responsibility for your suffering as due to a temporary or uncharacteristic act that the person did under pressure of circumstances or external forces. As we saw in the last chapter, this is how perpetrators themselves prefer to regard the misdeeds they acknowledge. They say, yes, I did something wrong that hurt someone, but I couldn't help it, and it was quite unlike the way I normally act—so I shouldn't be judged too harshly.

Yet, as we also saw, that is not the way victims prefer to see things. We are understandably reluctant to give the benefit of the doubt to someone who has just hurt us. Emotionally, this may be the least satisfying response, because you conclude that the perpetrator played a decisive causal role, yet you cannot allow yourself to feel outraged by it. You are supposed to maintain fair, positive, respectful feelings toward the person who has just wronged you, even while you are feeling the effects of this presumably isolated bad action the person has performed. This is tough, especially when you are angry and in pain.

The other alternative, then, is to blame the perpetrator for being a bad person. This explanation corresponds most closely to the myth of pure evil: The perpetrator is responsible for what he or she did to you. You (the victim) condemn him or her along with the act, because the act is something that expresses what the person is truly like. The transgression is seen not as isolated and uncharacteristic (which is how perpetrators usually depict their wrongs) but as typical, or at least as something that reveals the true inner self, which may be held in check or concealed (hypocritically) most of the time. Naturally, if you didn't do anything to provoke the other's attack, the question of why that person attacked you will arise. Here again, the myth of pure evil is helpful: He attacked you because he is wicked. He is the sort of person who attacks innocent people for no reason, or for his own pleasure or benefit. There is no need to think that you did anything to deserve or provoke the attack.

Thus, the explanation that corresponds most closely to the myth of pure evil is also the explanation that people prefer, when they have a choice. In particular, victims and their friends and supporters[47] seem likely to favor an explanation that absolves them of all responsibility for their suffering.

In general, people maintain their self-esteem by blaming their troubles on external factors and on other people.[48] Victims of aggression are no different, and they have a ready-made target to blame. It is more comforting to conclude that the world contains evil, malicious people who attack innocent victims for no reason than to believe that one's sufferings are the result of one's own poor judgment and ill-advised actions that provoked a violent response from someone else. This brings us back to the vital issue of reciprocal violence, which we will now consider once more.

But What about Reciprocal Violence?

I noted that most violence and aggression involve reciprocal, mutual grievances and provocations. The most common pattern is for two people (or groups) to offend, provoke, and attack each other in escalating rounds until one of them kills or injures the other. At the same time, I concluded that the most common way of thinking about violence—the myth of pure evil—puts all the responsibility on one side and absolves the other side. The myth of pure evil depicts sadistic, malicious forces that arbitrarily and randomly attack innocent, virtuous victims.

This difference is perhaps the most radical discrepancy between the image and the reality of evil. Can our image of evildoers really be irrelevant to the majority of actual cases of violence?

No. In fact, what seems to happen often is that both sides of a conflict perceive it through the lens of the myth of pure evil—but in mirror images. Each side sees itself as the innocent victim and the other as the evil attacker.

This point was made vividly in one of the classic psychological works on violence, Hans Toch's *Violent Men*.[49] Toch divided his attention about equally between studying police who deal with aggressive criminals and studying the criminals themselves. Both groups tended to see themselves as well-meaning, innocent people who had to cope with arbitrary, provocative behavior by the other group.

Consider a typical story from Toch's book.[50] Two policemen, according to their report, get a call about a fight going on at a house. They arrive, self-conscious about being white authority figures in a black neighborhood. A black man is sitting on the hood of a car outside the house where there was the complaint. They begin to ask him questions. He insults them and uses racial epithets. His hands are inside his pockets, which seems both defiant and threatening, because he could be carrying a weapon. They ask him to remove his hands from his pockets. He refuses defiantly and obnoxiously, calling them more insulting names and insisting on his rights. He makes vague threats that he and his friends are going to kill the policemen. Some of his friends are beginning to gather around, voicing criticisms of the police, and the cops fear that a riot could be starting. They attempt to take the man into the back seat of the squad car, but he resists, and they end up having to force him—to hit him and put him in handcuffs. All the time he is screaming angrily at them. Finally, to defuse the explosive situation, they drive off with him.

Now consider the young man's story. He was not involved in the domestic squabble and did not even know the police were called. From his perspective, he was sitting quietly in his neighborhood when two white policemen came up and began to question and hassle him. In response to their questions about the incident, he said (truthfully) that he did not know anything, but they refused to accept that as an answer. One of them ordered him to take his hands out of his pockets. He asked whether he was being arrested or charged with anything, but they dodged this question and continued to command him to remove his hands from his pockets. Looking back, he said that if they had simply explained why they wanted him to remove his hands, he would have done so, but they refused to explain their command and merely insisted on it. Then they seized him and one of them struck him. (When asked by the interviewer why the policeman would strike him for seemingly no reason, he did recall the additional fact that he had just called the policeman a "stupid bastard." And indeed one assumes that according to police policy such a remark, while certainly uncharitable, is not supposed to be grounds for striking a citizen. But you could also understand that a nervous young policeman might be moved by such a remark to think that he had better reassert control over the situation.) By now several of the man's neighbors were gathering to watch, and it was obvious to them that the police were behaving in an unjustified and inappropriately aggressive fashion. Some of them began making angry comments, pointing out that what the police were doing was wrong. Becoming fearful of police brutality, the man began to scream for his rights, but they beat him and wrestled him into the car and drove off with him.

The point of this example is that both the young man and the two policemen[51] described the event in terms of unprovoked, unreasonable, aggressive behavior by the other side met with a reasonable and well-meaning response on their part. Each man described his own aggression as something that he was forced to do, reluctantly, in response to the brazen, threatening, unjustified, offensive acts of the other. In other words, both descriptions of the incident roughly corresponded to the myth of pure evil—except that they exchanged the roles of evildoer and innocent victim. From the policemen's point of view, they were simply trying to do their job to investigate a complaint, and the young man became hostile because of his racism and general disrespect for authority. From the young man's perspective, he was innocently minding his own business when two white policemen attacked him for little or no reason (except, again, racism), violated his rights, and tried to embarrass him in front of his neighbors.

Who is correct? As we saw earlier, the answer is difficult to ascertain without some objective record, but it seems likely that both accounts shaded the facts to favor a certain interpretation. The aggressive policeman mentioned in passing that he responded to what he saw as a disrespectful attitude taken by the young man: "His attitude bothered me a little bit, so I asked him if he would take his hands out of his pockets."[52] Perhaps, then, it was not an overt threat that led him to begin the business about the pockets, but only a perception that the young man was being insufficiently deferential and therefore needed to be put in his place. Moreover, he described his first comment about the hands as being a polite request, which of course is quite different from the way it appeared in the young man's version. Meanwhile, the young man left out his calling the policemen "stupid bastards" until the interviewer asked. Both parties perceived the other, but not themselves, as motivated by racial antagonism.

The myth of pure evil, then, is surprisingly durable and elastic. Even when each side provokes and antagonizes the other, the myth can be invoked. Ironically, the myth fails to acknowledge mutual provocation, but it appears that both sides in a conflict are quite capable of seeing themselves as innocent victims and the other as unreasonably, gratuitously wicked.

Similar patterns are found over and over. Cases of mutual aggression are described by the participants as if the other side were unreasonably, gratuitously violent whereas they themselves were merely innocent, well-intentioned victims who were ultimately forced to defend themselves.

Even terrorists, who would seem to be the most obvious example of a group that attacks and kills innocent people, conform to this pattern. Terrorists see themselves as victims. One scholar observed how striking it is that despite the great diversity of causes that terrorists represent, their rhetoric has broad similarities. They all tend to speak as if they were engaged in a battle against the forces of evil, who have somehow amassed great power and numbers on their side. To the terrorists, they are the ones fighting for the real victims, and their just cause is so desperate that they need to resort to any tactics they can find.[53] Another scholar who studied terrorists in Germany observed that they all felt themselves to be victims of the oppressive and repressive government.[54]

If one concedes that terrorists have at least the one valid point—namely, that they are relatively weak and helpless in comparison with the huge governments and security forces they oppose—then one would think that repressive governments might be the ones who finally acknowledge their own oppressive nature. Surely, they if anyone could see that they are the aggressors, especially when they arrest, torture, and kill the relatively helpless, innocent citizens who end up as their victims. But they do not. Studies of repressive governments repeatedly find that they too perceive themselves as virtuous, idealistic, well-meaning groups who are driven to desperately violent measures to defend themselves against the overwhelmingly dangerous forces of evil. These patterns can be seen right from the earliest Western examples of institutional terror, in which committees gave lists of names to police forces who arrested, prosecuted, tortured, and executed the people on the lists. The Spanish Inquisition saw itself as needing to defend Christianity against internal enemies: heathen unbelievers, dissenters, and heretics who pretended to be normal, faithful Christians. The Terror following the French Revolution was driven by the paranoid view that the forces of reaction and subversion were trying to infiltrate the new government and destroy it before it could initiate its reign of virtue in its envisioned utopian republic. The Khmer Rouge believed that Cambodia was threatened by both internal and external enemies and needed desperate measures to survive. The century's bloodiest killing campaigns—the Stalinist and Maoist purges in the Soviet Union and China—were both fueled by fears that the utopian revolution was succumbing to the evil machinations of internal enemies who (aided by hostile foreign powers) were sabotaging and undermining the leaders' efforts to serve the people.

So far, I have argued that the myth of pure evil tends to blind people to the reciprocal, mutual causes of violence. Even people who appear to outside observers to be clearly the aggressors, such as by participating in large-scale violence against relatively innocent and helpless victims, tend to see themselves as being the virtuous victims. They too see evil as a powerful invasion of their good and peaceful society. Their victims do not seem to them like helpless innocents. Rather, they appear to be representatives of the forces of evil.

The tendency for perpetrators to claim victim status is easier to understand in light of the myth of pure evil. On the face of it, it seems preposterous that former Nazi killers or Argentinean torturers could define themselves as victims. But the fact that violence generally has reciprocal causes means that they can usually find some respect in which they were attacked, too (if only by being the targets of what they see as unfair, selective prosecution and stigma afterward). If they focus heavily on what has happened to them, they can still manage to see evil as the force that attacks them rather than as part of themselves.

A vivid example was provided in Dan Bar-On's book, which consists of interviews with children of the Third Reich. One of the women, Renate, told about her father, who was arrested nearly two decades after the war ended. She said her father complained about being arrested and prosecuted when others who had done far worse things went free. He expressed humiliation that he, a decent and proper German who had always done his best to serve his country effectively and had led a blameless, correct life, would find himself thrown in jail with common criminals. He had never even padded an expense account, but here he was being treated like an ordinary lowlife. Renate said she eventually became unable to bear his complaining because even though there was some merit in his claims to being a victim, he never said anything at all to acknowledge what he had done wrong. He had been a leader of one of the *Einsatzgruppen*—the small contingents who moved through conquered territory in Russia and executed Jewish citizens by shooting them, long before the gas chambers and crematoriums were built. She said he never expressed any regret or remorse or compassion for the people he shot, and this fact eventually revolted her to the extent that she could no longer even speak to him. The family began to regard her as a traitor because she failed to stand by her father in his time of trouble. She said she might have been able to support him if he had acknowledged some guilt or remorse, but he never did.[55] He never mentioned his own guilt or admitted that he deserved punishment, while he constantly harped on how he was the undeserving victim of excessive persecution.

In general, then, the myth of pure evil conceals the reciprocal causality of violence. By doing so, it probably increases the violence. The myth of pure evil depicts innocent victims fighting against gratuitously wicked, sadistic enemies. The myth encourages people to believe that they are good and will remain good no matter what, even if they perpetrate severe harm on their opponents. Thus, the myth of pure evil confers a kind of moral immunity on people who believe in it. As we will soon see, belief in the myth is itself one recipe for evil, because it allows people to justify violent and oppressive actions. It allows evil to masquerade as good.

PART 2

The Four Roots of Evil

CHAPTER 4

Greed, Lust, Ambition: Evil as a Means to an End

We turn now from the image of evil to the reality. There are four main root causes of evil, and the next four chapters will examine each one in turn. We will begin with the most obvious: evil as a means to an end.

The Killer Horsemen

To several million medieval Christians and Moslems, the Mongol hordes of Genghis Khan and his successors were the embodiment of evil. To Europe, the Mongols were demons incarnate, but they thought of themselves as supremely practical. This practicality included killing. The nomadic Mongols were sheepherders, and the act of killing sheep was a routine familiar to just about everyone. Nomads don't think of their animals as pets, precisely because it is fairly often necessary to kill one of them.

According to historian David Morgan, the Mongols debated killing everyone in northern China.[1] The idea was to make pastureland and prevent uprisings. Finally, the Mongols decided against the plan, convinced by arguments that the loss of tax revenue and tribute would not be worth it. It made more sense to leave the people alive so they could send money. Again, the Mongols weren't bloodthirsty—they were practical.

The Mongols conquered city after city throughout the so-called civilized world to the west of their homelands. Besieging, storming, and conquering these cities was costly and time-consuming, and the Mongols had no particular need to lay everything to waste, although they were quite willing to do so when necessary. But that too was a matter of practicality. The Mongols wanted two things: They wanted their superior authority and power to be accepted, and they wanted material wealth. Fighting battles and storming cities were means to these two ends.

The Mongols gradually developed a standard policy toward the cities that lay in their path.[2] Each city was presented with a choice. It could open its gates, let the Mongols in, submit to their rule, and agree to pay them tribute, in which case the Mongol army would move on peacefully. Or the city could offer armed resistance, in which case defeat meant the destruction of the city and large-scale or even complete massacre of the inhabitants. In some cases, such as if the siege were long or costly, the Mongols would spend an entire week killing every living thing within the city. The Mongols wanted this policy to become generally known, of course. The point was to get some of the cities to let them in with no resistance and hence no casualties on their side. An occasional freebie of that sort would be a nice picnic for the troops, especially as compared to the tedium and privations of a siege.

Still, some cities did resist. After all, cities were built precisely to hold out against such predatory invaders, and so to surrender meant belying the very purpose of the city. What, then, may we assume went through the minds of the Mongol invaders on the day they finally entered a resisting city and began to massacre the inhabitants?

It may be unrealistic to surmise that they were totally detached and unemotional about it. They might have felt some anger and frustration toward the people who had killed their friends and forced them to suffer the deprivations of siege warfare. They might also have found some pleasure in looting, pillaging, and other violent acts that finally relieved the intensely monotonous boredom of the siege. Sexual pleasure was rare for a lowly soldier in a traveling, besieging army, but of course on this day the women of the city were at the Mongols' mercy. If the women were going to be killed anyway, or even just sold as slaves to some rich stranger, one might as well see what they had to offer. One could even suggest that it is wasteful (from a practical point of view) to kill a pretty woman without raping her first.

What about showing mercy —what the great thinker Hannah Arendt called "animal pity," the basic sympathy that one feels with the suffering of another human being like oneself? Being utterly merciless no doubt contributed to the Mongols' reputation for being evil. Yet from their point of view, it was the only practical thing to do. To take pity on the citizens would be counterproductive and hence impractical and hence stupid. It was not just that the Mongols didn't feel like taking pity: They knew they weren't supposed to take pity. Taking pity was bad for business and was very costly. Killing them all was essential to prevent having to go through the whole miserable siege business at the next town.

The Mongol policy (later adopted by many other siege campaigns in Europe) is a compelling example of violence as a means to an end. To their victims they may have been evil, but in their own eyes and, perhaps, to objective observers they were merely pursuing a rational, sensible strategy for getting what most people want: wealth and respect. A great deal of crime and violence falls into this category of instrumental activity. The hurting is not done for its own sake but rather to further one's goals.

The defining criterion of instrumental violence is that the perpetrator would be willing to abandon violence if he or she could achieve the same goal without it. This puts the victim in a relatively good position, at least as compared with victims of other forms of violence such as hate crimes, where the victim's suffering is the essential point. To an instrumentally violent person, the material gain is the point, and if the material gain can be had without violence, so much the better. That was the essence of the Mongols' policy: If the city would open its gates peacefully, it would be spared the slaughter. From our historical vantage point, it is clear that the cities that capitulated peacefully were much better off. The Mongols' demands amounted to a stiff property tax—which is better than being pillaged and massacred.

Evil Means to Acceptable Ends

Some evil undoubtedly does derive directly from the craving for material gain. The desire for money, pleasure, power, and similar gains is deeply rooted in the human psyche. Countless means are used to pursue these desires, and some of them are evil.

Although I emphasize that the means, not the ends, are evil, it is important to recognize that these goals have been sufficiently problematic and disturbing to society that from time to time the ends have been condemned, too. The desire for money and the desire for sexual pleasure have both been condemned by the Catholic Church, which has listed them (as greed and lust) among the seven deadly sins. Envy of someone else's wealth is another. Ambition, in the sense of a desire for power and success, has also often been recognized as an unsavory and dangerous motive, and at least the anarchists (strong utopians and idealists themselves) have believed fervently that power is inherently bad.

Yet these condemnations are overstated. Money, pleasure, and power are not inherently bad, nor is the pursuit of them invariably destructive. In fact, it is doubtful if there have ever been human beings who were free of such desires, and if so these exceptional individuals (saints and Zen masters, perhaps) could exist only in a society kept going by masses of people who operated on those motives constantly. Even the Catholic Church, at the height of its power, had to change its views to allow people to desire and receive sexual pleasure in marriage, as well as to allow people to make a profit on their work. Power clearly can be sought through peaceful, constructive, and socially acceptable means. Moreover, an effective government is essential to the health, prosperity, well-being, and probably even the survival of the people.

Evil thus attaches only to the means by which these ends are pursued, not to the ends or desires themselves. Attempts to condemn the ends are generally foolish and futile. The first root of evil is instrumental: It is a resort to objectionable techniques as a way of achieving acceptable ends.

To think of evil as the use of wrong means toward acceptable ends is already far afield from the myth of pure evil. According to the myth, evil people seek to do harm for its own sake and derive direct pleasure from doing it. In contrast, an instance of purely instrumental violence involves someone who may take no pleasure at all from hurting others and may even be reluctant or unhappy about it. The myth of pure evil sees harm as a vital end in itself, not a means, and certainly not a means toward goals that are common and acceptable.

Turning Bad

We can understand instrumental evil as the use of a particular set of means to pursue goals that, alternatively, might be pursued with acceptable means. The key question for understanding this form of evil then becomes: What makes people choose evil means rather than other, more acceptable ones? This question goes to the heart of crime: Why would someone rob people rather than try to earn a living through legal and accepted means?

The goal of this book is to understand how otherwise decent people, much like you or me, can come to participate in evil acts. Let us begin by examining one of history's most famous and widely condemned sources of evil, the so-called Free Companies who ravaged central Europe during and after the Hundred Years' War. These roving gangs of bandits would descend on an innocent, unsuspecting farming village. They would steal its food and other wealth, leaving the poor peasants at best destitute, at worst brutally killed. Homes were burned and women were raped. According to the chroniclers of the fourteenth century (who admittedly were somewhat prone to sensationalism and probably exaggeration), the Free Companies destroyed entire villages, held others for ransom, violated nuns and mothers, destroyed the peasants' meager farm equipment (thereby preventing them from growing more food), and engaged in assorted other abuses. The peasants came to see them as comparable to the biblical plagues. The Pope issued several edicts condemning and excommunicating them, to little avail.[3]

Who would willingly choose a life as a member of one of these cruel and vicious bands of outlaws? Surely no one like you or me. But imagine yourself in the following scenario. You are a regular soldier in the British army fighting in France during the Hundred Years' War. Your commander, the Black Prince, is widely admired as "the Flower of Chivalry," and the war is driven by seemingly legitimate claims of the English to territory in France, which has been stolen by the French crown. The current expedition is a punitive raid intended to punish rebellious towns and villages who have gone over to the enemy (French) side, which stands to gain major advantages from the rich lands. The French army does not show up to oppose you. Following orders, you help punish the rebel towns by looting and burning them.

Punishment is not the only goal of your army's raids: The loot from the villages is an important source of revenue and even food. Medieval armies had only the most primitive notions of logistics and supply, and you could hardly count on food reaching you regularly from supply bases back in England. "Living off the land" was the polite phrase for the standard procedure of enabling the army to survive by looting and pillaging the unfortunates in its path. Procedures for paying the soldiers' wages were not much better than procedures for supplying them with food, and the wealth pillaged from conquered towns was often a crucial substitute for regular pay, welcomed by both the troops and their commanders. As for feeling guilty about this—well, war was war, and indeed the French themselves seemed no more sensitive about their villagers. The French tried to repel the British with a scorched-earth policy of destroying the farms and villages that the British might conquer. The peasants and townspeople lost out either way.

A major turning point came in September 1356. The French king brought a large army into the area and finally caught up with and trapped the Black Prince at Poitiers. Badly outnumbered and cut off from escape, the British dug in and tried to make a deal, but negotiations fell through. The French launched a frontal assault and were cut to pieces by the British archers. After many hours of fighting, a counterattack by the British captured the French king and drove off the remnants of the French army. Between the death or capture of its major leaders and the decimation and humiliation of its army, France was left without means of carrying on the war.

The unexpected and complete victory left the Black Prince with a new problem—a lack of opposition. He did not need all his soldiers and could not afford to pay them, and so he did what other generals in the same position did in those days: He simply released many of them. These former soldiers were the beginnings of the Free Companies.

And what would you have done? You are a British ex-soldier in western France, living among your nominal enemies. Even if the people did not hate you, there would be no jobs available, because the main occupation is farming and the farms are all taken. You have no skills other than fighting, and so even if you could get a farm you wouldn't be able to operate it. Nor do you see any realistic hope of getting back home to England.

Meanwhile, the chance to join one of the Free Companies is a feasible and even attractive alternative to starvation. You can remain with your friends and comrades, and you can use your military skills. You would be doing what you have been doing already, namely, attacking farming villages. There is some danger but not much: The villages cannot defend themselves, and with the total defeat of the French army there is no serious force to oppose you (indeed, there is hardly any authority in the area at all). It certainly seems as safe or safer than trying to make your way home alone, through a hostile countryside and across the Channel.[4]

Seen from a distance, then, the members of the Free Companies appear as ruthless, bloodthirsty criminals preying on defenseless peasants, and perhaps that is an almost entirely fair description. Yet it is also understandable how an ordinary person might have ended up among them, given the circumstances. They were not necessarily men who were innately wicked and attracted by a life of easy plunder and sadistic pleasure. (Indeed, probably the life in one of those outlaw brigades was anything but easy.) To many, perhaps, such a life was a way of obtaining food, safety, and money. There is nothing inherently evil about those desires, and in fact their victims probably wanted the same things. The difference between them and their victims was that they saw violent, evil means as their best and perhaps only chance for getting them.

Why Choose Evil Means?

We can now return to the broader question of why people resort to evil means toward acceptable ends. Certainly in a peacetime society such as today's United States there are ample legal ways of getting food and shelter. Why turn to crime?

One answer is that the criminal does not perceive the legal and legitimate means as feasible. As with the Free Companies, violence seems the only way to get what one needs. The memoirs of Kody Scott and Nathan McCall state that they felt that they, as young black men, were rejected and excluded from the legitimate system and hence the only way to get by was through crime.[5]

Another answer is that evil means often appear to be easier than legitimate ones. Michael Gottfredson and Travis Hirschi[6] pointed out in their important book, *A General Theory of Crime*, that most crimes require little in the way of skill, patience, institutional credentials, or planning. To make money through standard, legal work one must often acquire credentials and abilities, all of which may take years of schoolwork and other training. In contrast, very little is necessary to hold up a convenience store or rob a pedestrian. A gun or other weapon and a few minutes are sufficient to accomplish the deed. You don't even have to know how to shoot; just holding and pointing the gun will probably be enough.

Careful planning of career strategies is also necessary for success in many legitimate occupations. Crimes, in contrast, tend to be spontaneous and unplanned (unlike the elaborately planned capers featured in movies). In explaining how spur-of-the-moment crimes often are, Gottfredson and Hirschi cited interviews with prisoners who recounted that in many cases they had passengers waiting outside in their cars who had not even suspected that a crime was going to be committed. No well-planned crime involves bringing along innocent, unaware witnesses who might conceivably make trouble or raise objections.

Thus, evil means may be chosen because they seem easier and more feasible than conventional means. You can get rich by performing brain surgery *or* by mugging passersby. Elaborate skills and long years of hard work are required for the former; hardly any training is needed for the latter.

Related to the perception of ease is the perception of effectiveness. Evil means may be used because people think them more likely than other means to be effective. For example, the twentieth century has seen countless examples of insecure regimes that have instituted official terror policies to maintain their hold on power. People who oppose or even criticize the regime are arrested, tortured, and sometimes executed. Torture is sometimes defended as a necessary means of gaining information, but in practice most torture is conducted without the intention (or the result) of gaining any useful information, and the framework of interrogation is merely a pretext.[7] Torture is used to bully, intimidate, and punish dissent, as a way of shoring up the power of the torturer's organization.

From the other side, terrorists and others operating outside the political structure likewise tend to believe they have no alternative. They have often tried (sometimes sincerely, sometimes perfunctorily) the standard, legal options for redress of grievances and found them unsatisfactory. Such people do not turn to terrorism out of a love of violence, or at least not primarily. They believe that they have no choice, because their grievances are serious and real and because the system offers them no way of dealing with them.[8] Whether they believe that setting off bombs to kill civilians is likely to bring about political changes is hard to ascertain, but they can at least be reasonably sure that their cause and their problems will gain some attention by terrorist acts—which is more than they think they will get through legitimate channels.

The case of terrorism shows that even when legitimate means of protest are available, people may reject them as hopeless and ineffective. Hence, the temptation to resort to evil, violent methods can be understood in the context of circumstances that appear to lack other methods—and, in fact, sometimes that appearance is correct. Most people are probably reluctant to resort to crime or violence, but sometimes that is the only option.

A fascinating study by Diego Gambetta of the origins of the Sicilian Mafia makes this point clear.[9] Gambetta notes that traditional analyses of the Mafia have called it the "industry of violence," but this is misleading: What the Mafia really provides is *protection*. Normally, citizens of modern countries are protected by the government and the police, but when these are inadequate to do the job, people will turn to other sources of protection. The Mafia came into being to provide just such services in Sicily, where government and police were unequal to the task.

Consider a simple example. One man wants to sell a horse, and another wants to buy it. The seller wants to charge too high a price, and indeed he may be concealing the fact that the horse is sick or weak. The buyer wants to pay too low a price, possibly by misleading the seller about the market value of such a horse, or perhaps he wants to pay with counterfeit money or a bad check. It is illegal, of course, for either to cheat or defraud the other, but suppose the government is not able to provide a guarantee that the transaction will be within the bounds of fairness. Then each of them is vulnerable. The risk and fear of being exploited may be large enough that even honest transactions are avoided, simply because one cannot be certain. That is, even if the buyer wants to buy and the seller wants to sell and the price is fair and both are honest, they may fail to make the deal because each worries that the other might be trying to cheat him. But being under the protection of a mafioso enables the person to make the deal with some peace of mind. If the horse turns out to be sick, the buyer can turn to his Mafia connection to get his money back. In fact, merely having such a connection will tend to deter such frauds. Only a fool would use a sick horse to cheat someone who is protected by the Mafia.

What creates situations in which there is a specific need for illegal protection? Sometimes legitimate authorities are weak or corrupt. Police tend not to intervene until a crime has been committed, which is unfortunately too late for the victim in many cases. According to Gambetta, the Mafia originated as a way of protecting Sicilian farmers on the dangerous journey through open country to the market in the distant city. A lone individual with a carriage full of farm produce would be an easy target for bandits, because the police could not guard the long, deserted roads. But the same man accompanied by two hired guards would be much safer. The profits from selling his produce in the city might well be enough to make it worth his while even after paying the guards.

One might object to this analysis by saying that, although it works fine for nineteenth-century Sicily, it has little relevance to the modern United States, because the police are well organized and able to provide protection to everyone. This is not completely true, however; there is still a market for private protection. In particular, criminals themselves often need protection. Suppose, for example, that you make your living by selling drugs, and your supplier cheats you or your customer robs you. You cannot go to the police to get your drugs back from the customer who didn't pay. You cannot call the Better Business Bureau and file a complaint against the cocaine supplier who swindled you, nor can you sue him in civil court. Similar problems apply to prostitutes whose customers cheat or rob them, to burglars who need to sell the items they have stolen, and many others.

Criminals, after all, are often trying to make money, yet their transactions are not protected by law. Links to the Mafia may be of considerable value to them. Your drug supplier would be reluctant to cheat you if you were known to be protected by the Mafia. And if he did cheat you, you would stand a fair chance of getting your money back.

Thus, one set of explanations for the resort to evil means has to do with fairly rational considerations. People choose violent or destructive means because these seem easy and effective, or because they do not perceive legitimate means as feasible for them. Evil looks like an appealing shortcut to get what one wants. It holds out the promise of reaching a highly desired or attractive goal, and in a rather short time. It is quicker and in some ways more exciting and even more fun than legitimate ways of satisfying one's material needs. Sometimes it is the only way that looks like it might work. That brings up a central question: Do evil means work?

Are Evil Means Effective?

So far, we have seen that people sometimes resort to evil because they think it will get them what they want. Are they right? Are evil means—criminal, destructive, socially condemned methods—effective? The answer is not simple.

For one thing, the answer seems to depend on the time frame one adopts. Assassinations do succeed in eliminating the detested ruler, but they do not usually succeed in bringing about the governmental changes that the assassins want. Crime may bring short-term gains, but in the long run most criminals do not end up wealthy. A recent study concluded that the average pay from crime for young black men in Boston was between $10 and $20 per hour, whereas the after-tax wage for legitimate employment was only about $5.60.[10] Thus, crime (especially selling drugs) seems to pay much better. But if the risk of imprisonment and violent victimization are included in the calculations, the economic superiority of a criminal career may be eliminated or even reversed.

More generally, the question of the effectiveness of evil and violence has been examined by many different scholars in many different spheres, by looking at the results of particular kinds of crimes or other objectionable acts. Over and over, they seem to come to the same conclusion: Evil is not very effective, especially when viewed in terms of fulfilling long-range objectives. At most, violence and cruelty help one gain temporary advantage over some adversary or obstacle. Consider some of the evidence.

The Rewards of Stealing

One logical place to start is with the monetary income from robbery.[11] Does crime pay? The best answer is sometimes, and not very much. Many crimes are attempted but do not succeed. Even in successful crimes, the payoff for the criminal is often quite small. According to victim reports, the median loss from robbery is under $50 and the median loss from burglary is under $100. Shoplifting generally involves items of low value. Embezzlement usually involves taking money from a small business or fast-food store, and such crimes are unlikely to yield much.

Another recent review of criminal profits came to a similar conclusion.[12] The average loss in robberies and burglaries was around $80. Losses above $250 were relatively rare, reported by less than one-fourth of robbery victims. Robbing institutions instead of individuals yields more money, but not a great deal more. From police statistics, the average amount stolen from gas and service stations was only $303, and one must assume that the true average is even lower, because the smallest losses are the least likely to be reported to the police. Bank robbers average significantly higher amounts of money—sociologist Jack Katz gives an average of $2664—but this must be offset against the fact that they are also significantly more likely (around 80 percent, or four out of five) to get caught.

These data are mostly compiled from victim surveys, police reports, and insurance reports, so they look at the value from the victim's side. The victim's loss is not necessarily equal to the perpetrator's gain—but unfortunately for the perpetrator, the typical difference merely reduces the already low yield of robbery. Most stolen items lose much of their value by virtue of being stolen, for the pawn shop's price or the resale value of used appliances or jewelry is generally much lower than the actual legal value reported to the insurance agent or police. A burglary loss of a videotape machine worth $300 in terms of insurance replacement value may result in only a $50 gain for the burglar.

These differences in the cash value of stolen items exemplify the magnitude gap between victims and perpetrators. As we have seen, there is a general pattern in which the victim's loss is larger than the perpetrator's gain. Often the magnitude gap involves intangible factors such as the victim's suffering compared to the perpetrator's pleasure. With robbery and burglary, however, the difference can be measured financially. The act of stealing substantially reduces the value of the item that is taken.

Katz emphasizes one more fact about robbery that is worth considering. It is already apparent that most crimes yield fairly low amounts of money and that the amount obtained depends to a great extent on chance (that is, how much cash the victim happens to have). Still, every now and then, a robber or burglar will get lucky and succeed in garnering a substantial amount of money.

Even in such cases, however, the money is soon gone. Katz talked to many criminals about their biggest scores, and they typically said that afterward they went on a euphoric spree and ran through the money in a few days. They spent money on clothes, gambling, women, fine food, and other indulgences that soon exhausted their ill-gotten riches, leaving nothing behind. They did not invest it in real estate or mutual funds or anything that would have led to long-term improvements in their lives. Instead, they became high-rolling big shots for a few days and then were poor again, which put them in a position of needing to commit another crime to look and feel good again.

Organized Crime and Drugs

Organized crime differs in several ways from casual or impulsive crime. According to recent accounts of organized crime syndicates,[13] the profits are often immense. In that sense, participation in organized crime does have instrumental benefits. Still, in the long run, the payoffs are counterbalanced by the vulnerability to being imprisoned or murdered. Members of the Mafia or other such groups may have steadier and higher incomes than other criminals, but their chances of staying out of prison and dying of natural causes are much lower than those of the average person.[14]

The same applies to selling drugs, which is probably the most reliably lucrative criminal activity on today's scene. Many people would debate whether selling drugs should even be considered as a form of evil: It simply provides people with a product they want and that gives them pleasure, it is akin to selling cigarettes or alcohol, and so forth. Still, selling drugs is illegal and is associated in the popular mind (somewhat unfairly, perhaps) with violence, and so it is worth considering as a possible form of evil.

By all accounts, there is an immense amount of money to be made in selling drugs.[15] As a way of acquiring cash, selling drugs is hard to beat—especially for someone without education, training, connections, or marketable skills. Yet it is clear that the long-term prospects are poor. Few pushers find the business to be a reliable path to the American dream of respectable financial security. The risks of being killed by rivals or captured by police are substantial, and probably they are compounded if the seller begins to take drugs, because drug use may lead to errors in judgment. Addiction is another occupational hazard.

So, selling drugs is an effective short-term source of money, but it is a high-risk occupation with relatively poor long-term prospects. You make very good money for a while, but you do not retire wealthy and bequeath a fortune to your children.

Political Murder

Another form of instrumental evil, political murder, has already been brought up in several examples. Political murder (including terrorism, assassination, and the like) is usually instrumental: the pursuit of power or other political ends by violent means. Franklin Ford's survey of political murder across many lands and eras[16] concluded that it has rarely brought about the lasting effects desired and intended by the perpetrators. Usurpers who seize power by assassinating the existing ruler tend to become victims themselves. Societies devoted to political assassination to achieve political changes, from the Moslem Assassins to the

Jewish Sicarii ("Daggermen") to the nineteenth-century anarchists, succeeded in killing quite a few eminent and powerful citizens but failed utterly to achieve the kind of sociopolitical arrangements they envisioned. Terrorists have failed to inspire popular sympathy and support; instead, there is a growing popular resentment and backlash against them.[17]

Government Repression and Torture

In a sense, government repression is the inverse of terrorism. Faced with internal enemies, some governments resort to evil means of clinging to power. They imprison, torture, and execute their opponents. Governments have many obvious and substantial advantages over individuals or small rebellious groups who seek to use violence to further their political ends. These advantages include the sovereign power that exempts them from foreign interference (or at least makes it less likely), legality, and control over information. The last of these can often enable them to keep most of the world from finding out about their violent acts, or at least from learning the extent of them. Probably the most dramatic illustration of this point was the Cultural Revolution in China during the 1960s. Outsiders knew that repressive measures were being taken and that people were being imprisoned, but it was not until several decades later (and, not incidentally, until after Mao, who presided over the Cultural Revolution, was dead) that the extent of the violence came to light. By early estimates, there were 2 million victims of the Cultural Revolution, which is certainly a great deal of human tragedy. More recent evidence has indicated that the true number of victims was around 10 times that many, which places the Cultural Revolution alongside the purges of Stalinist Russia as the most lethally successful mass murder campaign of all time. The Chinese rulers had managed to conceal about 90 percent of their killings from the rest of the world for decades, thereby temporarily making the Cultural Revolution seem more like a grisly internal purge than a holocaust.

How successful is government repression, in general? It must be conceded that government terror does seem to help prolong and strengthen a regime's power, at least for a period of time. There is a substantial cost, however, in loss of legitimacy and erosion of genuine popular support. Over the past decade, most of the world has witnessed a dramatic political shift. Military dictatorships, Communist tyrannies, and other repressive governments have given way to much freer and more open societies. As this is written, the Communist regimes of Europe are almost all gone, replaced by largely democratic societies. South America and Asia have reached broad levels of political freedom almost without precedent in their authoritarian pasts. Of the remaining continents, North America and Australia have been relatively free of repressive governments for a long time, and only Africa remains as a bastion of violent, repressive governments—and even long-suffering Africa has taken some steps away from its harsh authoritarian patterns. Thus, the global picture at present suggests that terror and tyranny are somewhat unstable, temporary forms of government. They can succeed for decades, which is perhaps greater success than other forms of evil can claim, but they do not seem to be feasible as a permanent basis of power.[18]

If internal terror is designed to defeat internal opposition, then one can measure its success by how that opposition fares. Judging by the experience of the former Communist nations of eastern Europe, it seems reasonable to propose that internal opposition can be *silenced but not eliminated* by repression and terror. The same lesson emerges from the South American tyrannies. Public criticism of the government can be almost entirely eliminated (for example, by jailing journalists who publish disagreeable stories or opinions), and private expression of dissent can be extensively suppressed if people learn that even their friends and family may betray them. But silencing dissent is not the same as generating support. When such countries do become free, there is generally an abrupt outpouring of retroactive criticism of the repressive regime. Terror seems to increase public compliance with the government, but not genuine support.

Government terror may also be analyzed in terms of specific acts of violence and oppression, as opposed to looking merely at the campaign as a whole. Torture is notably ineffective in its stated goal of gaining information. As Amnesty International has concluded, the vast majority of torture victims do not have any secret information about opposition groups to reveal to their captors, however much they may want to reveal such information to end their suffering.[19]

A cynic might say that torture does succeed in eliciting information that, although inaccurate, is useful to the authorities in a twisted fashion. What generally happens is this.[20] An innocent person is taken prisoner and is accused of being an enemy of the regime (or, in the case of the Spanish Inquisition and similar torturing groups, an enemy of the dominant religious authorities and faith). Torture is applied to elicit a confession of subversive activities and information about accomplices. To believe that anyone can resist torture indefinitely is naive: Almost inevitably the body breaks down under the relentless onslaught of pain and harm, and the victim wishes to cooperate. Then ensues a hideous game: The torturers will not tell the victim what to confess (because they regard themselves as wishing to gain the truth, and forcing someone to sign a phony confession is usually not acceptable) but will not stop the torture until a satisfactory confession is produced. The victim ends up trying to guess what false confession is wanted and starts to invent all sorts of crimes, which the torturers dutifully record. They also require the victim to name accomplices, and so the victim starts naming various acquaintances as having participated in these imaginary crimes. (That is probably what led to the person's arrest in the first place: Previous torture victims named him or her as accomplices in their phony crimes.) Although the information may be entirely false, it does give the torturers and their bureaucracy something else to do; namely, to arrest and interrogate these new accomplices until they confess, too. Many of the bloodiest purges have been sustained by this sort of domino effect in which innocent people invent crimes and name other innocent people as accomplices; the torture apparatus is kept busy and an ever-widening circle of internal enemies is identified.

Still, the identification of new victims can hardly be sufficient to label a torture operation a success. Yes, people suffer and die after confessing to crimes, and more people are arrested on the basis of those confessions, and the torture bureaucracy can get its budget increased because there seem to be more enemies than anyone suspected. But the information is mostly false. The regime gains little or nothing from torturing and executing an innocent civilian, and indeed each such death brings a small cost in terms of social disruption, weakening of legitimacy, and harm to the social fabric. In extreme cases, a large number of innocent deaths can leave a society weakened by sheer loss of manpower, as in the nearly fatal destruction of the Red Army by Stalin's purge during the 1930s, which did more damage to the Russian officer corps than all the horrific battles of the Second World War combined.[21]

Warfare

War is another form of violence that is used to solve problems. In many cases it certainly does lead to some resolution of the dispute that started it. Yet whether it is a suitable long-term solution is debatable. It is necessary to consider mainly the countries that start the wars, because their opponents then have little choice except to defend themselves. Among the countries that start wars, some (such as Iraq in the memorable 1991 war over Kuwait) certainly end up losing, and so for them the resort to armed force was not an effective means. Even among the victors, however, it is likely that the hard-won benefits and advantages fall short of what they initially sought. Lands and cities are often seriously damaged by the process of conquering them. People resent ideological and institutional changes that are imposed on them by force. The victors' human and financial costs may outweigh the value of what is gained. Sometimes, international objections or internal outcry pressure the victors into giving up part or all of what they have conquered. In general, it is not easy to find examples of modern wars in which the initial aggressor ends up fully satisfied with the outcome.

Once a war has begun, there are certainly wide variations in the extent to which combatants resort to especially evil means. Atrocities, crimes against helpless noncombatants, and the like can be examined as instances of particular evil within war. These, too, appear not to be very effective. Military prisoners were periodically massacred by the Christians during the Crusades, but it does not appear that the Christian side benefited from these outrages. The Germans executed Russian prisoners during the Second World War, but these executions did not give Germany victory. In the American Civil War, the South executed Northern officers who commanded black troops.[22] In the Spanish Civil War, both sides appear to have executed some prisoners.[23] In general, such tactics appear to reflect a policy of desperation in a losing cause, rather than being effective means to increase the likelihood of victory. Word soon gets out that prisoners are being killed, and so the enemy soldiers cease to surrender—which makes winning battles that much harder.

There is some evidence that crimes against civilians tend to be counterproductive. The Germans in World War II pioneered various tactics of total war, including the policy shift during the Battle of Britain to downplay the military targets and concentrate on breaking civilian morale by bombing London. Instead of producing a demoralized capitulation, this tactic apparently stiffened the British resolve. In the Ukraine, the German oppression against civilians was, in retrospect, a catastrophic blunder for them. Indeed, many Ukrainians hated the Soviet regime and initially welcomed the Germans as liberators, but when the Germans began killing civilians they had no choice but to side with the Russians. Later in the war, the British copied the unsuccessful German tactic. Their famous bombing of Dresden, a beautiful city without military significance, was reportedly intended to demoralize the Germans, but instead it outraged them and temporarily increased the resolve to fight on. The American bombings of North Vietnam during the Vietnam War were apparently equally useless in undermining popular support for the war; they may have just increased the will to resist, thereby contributing to the eventual American defeat.

To be sure, one can find some exceptions where systematic and atrocious massacres did reduce the will to resist. In these cases, presumably, the aggressor demonstrated that he had the power and the will to destroy all who opposed him, and so others capitulated because they realized that resistance was in fact useless and would lead only to death. The American bombings of Hiroshima and Nagasaki did lead to the prompt surrender of the Japanese. The Mongol massacres of cities that resisted did cause some other cities to surrender without putting up a fight. Sherman's march through Georgia and South Carolina late in the Civil War drove home the fact that the South could no longer defend itself. The Zulu empire in southern Africa grew in part after several attention-getting massacres of resisting tribes convinced other tribes that it was better to join up voluntarily than to resist.[24] Indeed, the draconian practice of some occupation forces of executing innocent citizens as reprisals for partisan resistance does seem to have some effect of discouraging resistance, although in the long run it is hardly conducive to securing the cooperation of the conquered population.

It is apparent that excessive cruelty in war does force an enemy to realize that he is thoroughly outclassed, when the power differential is substantial and genuine. Dropping the atomic bomb on Hiroshima was in fact a demonstration that the Allies had a weapon that could destroy Japan if necessary. (It also demonstrated that they were willing to use it.) Fighting on under those circumstances was indeed doomed, futile, and suicidal. In the London and Dresden bombings, however, and in the case of periodic massacres of prisoners or hostages, no such irresistibly superior power is proved. Under those circumstances, atrocious cruelty seems merely to increase hatred and make people less willing to surrender or capitulate. Evil is thus counterproductive as a means of winning the contest; it is only useful, apparently, as a way of getting across the message that the contest is no longer a contest.

Murder and Other Violent Crimes

One more class of cruel and criminal actions needs to be examined before we can draw broad conclusions about the effectiveness of instrumental evil. This class consists of individual violent crimes, ranging from domestic violence to murder. When people resort to such violence, they sometimes do seem to succeed—at least to the extent that they manage to hurt or kill someone.

The long-term effects of these actions are often very counterproductive, however. People who commit murder get arrested and find themselves in prison (and, later, burdened with a criminal record), which generally far outweighs anything they gained from the killing. A husband may win a domestic argument by beating up his spouse, but in the long run the relationship is damaged or ruined. The perpetrator's chances of getting the victim's love—which is a major motivation in domestic violence—are severely diminished.

There are two typical patterns of murder.[25] In the first, two people who know each other get into an argument, often over some seemingly minor or trivial matter. The argument escalates through nasty verbal exchanges to threats or minor physical violence. Finally, one pulls a gun or a knife and kills the other. Was this violence effective? The murderer can claim to have won the argument, I suppose. Still, the long-term costs tend to outweigh any benefit from winning, especially if (as is often the case) the initial dispute was indeed a trivial one. People are often sorry after they have killed or injured a family member, which is one of the most common violent crimes.

The other common pattern of homicide involves a robbery or burglary in which unexpected resistance by the victim prompts the perpetrator to use violence to get his or her way, resulting in the victim's death. Thus, a robber may point a gun at someone and demand money, and if the victim refuses the robber may actually fire it. Or a burglar may think the house is temporarily deserted but is startled to be discovered by a member of the household and shoots that person in panic or desperation. Here again, the killing does help solve the immediate problem and facilitate the successful crime, but in the long run the perpetrator derives minimal gain and often considerable risk and cost from the murder. Objectively, after any given burglary, the burglar is worse off if he killed somebody than if he didn't. Killing somebody brings intensive police attention, which is bad for business.

Thus, murder in general does not typically provide much benefit to the killer. Murderers are more likely than most other criminals to be caught, and so the costs and penalties associated with killing are substantially larger. The benefits, meanwhile, tend to be short-term or even negligible.[26]

Adding It Up

Taken together, the evidence is consistent and convincing: In the long run, violence is not a highly effective means of achieving material gain. Robbery, burglary, and other forms of stealing generally net only small amounts of money, and even people who happen to steal a large sum generally run through it quickly. There is more money in organized crime and selling drugs, but the costs are high, too, and the rate of imprisonment or premature violent death would be enough to dissuade most thoughtful people from choosing that line of work. Murder is usually regretted as a pointless and self-defeating act that brings the killer little satisfaction or benefit but produces serious problems and risks.[27]

Assassination may remove a detested ruler or eliminate a rival, but it does not generally produce the desired effect in the long run; indeed, it is common for those who gain power by killing rulers to end up being killed or otherwise violently deposed themselves. Terrorism rarely or never brings about the desired political changes. Torture hardly ever elicits useful or accurate information. Severe government repression tends to turn the population against the regime, and although it can prolong such a regime's tenuous hold on power, it does not seem to work in the long run. Starting a war often leads to defeat, and even successful wars usually carry a huge cost in terms of people, money, and property. Excessive violence within war tends to increase rather than break down resistance, except for the final stage when it can help to convince a beaten enemy that further resistance is hopeless.

This is not to say that violence never produces benefits or that it is always self-destructive. (Indeed, violence is often necessary and effective to defend oneself against violent attack. Then again, most people would not regard violent self-defense as evil.) Still, the resort to violence or other evil actions as a means toward some end is usually ineffective. Evil has a low success rate in the long run.

One must admit, however, that evil and violence do often achieve a significant measure of success in the short run. The violent person does win the argument, get the money, establish dominance, eliminate the rival, make good his claim to the disputed territory, silence dissent, or accomplish whatever other short-term goal prompted the violent response. These benefits may evaporate or seem trivial in the long run, but in the short run they are sought and gained. It is only from a broad, long-term perspective that one can say that evil means are not generally effective. They score much higher if one looks only at immediate payoffs and benefits, however small or trivial these may be.

What evil accomplishes best is to make someone else suffer. War may be a dangerous and unreliable way to benefit one's own nation, but it does make life miserable for the enemy. Murder ends a life. Torture produces extreme states of pain and woe. Rape may not bring sexual pleasure to the rapist, but it does inflict degradation and suffering on the victim, sometimes lasting for years. (This fact, incidentally, may help explain the use of rape in war, such as the recently publicized incidents in which the various warring factions in former Yugoslavia have been reported to engage in the systematic rape of women in conquered villages. The rapes may not bring much pleasure or advantage to the victors, and they certainly do not help further the political cause, but they do dramatically compound the misery of the conquered people.)

These patterns reveal the broad scope of the magnitude gap. Victims of torture, rape, murder, and other crimes suffer losses that are large compared to the benefits garnered by the perpetrators. A rape victim, for example, may suffer trauma, distress, and injury, along with a loss of sexual responsiveness, for many years thereafter. The rapist gets just a few minutes of rather limited pleasure. No matter how good those moments could feel—and apparently they typically are not that great anyway—they could not possibly measure up to the negative effects on the victim.[28]

The broader implication is that evil and violence, while not generally effective in producing positive outcomes for the perpetrators, succeed in producing negative outcomes for the victims.

Even if we ignore moral issues and give full recognition to what perpetrators may gain from their violent acts, the net effect is profoundly negative. Evil makes the world a poorer, uglier, worse place, not just for the victims, but for everyone—even the perpetrators. The magnitude gap thus shows something essential about the nature of evil: Evil means are mainly effective in causing the victim to suffer seriously and disproportionately. Evil is a costly and inefficient means of securing material ends, but if one's goal is to make the victim suffer, evil means can be quite effective.

Suffering, Dominance, and Power

So, violence may not bring much in the way of direct material rewards to the perpetrator over the long run, but in the short run it can cause real harm to the victim. As a way of making people suffer, violence is thus a useful and effective way to establish dominance over another person or to defeat the other person's dominance over you. In simple terms, violence is a tool for taking power.

At the individual level, the violent person in a relationship gains power over the other. Although there are many complex and elaborate theories about why men have generally been the rulers of their families, the evidence keeps pointing back to the simple fact that men are bigger and stronger than women and hence have always been able to enforce their superior position. Research on domestic violence tends to show that the husbands who batter their wives do so to establish their power in the family. Batterers are often men whose wives outclass or outrank them in some way, such as by earning more money or having a better education. Battering husbands also tend to adhere strongly to the belief in male superiority. They beat up their wives to shore up a weak or slipping hold on power in the family. "I have to hit her now and then to show her who's boss" is a fairly standard comment made by such men to justify beating their wives.

Violence between parents and children follows the same pattern. Researchers have found, for example, that mothers tend to hit their young children much more than they hit their teenagers. The discrepancy is not because teenagers are so much better behaved than the younger ones; in fact, the opposite is often the case. But a woman can beat a child without fear of consequences, whereas she does not have the physical superiority to impose the same kind of physical dominance over a large teenager.[29]

Looking beyond individuals, one can see the same pattern: Violence is used to gain or maintain power. There are probably very few countries in the world that do not owe their independence or current form of government to some act of violence, such as a war, revolution, or coup. Even the supposedly peace-loving United States was created through several wars: a revolution to throw off the dominance by England, a civil war to prevent the southern half of the country from seceding, a series of wars against native peoples to conquer additional territory, and a few very brutal military actions to maintain control over rebellious slaves or recalcitrant Indians.

Sociologist Jack Katz took an enlightening and detailed look at the use of violence to support interpersonal power in his analysis of the *badass*.[30] The badass is someone who cultivates an image of being supremely wicked, mean, and violent. Tattoos of swastikas, skulls and crossbones, snakes, bloody daggers, and other insignia may be used to create the image of a violent, evil person. The person may pick fights with others or be gratuitously mean and nasty to helpless, innocent people, among other ways of cultivating this image. The badass seeks to use violence (and related patterns) in a quintessentially irrational fashion. The badass will do nasty things that seem to have no reason and carry no practical benefit to himself.

Yet the badass does have a deeper purpose: He gains considerable power over other people by getting them to perceive him as irrationally violent. A badass is recognized as capable of turning wildly, senselessly violent for no apparent or predictable reason, and so everyone else has to be extra careful around him. Just as one might take precautions to avoid being the victim of a hurricane or tornado, one must be careful around a badass. In particular, one must take care not to offend or frustrate him, and this allows him to get his way. If his reputation is solid enough, the badass will scarcely have to do anything to use this advantage. This is the irony of the fighter who never fights because he is known to be such a dangerous fighter that no one is willing to challenge him.

The egotism of the badass is thus intimately linked with his violent nature—or rather with his violent image. So far, we have seen violence as a common response to a threat to one's egotism, and this egotism often consists of claims to superiority that have little or nothing to do with aggression or fighting ability. With the badass, however, violence is central. The badass claims and gets respect precisely because of his aggressive nature. He represents danger and harm, and that is what gives him influence, even dominance, over other people. Violence is what makes him superior. (This superiority also raises the issue of self-esteem and egotism, which will be the theme of the next chapter.)

The badass is an especially interesting case because he applies the myth of pure evil for his own benefit. The tattoos of skulls with bloody daggers thrust through them, the swastika pendants, and the other cues convey the idea that the wearer has embraced evil. Moreover, they suggest that the badass may enjoy inflicting harm on others, which is one of the central aspects of the myth of pure evil. The badass also cultivates this impression through his actions. Being mean and cruel for no apparent reason helps to reinforce the impression that he acts for the sadistic pleasure of the action, and not for any pragmatic gain. Katz gives the example of a group of young men who supported their badass reputations by entering the public library during open hours, knocking people down, making a mess, creating turmoil, and even starting a fire before running out. A couple of them were laughing so hard by the end that they could hardly keep running. Obviously, they gained nothing in practical or material terms by their acts. But that is precisely the point: They showed that they do such things for the mere pleasure of it. The elderly people walking into the library, for instance, would otherwise seem a poor choice as victims because they have little money to give and hurting them does not prove one a great fighter. Hurting them, however, does prove one to be an irrationally violent person who inflicts harm randomly for the pleasure of doing so, and that is a key part of the badass image. The innocence of the victim is, of course, another part of the myth of pure evil.

The badass uses one more crucial aspect of the myth of pure evil: chaos. As we saw in Chapter 3, the eternal images of evil combine hurting with chaos in the sense of irrationality and lack of stable order. As Katz emphasizes in his portrait of the badass, the irrationality is vital for conveying to everyone that the badass cannot be controlled or predicted, let alone understood. Most people want to live in a stable, orderly, predictable world. The badass makes it clear that he is not part of that world and does not live by those rules. By refusing to be rational, he forces other people to think irrationally and adjust themselves to him. The fear of unreasoning chaos is almost as deeply rooted in human nature as the fear of harm, and the badass plays on both fears.

Thus, we can see some benefit to violence if we look at interpersonal relations instead of material gain as the outcome. Violence, including even the mere threat of violence, is one of the main ways that people take power. Violence does not get people the material ends that they want, but it does help create and sustain a pattern of interpersonal relationships marked by power and dominance that can produce a desirable stream of minor benefits. Power pays, and violence produces power.

To be sure, violence is not always effective as a means of creating power relationships. Governments that violently repress their populations tend to lose rather than gain popular support, and in many cases this contributes to their downfall. Likewise, domestic violence does not strengthen family ties, and eventually many victims of such violence do leave the relationship if they can. Still, interpersonal dominance is probably the one outcome that violence is most effective at securing.

Violence as Self-Destruction: The Price of Living in the Present

There is one more crucial point to be gained from this survey of the costs and benefits of violence that will help us understand why people perform evil acts if they are generally so ineffective. We have seen that evil can sometimes produce benefits in the short run even if these benefits tend to evaporate or be canceled in the long run. The choice of evil as a means to an end signifies a victory of the narrow over the broad time perspective. It is a victory of the present over the future, so to speak. Violence or other evil action may be an appealing or even a rational means of solving a problem, but only if the perpetrator adopts a very narrow time frame. As we saw in Chapter 2, victims have much longer and more inclusive time frames than perpetrators.

The implication is that evil is most likely to result when people are focused narrowly on the immediate present. If a perpetrator could stop and appraise the long-term effects of his actions, he might well refrain from violence. But the more he is immersed in the here and now, ignoring the long-term considerations, the greater the chance of violence.

There is another well-established pattern in which short-term gains are pursued at the expense of long-term benefits, and this is the broad category of self-defeating or self-destructive behavior. In my previous work, I have reviewed many studies of self-defeating acts, from case studies of political disasters to laboratory experiments with college students.[31] Over and over, the same pattern emerges: People mess up their chances, lose their money, make fools of themselves, and generally bring various forms of unhappiness down on their own heads by making the standard mistake of focusing excessively on short-term factors and ignoring long-term ones.[32] Other scholars working with similar facts have reached the same conclusion. Self-inflicted wounds are generally the result of adopting a very short-term focus.

The parallel between evil and self-destruction is not just a coincidence. Evil is often destructive to the perpetrator in the long run, despite the short-term goals that may be achieved. Take the all-too-familiar case in which an angry dispute between acquaintances becomes violent, resulting in the death of one at the other's hands. Typically, the killer is sorry afterward and has nothing much to show for having won the argument. At most, perhaps, the victim has been prevented from making further insulting remarks. Meanwhile, feeling sorry is probably the least of the killer's problems, as he is likely to face arrest, prosecution, and imprisonment, with accompanying disruptions of career and family life. Had the perpetrator been able to pause a moment during the argument and consider all the misfortune that he would be bringing down on himself by killing his acquaintance, he probably wouldn't have done it. But the "heat of the moment" (in the common phrase) means precisely that: One does not pause to consider the long term. Being emotionally upset increases the tendency to make impulsive, risky, short-term decisions.[33] The violent person focuses only on the immediate situation, including whoever is upsetting him and the emotions that result from feeling that the other person is making him look bad. The violent act is a response only to the immediate situation.

The Victim's Lot

Unlike the other roots of evil, instrumental evil reduces the victim's suffering to a peripheral, secondary position among the perpetrator's concerns. The perpetrator wants something and is using violence or harm to get it. If he gets it, presumably it doesn't matter much to him whether the victim suffers or not. The victim's suffering is merely a means to an end. The evildoer may be totally indifferent to the victim's fate or may even conceivably feel sorry for the victim. The perpetrator may tell himself with some truth that he did not want or intend his victim to suffer.

In an important sense, the relationship is much more casual for the perpetrator than for the victim (another sign of the magnitude gap). The perpetrator's ability to hurt the victim is the central aspect of their relationship from the victim's perspective. The perpetrator, however, is focused on what he may gain by that harm, and the extent of the victim's suffering is only meaningful insofar as it promotes that goal. To care about the victim only makes the perpetrator's task harder and more unpleasant.

The perpetrator's indifference has several important implications for the victim. On the negative side, it means that perpetrators of instrumental evil are likely to cultivate a moral and emotional detachment from the victim's suffering, and so it may be hard for the victim to reach the perpetrator. To the perpetrator, the victim's life or death becomes a pragmatic rather than a moral issue. Killing the witnesses to a crime is one illustration of this attitude. The perpetrator may be reluctant to kill them and indeed probably has no personal reason to wish them any harm, but he may think that killing them is the safest course of action. Thus, small, seemingly accidental circumstances may become matters of life and death for the victim. One just happened by coincidence to witness the crime and so one's fate is sealed, even though one had nothing to do with it other than the accidental fact of witnessing it.

This indifference was vividly illustrated by a news story several years ago. During the civil wars in Uganda, the rebels at one point took control of the capital after a fierce battle left much of it in ruins. The occupying force was busy looting the city and executing enemies. Gradually, the soldiers developed a new pastime. They would set up a small camp on the roof of one of the tall buildings and then head out to search for attractive young women. When they found one, they would tie her hands behind her back and take her at gunpoint up to the roof. Once there, several of them would rape her. When they finished, they would throw her off the roof to her death, her hands still tied behind her back.

One is tempted, as usual, to imagine this scenario from the victim's point of view: hiding for days, hungry, scared, then captured by the enemy soldiers, being tied up, the escort at gunpoint through the town. Up to the roof, being undressed, probably beaten if you resist the rape, the pain and disgust as several men take their turns, just trying to get through that part of the ordeal, then perhaps the horror of discovering what the men will do with you when they are done. The intense screaming fright of the long fall.

Let us imagine the scene from the men's point of view: the receding memory of the desperate fear of battle, the luxury of having a city to inhabit instead of sleeping on the ground. The gradually growing boredom of the long hot days guarding the defeated, occupied city. The close bond with the few ragged men who have shared your risk and fear and now can share whatever fun you can find. The casual killing of suspected enemies, and then the discovery of the game of hunting girls. Possibly the gang rape helps to strengthen the sense of camaraderie. Talking to one another during the event, never to the silent girl. And then, after the girl has been thrown to her death, the sense of letdown, of wondering what to do next, probably not unlike the way a group of men feels after they watch a big game on television that is over too early to go home. Perhaps they will play cards.

Presumably, the rape hunt was a sufficiently absorbing pastime to take the boredom out of the long days. Searching the houses for a suitable girl, capturing her, taking her up to the roof, undressing her, and so forth, would certainly be as absorbing as a challenging game. Rape does not usually bring a great deal of sexual pleasure, but the rapist does anticipate pleasure in advance, and at least some rapists testify that the process becomes compelling, even addicting, once one gets used to it. Even the ones who did not take part in a rape might get some stimulation, even pleasure, out of seeing an attractive girl naked, and if nothing else this would be a big improvement over the deprivation and discomfort that a rebel army has to put up with while on the move or in the field.

Yet it is shocking to imagine how someone with whom you have just had sex could mean so little to you that you could casually put her to death in such a cruel fashion. To throw a human being off a tall building, as you might throw a stone off a bridge or toss a food wrapper into a trash can, shows how extreme cruelty can derive from extreme indifference. Falling is one of the most deeply rooted innate fears in the human organism, and the moment of the fall would certainly generate an intensely horrible feeling. It is not surprising that perpetrators learn how not to empathize with the suffering of their victims. Obviously they managed to engage in sexual intercourse without feeling a shred of intimacy, for any lingering sense of connection with the victim would make it painful to kill her in such a casually cruel way. The contrast with the American rapist and murderer quoted in Chapter 2 is striking: Despite committing his horrible crimes, he said he tried to be gentle with the victims and to kill them relatively painlessly. In his own twisted fashion, he still seemed to feel some connection to his victims, enough to impel him to make a gesture toward reducing their suffering. Not so the soldiers on the roof.

Once again, it is necessary to invoke the magnitude gap. Each of these incidents meant a horrible death for the young woman, whereas to the soldiers it was only an afternoon's diversion. In no sense did the pleasure or gain the soldiers got from hunting, raping, and killing these girls add up to anything like the loss and suffering that the victims endured.

The indifference to the victim can have a positive side, however. Victims of instrumental evil can ironically end up better off than victims of other forms of evil. Some victims may be able to save themselves or reduce their suffering by capitalizing on the pragmatic concerns of the perpetrator. The perpetrator wants something in particular, and if you give it to him there is no need for him to harm you further. The obvious example would be a robbery at gunpoint. He wants your money, not your death, and this fact does offer you a crucial chance for survival.

To be sure, it doesn't always work. Criminologists have noted that some armed robbers seem to harm or kill their victims for no apparent reason. Even if you willingly give him your wallet and car keys, he still might shoot you.[34] But these are the exceptions. By and large, the harm stops when the perpetrators get what they want. Victims can use the perpetrator's indifference as an opportunity to get through the incident with a minimum of harm and loss.

The dilemma may fall most heavily on victims of rape, if only because many legal rape cases turn on the issue of voluntary consent. Once she finds herself in his power, her best chance to get through with a minimum of harm may be to give him what he wants, yet if she fails to resist she may be letting him escape punishment if he is caught. The official advice to young women and girls on how to react to rape has wavered between advocating resistance and advocating submission. In the 1970s, because of the legalities, women were counseled to put up a fight, but the subsequent cost in terms of badly beaten or murdered victims has resulted in a shift toward advocating greater acquiescence.

Apart from such cases, though, the pragmatism of instrumental evil does have its advantages for the victim. The perpetrator does not primarily or essentially want the victim to suffer, and so the victim may minimize suffering by appealing to this pragmatic sense. For many victims, the difficulty may be in setting their own perspective aside and understanding the situation in the perpetrator's instrumental terms. It is quite hard to set aside concern over one's own suffering and possible death. But if the perpetrator can achieve his goal without the victim's suffering, the victim may manage to avoid the worst.

CHAPTER 5

Egotism and Revenge

Two centuries ago, in southern Africa, before anyone took notice of the handful of white settlers, an independently minded young woman developed a romantic crush on the prince, who was just ascending to the chieftain's throne. They were from the same clan and distantly related, so marriage was impossible, but flirtations were allowed, and indeed local customs among the Bantu permitted unmarried young men and women to have sexual contacts as long as they did not actually have intercourse. The woman contrived to meet the young chief on the road one day, and they had a very pleasant and passionate fling that afternoon.

Unfortunately, they did not manage to stay within the permitted bounds, and the chief soon received the unwelcome message that the young lady was pregnant. Acknowledging the pregnancy would mean disgrace and humiliation for the clan, and so the elders sent back word that the woman must merely be suffering from an iShaka, that is, a small beetle that in Bantu folklore was regarded as the cause of menstrual cramps and problems. Several months later, the chief received another, slightly sarcastic, message that it was time for him to collect the woman and her menstrual bug.

The chief tried to do the decent thing. He quietly brought the woman to live with him as his third wife, but the relationship was tempestuous, and the stigma of disgrace lingered over the woman and her infant. Some years later, he had finally had too much—some reports suggest that the boy had now become troublesome, too, losing one of the chief's goats through carelessness—and so he sent her back to her people. Good riddance, he thought. He had other wives and other sons, one of whom was clearly the heir to the Zulu throne. (At the time, the Zulus were a small Bantu tribe.)

Back in her village, the woman was treated badly. She had disgraced the village, and she had no man to support and protect her. To make matters worse, her strong-willed, opinionated, argumentative nature and sharp tongue made enemies. She and little Shaka (the unfortunate name had stuck) spent years living among people who despised and tormented them. The fatherless, stigmatized boy was regarded as fair game, and the other boys beat him up and humiliated him regularly for sport. By some accounts, he was also unfortunate in having very small genitals, which everybody could see given the near nakedness in summer, and they humiliated him about this, too. He grew up without friends, a lonely and bitter lad who was routinely picked on by everybody else. He was constantly reminded that he held the lowest status and esteem in the village and that everybody was above him and his grumpy, outcast mother.

The story probably would have ended like most such stories, with the boy either being driven off and killed or gradually accepted into a peripheral role in the village, but for one unexpected development: Shaka grew up to be a formidable giant of a man, nearly a foot taller than the average and well muscled from the years of having to fight all the other boys. Also, although it was not evident yet, he was intellectually brilliant, which had probably helped him through a few rough scrapes. The distant emperor was always looking for warriors, and Shaka was recruited to fight for him. By some accounts, he escaped the village at the last minute, when his enemies were plotting to kill him because they thought he was becoming dangerous to them.

He was remarkably successful in the military. Not only was he one of the most fearsome warriors in the army, he also proved to be extremely intelligent and creative. Bantu warfare at the time was highly ritualized, but the bitter young man detested the local traditions as much as he hated his many enemies, and when given a small command he began to introduce innovations to make his battles much more efficient and devastating.

He liked being in charge. Following traditional customs for ritualized, half-assed war was a waste of time, he thought; far better to attack with planning and *annihilate* your enemies. His troop racked up the victories.

After years of service, the emperor decided to reward Shaka by making him king of the Zulus after their current chief (Shaka's father, who had repudiated him) died. The Zulus were minor-league nobodies far from the center of the empire, and the emperor wanted Shaka to build a friendly buffer state between him and his distant enemies. Shaka quickly arranged for his father's official heir (his half brother) to be murdered, and he consolidated his power. He then began to transform the sleepy clan into a powerhouse, using the military techniques he had developed in the emperor's army. Once his new army was ready, he began to conquer his local neighbors. He offered them the chance to join him or fight him, and as his reputation spread, many took the option of joining him, even though it meant submitting to a foreign power without a fight.

And so it came to pass that the village where he had grown up as a lonely outcast boy lay in his path. What happened next reads like the fantasies of a child who has been tormented and beaten for years with no recourse. Shaka's crack troops surrounded the unsuspecting village before dawn. When the sun came up, the Zulus entered, and there was almost no resistance. Normally, the towns that surrendered without resistance were allowed to join the Zulus with no casualties, but Shaka had scores to settle. The entire population was made to assemble in front of him. Everyone he remembered was made to stand in one line.

Shaka went through the line and identified the handful of people who had ever done him a favor or been kind to his mother. These few individuals probably could not remember what friendly good deed they might have done casually many years ago, but he remembered. Each one received a nice gift and was set free—but Shaka advised them to stick around and see how much their past kindness was worth.

He then turned to the rest, the ones who had picked on him, teased him, beaten him up, played mean jokes on his mother, snubbed him, or otherwise humiliated him. One by one, they were impaled on sharp stakes taken from the corral fences. Those big and sharp wooden stakes were pounded very far up into the victim's rectum, causing internal bleeding and tissue damage and making for a sure but slow death. The people he hated suffered in the hot African sun all day. As evening fell, Shaka ordered his men to set fire to the wooden stakes, and those of his enemies who had remained alive through the day were burned to death.[1]

Shaka's story is a classic of revenge. He had suffered over years, and the suffering included both physical pain and the less visible injuries of humiliation and disgrace. He was the son of a king, a chief, but he was treated as an outcast and a bastard. Years later, he came back as a king and a commander of a small but superb army, and he exacted his full measure of revenge. The historical record is silent on what he did between the dawn raid and the evening bonfire, but it is safe to bet that he spent much of the time watching and listening to these people he had hated for years. (He was not a squeamish man.) He probably wanted to see them realize how wrong they had been to show disrespect to him, to underestimate him, to treat him in a humiliating or condescending way.

In the last chapter, I assessed the pragmatic effectiveness of violence. That effectiveness is generally low and erratic. The main exception is that violence is an effective way to make the other person suffer. By and large, one can conclude that violence and other evil means are unreliable for gaining material rewards or changing circumstances to fit one's preferences, but they are good for causing someone else to feel pain. The exception is far from trivial, and it is especially important when what the perpetrator wants is precisely to make someone else suffer.

One such case is that of revenge. Sometimes people believe they have suffered some grievance or affront. Maybe there is no way to undo the harm or loss they have suffered, but they still want to make the person who hurt them suffer. Violence and similar measures are quite effective in such cases.

The death penalty provides a good example. When someone has been murdered, the victim's family often wants the killer to be given the death penalty. Clearly, this measure will fall far short of undoing the loss they have suffered. As opponents of capital punishment like to point out, killing the murderer will not bring the victim back to life. In fact, it seems that the victim's family gains very little in most cases by having the murderer put to death. They do, however, get revenge and any satisfaction that goes with it.

Families of victims often take this very seriously. Indeed, occasionally there is someone among the victim's family who does not believe in the death penalty and says publicly that the killer should not be executed. Such individuals are often subjected to extreme pressure by others, including even the families of other victims having no relation to the case. They are told they are traitors. They get insulting phone calls late at night, even threats. Sometimes people suggest that they must not have loved the victim very much if they fail to demand the death penalty for the killer.[2]

What prompts people to take strong measures to get revenge? The main answer appears to be threats to their self-esteem. A great deal of human violence is perpetrated by people who feel that someone has threatened or damaged their self-esteem. Being humiliated, embarrassed, treated with disrespect, made a fool of, or otherwise attacked on this dimension of worthiness is an important cause of violence, because it creates strong urges to take revenge.

Pride—love of self, self-esteem, egotism—is an important element in Shaka's story. He was not simply getting even for having been cheated in some practical or material way. He was getting back at people who had put him down. As we will see, egotism lies behind most of the violent acts of revenge.

In Christian scripture and theology, Satan's first sin was neither murder nor rape, nor was it greed or sloth. It was *pride*. Satan, the ultimate incarnation of all things bad, embarked on his evil career by loving himself more than God.[3]

Although the religious view of evil has often emphasized arrogance and self-love, modern views have become more complex, and modern Western culture has come to regard self-esteem as a valuable resource and virtue. The difference in attitude is apparent in the connotations of common terms: *self-esteem* is seen as positive and desirable, whereas *conceited* or *arrogant* still carry a negative value. Yet both refer to what can simply be called *egotism*—the attitude of thinking very well of oneself.

This chapter will focus on revenge and egotism as causes of evil. In principle, revenge and egotism are two separate things. Revenge involves getting even for some wrong or loss, and egotism involves thinking well of oneself. Certainly, one can pursue revenge for something that has no element of egotism, and feelings of superiority could lead to violence even when there is no clear element of revenge. But such cases turn out to be relatively uncommon. Egotism and revenge probably overlap most of the time. Threats to self-esteem form the main category of things over which people seek violent revenge.

The link between egotism and revenge was shown by an important laboratory experiment conducted by Bert Brown.[4] This clever experiment, which was Brown's doctoral dissertation, was designed to see when people would become so intent on getting even that they would be willing to incur costs to themselves. Participants in the experiment, all young men, were told to pretend that they owned a small trucking company. They could earn real money by driving their trucks along a road, in a sort of primitive video game. The catch was that one of them controlled a stretch of the road that both of them needed to use, and he had the option of charging the other a toll to use that section of road. One person thus had the opportunity to take advantage of the other. In the experiment, this person was actually a confederate working with the experimenter and merely pretending to be another subject. He used his advantage frequently, so that the real subject lost out on a fair amount of the money he could have earned.

In the second part of the experiment, the roles were reversed. Now the real subject had the opportunity to control that precious stretch of road and to charge tolls. Obviously, this gave him a chance to get even. The experimenter told the real subject, however, that if he charged tolls he would have to pay "road taxes" on a sliding scale. Low tolls carried small taxes and so were still profitable. High tolls, however, carried larger and larger proportional taxes, and in the extreme case the subject who charged the maximum toll would lose money: He would pay taxes exceeding his total income from tolls. Thus, the subject could get even in the sense of hurting the other guy, but it would cost him money rather than benefiting him. Moreover, the only reason he was doing the experiment was to get money; it didn't make sense to spend that money just to punish somebody he'd never see again. It would be a costly form of revenge.

Most of the participants in the experiment did not want revenge that badly. They charged their opponent low tolls to recoup some of their losses, but they stopped short of the high tolls that would have cost them money, too. Thus, they sought only a limited form of revenge: They wanted to use their advantage to make back some of the money they had lost when the other guy had been in control, but they only wanted to hurt him as long as there was direct benefit to themselves.

There was, however, one crucial exception, in which people went all out to get revenge on the other person even if they themselves would lose real money on the deal. These people had been deeply affected by one further feature of the experiment. During the intermission, the experimenter told each subject that there was an audience of observers who were forming impressions of the subjects, and the experimenter told the subject what the audience had thought of him. Actually, these evaluative messages were also part of the experiment; they were prepared in advance and assigned to the subject at random, regardless of what he had done. Some subjects were told that, even though they had lost money when the other charged tolls, they still made a good impression for "playing it straight." Others, however, were told that the confederate had made them "look like a sucker" by charging those tolls. Think of it: the other guy had made a fool of you, in the opinion of several other people who had observed the whole thing.

These summaries about how the subject had supposedly come across made all the difference. Over and over, the guy who believed that he had been humiliated, made to "look like a sucker," went all out for extreme revenge. He charged the highest tolls even though to do so cost him money instead of bringing him profits. He was willing to give up some of his own money to punish the confederate who had embarrassed him. In contrast, those who were told that the audience still respected them did not seek the extreme revenge.

These experimental results have important and far-reaching implications for understanding the psychology of violence, oppression, and other evils. When someone does something bad to you, you are likely to seek to get even, but your efforts probably remain pragmatic and rational: You want to get back what you have lost, but that is normally the extent of it. You certainly do not want to lose any more money (or time or other resources) just to punish the person whose actions cost you. In contrast, however, if the person has not only taken your money but also hurt your pride, you will go to much greater lengths to get even. When responding to a blow to one's self-esteem or public image, people will accept further costs and losses to hurt the person who humiliated them.

The laboratory experiment involved only a simulation, but the dilemma is comparable to one that is often faced by people who have suffered some grievance at the hands of another. Often the quest for revenge involves significant costs and risks to the self. An individual who pursues someone out of a grievance puts considerable time and effort into that pursuit, and attacking that person often carries the risk of being hurt or even killed in the process. Likewise, nations that start wars over blows to national pride incur the costs of war, including the deaths of soldiers, the often huge expenses of paying for war, and damage to property. There is also the risk of losing the war, in which case the costs might far exceed what was suffered in the initial provocation.

A common and important cause of evil is the quest to avenge blows to one's pride. Dangerous people, from playground bullies to warmongering dictators, consist mainly of those who have highly favorable views about themselves. They strike out at others who question or dispute those favorable views.[5]

But What about Low Self-Esteem?

Before we proceed to examine the links between threatened egotism and violence, it is necessary to acknowledge that many people hold the opposite belief. My conclusion that violent people tend to have highly favorable opinions of themselves runs directly contrary to a well-entrenched view that *low self-esteem* is a major cause of violence. The argument runs something like this. Those who commit crimes and other acts of violence suffer from an inner sense of worthlessness. They believe that the world fails to appreciate them. By striking out, they are trying to gain esteem and prove their positive worth to a doubting world. If society could only provide these unfortunates with a good feeling about themselves, they would not act violently, and crime would be vastly reduced or even ended. This argument is plausible on the surface. It has wide-ranging appeal because it helps people to sympathize with those who commit evil acts and because it fits the attractive notion that we are all doing a good deed by loving ourselves more.

The view that low self-esteem causes violence and aggression has become commonplace. Many scholars assert it routinely, without even bothering to provide evidence or support for it. Consider just this smattering of examples from recent scholarly works that have reiterated that claim. David E. Long[6] said that low self-esteem and feelings of inadequacy are prominent traits among terrorists. Elijah Anderson claimed that low self-esteem is a major cause of violence among youth gangs. Claire Renzetti summarized the prevailing view that low self-esteem creates jealousy and possessiveness in close relationships, and these in turn lead to domestic violence (her work was on lesbian relationships). Edward W. Gondolf said that most researchers on domestic violence by men assume that low self-esteem prompts these men to beat their wives, although he added that the evidence to back up this assumption is very weak. John M. MacDonald said that armed robbers "lack self-esteem." David D. Kirschner discussed several cases in which adopted children had killed their new fathers, and he proposed that the young killers suffered from low self-esteem. Martin Sanchez Jankowski said that violence among gang members resulted from "self-contempt." Jack Levin and Jack McDevitt noted that low self-esteem is generally understood to be an important cause of hate crimes. Vernon Wiehe said that low self-esteem is one possible reason that children beat or hurt their brothers and sisters. Hans Toch said that men who get into violent fights with strangers suffer from low self-esteem. C. G. Schoenfeld proposed that the high crime rate among modern American black citizens is a result of the low self-esteem among blacks that can be traced back to slavery. R. Kim Oates and Douglas Forrest asserted that abusive mothers have low self-esteem. Erwin Staub's book on genocide said that the traditional view among a broad assortment of researchers is that low self-esteem is responsible for all manner of violence.[7]

Staub is right: That is surely the traditional view. But that doesn't mean it's correct. Could the link between low self-esteem and violence be a mirage?

There is ample reason to question whether low self-esteem is to blame for violence. Think of the obnoxious, hostile, or bullying people you have known—were they humble, modest, and self-effacing? (That's mainly what low self-esteem is like.) Most of the aggressive people I have known were the opposite: conceited, arrogant, and often consumed with thoughts about how they were superior to everyone else.

If one looks away from one's own acquaintances to the world's most notoriously violent individuals, the same pattern can be seen. When embarking on their aggressive campaigns, Saddam Hussein and Adolf Hitler were enormously confident and arrogant, adored by millions of followers. Indeed, the Nazi claim to be the "Master Race" suggests that they believed in their collective superiority, not inferiority. Idi Amin was hardly a shy or humble person. Stalin and Mao had high opinions of themselves. One can easily go on listing such cases. Meanwhile, it is hard to find contrary examples. Few of history's great conquerors, oppressors, or butchers were humble or modest or showed other clear signs of low self-esteem.

If low self-esteem causes violence, then one would expect that large groups or categories of people who have low self-esteem would also show high rates of violence. Indeed, it would be worth comparing the crime rates of groups that are known to differ in self-esteem. These comparisons almost uniformly point to the opposite of the low self-esteem theory.[8] Let us consider a few of them.

The obvious place to start is to compare men and women. Men have somewhat higher self-esteem than women, as reflected in the arrogance of "the male ego" and the female patterns of insecurity, lack of assertiveness, and depression. Yet on almost any measure of violence or aggression, men score higher. In laboratory studies using identical situations and provocations, men tend to respond more aggressively than women by about one-third of a standard deviation. Outside the laboratory, the differences are much larger. Men commit the majority of crimes and the vast majority (around 90 percent) of violent crimes. In fact, a woman's chances of being severely beaten up or murdered by another woman whom she doesn't know are negligible. A man's chances of being similarly hurt by a male stranger are much larger, and among young men such violent contacts between strangers are one of the leading causes of death. The only kind of violence in which women approach or equal men is domestic violence, and we will return to this shortly. In general, there is no question that women are less violent than men.

Another test would compare depressed people with those who are not depressed, because there is fairly solid and convincing evidence that low self-esteem is correlated with depression. Certainly, mental illness in general can be linked to violence and aggression, and criminals score higher than the general population on several measures of mental illness. But depression is not one of them. According to the report of the National Research Council,[9] depression has not generally been linked with crime or violence (unlike other mental disturbances). The only exception was that there seemed to be some link to domestic violence, and even those findings were inconclusive or ambiguous. In particular, it seemed likely that depression was the result rather than the cause of family violence.

Psychopaths are another relevant group. They form a small minority of the population but commit a disproportionately large share of the crimes, especially violent crimes. Although some experts regard psychopaths as abnormal, they are not mentally ill in the usual sense. They function reasonably well in society, they are well in touch with reality, and their actions are freely chosen rather than being driven by compulsions or irresistible urges. Do these nasty, callous predators show any signs of low self-esteem? One expert, Robert Hare, who thinks they commit about half the serious crimes in the United States and Canada, describes them as having a "narcissistic and grossly inflated view of their self-worth and importance." He adds that they regard themselves "as superior beings" and generally seem to think and act as if they were the center of the universe.[10] In fact, one reason they seem to feel no regret about using or exploiting other people is that they regard other people as inferior.

Comparing blacks and whites in the United States is a sensitive issue, partly because some possible conclusions may be unacceptable for political reasons. Yet those comparisons are especially valuable for examining the link between self-esteem and violence, for one important reason. The past century has seen a big shift in self-esteem between blacks and whites. For many years, white Americans were secure in their sense of racial superiority over blacks. It is generally agreed that this white self-confidence has eroded, partly due to collective guilt over having exploited and oppressed black people. In addition, various movements to boost black pride started around the 1960s. They seem to have succeeded very well. A recent overview of scholarly research studies on self-esteem concluded that, if there is any difference at all, it is black Americans who have higher self-esteem. Many studies have found no difference, and some have found blacks to score higher on self-esteem than whites.[11]

Thus, the self-esteem of black citizens has risen substantially, relative to that of whites, during the twentieth century. And the shift in relative self-esteem has been accompanied by a shift in crime rates. But the shift goes directly opposite to the theory that low self-esteem causes violence. Although precise statistics from the 1800s are hard to come by, it is fairly clear that white people killed black people far more often than the reverse. Even into the 1920s, the pattern of whites killing blacks was more prevalent than blacks killing whites.[12] Recent murder statistics show a dramatic reversal of this trend. Today, blacks kill whites 5 to 10 times more often than whites kill blacks.[13] The meaning of this statistic may be debated, but it appears indisputable that there has been a major reversal in the statistical pattern of interracial murder.

The same shift can be found in statistics on interracial rape. Historians believe that, despite all the hype about black men raping white women (for example, in the Old South), such rapes were actually quite rare. In contrast, white men raped black women with much greater impunity and frequency, dating back to the days of slavery.[14] Even white Northern soldiers who were fighting to defeat the South and free the slaves committed rape against some of them. The Union soldiers by and large raped very few of the Southern (white) women in the areas they conquered, especially in comparison with other armies in civil wars and comparable circumstances. But they did engage in a certain amount of raping of black women. Somehow it just seemed OK, because black women were considered inferior beings and hence fair game.

Today, however, black men rape white women about 10 times more often than white men rape black women.[15] One scholar, Gary D. LaFree, compiled a great many studies of interracial rape statistics and showed an impressive pattern of temporal change. Earlier in this century, all studies found a preponderance of white-on-black rape. Studies done in the 1950s found that the numbers of white-on-black and black-on-white rapes were about equal. Since 1960, every single study has found black-on-white rapes to be more common than white-on-black.[16] The key point is that the sharp rise in black violence toward whites coincided roughly with the movements aimed at raising pride and self-esteem among blacks. High self-esteem apparently leads to more raping, contrary to the low self-esteem view.

Now, I don't want anyone to use these statistics to fan the flames of racial antagonism. Personally, I do not see that there is any moral high ground in these numbers to be claimed by either group. Both blacks and whites have committed far too many horrible crimes, and both should concentrate on their own shame rather than pointing fingers elsewhere. The relevant point is this: Racial pride and feelings of superiority seem to go with violence toward others, and this is apparently true of both blacks and whites. Perhaps it is merely one of the sadder, uglier signs that basic human nature is the same in whites and blacks.

Parallel evidence about temporal patterns in violence and self-esteem can be seen by looking at people who suffer from manic-depressive (now called bipolar) disorder.[17] This illness is marked by wide mood swings. On some days, the person feels euphoric, energetic, eager to tackle new challenges and ready to conquer the world. On other days, the person feels hopeless, helpless, worthless, and miserable. Feelings of self-esteem ride right along on this roller coaster. Which phase is associated with violent, aggressive actions and hostility toward others? Mainly the manic state—that is, the one marked by exaggeratedly high self-esteem.[18]

A last group worth examining is people who have consumed alcohol. The evidence about alcohol and aggression is extensive and quite clear. Alcohol is neither necessary nor sufficient to cause violence, so it is just a contributing cause (a moderator)—but it is a big and powerful moderator nonetheless. Numerous separate studies of murder, rape, and assault have repeatedly found that the majority of violent crimes are committed by people who have been drinking.[19] Laboratory experiments have likewise confirmed that alcohol intensifies aggressive tendencies.[20] That is, although alcohol does not by itself make people act aggressively, intoxicated persons will respond more aggressively when provoked than will sober persons.

The question then is what happens to self-esteem under the influence of alcohol. Several recent studies have found that alcohol makes people more egotistical.[21] After drinking, people rate themselves more favorably. In short, drinking alcohol causes a temporary boost in self-esteem.

Over and over, then, we find that groups with higher self-esteem are more violent and aggressive than others. When self-esteem rises, violence rises too. These patterns do not quite prove that high self-esteem causes violence, because they are mostly based on groups, and it could be that the violent acts are committed by the few people in the group who do not share the egotism of the rest. Then again, if low self-esteem really causes violence, it would be reasonable to expect that most groups with higher self-esteem would have lower rates of violence. But the opposite is the case.

Thus, the widespread and traditional theory that links violence to low self-esteem should be discarded. Many researchers have alluded to it, and some recent social policy in the United States appears to be based on it, but on close inspection not much is provided in the way of proof or evidence. The low self-esteem theory is contradicted by everyday experience and by large masses of statistics. Low self-esteem does not cause violence.

Ego Threats and Insecure Arrogance

Is there is any connection between how people regard themselves and how they treat others? We have seen that groups that have a sense of superiority tend to be more violent than others. Does this mean that high self-esteem causes aggression?

No. At least, not by itself. Plenty of people have high self-esteem and don't go about harming strangers or taking advantage of their neighbors. High self-esteem, by itself, is not always or inevitably a cause of violence. As we will see shortly, most violent people have high opinions of themselves, but most people with high opinions of themselves are not violent. Violent people are an important but distinct, atypical minority of people with high self-esteem.

The most potent recipe for violence is a favorable view of oneself that is disputed or undermined by someone else—in short, *threatened egotism*. The roots of violence lie in the gap between a highly favorable self-appraisal and a bad appraisal by somebody else. The person you hit is the person who has just told you that you are not as wonderful as you thought.

There are two possible ways to react to a bad evaluation.[22] One is to accept it as correct, which means revising your opinion of yourself downward. In general, people hate to do this. Damage to self-esteem is usually accompanied by unpleasant emotional states: sadness, depression, disappointment, anxiety, shame. These are all feelings that are focused on the self, and they are miserable.

The other option is to reject the bad evaluation as wrong. This choice allows you to preserve your favorable opinion of yourself, and it is the one that people prefer. It does leave the evaluation hanging out there, however: How could that person say that to you, if it is not true? The usual answer is that there is something wrong with that person. He (or she) must be obnoxious, unfair, biased, stupid, or unreasonably antagonistic toward you. The most common and appropriate emotional reaction to such an evaluation is anger. Anger is unpleasant, but it is directed outward at the other person, not at yourself. That is how aggression gets started.

This choice point can be seen almost anywhere people receive bad evaluations. Romantic rejection is as good a place as any to provide examples. Consider the fairly common case in which a young couple goes on several dates, but when the man wants to continue and get more serious, the woman declines and says they should stop dating.[23] There are two ways for the young man to react. One is to feel depressed and humiliated: He wasn't good enough for her. He may lose confidence and withdraw socially for a while. He may wonder what is wrong with him, or he may ruminate about what he did wrong and why he didn't measure up to her standards. He may contemplate his future in terms of less desirable women. These are depressing thoughts.

Alternatively, he may simply get mad at her and blame her. Her expectations were unrealistic, absurd, unfair. There was nothing wrong with him. This response allows him to go on thinking well of himself, and indeed he may believe that his next romantic partner will be just as attractive and even more desirable overall than the one who dumped him, because he tells himself he will make sure not to get involved with "another neurotic bitch." If he had known from the start that she would turn out to be some kind of frigid, ambivalent, man-hating nut case, he wouldn't have wasted that much of his time and money on her. Fortunately, such reactions do not lead to physical violence in most cases, but insults and other verbal abuse are common.

Psychologists have long recognized that emotions are linked to aggression, but theories about this link have changed repeatedly. A standard view for several decades was that frustration led to aggression, but closer study has shown that it is not that simple. Not all frustrations produce aggression, and not all aggression derives from frustrations. Another standard view is that anger leads to aggression, but again the evidence shows that some anger doesn't produce aggression and some aggression doesn't involve anger.[24]

These facts can be explained by exaiming the bad evaluation and the choice of responses. There will be unpleasant emotional reactions in either case, because receiving a bad evaluation is just one of those experiences that is likely to make one feel bad. But aggression follows only from the reaction that denies the validity of the bad evaluation and produces emotions that are directed toward the other person. If you blame the other person for frustrating you, you may want to hit that person; but if you blame your own inadequacies for your frustrations, you are less likely to want to attack anybody else.

Envy provides a good example, because it can lead to either reaction. Envy is what you feel when someone else has something you want. The fact that somebody else got the promotion, the house, the girlfriend, or the award you wanted could mean that the other person was more deserving than you—or it could mean that the other person used some kind of unfair advantage.

Thus, envy presents us with a threat to self-esteem and a choice point. Researchers have found that the choice of response makes a crucial difference in whether hostility ensues.[25] If you decide that the other person got what you sought because he or she was more worthy or deserving, you may feel depressed or disappointed, and your self-esteem may suffer, but you do not tend to become hostile. In contrast, if you preserve your self-esteem by concluding that the other person got what you sought unfairly, unjustly, or inappropriately, then you are more likely to feel hostility toward him or her.

Riots, revolutions, and other violent uprisings by poor people also illustrate this difference. Poor people have probably always envied rich people, but they have not always reacted by burning, looting, and killing. It is injustice, not inequality, that breeds riots. It is mainly when poor people come to think that their poverty is unfair that they burst into violence.

Who Turns Violent, and When

I have proposed that ego threats—that is, the combination of high self-esteem and an external, unflattering evaluation—are the principal cause of violence. This formula provides a useful key for predicting just which people are most likely to become violent and aggressive. Specifically, the people who are most prone to encounter ego threats are the most likely to respond violently. Anything about a person that makes him or her more likely to receive bad evaluations from other people will increase the odds of a hostile response.

Inflated Self-Esteem

One simple conclusion would be that high self-esteem per se leads to aggression. Suppose on a scale of 1 to 10 you rate yourself as a 9. Then any time someone tells you anything else, from 1 to 8, it will be an ego threat, because the evaluation is lower than your self-appraisal. In contrast, if you only rate yourself as a 3, then ego threats are limited to ratings of 1 or 2. If somebody rates you as a 5, you will be pleased and flattered if your self-appraisal was a 3 and deeply insulted if you regarded yourself as a 9. By this reasoning, the higher your opinion of yourself, the more likely you are to get ego threats, and hence the more prone to violence you would be.

There is one flaw in that reasoning. Feedback is not random. It seems fair to assume that there is a large dose of reality underlying the feedback we receive. Maybe the person who thinks he's a 9 is in fact so competent that he will never be evaluated as a 5—he will receive evaluations mainly of 8, 9, or 10. (If only life were so fair and consistent!) It seems likely that, on average, everyone receives evaluations that cluster around his or her true level. In that case, everyone would receive about the same number of ego threats.

There is one important exception to that argument, however. Yes, if you think you're a 9 and you really are a 9, then maybe you will mostly hear favorable evaluations. But if you think you're a 9 and you're actually only a 6, then you are likely to receive ego threats quite often. That is, your daily experiences will tend to be telling you that you are a 6, and this will constantly upset you if you think you are a 9.

The point of this argument is that those who harbor inflated self-esteem will be likely to encounter a relatively large number of ego threats—and hence be prone to hostile, aggressive, or violent responses. It is conceited people who will be the bullies. People who think they're better than they really are will be the dangerous ones.

Violent people certainly do show plenty of signs of inflated self-esteem, even apart from the few maniacs like Adolf Hitler and Saddam Hussein who seemed to think they were gods. Some remarkable comments emerged from Diana Scully's interviews with convicted rapists.[26] She said many of these men spontaneously bragged to her about both their sexual prowess and other supposed accomplishments. Many of them described themselves as "multitalented superachievers," a claim that seems quite out of touch with reality when coming from someone who is in prison.[27]

The gap between self-concept and reality has become a new focus of research on domestic violence. Most of this research has examined violence by men, partly because male violence is a more serious social problem than female violence. Early studies assumed that low self-esteem must be a cause of domestic violence, and indeed some comments by victims did depict their male partners as suffering from low self-esteem.[28] Yet, as we have seen, one cannot rely solely on victims' interpretations. A female victim of battering may say that her abusive husband suffers from low self-esteem, because that is much more optimistic and also better for her than to say that she has married an irresponsible, violent pig who lacks self-control. When researchers began to conduct careful prospective studies of family violence, however, the evidence for low self-esteem disappeared.[29]

The new buzzword among researchers on family violence is *status inconsistency*. Status inconsistency refers to some serious contradiction among the various signs of the man's status. For instance, a man might hold a Ph.D. while his job is driving a taxi. Several important and carefully conducted studies have found that status inconsistency is a typical part of the picture of the violent, abusive husband.[30]

Status inconsistency is an important step forward in understanding domestic violence. I think, however, that the concept is misleading in one crucial respect: Not all status inconsistencies lead to violence. In fact, some kinds of status inconsistency seem to *reduce* family violence.

This problem with status inconsistency was apparent in the landmark study that introduced the concept.[31] The researchers certainly did provide a great deal of evidence to show the importance of some forms of status inconsistency. For example, conventional wisdom supposed that housewives would be victims of battering more often than working wives, but the researchers found the opposite to be true. The reason, they concluded, was that nonworking housewives do not threaten their husband's superior status. But a woman who earns her own money could create status inconsistency for her husband, who might regard himself as the breadwinner but then find that his wife is bringing home a bigger check.

The most important findings, however, involved gaps between education and occupation (for example, career prestige and salary). In these findings, inconsistency had strong but opposite effects. On the one hand, men who had earned high qualifications but who had poor careers were exceptionally violent as a group. In fact, they were six times more likely than average to perpetrate severe violence against their wives. So far, so good for the status inconsistency theory: inconsistency breeds marital abuse. On the other hand, though, men who had poor qualifications but exceptionally successful careers—for example, someone who had dropped out of school but then worked his way up to a high executive position in a corporation—were six times *less* likely than average to beat their wives severely.

The status inconsistency is the same in both cases: high education and unsuccessful career, or low education and successful career. Yet the effects on violence are opposite. How can this apparent paradox be resolved?

Threatened egotism provides a key. The men who had impressive qualifications probably thought they deserved to be successful, and when life failed to confirm these expectations, they tended to turn violent and take it out on their wives. In contrast, men who had poor credentials most likely had much lower expectations. When their career success surpassed those expectations, they may have noticed the inconsistency, but their egos were not threatened. Thus, the violent husband is the man who thinks his daily life is not confirming his exalted opinion of himself.

A historical study of wife beating around the beginning of the twentieth century shows the same results and points to the same conclusion.[32] The historian, David Peterson, began with the standard view that the typical wife-beater would be an all-powerful family tyrant, but the evidence painted quite a different picture. Most of the abusive husbands turned out to be men who lacked money, education, and other resources or signs of status. In particular, many lacked status relative to their wives, such as if the wife came from a richer family or had a higher level of education than the husband. Peterson thought that this lack of status would lead to low self-esteem, and so he was puzzled to find that everything these men said indicated that they believed strongly that the man should be king in his own house. They believed in the traditional family concept, including especially the idea of male superiority. Peterson said that the implications for self-esteem were thus contradictory.

They are not contradictory, though, in terms of threatened egotism. In fact, they make perfect sense. The men Peterson studied believed strongly in male superiority, but they found themselves in a situation in which their wives surpassed them in some way. They probably feared that other people might think they were not kings in their household, because their wives had a better education or more money. They may have feared that their wives would not look up to them, as they thought a woman should. And so they dominated their wives physically.

A good illustration of this pattern is provided in a recent study of marital rape, published by David Finkelhor and Kersti Yllo.[33] Ross, the man in the story, was in his late 30s. He had a good education, but his business had not gone well, and indeed at the time of the study he had lost his insurance agency and was trying to start a new small business. He had not had much experience with girls, and he clung to his one high school girlfriend all through college, finally marrying her afterward. Her family was richer than his, and he felt that they looked down on him. "I wasn't good enough because I didn't go to Harvard or Yale" was how he recalled their condescending attitude toward him.

The marriage was a struggle right from the start. He thought that she wanted to control everything and that this desire caused her always to insist on something contrary to whatever he had decided. Reading between the lines, one can infer that he was just as intent on being the boss. Looking back after the divorce, he described the marriage as "an endless battle of wills"—and one in which she was usually the victor. They had many arguments and fights, and he began to perceive everything she said or did as an attack on his pride. She gloried in humiliating him, he thought.

She also withheld sex from him. In his view, her prudish Victorian upbringing had left her with only a minor interest in sex for her own sake, and so she used sex to manipulate him. She told him sometimes that if he wanted to have sex he ought to earn it, and he took this to mean that he wasn't making enough money in her opinion. Once she discovered him masturbating and told him that it was disgusting and he should stop, but later on when she didn't want to have sex, she would condescendingly tell him to masturbate.

One night they were having another fight. She was wearing her nightgown, and for some reason he became sexually aroused. Right during the argument he reached out for her breast. She slapped his hand away. That did it. He told her she was going to get it whether she liked it or not. "Oh, no you don't," she said, and she fought him as he seized her and tried to push her down on the bed. Finally she saw that she was outmuscled and resigned herself to it. "I had the best erection I'd had in years," he said later. He forced himself on her. Afterward she cried and called him names, but he knew that for once he had won. "I'm not proud of it, but, damn it, I walked around with a smile on my face for three days," he recalled.

There were a couple more marital rapes. Then they went for marriage counseling, and when that failed they divorced. Looking back, Ross felt he had done something wrong, but not too wrong. He emphasized that he had never struck her or harmed her. As for the rapes, he felt that he had received sufficient provocation to justify them: "a just cause," he said. She had tried to emasculate him and take control of the marriage. Raping her was his main way of reclaiming the superior position that he thought a man should have.

Thus, one general category of violent people is made up of those who overrate themselves. Someone whose opinion of himself (or, less often, herself) is unrealistically positive is likely to be vulnerable to frequent ego threats. Whenever reality intrudes, it will tell him that he's not as good as he thought. And he may be prone to respond violently against whoever tells him that. The alternative of lowering his opinion of himself is typically avoided whenever possible. Hence, conceited people will tend to be hostile and dangerous.

Unstable Egotism: Insecure Grandiosity

Another form of high self-esteem that may contribute to violent outbursts appears in people who think well of themselves most of the time but who are vulnerable to frequent or large fluctuations in their self-esteem. For these people, that miserable sinking feeling that goes with a drop in self-esteem is all too familiar, and they are on guard to avoid it. Even a slight hint or mild implication that questions their personal worth may elicit a strong response. Fluctuating self-esteem makes a person hypersensitive to ego threats, and a basically high but somewhat malleable self-esteem is probably the most dangerous.

People with this pattern are particularly sensitive for the same reason that violence occurs when anger is directed outward to avoid a loss of self-esteem. If your self-esteem rides a roller coaster, so to speak—high one moment, low the next—then you are probably well acquainted with the risk of it dropping. If your self-esteem is mostly low but volatile, then perhaps there is no place to go but up, so a modest person with fluctuating self-esteem is not likely to be violent. But if you mostly think well of yourself and yet are vulnerable to fluctuations in that belief, you are vulnerable to losses in self-esteem.

It is the threat of losing self-esteem that makes the difference. A person with a firm, *unshakably* high opinion of himself is not going to be threatened by anything. No matter what happens, he will still think he is great. That firm belief will make him largely immune to ego threats. But there are precious few such individuals. Most people with big egos feel there is a pervasive risk that their good opinions of themselves could be ruined. They also worry that other people will get a bad impression of them, which they think would be tragic.

The evidence about the stability of self-esteem is quite convincing. Researchers led by Michael Kernis have studied such effects by measuring each person's self-esteem on several occasions to track fluctuations.[34] With such measures, people can be sorted into four groups, based on whether their basic self-esteem is high or low and on whether it remains constant or is subject to fluctuations. The rates of hostility and defensiveness of these different groups can then be compared.

One of the four groups stood out as the *least* prone to hostile reactions, and that was the group with high and stable self-esteem. Such people seem to like themselves no matter what. Bad evaluations, failures at work, or insulting remarks by others do not seem to threaten their self-respect.

The *most* hostile group was the one with high but *unstable* self-esteem. These people think well of themselves in general, but their self-esteem fluctuates. They are especially prone to react defensively to ego threats, and they are also more prone to hostility, anger, and aggression than other people.[35]

These findings shed considerable light on the psychology of the bully. Hostile people do not have low self-esteem; on the contrary, they think highly of themselves. But their favorable view of themselves is not held with total conviction, and it goes up and down in response to daily events. The bully has a chip on his shoulder because he thinks you might want to deflate his favorable self-image.

There is plenty of evidence to fit this view. We have already noted that people who show temporary, artificial highs in self-esteem are prone to be aggressive. Manic-depressive people are more aggressive when they are in the manic state, and alcohol gives a temporary boost to both self-esteem and violent reactions.

A classic study by Hans Toch[36] entitled *Violent Men* drew just such a picture of insecure arrogance and egotism, although Toch himself did not quite see it that way. The original study was done several decades ago, and its statistical basis would not pass muster today, because he wanted to propose several categories of violent men, but his data did not really support the view that the different categories in his theory were actually different. Looking at his data with modern statistical knowledge, one would say that he basically found one main category of violent men, plus a few exceptions. The main category can best be described as threatened egotism. These men encountered, sought out, or deliberately instigated challenges to their egos, such as by getting into arguments in bars or insisting on deferential treatment by policemen. As soon as anyone showed any disrespect, questioned them, or offended them in any way, they would respond with violence.

The same conclusion emerged from an interview study of British men imprisoned for violent assault. Leonard Berkowitz, who ran the study, was looking for evidence to support the then-popular theory that "subcultures of violence" promoted aggression. He did not find any such evidence. Instead, most of the men had gotten into trouble because they reacted with their fists to someone who insulted them. Berkowitz came away from the interviews with the strong impression that "their egos were fragile indeed,"[37] because they were so easily offended. A fragile ego is another term for a favorable but vulnerable self-opinion.

Many of these violent men react to what would seem to be a very slight or trivial offense. Indeed, the researchers in a number of these studies felt moved to wonder over how little it took to make these men hit or harm someone. The extreme, irrational sensitivity to a stranger's slightly disrespectful tone or remark may be what caused some earlier observers to conclude that low self-esteem must be at work. But it is not low self-esteem. It is high self-esteem that is vulnerable to fluctuations. Once you know the miserable feeling of anxiety and sadness that comes from a sharp drop in self-esteem, you will be on the lookout to avoid any such drop. You won't wait for a thorough and detailed attack on your worth as a person, because by then it will be too late to avoid that horrible feeling. Instead, you will want to stop any such criticism or attack before it gets started. As a result, you will overreact to any slight or incipient hint. The problem, of course, is that you end up lashing out at people who meant nothing bad or were only making a friendly joke. Sometimes the victims are surprised that you became violent and hostile over nothing.

The problem is undoubtedly most acute for the people who live with these hypersensitive egotists. Battering husbands differ from other husbands in precisely this hypersensitivity to blows to their esteem. In one study, researchers asked several groups of men whether they would be offended in various ambiguous situations, such as if a wife disagreed with her husband about something in front of other people. The abusive, battering husbands were much more likely to see these minor acts by the wife as attacks on the husband's pride.

Romantic jealousy is another experience in which people become irrationally oversensitive because of implicit blows to their pride. Much violence between spouses or dating partners is driven by jealousy, and much of it is unwarranted. If a woman merely smiles in a friendly way at a man, her husband may think that she is sexually interested in the outsider—which the husband may find to be an attack on his own sexual adequacy. Accordingly, he may strike her.

Jealous violence is not limited to men, either. In a ground-breaking study of violence in lesbian relationships, jealousy emerged as major reason that some women beat their partners. Claire Renzetti, the author of the study, described the abusive partners as prone to "delusions of infidelity," which made them think their girlfriends were betraying them. In one sad but revealing incident, a woman described how one of her partner's friends had casually suggested that they have lunch. "You want me to die or somethin'?" she replied. If her abusive, possessive partner knew she had lunch with another woman, she would beat her up, or worse.[38]

The ego threat, in fact, is especially strong when jealousy arises in same-sex relationships, as Renzetti pointed out. If you and your lover are both females, then another female could be interested in either of you. So when she flirts with your partner, she has implicitly rejected you. In a sense, then, the blow to one's pride is doubled. Both your partner and the outsider have made some negative judgment about you.

In other respects, violent lesbians are quite similar to the violent husbands we discussed earlier. Status inconsistency is apparent in that the abusive women find that their circumstances fall short of their egotistical expectations. Renzetti observed that the violent lesbian typically wanted to be the boss and the dominant partner, but she found herself the one who had less money or less education. Hitting her partner was a way to claim the dominant position that she wanted but didn't feel she could claim securely on other bases.

The link of fluctuating self-esteem to emotion is implicit in other studies that show shame-prone people to be the ones most likely to become angry and violent. Shame is defined as the emotion that occurs when one feels that one is a worthless, terrible person in general—as distinct from guilt, which is a feeling that one committed one particular wrong action.[39] People hate to feel shame, and those who are especially vulnerable to it are also the ones who are most likely to feel rage and hostility toward others.[40] The reason seems to be that getting mad at others is a way of avoiding or escaping the terrible feeling of shame.

The sequence goes something like this. Someone tells you that you are not very competent at something. If you are a shame-prone person, you start to experience that sinking feeling that the other person may be right and that maybe this is not the only thing you are bad at, and maybe you are just a worthless loser in general. You start to feel panic, anxiety, and misery, and your heart beats faster. To break free of those feelings, you reject the premise. You are not incompetent in the way the other person said. The other person had no right to say that to you, and he's completely wrong. Your feelings are now directed outward at him, instead of at yourself, and the effects of your faster heartbeat and general arousal transfer into intense anger at the person who has so unfairly insulted you. You want to hit him.

Feelings of vulnerability about one's own superiority are not limited to individuals. Whole nations show the same pattern. The political historian Franklin Ford offered this generalization based on his survey of political murder and terror across many centuries and cultures: "Ancient history—and later history as well—suggests that official terror is usually the mark of a regime that may appear brutally self-confident but is in fact insecure."[41] The claim on superiority is important, but so is the fear that it could be undermined easily.

Still, insecurity carries a connotation of lack of self-esteem. I have proposed that violent, evil people tend to be marked by feelings of superiority but also a fear that they could lose their superior position. Could this mean that they have low self-esteem after all? We will now consider this question once more.

What about Deep Down Inside?

Violence emerges from a tension between two views of the self, one of them favorable and the other less favorable. Some readers might take this to mean that violent people really suffer from the low self-esteem that lies buried behind or underneath the veneer of confidence and superiority. Indeed, when I described my findings about the psychology of violent, evil people to various colleagues and students, some of them asked, "But aren't they really suffering from low self-esteem deep down inside?"

The answer is no, for several reasons. One of them is the direct weight of the evidence. Several researchers who have devoted considerable study to violent individuals have explicitly addressed this question, and their conclusions are clear. Psychologist Dan Olweus spent years studying childhood bullies, who are aggressive toward other children and who often go on to become juvenile delinquents and then violent criminals as adults. Multiple studies with a variety of research methods found plenty of evidence of low self-esteem among the *victims* of bullies, but little or none among the bullies themselves. Moreover, there was no sign of hidden or secret feelings of low self-esteem. As Olweus wrote, "In contrast to a fairly common assumption among psychologists and psychiatrists, we have found no indicators that the aggressive bullies (boys) are anxious and insecure under a tough surface."[42]

Nor do members of violent youth gangs have low self-esteem deep down inside. Martin Jankowski, a sociologist who lived with several dozen of these gangs for more than a decade, made that clear. He too noted that some theorists had proposed "that many gang members have tough exteriors but are insecure on the inside. This is a mistaken observation."[43] Individually and collectively, the gang members think very highly of themselves.

One clarification is necessary, because I have characterized violent people as insecure about their high self-esteem. Jankowski, Olweus, and others use the term *insecurity* by itself to refer to a broad pattern of low self-esteem, which is something quite different from holding high self-esteem that is vulnerable to fluctuations. My own usage of the term here refers to insecurity about the egotism, not insecurity in the sense of lacking egotism altogether.

Another way to look at the issue is to consider how people react to problems and setbacks. Researchers have established that self-esteem makes a clear and reliable difference in such reactions. People with low self-esteem tend to blame themselves when things go wrong. People with high self-esteem tend to blame external factors, such as other people, the situation, or various obstacles.[44] These attitudes are not too surprising, because they are likely to cycle back and affect self-esteem. Thinking that all your problems and failures are your own fault is a style that fits low self-esteem. Thinking that nothing bad should ever reflect on you is an integral part of high self-esteem. So which style do violent people use?

Quite simply, violent people seem to follow the high self-esteem pattern. Jankowski observed that the members of teen and young adult gangs always blamed something else for failure, rather than their own error or inadequacy. More ominously, the bloody purges of violent groups show the same pattern of finding scapegoats rather than blaming themselves. The Khmer Rouge, for example, were never willing to admit that they could be wrong or make a mistake. Whenever there was a failure anywhere, somebody had to be blamed as an enemy.[45]

This blaming of enemies is one of the driving forces behind many deadly purges. Elizabeth Becker's account of the Khmer Rouge is one prototype, but the same conclusion could emerge from examining the Stalinist or Maoist purges, which had much greater body counts. Becker put the tragedy in perspective. The Khmer revolution never really had a chance. They wanted to make their country self-sufficient by eliminating all foreign influence. In fact, however, Cambodia's economy had only been viable by virtue of large infusions of foreign aid money, and once the Khmer refused foreign aid, there was no hope. The idea that modern city dwellers could be converted into successful rice farmers in the countryside was absurd, and the chances for a moderately large population to feed itself (let alone grow enough food to make the officially forecast profits) without modern technology were likewise minuscule. Inevitably, there were shortages and other failures. But it was not permitted to blame the party's plan. Instead, the only permissible explanation was that enemies had sabotaged the people's efforts. And so they began to shoot people—people who were in fact mostly well-meaning, hard-working, loyal individuals—because any person in a position of responsibility was suspected of contributing to the failure. Saboteurs had to be found, and since hardly any real saboteurs existed, innocent people were arrested instead. And executed.

There is also a subtle but important logical flaw in the argument that violence is caused by hidden low self-esteem. It is clear that genuine low self-esteem does not cause violence. The accumulated mass of research findings is quite convincing about this. After all, there are plenty of people who have low self-esteem that is not hidden, and they tend to be nonviolent.

Thus, anyone who wants to salvage the low self-esteem theory has to argue, oddly, that *overt* low self-esteem is nonviolent and only *covert* low self-esteem is violent. In other words, they have to say that low self-esteem is bad only when you can't see it. Aside from the theoretical vacuousness and apparent absurdity of that argument, it begs the question. If low self-esteem is only linked to violence when it is hidden, then one must look at the hiddenness itself as the decisive cause. What is hiding the low self-esteem is, of course, the veneer of egotism and pride. Low self-esteem is only violent when it is combined with a surface pattern of arrogance, confidence, or egotism. Thus, we are back to where this argument began. The favorable opinions about the self are the decisive ones in causing violence.

Playing to the Audience

We have focused on how self-esteem affects violence, but sometimes the self's opinion is not the only one or even the most important one. When there is an audience, people often worry about what the audience may think. Even if they are unruffled by a private insult or disrespectful treatment, they may turn violent if they think someone else will witness the incident and think less of them for backing down.

A man gets on a bus in a Brazilian city. He is in a bad mood. He pushes his way to the middle of the bus. A younger and smaller man, the one who later tells the story, is standing in his way. The older man resents the younger man's clean shirt, or maybe he is just frustrated with people standing in his way and feels an impulse to take it out on this particular one. He gives the young man a rough push in the back with his elbow.

The young man turns and looks at the other man. In a fair fight, he would probably lose, so getting into a fight is not a good idea. But he has his own angers and frustrations, and he doesn't want to back down. He looks the other man in the eye with an intimidating, dangerous look that he has practiced for just such occasions. The older man is a little surprised at this show of fearlessness. The young man asks him what he wants. The older man, despite his seeming physical superiority, lowers his head in a slightly submissive gesture of apology. Nothing further is said. What could have turned into a violent or even deadly argument is instead defused and ends peaceably.[46]

When the young man told the story to the anthropologist Daniel Linger, he made one crucial point. When he spoke to rebuke the older man, he did so in a very quiet voice, so that none of the other bus passengers could hear what he said. This was probably the only way that the incident could have ended without violence, in his view. In effect, the other man backed down and accepted a small humiliation, but he would not have done so if the other passengers had seen it. As the young man put it later, "If the thing becomes public it can get much worse, because then it isn't just between us two: Then you've got the obligation to give some satisfaction to the people who are watching."[47]

Concern over the opinions of others is often a driving factor in violent, aggressive, or other evil behavior. Indeed, we saw earlier in this chapter that the opinions of the audience made all the difference in how far people would go to seek revenge.[48]

You might think that murders would be private affairs because killers would not want witnesses, but some studies have found that a high proportion of them occur in the presence of other people. A fairly extensive study of California homicides by David Luckenbill found that an audience was present in more than half the cases.[49] In some cases, audiences egged on the people who were arguing, such as by asking, "Are you going to let him get away with saying that?" Sometimes the audience even gave the killer the weapon.

Still, the most important function of the audience is probably just that it makes the offense harder to ignore. People seem to feel that they cannot ignore, dismiss, or otherwise "take" an insult if other people see it.

Audiences lend *social reality* to events. If no one else knows about it, you can pretend it never happened.[50] Self-esteem can usually bounce back. But people are very concerned with what other people think of them, and if someone else knows about an ego threat, the option of ignoring it is lost. There is no longer any way to pretend it didn't occur.

People are sometimes sensitive to the broader implicit audience of everyone around them who might find out some day. Thus, different patterns of culture and society can produce very different levels of proneness to violence. Richard Nisbett, in his work on regional cultures in the United States, points out that the South traditionally had fewer routes to individual success than the North, because educational and industrial institutions were slower to develop in the South. As a result, he thinks, Southerners—particularly young white men—developed a greater tendency to focus on the need to gain and defend personal prestige by fighting.[51] This is one explanation for the higher rates of murder and violent crime in the South. It is not simply that the South is lawless; its crime rates are comparable to those of the North in other respects, and in some cases lower. But personal violence is high, partly because Southerners are more prone to think that physical retaliation is called for whenever someone insults or offends you.

The Logic of Revenge: When Getting Even Isn't Even

Revenge is based on some concept of equity. An eye for an eye, a tooth for a tooth; the wrongdoer should suffer to the same extent that he or she has hurt the victim. People who favor capital punishment generally want it used to punish murderers and comparably evil people. Killers should be killed, is the attitude. After all, if capital punishment is merely a rational policy of deterrence, why not use it to punish embezzlement, plagiarism, tax fraud, and other such crimes?

Revenge is the flip side of the Golden Rule of doing unto others as you would have them do unto you. Revenge does unto someone what he has already done unto you.

In social transactions, however, the computation of fairness is far from an exact science even when practiced by the most disinterested, objective judge. When practiced by people who are centrally involved in an upsetting episode, it is even more elusive—far more. The social problem with revenge is that retaliations will tend to exceed the original transgressions, often by a great deal.

As an example, consider this story told by George Anastasia in his account of the Philadelphia Mafia.[52] Nicky Scarfo was a ruthless and ambitious young gangster (who later became the chief underworld boss in the city). The older bosses saw him as potentially useful but also as difficult to control. To punish him for overstepping his authority, they sent him to work in Atlantic City, a relatively small-time operation then. He busied himself with various local projects, including involvement in both legitimate and illegitimate businesses. His nephew, Philip Leonetti, wanted to get into cement contracting work, and Scarfo got him a good job in a contracting company. Leonetti learned the ropes from Vincent Falcone, who was also in the cement business.

The young man did exert himself to learn the business, but either he did not work hard enough or he lacked the aptitude. That, at least, was the judgment of Falcone. Falcone ceased to be helpful to Leonetti and was heard to make various insulting remarks about Leonetti and, more important, about Leonetti's uncle. Some of these remarks were repeated to Scarfo, who began to dislike Falcone. Another cement contractor told Scarfo that Falcone was now going around saying that Leonetti was incompetent and Scarfo was crazy. Scarfo replied that he was going to kill him.

And he did. He invited Falcone for drinks at a friend's apartment, supposedly for a friendly business discussion and relaxation. Following Scarfo's plan, while the five men were sitting with drinks in their hands and watching football on television, Leonetti quietly pulled out a gun, pointed it at the back of Falcone's head, and shot him. Scarfo made a few obscene jokes about the body on the floor. Leonetti fired another bullet into the heart for good measure. Then Scarfo produced the blankets and rope he had stashed for this purpose, and they hog-tied the corpse ("I love this, I love it," Scarfo is alleged to have said while they were working on the body) and rolled it up in the blanket. They carried the roll downstairs and put it in the trunk of the victim's car, where it was found the next day. Meanwhile, that night, Scarfo and the others headed for the casinos to have a good time. Scarfo was ready to forget the whole episode, except that he wasn't entirely satisfied. "If I could bring the motherfucker back to life, I'd kill him again," he remarked to his buddies.

Out of Proportion to the Offense

This example is revealing because the revenge seems so disproportionate to the initial offense. After all, who has not occasionally said that someone was crazy as a form of mild insult? The term *crazy* in its colloquial sense of being wild and irrational would not be entirely amiss when applied to Scarfo as he was depicted in Anastasia's book.

The accusation of craziness was certainly not contradicted by his response of having Falcone killed, any more than the murder proved that Leonetti had talent for the cement contracting business. It was not a rebuttal to false accusations, in any sense. Indeed, killing someone who has called you crazy would seem to prove the accusation right, not wrong. But of course Scarfo was not trying to provide convincing proof of his sanity. He was getting revenge.

The story about Scarfo is especially relevant because the killing was revenge over a threat to his esteem. It is easy to articulate a principle of an eye for an eye, but how does one determine the equivalent of a blow to one's ego? The legal business of defamation and libel lawsuits reflects the problem of determining the cash equivalent of an insult or loss of face. Undoubtedly, some people's images matter more than others, and so identical insults might have different financial implications. We saw already that the Mafia, as a protection business, depends crucially on image, although being thought to be "crazy" might be either a liability or an asset in such a context.

In addition, a deeper obstacle blocks the equity of revenge in cases of ego threat. Even if it were possible to calculate precisely how much retaliatory suffering would be fair recompense for humiliating someone, that person might not be calm and rational enough to make those calculations. A blow to one's pride produces anger, rage, and other emotions that are not conducive to thoughtful assessments of fairness.

Movies (like other art forms) have long embraced the theme of revenge. Usually, killers are hunted down and killed in turn, often by the friends or loved ones of their victims. In some cases, however, the revenge is disproportionate, and this does not seem to bother movie audiences very much. One standard theme, for example, involves a woman who is raped by several men and then later tracks them down and murders them one by one. The literary critic Carol J. Clover says that this genre began with the low-budget classic *I Spit on Your Grave*, but the theme can also be seen in big-budget films such as *Sudden Impact*.

A popular series of revenge films began with *Death Wish*. Charles Bronson, already an accomplished avenger from a series of Westerns, played a peace-loving modern citizen whose aversion to killing was so strong that he had been a conscientious objector in the war. Then street punks broke into his apartment, murdered his wife, and raped and traumatized his daughter. Bronson became a vigilante, traveling alone at night through dangerous areas in the hope that street punks would accost him, to which he would respond by shooting them. In some vague fashion, killing these street punks operated as revenge for his wife's death, although he killed plenty of people who had had nothing directly to do with her murder.

Of course, revenge does not always involve death or even crime. In everyday life, people find many small and legitimate ways of getting back at those they think wronged them. Divorce cases provide many examples of such seemingly small but gratuitously nasty acts of retaliation.

A couple I know went through an unpleasant divorce, and part of the agreement was that the man was to take possession of the house they had owned jointly. The woman was living there while they were separated, and so she had to vacate the house on a certain day. The man arrived on the appointed day anticipating that he might have to face some unpleasant words from her, but she was already gone. In fact, she had left a week earlier. When he went in, he found that she had left the thermostat turned up to the maximum temperature—and left all the windows wide open to the cold winter air. The heating bill had been assigned to him, and it cost him the equivalent of two months' salary. Obviously, this gained the woman nothing of material value, but it certainly cut deeply into the meager savings he had left after the split.

Sometimes, revenge may seem to have divine sanction. In a famous passage in Deuteronomy, the Judeo-Christian God speaks of taking "vengeance upon my enemies. I will make my arrows drunk with blood, my soul shall devour flesh, blood of slain and captives, the heads of enemy princes."[53] The killing of captives is regarded today as a war crime, yet the author of Deuteronomy believed that God not only would approve such an atrocity but would boast about committing it.

The Spiral of Revenge

The logical structure of revenge is, at its center, a simple reversal of victim and perpetrator roles. The victim becomes the perpetrator, striking back for what he or she has suffered.

The exchange of roles contains considerable danger, however, because of the crucial differences in perspective between victims and perpetrators. Foremost among these differences is the gap in magnitude: Offenses seem much greater to the victim than to the perpetrator. This will almost inevitably lead to disproportionate responses, especially if a cycle of retaliation develops.

Suppose you disgrace me by telling some very unflattering story about me to a number of important people. As victim, I see the incident as very damaging. I think the story was untrue or at least unfairly exaggerated and out of context, and I fear that people will avoid or reject me if this story becomes misinterpreted as evidence that I am incompetent or untrustworthy. To you, however, the offense was probably small. You merely repeated a story that you thought was accurate in the main facts. If I retaliate in some violent fashion, such as by destroying your car or breaking your leg, you are likely to think that this is far beyond what is appropriate. And so just when I think we are even, you think you have a major grievance for which you are entitled to revenge. At your next opportunity, you may seek to injure or kill me. Such an attack may make you believe that the score is settled, but to me (or my associates who survive me), your attack is an outrage and a rekindling of matters that had been settled. Now my side has a grievance to avenge, just when you thought the matter was settled.

In this way, grievances can snowball and indeed can be passed down in families for generations, as in the famous feuds and vendettas of history. Because of the magnitude gap, the victims will maximize their own suffering and the perpetrators will minimize the harm they inflict. And so each time they exchange roles, they will think that there are unpaid debts that call for ever more severe retribution.

The myth of pure evil is also an important factor. Victims will tend to see the people who have hurt them as evil—as committing wicked deeds for no valid reason and getting sadistic pleasure out of breaking rules or inflicting harm. To respond with zeal, maybe even going slightly beyond the extent of one's original suffering, seems appropriate if one is dealing with an evil character. There is no sense in practicing forbearance, restraint, or mercy if one is dealing with a truly evil person.

Suppose Adolf Hitler came back from the dead, ran a red light, and bumped into the back of your car. Undoubtedly, you would want to sue him to the maximum extent allowed by law, and if your lawyer suggested exaggerating your injuries a little you would probably be willing to do so. (In contrast, if Gandhi came back and dented your fender, you'd be likely to forget the whole thing.) Extreme measures seem appropriate when one is retaliating against a thoroughly evil person. Unfortunately, because victims tend to see those who harm them in extreme terms, they will unusually be prone to think that extreme retaliations are appropriate.

The Goal of Revenge

I have pointed out that revenge often brings little or no direct benefit to the avenger. The goal is not to get back what belongs to one or to recoup losses. Rather, the goal is more often seen in such vague terms as teaching the miscreant a lesson. Unfortunately, this attitude also may promote extreme measures, because people believe that vivid and dramatic lessons are more likely to be learned than subtle ones.

Most people who seek revenge are clearly looking to teach somebody a lesson. To return to the Mafia, they sometimes use symbols to indicate what observers or others should learn from a particular killing, such as in the famous practice of stuffing cash into the mouth and anus of a corpse.[54] One would think that when killing is motivated by financial disagreements, the killers would want to keep all the victim's (presumably disputed) money that they could find, rather than wasting it. But the grisly display of cash is intended as an explanation and an implicit warning. It means that the victim got too greedy, such as by cheating his associates or the organization by skimming too much cash from an ongoing operation. It tells others what they can expect if they let personal greed get in the way of organizational duties and loyalties.

Adding extra brutality to teach someone a lesson will often backfire, however. It does certainly create a basis for the victims to feel that they now have a legitimate grievance, and so they may become all the more eager to resist or strike back. In World War II, the bombings of Pearl Harbor, London, and Dresden were all expected to weaken the morale of the target populations and push them to give up. Instead, these bombings inflamed the resistance of the victims and increased their determination to fight.

The bottom line is that revenge can contribute to violence and cruelty because the avenger, who is perpetrating harm, acts with the clear conscience and self-righteous zeal of the victim. If you are only striking back, you seem to have a right to do so, and so you do not blame yourself for your actions.

Suffering and Satisfaction: Why Does It Feel Good to Get Even?

The whole point of revenge is to make the other person suffer. The victim of revenge is therefore in a very poor position to hope of getting off lightly. The avenger's experience is similar to the sadist's in that the harm is done to bring pleasant, positive, satisfying feelings to the perpetrator.

The victim's plight is made worse by the magnitude gap between victim and perpetrator views. In revenge, the perpetrator is inflicting harm to reach a certain level of satisfaction, and the victim has to suffer enough (assuming that's possible) to provide that satisfaction. Because victims suffer more than perpetrators gain, the victim of revenge will probably have to suffer far more than the perpetrator realizes.

One of the few options the victim has is to apologize, as sincerely and thoroughly as possible, for the original (provoking) offense. Research has established that apologies do reduce victims' vindictive feelings. Indeed, showing that one feels guilty seems to operate as a kind of "down payment" on one's suffering, so that people will think that a perpetrator deserves to suffer less if he or she feels guilty than if there is no sign of guilt. Given the extremes that revenge can take, it makes sense that people have learned very well how to apologize and express remorse or other feelings of guilt.

As we have seen, much of the violence in revenge occurs when the original offense brought humiliation. Therefore, treating others with respect may also be a way that one can reduce or deflect the brunt of another's quest for revenge against one.

No doubt the perpetrator's satisfaction and the magnitude gap are responsible for the remarkable excesses of cruelty that are sometimes observed. Robert Ressler, the FBI's leading expert on serial murderers, has noted that many of these killers are driven by some fairly vague desire for revenge. Most commonly, the killer is a man who wants revenge against females in general for some grievances that he may have formed while still young. The satisfactions of revenge are presumably the only way to explain what Ressler described as literal "overkill" in some of these murders, such as cases in which the victim was stabbed 200 times or in which the victim's head was cut off after she was already dead from other wounds. Obviously, there is no practical reason to continue stabbing someone who is already dead. But perhaps the killer continues to get some pleasure or satisfaction by continuing to inflict damage, thereby prolonging the moment of revenge.

Still, that brings up the question of whether avengers really do get the satisfaction they seek. Because of the magnitude gap, retaliation that would satisfy an avenger would normally have to be so much greater than the original offense as to be almost impractical.

Revenge for damage to one's image or esteem would seem to be much more achievable—although it, too, is likely to seem excessive to anyone else. A good example is Scarfo, the Philadelphia gangster who killed a man for calling him crazy and criticizing his nephew's cement-working skills. One suspects that avenging an insult by killing the insulter would be satisfying to the person insulted, although nearly everyone else might think it is far too extreme. It is noteworthy, however, that even in that story the gangster seemed less than fully satisfied, as reflected in his remark that he wanted to bring the man back to life to get the satisfaction of killing him a second time.

Serial killers seem to find the same dissatisfaction, according to Ressler and other experts. We will return to this point in Chapter 7, but for now I will note that serial killers often report that they found the actual killings less than satisfactory. Indeed, Ressler believes that the lack of satisfaction is paradoxically one reason for the serial killings. If the killer's desire to get revenge against his mother or some other offending woman were satisfied by killing the first victim, there would be no need to kill more of them. According to Ressler, however, the first killing is often so unlike the killer's fantasy of it that he is upset and decides not to do anything like that again. After a while, however, he begins to think that he must have done it wrong and that these procedural errors were the reason it failed to bring the satisfaction he envisioned, and so he begins to plot another murder.

Many avengers want their victims to know who is hurting them, and why. Part of this is undoubtedly due to the aspect of "teaching them a lesson," in the familiar phrase. In other words, the revenge should operate to discourage the person from mistreating you that way again. But it goes deeper than that. People want their victims to recognize the revenge even if there is no need for a lesson, such as in the extreme cases in which the victim dies.

A memorable story from Annette Lawson's book on adultery shows how someone can take some satisfaction in revenge even if the target never realizes that revenge has taken place. The story is about a middle-aged woman whose marriage had various conflicts and arguments. When her husband wanted to punish her for what he considered wrongdoing on her part, he adopted the strategy of just refusing to speak to her. She found this quite painful and upsetting, as do many people who are given the "silent treatment." But from his point of view, the beauty of the weapon of silence was that it defused all her weapons. Whatever she yelled at him or said to him would merely increase her own punishment, because he would not reply.

And so to strike back at him she devised another tactic, which was to have an affair. The woman described with vivid pleasure the satisfaction she gained from lying next to her husband in bed during one of his silent treatments. He thought he was punishing her, shutting her out, but she could smile to herself that just hours earlier that same day, another man had lain in that same bed with her—and not only spoken to her but paid plenty of other attention as well. Indeed, she made a point of wanting her lover to come into her marital bed, as opposed to having a rendezvous in a motel, because that increased her sense of having won a victory over her cuckolded but unsuspecting husband.[55]

This brings us back to the broader issue of just what vindictive violence accomplishes. We have said that a blow to one's esteem drives people to attack the person who humiliated them. But how does violence restore their esteem? Or does it? In practical terms, of course, revenge often brings little benefit and is costly. Capital punishment of a killer does not bring the victim back to life, and capital punishment as currently practiced in the United States costs the taxpayers more than life imprisonment. There must be some important nonmaterial satisfactions in revenge, and when revenge is associated with humiliation (as it usually is), we might assume that some benefit to the ego is involved. But how?

There are a few obvious cases in which the threat to self-esteem concerns one's physical prowess. When one gang member insults another as a poor fighter and the other responds by fighting, it is easy to see that winning the fight provides visible proof of who is the better fighter. In such cases, the violence does contribute directly to restoring esteem.

Additionally, some cultures regard the outcome of a fight as proof of who was in the right. During the Crusades, the Moslems, whose culture was more advanced than the Christians', were fascinated and amused to see the Christians settling disputes with a trial by combat. To the Moslems, this was an absurd superstition. The Christians, however, believed that God would not allow the person who was in the wrong to win the fight.

In most cases, however, the fight is irrelevant to the esteem threat and the surrounding dispute. Whether you are a seventeenth-century aristocrat fighting a duel or a modern teenager in a gang-related fight, the same irrelevance remains: Hurting or killing someone who has insulted your mother does not prove your mother's virtue.

It does, however, establish whether the person has the right to humiliate you, and this may be the key. Winning a fight establishes a palpable physical dominance over the other person. Stripping away the layers of ritual and material concerns, many violent interpersonal conflicts are about relative prestige. In actuality, of course, the other person really doesn't know or care much about your mother. The point of his insult was to make you look bad. By hurting and defeating him, you deflect the challenge to your image. You make *him* look bad.

A recent article on black street gangs by sociologist Elijah Anderson added a further dimension to the understanding of esteem and aggression. In his analysis, there is a limited and fixed amount of prestige to go around, making what social scientists call a zero-sum situation. The term *zero-sum* comes from game theory and refers to games in which players' outcomes add up to zero. In most two-player games, for example, there is one winner and one loser, and a win (+1) plus a loss (−1) add up to zero. In contrast, there are non-zero-sum games and situations, in which everyone might win or everyone might lose. Putting together a jigsaw puzzle with other people would be one example.

By saying that esteem in gangs (or in the ghetto generally) has a zero-sum character, then, Anderson was making a key point: The only way that one person can gain esteem is if someone else loses it. Anderson emphasizes that poor black communities and other disadvantaged groups may feel this way because there seems to be far too little esteem and respect to go around. Hence, it is necessary to raise oneself up by knocking others down.

There is not a great deal of systematic research on the idea that esteem or prestige fits a zero-sum pattern in groups, but there are certainly enough observations to suggest that some people (at least) think that way. Thus, people may resent someone else's successes or air of self-confidence, because whatever esteem is claimed by someone else is unavailable to you. If someone moves up a few notches in status, then you and several others may have to move down.

These resentments may lie behind the "tall poppy effect"[56] described by the famous Australian social psychologist Norman Feather. The tall poppy effect refers to getting pleasure or satisfaction from the downfall of someone high up. Certainly this effect is not confined to Australia; Americans, too, love to read about the downfall of the high and mighty. Undoubtedly, many Americans felt some pleasure or satisfaction when President Nixon resigned in disgrace, or when the arrogant billionaire Donald Trump filed for bankruptcy, or when various celebrities were exposed or arrested.

A more sinister side of the zero-sum pattern can be seen in the studies on rape. Several of those studies asked rapists how they had chosen a specific victim, and among the many comments there was usually something that suggested a desire to raise oneself up by bringing someone else down. One of these men would see a woman walking along, happy and self-confident, and he might get the feeling that she thought she was better than others, and in particular better than he. He would then follow her and rape her, to disabuse her of any such feelings of superiority. "I felt like I had put her in her place,"[57] these men say afterward. Or, as another rapist said, "I wanted to knock the woman off her pedestal, and I felt rape was the worst thing I could do to her."[58] Another thought he was offering a positive explanation that would reduce his guilt when he said, "I didn't want to hurt her, only to scare and degrade her."[59] The same sort of motive may have been behind the pattern of raping black women that the Ku Klux Klan seems to have (informally) adopted during the period after the Civil War, when the freed slaves represented a threat to the comfortable sense of superiority that white Southerners had nurtured for a couple of centuries.[60]

At present, it is not known how pervasive zero-sum thinking is and how often it leads to violence. It is, however, an accurate description of the situation whenever there is a fixed hierarchy, such as in some fighting groups or gangs, and whenever the number of people is limited and there is little or no movement into or out of the group. Such groups are the prototype of the male dominance hierarchy in a fighting tribe or gang: One can move up only if others move down. Fortunately, most of the world does not currently operate on this principle.

The Trivial Victim

Favorable self-images can lead to violence and evil in more ways than just the seeking of revenge over an insult or humiliation. In particular, regarding oneself as superior can cause people to be indifferent to the suffering of others. Sometimes people don't care about others because they think those other people don't matter. The highly conceited person may hurt or exploit others out of plain indifference.

Yet to wonder what makes people insensitive to the suffering of others is perhaps to approach the problem backwards. One remarkable thing about human beings is their capacity to feel empathy with the suffering of others, even if this empathy is confined to a small group. In fact, there is some evidence to suggest that people mainly feel empathy toward those who are most similar to themselves. The majority of guilt occurs in the context of close relationships between family members, other relatives, and friends. Empathy and guilt are both linked to the communal sense of feeling that one belongs to a certain group of similar people.[61]

Hence, people restrain their selfish impulses more when dealing with those close to them than when dealing with strangers. You feel guilty about neglecting to return your mother's phone call, but you feel much less guilt over neglecting to return a call from an insurance agent.

Thus, scruples seem to be felt most acutely toward members of one's own group. Other groups are generally regarded as inferior, or at least as less important, and so one does not feel as much regret over mistreating them or taking advantage of them. Most people have several levels of identification: a strong one with family, a weaker one toward special groups and organizations to which they belong, another weak one toward nationality, and an even weaker one toward the human race in general.

And so one danger of egotism is that people see nothing wrong in hurting others who are sufficiently different and inferior. Indeed, as we will see when we examine the processes of justification, one way to make oneself feel better about hurting people is to devalue them. Some categories of killers denounce their victims as vermin or as other subhuman creatures, whose killing is thus compared to the extermination of insects.

The extreme case of lack of empathic concern over hurting others can be found in the psychopath. Robert Hare, in his book on psychopaths (revealingly titled *Without Conscience*), depicted them as fitting the following image: "A self-centered, callous, and remorseless person profoundly lacking in empathy."[62] They look down on other people as means to an end or as problems to be solved, not as fellow human beings with whom they can share community spirit or intimate bonds of mutual caring. Socially, they are *users* in the most explicit and heartless sense of the word: They use people to get what they want. They take what-ever they can get and then they move on, and the people left behind with broken hearts or empty wallets are regarded, if they are thought of at all, as suckers.

Perhaps the quintessential example of this attitude can be seen in Hare's account of an interview with a young man who had swindled his own mother. He had persuaded her, a widow, to get a second mortgage on her house, and then he took the money for himself and left her trying to pay it off with her paltry wages from working as a checkout clerk. When asked about his mother, the psychopath (interviewed in prison) expressed loving concern: "She works too hard. I really care for that woman, and I'm going to make things easier for her." But when asked about the money he had stolen, the man forgot his concern about his mother: "I've still got some of it stashed away, and when I get out it's party time!" The interviewer was shocked at the man's failure to connect his mother's overwork with his own intention to spend the money he had stolen from her on his own fun, and so tried to point out that the stolen money could greatly ease the mother's burden. The man replied, "Well, yeah, I love my mother, but she's pretty old, and if I don't look out for myself, who will?"[63]

Obviously, such an attitude is extreme. But self-serving is often at the expense of others, and people must have an implicit policy about how to balance their own welfare against the welfare of others. The greater the egotism, the more that balance shifts in favor of self.

6

True Believers and Idealists

"It's always the good men who do the most harm in the world," Henry Adams said with reference to Robert E. Lee.[1] The point is overstated— it would require quite a stretch to define Saddam Hussein or Idi Amin, let alone Hitler or Stalin, as good men. Yet there is an important kernel of truth in the statement. Good men with lofty principles and admirable intentions have occasionally done a great deal of harm. Many of the greatest crimes, atrocities, and calamities of history were deliberately perpetrated by people who honestly and sincerely wanted to do something good. This chapter will focus on the seeming paradox of how doing good can lead to evil.

The truth of Adams's point lies in the very thing that makes "the good men" good: their moralistic, virtuous idealism. Under normal circumstances, morality, virtue, and idealism are powerful internal brakes that prevent people from harming others. Morality supports self-control and, by doing so, helps to prevent evil. In Chapter 4, we saw that these internal barriers seem to be circumvented in instrumental evil. Somehow they get turned off.

In idealistic evil, on the other hand, moral virtue and idealism remain in force—but they support the committing of violent or evil deeds. That is what often makes idealistic evil especially bad: The traits of inner conscience and strength of character operate to spur the perpetrator on to more severe and intense deeds. It is not simply that it becomes acceptable to hurt others—it becomes one's sacred obligation to do so. When inflicting violent harm goes from being a right to being a duty, it is fair to expect that the violence will become relentless and merciless.

The role of fanatical idealism can be seen when violence loses its practical, instrumental benefits. A chilling example was furnished by the Khmer Rouge after they gained control of Cambodia. Conceivably, one might argue that the mass executions of educated or "intellectual" Cambodians (in some areas, "intellectual" was defined broadly enough to include anyone who wore glasses) had some practical advantage of silencing opposition to their power—but that would not explain a need to target expatriates. The Khmer Rouge announced to the world that they needed the skills and knowledge of educated Cambodians who had left the country and called upon them to return to serve their country and build a better society. Many responded to the call, out of homesickness and patriotic obligation, even though they must have had some worries and fears about what was going on in Cambodia. In reality, the Khmer Rouge had no use for these people but regarded them as enemies, and they were quickly imprisoned and executed. In some cases, the returning Cambodians were met immediately upon arrival and taken directly from the airport to the prison and torture center. It is hard to see any pragmatic motive for such killings. It is not hard, however, to believe that a group might do such things out of a passionate belief that its noble cause requires the elimination of people who have been identified as its enemies.

Noble Ideals, Evil Actions

How can virtue and idealism lead to cruel, violent, or oppressive acts? How can good cause or create evil?

On the face of it, there seems to be a contradiction in saying that good acts can be evil. But this contradiction is easily resolved. It is only necessary to recall that evil is in the eye of the beholder. It is sad, but hardly impossible, to recognize that some people who commit evil deeds are motivated by high ideals and a zealous desire to make the world a better place, as they see it. It is mainly from the perspective of their victims, and perhaps neutral observers, that these acts are bad.

Religion provides one persuasive example. Most people who do what their gods and their spiritual leaders tell them feel certain that they are doing what is right and good, even if this includes hurting others. An important trend in the past few years has been violence at abortion clinics, even to the point of murder, perpetrated by people who have strong religious beliefs that abortion is evil. They think God wants them to beat or kill a physician who is performing abortions, or even a receptionist who works at the clinic.

People with very different religious beliefs may not share the perpetrator's faith in the divine justification of such acts, however. God is the ultimate good, and what God tells you to do is therefore unimpeachably in the service of good. But someone who does not believe in your god will doubt your divine authorization, and your acts are suddenly judged by different standards. Because most readers of this book will be familiar with the Judeo-Christian tradition, let us consider several examples of acts that may seem good and proper when viewed from inside that tradition but could easily seem cruel and evil to anyone who does not accept its basic assumptions.

The Bible contains ample evidence of stories that seem morally questionable and objectionable if one abandons the assumption that anything God commands is automatically good. The story in which God tells Abraham to kill his son Isaac, relenting only at the last minute when Abraham is already standing at the altar holding a knife over the poor boy's throat, creates a remarkable image of what one scholar has called "God as a despotic and capricious sadist."[2] Certainly to anyone who doesn't share the belief in divine legitimacy, Abraham is a child abuser who is about to commit a horrible act of deadly violence against a defenseless family member. That Abraham must be a real sicko, you'd think, if you saw that story on the news today, even if it had the same happy ending. But to devout believers, Abraham's willingness to kill his son was a good thing, a positive proof of his moral faith in God.

Later, the Israelites believed that God gave them the land of Canaan, and it appeared that extensive and violent ethnic cleansing was necessary to accept this gift. The native inhabitants of Canaan had to be subdued brutally and in many cases massacred. After a while, the Israelite armies developed the habit of mutilating the genitals on the corpses of their defeated enemies, cutting the foreskins off their penises and bringing the lot in a bag to the king or queen. Without the sacred context—which is to say, in the eyes of anyone who does not fully accept the Judeo-Christian religion—the massacres and slaughters of the Old Testament are no less evil than many of the genocidal holocausts, atrocities, and collective brutalities of history.

Yet the difference to the perpetrators is crucial. Earlier we considered the example of Genghis Khan, whose violence was largely practical and instrumental. He offered cities in his path the choice of immediate surrender followed by merciful treatment, or resistance to a siege which, if the Mongols prevailed, would be followed by a massacre of the inhabitants. The cruelty was a pragmatic policy that helped to discourage further resistance by other cities. Moral scruples were irrelevant except perhaps to restrain the brutality here and there. In contrast, the massacres committed by the Israelite troops were intended to serve the glory of their God and to carry out his instructions. The perpetrators' moral scruples encouraged brutality and might even have intensified his cruelty.

The Crusades were an extremely important instance of divinely sanctioned brutality involving millions of people over hundreds of years. Devout Christians heeded the Pope's call to do God's work in the Holy Land, which meant to wrest control of it back from the heathens. From the first knights who set out in the 1100s, to St. Louis and other participants in the later Crusades, it is clear that many (although certainly not all) of these Christian soldiers were guided by the highest motives of religious duty. Some of their fellows were apparently selfish and lacking in religious motivation, and sometimes the violence used by the Crusaders was excessive, but most Christians shared a firm belief in the basic goodness of the Crusades. Even the term *crusade* has retained its positive meaning in Christendom as a large movement in the service of high principles and attacking the forces of evil. Dwight Eisenhower titled his memoirs of the American invasion of Europe during World War II *Crusade in Europe*.[3] Today the media speak of crusades against crime, drugs, and other social ills.

Yet anyone who is not dazzled by the Christian faith is certain to see a much darker side to the Crusades, and the label of evil is difficult to resist. This is true even for the supposedly good Crusades, let alone for the moral nadir reached by the Fourth Crusade, to which we will return later. The most idealistic and well-intentioned Crusades were marked by frequent and remarkable atrocities.[4] Prisoners and hostages were massacred. Villages were destroyed. Noncombatants were slaughtered, and there were multiple reports (whether true or untrue) of Christian soldiers roasting and eating Muslim babies. Captives, including noncombatant religious figures, were tortured and mutilated.

In the fourth month of the desperate siege of Antioch, early in the First Crusade, the neighboring town of Aleppo sent an expedition to try to break the siege. Poor leadership rendered the traditional cavalry tactics of the Arabs ineffective and left them fighting hand to hand against the Christian knights, who in their heavy armor easily outclassed them. After the victory, the Christian soldiers hacked off the heads of the Aleppo soldiers, piled them into catapults, and shot them over the walls into Antioch. They hoped this would discourage the inhabitants of the city and prompt them to open the gates and surrender. (It didn't.)

The climax of the First Crusade came in the siege and conquest of Jerusalem, the Holy City. After the Christians managed to break into the city and subdue the garrison, there was a long and frenzied massacre of the miserable Muslims living in the town. While this was going on, the frightened Jews gathered their entire community in the main synagogue to pray. They didn't know what the Christians had in mind for them after the killing of the Muslim enemies was done. They had not opposed the Christian forces, and so they had some hope for mercy, but this did not pan out. The Christian soldiers barricaded the doors of the synagogue, stacked wood against the building, and set fire to it, burning alive most of the frightened people inside.

Although these Christian atrocities cannot be condoned, they can be understood. The crusading soldiers were mainly uneducated people serving their God and trying to stay alive. They had endured hardships far beyond their imagination; most of them had walked all the way from central Europe. Now this great victory seemed to prove that their several years of struggle had been the right thing all along. Of course the heathens should all be killed; God didn't lead us through those years of desperate ordeals just to come and shake their hands.

Through the ages, religious wars have been marked by a similar intensity of cruelty. Religion has shown exceptional power to divide people and set them against one another, even contrary to their mutual interests. At the time of the Crusades, for example, there were many Christians living in the Holy Land, and many of them sided with the invaders against their own countrymen, thus providing valuable assistance to the very people who nearly destroyed their way of life. Religious differences have continued to produce violent battles inside countries, occasionally escalating into terrible civil wars. The Thirty Years' War devastated much of Germany as Catholic and Protestant troops marched back and forth, destroying the lands where the other version of their faith was practiced. In our own century, sectarian violence has produced a seemingly unstoppable sequence of bloody incidents in Ireland and India, both of which split apart under the force of savage religious differences. Sadly, even those divisions failed to bring an end to the violence. Religious differences have also fueled the savage brutality in Bosnia, Serbia, and the other pieces of former Yugoslavia.

The grisly record of religious violence reveals the core paradox of holy war. The idea of a holy war is that one resorts to military violence in the service of sacred, spiritual ideals. One might hope that a divinely inspired war would be somehow "better", less evil, than ordinary wars. Leaders who call for a holy war mean to set their undertaking apart from ordinary, mean-spirited wars, and in particular they claim that holy war occurs on a higher plane. Yet the record suggests that holy wars are often dirtier, more brutal, and fuller of cruelty and atrocity than ordinary wars. The usual effect of religiosity is to make war more brutal, not less.

Indeed, as we move into the twenty-first century, it may be necessary to have two sets of rules of war: one for ordinary wars and another for holy wars. If your opponent declares a holy war, you are likely to be treated to much greater brutality. Declaring a holy war seems to mean that the ordinary rules, such as the Geneva convention, are suspended.

A key to understanding this link between idealism and violence is that high moral principles reduce the room for compromise. If two countries are fighting over disputed territory and neither can achieve a clear victory on the field, they may well make some kind of deal to divide the land in question between them. But it is much harder to make a deal with the forces of evil or to find some compromise in matters of absolute, eternal truth. You can't sell *half* your soul to the devil.

This refusal to compromise is evident in the same examples we have discussed. The Thirty Years' War was one of the most miserably ruinous wars ever fought, especially if one adjusts its devastation to account for the relatively primitive weapons in use. On several occasions, the war-weary sides were both ready to negotiate an end to it, but ideological commitments to one or the other version of Christianity scuttled the deal and sent everyone back to the battlefield. Indeed, the war had started as a local affair, but it escalated beyond hope in 1620 (the third year of the war) when Emperor Ferdinand II abolished religious tolerance and set out to impose strict Catholic practice and belief everywhere.[5] Ferdinand was himself a sincere and zealous Catholic who spent much of his time attending Mass and making pilgrimages, and whose nonmilitary actions were just as supportive of the Church as his warlike ones.

Absolutism played a key role in the Crusades, too, needlessly extending the brutality and suffering on both sides and, ironically, contributing to their ultimate failure.[6] The First Crusade conquered much of the coveted Holy Land, including Jerusalem, but the Christian forces that stayed there were too weak to defend all of the conquered region. The local Arab powers were often at odds with one another, which is why they had not been able to mount a unified defense against the invaders at the start. After a while, they seem to have accepted the Christian nation as simply one more local power, and it was drawn into the intrigues and wars between the neighboring lands. Adjusting to the reality of political life in the area, the Christians entered into trade and even military alliances with various Muslim powers, which were more worried about one another than about the small Christian state, especially after they got Jerusalem back and pushed the Christians to the coast.

Unfortunately, the arrival of new crusading forces usually spelled trouble for these agreements and alliances. The new arrivals persisted in seeing the issue as Christian against Muslim. Eager to fight for Jesus, they would attack Muslim friends as readily as Muslim foes. Ironically, the existence of a Christian nation in the Holy Land might have lasted much longer had it not been for the destabilizing influence of these new Christian troops from Europe.

The Christian country dwindled in size as the Muslims slowly conquered back a city here and there. The last Christian stronghold in the Middle East was Acre, which had been held by the Christians for two centuries. It was a center for trade with Christian Europe, and as such the Muslims might well have tolerated its remaining in Christian hands for a long time to come. But the arrival in 1290 of Crusaders from Italy brought trouble. Lacking any military target, they began killing peaceful Muslim peasants and merchants in the city itself. After an especially brutal massacre, the distant sultan insisted on justice. The rulers of Acre might yet have saved the town for Christendom if they had turned over the murderers to the sultan's courts as he demanded, but such accommodation with the heathen enemy was unacceptable to the Christian rank and file, and so they refused. The sultan vowed that not a single Christian would remain alive in Acre, and although he died during the expedition, his son pretty much fulfilled his vow, supervising the final conquest and destruction of the city.[7] That was the end of Christian power in the Middle East.

Ends Justify Means

Idealism leads to evil primarily because good, desirable ends provide justification for violent or oppressive means. Evil is not likely to result when people firmly believe that ends do not justify means. If they evaluate their methods by the same lofty standards by which they judge their goals and purposes, evil will be held in check.

It is easy to adopt a virtuous pose and insist upon rejection of the view that ends justify means. To do so is hypocritical, however. Most people regard lying as wrong, and yet they will tell someone she looks nicer, younger, thinner than they think she does, or they will lie to protect a secret (or a surprise birthday party), and indeed their utterances depart from the truth in many respects. They may think that killing is wrong, yet killing to protect oneself or one's family or one's country is often seen as acceptable. They may support freedom of speech and condemn censorship, yet they may approve censorship of violent pornography, hate speech, or other objectionable material.[8]

Idealistic evil thus shares an important dimension with instrumental evil: solving problems. Undoubtedly, idealistic, virtuous people would prefer to implement their commendable goals using only the highest, most respected, and virtuous methods. Unfortunately, these methods often seem inadequate, too slow, or ineffective. Something, or someone, creates a major obstacle that blocks something wonderful from coming true. Violence is a way of removing that obstacle.

Rarely has this point been put as bluntly as by Sir Alfred Milner, the British High Commissioner for South Africa at the turn of the century. This man was a dedicated servant of the British Empire who, along with others, saw the chance for the empire to absorb the entire southern tip of the African continent, which for decades had been divided among several powers including independent Boers (Dutch and other immigrants) and the native Zulus. This would bring glory and wealth to the empire he served, as well as help his country keep a step ahead of its main rival, the French.

Milner's predecessors had managed to start a war with the nearby Zulu empire, permitting the seizure of a great deal of land that, when the unsavory details came to light, was relinquished by the Crown and so passed into Boer hands. Milner's plan was to stir up a war between England and the Boers, which would enable his country to conquer the entire area. He succeeded in this, and in later years he was known to boast that the Boer War was "his" war.[9]

A thoughtful and far-sighted man, even before the war started Milner looked ahead to what would come afterward. It should be easy enough for the disciplined British troops to defeat the unorganized Boer rabble (although it turned out to be much more difficult than anticipated), but it would then be necessary for everyone to learn to live together under British rule. The needs and claims of the various parties had to be sorted out, and there would not be enough land and other resources to go around.

Milner came up with a simple and elegant solution: The various factions of British and Boer settlers could all get more or less what they wanted, but very little would be left over for the native black population. The white factions would reconcile their differences at the expense of the blacks. Milner explained this solution to a colleague in 1897: "You have only to sacrifice 'the nigger' absolutely, and the game is easy."[10] This ran contrary to the bulk of policy directives from Europe, where the Crown expressed concern that its colored subjects should benefit from British rule. But Milner saw that sacrifices had to be made, either shared ones by all parties (in which case no one would be happy), or drastic ones by one party. He opted for the latter.

It did not work out entirely as Milner had planned, but he had been correct about the necessity of accommodating the Boers to end the war, and the final agreement did conform to his plan of reconciling the white interests at the expense of the blacks. The painful history of South Africa in the twentieth century was decisively shaped by that historic compromise.[11] The native population lost land, sovereignty, and rights. In a final compromise with the Boers, a crucial word was added to the section of the agreement about giving blacks the vote. It was to be agreed that the natives would not be allowed to vote in elections until the introduction of self-government, which seemed reasonable enough at the time, except that the Boers were opposed. Milner added the word "after": no vote until *after* self-government, which imposed no obligation to share voting rights when self-government arrived in 1906–1907. The word *after* was sufficiently indefinite as to mean "never" for practical purposes.[12]

In retrospect, it would be easy to portray Milner as a racist out to degrade and exploit the native people of South Africa, but that would not be a full explanation. Milner's goals were compatible with at least some of his own nation's high ideals. He wanted to expand the empire he served and to strengthen its position, and so he stirred up a war to make that come true. And then he wanted to achieve a workable peace in which the strong parties who could ruin things might find a way to live together, and so he settled on sacrificing the weakest group to please the strong ones. The motives of patriotic loyalty and peace are lofty ones. The disastrous evil he brought on the native people was presumably just an unfortunate side effect of the way he solved the problems that stood in the way of his idealistic ambitions.

The use of violent or oppressive means to solve problems is a common feature in both instrumental and idealistic evil. There is an important difference, however, and that is the extent to which the ends justify the means. The thief does not generally claim that his desire for money makes his use of violent or illegal means right. In contrast, the idealist may feel that the means are justified. The goals of instrumental evil are generally acceptable ones, such as the desire to have money or power, but they are not normally endowed with sufficient moral force to make people think that it is right and good to use violent means. Idealism can make the methods seem right and good, or at least acceptable.

Because of the importance of perceiving the means as morally acceptable, there may be a strong ongoing need for justification in idealistic evil. The person is doing something that would normally be regarded as wrong, such as killing or hurting people. Somehow, the person must sustain the belief that it is right. This is often done by focusing on the goodness of the overriding goal. Throughout history, many soldiers have faced this dilemma. They have enlisted to fight for a cause or a country or another ideal in which they strongly believe, and then they are confronted with the ugly, sordid reality of combat. This includes killing other young men at close range on a cold day when you are soaked from the rain and have diarrhea and are tired from lack of sleep. It's all miserable, but it's all for a good cause, and so you do your duty and you do your best.

When the means turn even more cruel, such as victimizing defenseless people, the psychological burden on those who carry out the means becomes even greater. Their views are preserved in history only rarely, but these few cases enable us to understand how they struggled inwardly with doing what seemed and felt wrong in the service of what they knew was right.

Some examples survive from the extraordinary terror-famine that occurred in the Ukraine between the two world wars, as recorded in Robert Conquest's historical account.[13] The peasant farmers of the Ukraine had been an important source of Russian grain for centuries. Knowing well how to farm, they resisted the collectivization of farming that the Communist government prescribed. Force was used to move them to the collective farms as well as to destroy any allegedly "rich" peasants, a category that gradually expanded to encompass nearly everyone who was minimally competent or successful at farming. Rather than shooting them or executing them in other ways, Stalin's group created a policy of systematically confiscating all their food, including the seed grain. This measure, carried out fully over a period of many months, led to mass starvation. Starvation is a slow and awful death for the victims, but it does spare anyone from having to pull the trigger. Conquest estimated that this terror-famine killed 11 million people. Several additional millions died in labor camps.[14]

The unpleasant part of the work was carried out by local party members who conducted house-to-house searches for any remaining food. This was hard work, partly because it brought them into face-to-face contact with their victims. These moments brought them closest to the equivalent of pulling the trigger. One of these young party activists recalled the difficulty of taking the last food from starving peasants. He said that one of his friends in the group could not bear it. The friend asked him, "If this is the result of Stalin's policy, can it be right?" In other words, these means seemed so wrong that they even cast doubt on the end. The activist recalled that he "let him have it hot and strong and the next day he came to me and apologized."[15] Such doubts were not permitted, and presumably the man would be regarded as lucky to have had a friend who would provide moral leadership so that he could continue to carry out his small duties in the genocidal operation.

Another party activist was more explicit: "With the rest of my generation I firmly believed that the ends justified the means. Our great goal was the universal triumph of Communism, and for the sake of that goal everything was permissible"—which, he added, included "to lie, to steal, to destroy hundreds of thousands and even millions of people, all those who were hindering our work or could hinder it, everyone who stood in the way." He said they believed that to hesitate or entertain moral doubts was a sign of weakness, of "intellectual squeamishness" and "stupid liberalism." He said he managed not to lose his faith, although sometimes it was tough when he was rooting out the last morsels of food that some miserable family had. He had to force himself to close his ears against "the children's crying and the women's wails," reminding himself that this was all part of the "great and necessary transformation of the countryside." He reminded himself repeatedly that in the end everyone would be better off—except for class enemies, of course.[16] Still, he said, "It was excruciating to see and hear all this. And even worse to take part in it." Grimly he kept telling himself that to give in to pity was wrong. He was doing his duty for the fatherland and the Five Year Plan. It was unpleasant but it was unquestionably the right thing to do.[17] That faith kept him, and thousands like him, going.

Those who carry out brutal commands need to have plenty of such thoughts to fall back on. Otherwise, as suggested by the first activist's friend, the apparent evil of the method contaminates the utopian ideal itself. Another activist in Conquest's account recalled how he felt "emptied of hope" when he finally realized that all this cruelty was indeed part of the official policy.[18] Up until then, he had managed to believe that the cruelest acts were merely the excesses of brutal individuals who went too far. (The Soviet authorities encouraged this perception by periodically prosecuting and even executing the most zealous of those carrying out the policy, saying that they had not intended such "excesses.") Yet after a period of time, this activist eventually could no longer sustain that belief. "The shame of it had been easier to bear as long as I could blame . . . individuals," he said.[19] Still, although his faith in the Communist ideals was shaken, it recovered. He learned not to let these horrors bother him. In the end, his faith was strong enough to allow him to go on serving the state while it went on cruelly murdering millions of its citizens. This is an impressive example of the power of faith in the highest human ideals.

License To Hate

A powerful and important factor in idealistic evil is the attitude toward the victim. We have seen hints of this attitude already. Some perpetrators reported feeling guilty if they had any doubts or felt any sympathy toward the victims. Idealistic evil permits and sometimes even demands that its agents despise their victims.

The logic behind this attitude is built into the situation, and it is difficult to resist. If you think that you are doing something that is strongly on the side of the good, then whoever opposes you or blocks your work must be against the good—hence, evil. This conclusion is far more than just a convenient way of rationalizing one's violence toward certain people. It is central to the idealist's basic faith that he is doing the right thing. The enemies of the good are, almost by definition, evil. To perceive them as any less than that—to allow that one's opponents have a legitimate point of view, for instance—is to diminish one's own side's claim to be good. One is not fighting the good fight if the enemy is good, too. Therefore, to sustain one's own goodness, it is essential to see the enemy as evil.

Thus, idealism usually ends up conferring a right, a license, to hate. As we will see shortly, people do not generally need a great deal of urging to despise the groups that are arrayed against them, and so it would be too much to say that idealism is fully responsible for creating such hatred. But idealism does permit it. Once the collective understanding of good declares that it is correct to hate a certain category of others, people will readily oblige.

One consequence of this apparent duty is that it will tend to put the more extreme and fanatical members of the group into the positions of moral leadership. Consider the activist in the Ukraine who "let him have it hot and strong" when a colleague expressed some doubts or sympathy for the victims. The members with the firmest sense of hatred will end up being the ones that the others look to for support and guidance. Yet the activist who "let him have it" harbored his own private doubts, which suggests a very potent split between public statements and inner sentiments. He privately agreed with the other young man's doubts about the legitimacy of the whole process, but what he said publicly was to have no pity.

The duty to hate continues to be a source of vexation in modern society, despite the society's apparent commitment to tolerance, understanding, and moral relativism. For years, Americans felt comfortably entitled to be hostile toward Communists, from the Soviet and Chinese enemies who seemed ready to attack us with lethal weapons to homegrown Communists. The McCarthyist "Red scare" and persecutions of the 1950s emerged in part because it became safe and appropriate to direct hostility toward these internal enemies. Now, with the fall of the Soviet Union, one is no longer supposed to hate those poor Russians, and the adjustment is difficult for some dedicated American patriots.

Ironically, the very effort to tolerate and value diversity constitutes a license to hate those who disagree. One of the core paradoxes in the recent social evolution in the United States is how the broad desire to overcome prejudice and ethnic antagonisms has resulted in a society that seems more fragmented and prejudiced than ever. Each group firmly believes that it holds positive, inclusive, desirable values, and so other groups are gradually assumed to be inimical to these positive values. And if the other group is opposed to the good, then by definition it must be evil. Each group feels attacked by others, as in the current debate (as this is being written) on the future of affirmative action programs that support preferential hiring of members of disadvantaged groups. Each side perceives the others as selfishly and unfairly trying to benefit at its expense. In other words, both minorities and whites can see themselves as holding the values of fairness and equality and the other side as opposed to those values—and hence, wicked. Along the same lines, the 1995 World Conference on Women was held in China during the time this book was being written, and the American delegate Betty Friedan (author of *The Feminine Mystique*, one of the most influential works in the women's movement) felt compelled to argue in a national publication against the conference's strident and oppositional tendencies: "countering the hatred of women with a hatred of men" was a bad strategy, she emphasized, recognizing that such category antagonisms evolve all too readily.[20]

In many cases, the consequence of one's own presumptive goodness is more than a license to hate one's opponents: It is a positive *duty* to hate them. Sometimes it is difficult to ascertain how much this matters, because people are often willing to hate without needing much encouragement. Still, when dealing with members of the group who might have doubts or otherwise lack sufficient feelings of animosity, the others may feel entitled to put pressure on them to get with the program and summon up the appropriate degree of hostility. If you do not hate Satan, then there is something wrong with you.

Jeffrey Burton Russell discussed a topic of medieval debate: "Are we to hate the Devil as much as we love Christ?"[21] The answer was presumably no, but it was a close enough call to be worth debating. A good

Christian's emotional duties were said to include both hatred and love, directed toward the appropriate targets. The duty to love Christ is supreme, but the duty to hate the Devil may be almost as strong.

There is ample evidence that perpetrators of violence learn to detest their victims. Thus, state torturers are selected partly on the basis of their ideological purity, and they are taught that their victims are part of a dangerously powerful movement that aims to destroy their country.[22] They learn (and one must assume that they are willing to accept) that their enemies in general are evil, and so even if they can see that the particular individuals they are torturing have little useful information to offer and are ultimately just human beings in pain, the torturers can still feel it is appropriate to make them suffer. These prisoners belong to the evil group.

Likewise, terrorists are generally fervent utopians who see "the establishment" (the government they oppose, and its supporters) as evil.[23] President Clinton called the terrorists who bombed the Oklahoma City courthouse in 1995 "evil" for committing America's worst act of terror. Yet to them, or at least to many people like them, the government is evil. Terrorist groups attract people who are hostile to authority. (This is ironic, because terrorist groups tend to be quite authoritarian, with the leader having close to absolute power in the group.) Terrorists, too, feel that pity for one's victims is an unacceptable sign of weakness and a source of shame.

Terrorists have an interesting special problem of self-justification. They tend to choose random targets such as buses or public libraries, full of what most others regard as innocent victims. Terrorists cannot afford to accept that view, however. Acknowledging that the group really did kill innocent victims would undermine their faith in the goodness of their own cause. Hence, terrorists tend to adamantly reject the idea that those people are innocent. Sentiments such as "anyone who is not with us is against us" are popular with such groups, because they conveniently allow the group to despise all their victims as enemies. Likewise, terrorists tend to adopt very broad categories of enemies. If they regarded only the top government officials and the police as their enemies, they might find it difficult to avoid victimizing innocent people. But if they broaden the category to include anyone in the society who is not actively opposed to the government, then few innocents remain, and they can plant their bombs in public places without a guilty conscience.

Western history's most durable example of the license to hate is probably the attitude of Christians toward Jews. This antagonism has led to
oppression and violence for 2000 years, and the twentieth century can
hardly claim to have witnessed a diminution of it. Group rivalries and
hostilities are nothing new, yet somehow anti-Semitism has been bitter
and brutal over an exceptionally long span. How have so many Christians,
whose religion is ostensibly based on love, come to hate and persecute so
many Jews? What made it acceptable, typical, or even at times obligatory
to hate Jews?

That question formed the center of a recent book by Joel
Carmichael.[24] There are several parts to the answer. In the first place, of
course, Jesus and his followers were Jews, and so the early Christians
tended to think that the rejection of Jesus by those who remained Jews
was especially unforgivable, because Jesus lived among them and
preached to them. Christ's truth had been revealed to them, and they
had rejected it, which seemed to prove that they were in league with the
forces of evil (unlike, say, Greek pagans who simply did not know any
better). The Jews particularly distanced themselves from the Christian
sect during the century after Jesus' death, when they had their own
rebellion against Rome. The perception of the Jews as a people who had
been given a special chance by God but rejected it undoubtedly had
more personal and psychological roots as well, such as the fact that the
new Christians were being rejected by some of their countrymen,
including their relatives and friends.

Moreover, the Christians were understandably aggrieved by the execution of Jesus. Whoever kills the epitome of religious goodness and
truth must certainly be evil, and someone had to be blamed. In fact, the
Romans had executed him, with some minor complicity by the Jewish
authorities, who were relatively powerless anyway. Yet after the death of
Jesus, his followers found many Roman citizens interested in their religion and ready to convert, unlike the Jews, and so they wanted to find
some version of the truth that would not antagonize the Romans. Thus
developed the historically weak but psychologically attractive view that
the Jews were responsible for Jesus' crucifixion.

Over the years, two parallel views of evil Jewishness developed. One
was secular and mundane, depicting Jews as greedy. (Because of job discrimination and New Testament prohibitions against Christian money-
lending, Jews were often pressured into occupations such as lending

money and financing trade, which provided the basis for Christians to think that the Jews they encountered fit this stereotype.) The other view was cosmic and metaphysical, centering around the belief that the Jews had supernatural powers and were connected with exotic, unchristian, secret forces. The fusion of these two beliefs ran through the Christian perception of Jews for many centuries.

The belief that Jews enjoyed access to vast secret powers that were inimical to Christendom was important because it should have been obvious to anyone that Jews were actually relatively weak and powerless. Their country was conquered and destroyed, their people were scattered, they lived in ghettos, they had no weapons or political power, and they were subject to sporadic persecution by Christian (and secular) authorities that they were largely unable to resist. To believe, despite all these outward signs of weakness, that the Jews possessed dangerous mystical powers was not easy, but it became possible by virtue of the putative secret forces.

For centuries, the biblical figure of Judas was a major prototype of the Jew. He had betrayed his Savior for a mere thirty pieces of silver, a trivial amount of money. That event captured the supposedly greedy, money-loving aspect of Jews, as well as the disloyalty and treachery. It also suggested that Jews would do evil simply for the sake of doing evil—because the amount of money was relatively small; one surmises that betraying Christ presumably should have been worth immense riches. After all, had Satan made an offer, it seems safe to assume that the price he put on Jesus' head would have been a high one.

Doing evil for its own sake brings up the myth of pure evil, and that is an important aspect not only of the demonization of Jews but also of idealistic antagonisms in general. Idealists, perhaps in proportion to their ideological passion, tend to assimilate their enemies into that myth. As I have already said, idealists and utopians cannot easily acknowledge that their opponents have a legitimate, acceptable claim on being good themselves, because to do so would undermine their own claim to be on the side of good. The inability to see the other side as legitimate is consistent with what we saw in Chapter 2 as a general pattern among victims: They refuse to attribute good or even innocuous or acceptable motives to the perpetrators who harm them. This refusal leads directly to the myth of pure evil. If the other side has no good or decent motive, then it must be motivated by the sheer perverse wish to do evil for its own sake.

The Treatment of Victims

There are important implications of idealistic evil for the victims. Idealistic perpetrators believe they have a license, even a duty, to hate. They perceive the victim in terms of the myth of pure evil: as fundamentally opposed to the good, for no valid reason or even for the sheer joy of evil.

One implication is that ordinary restraints that apply even to severe conflicts may be waived. Holy wars tend to be more brutal and merciless than ordinary wars, and the reason for this is now apparent. When fighting against the forces of evil, there is no reason to expect a fair fight—and hence no reason to fight fair oneself. Idealists think they are up against a dangerous and powerful opponent who will stop at nothing to spread evil in the world, and so desperate and extreme measures are appropriate.

In a sense, this solves the problem of how ends justify means. If you are up against Satan, you should not expect the ordinary rules to apply. Murder may be acceptable if you are killing the most wicked and demonic enemies of the good; indeed, the state does that by executing the worst criminals and traitors. And the Bible is full of examples of how killing was all right when done in God's name and in the service of divinely sanctioned causes. After all, it is only because of broad conceptions of goodness that murder is seen as wrong. If Satan is your enemy, you know that the fight is not going to be conducted in line with those notions of goodness. Satan cannot be expected to obey Christian morals and similar rules.

Another implication is that the victim's options are slim. In instrumental evil, the victim can get off relatively easily by conceding whatever it is that the perpetrator wants. In idealistic evil, however, what the perpetrator often wants is that the victim be dead. The victim's suffering is not one of many means to an end, but an essential condition for the (ostensible) triumph of good, and that leaves the victim with much less latitude to make a deal.

Isn't It Just a Rationalization?

Whenever people attribute their violent or oppressive actions to high, pure, morally admirable motives, suspicion arises as to whether they are not simply concocting fancy rationalizations for what are at bottom self-serving motives. An adequate understanding of evil must look below the surface at idealistically motivated violence. It could be that the idealism merely dresses up or conceals what is in fact another form of instrumental evil: people using immoral means to do what is best for themselves. The veneer of idealism might be no more than a dishonest or hypocritical ploy to conceal selfishness.

It is abundantly clear that such hypocrisy has occurred. Individuals and groups have often sought to hide their greedy or grasping motives under such high-sounding assertions. For example, the European conquest of Africa was often justified (or rationalized) in terms of what Kipling, in another context, called "the white man's burden" of sharing the benefits of his culture with backward peoples. Europeans spoke often of bringing the "three C's" to Africans: civilization, commerce, and Christianity. Yet these were hardly the sole motives. The glory of empire and the anticipation of profits and riches were decisive, despite the fancy talk of bringing benefits to the natives. And once it became clear that the expected benefits were not forthcoming, the Europeans lost much of their interest in maintaining African colonies. Apparently, it was one thing to bring true religion and Western culture to the dark continent while turning a profit, but quite another when it turned out that Europe would lose money in the deal. These ideals still apply, of course, and Europe is still trying to do some good in Africa these days (with uneven success), but the sense of urgency for major involvement goes down when it is discovered to be a money-loser instead of a big money-maker.

At the individual level, it is even clearer that self-serving motives often operate under the guise of ideals. Historians of various ideological repression campaigns typically record that petty local grudges and animosities often lie behind the denunciations that feed a purge. This was true in the Spanish Inquisition, and it was still true in the modern Stalinist and Khmer Rouge purges. The notorious punishment of Lyons during the French Terror was run by a man who had a personal grudge against the wealthy people of Lyons. He had been an aspiring actor and stage manager there many years earlier, and he had not received the admiration that he felt was due him. He thought the local folks in general had treated him shabbily when he was down on his luck. Under his vindictive leadership, the Terror became much harsher in Lyons than in other regions of France.

Yet it would be a serious error to conclude that genuine idealism is always absent or irrelevant as a factor in promoting evil. The cases of deception and hypocrisy are important, but there also seem to be ample cases in which the enthusiasm for lofty or utopian ideals is indeed genuine.

One piece of evidence for this fact is that many violent utopian movements have been marked by a puritanical hostility to pleasure. When the brutal Khmer Rouge took over Cambodia, for example, they did away with most of the joys and pleasures of normal life—even for themselves. According to Elizabeth Becker, the leaders did live a more comfortable life than the miserable near-starvation of the rural peasants, but not by a great deal. She describes them as "a dour, puritanical group of people"[25] who rarely smoked cigarettes, abstained from alcohol, and regarded "unauthorized" romance as deserving of the death penalty. They occasionally smiled but were never seen to laugh aloud. They seemed fanatical about being clean and orderly at all times. (Their long years of desperate life in the jungle may have prepared them to adore cleanliness, just as it accustomed them to live without much in the way of sensual pleasures.) She says that they generally provided good examples of the "strict life" they sought to impose on the rest of the population. Pol Pot, the leader, was captivated from an early age by the ideal of purity, and the Khmer Rouge elite seemed to concur.

A similar picture emerges of the European Fascist leader Francisco Franco, who presided over the winning side in one of modern history's most brutal civil wars. The Spanish Civil War was marked by systematic mass executions of prisoners and civilians, machine guns being turned on refugee columns, and various other atrocities, some punctuated by the eerie chant of "Long live death!" Peter Wyden summarized several descriptions of Franco as a man followed a "puritanical life-style," which meant "no drinking, no smoking, no cards, no women,"[26] and as being generally a "pleasureless" individual.

The Chinese Cultural Revolution, which may have had the highest body count of any mass murder campaign in the bloody twentieth century, was also puritanical. The only jewelry allowed to be worn by anyone in the country was the little pin-on button with the likeness of Chairman Mao.[27]

In America, the Ku Klux Klan had a similar attitude during its heyday. William Simmons, the man who revived the Klan in the early 1900s and brought it to its all-time peak, urged Klansmen to live by a higher ethical code than other people, with special emphasis on sexual purity. The Klan sought to raise the moral purity of politics and other local affairs, and the women's Klan campaigned vigorously against liquor, vice, wife-beating, and other immoralities.[28]

The Nazis are of particular interest, too. It is clear that many of them benefited from the brutalities they inflicted on Jews and others who fell into their power. Yet they also maintained a commitment to an idealism that took self-denying, even puritanical forms. As we will see in Chapter 10, the SS leaders insisted that their brutal work be done in a sober, puritanical fashion that would support their claim to having high, pure motives. Although the reality was certainly not as scrupulous and selfless as the leaders contended, it is nonetheless probably true that the prevailing attitude was to avoid the taint of self-serving motives while carrying out these horrible deeds. As with Stalin's and Mao's purges, there was a general effort in the SS to keep the proceedings in the context of serving the noble cause and the beloved fatherland, as opposed to killing people for the sake of stealing their meager possessions.

Indeed, the SS was in every way an elite.[29] It was designed to be, and it regarded itself as, the purest and best of the organizations serving the country and party. Getting into the SS was quite difficult, and various criteria were imposed to ensure that only superior beings qualified: One had to have impeccable ancestors; be at least a certain minimum height; have a facial appearance that was free from any resemblance to Jewish, Slavic, Mongol, or other proscribed ethnic backgrounds; and so forth. (Himmler forecast that in 120 years, all the officers would be blond.) One's personal past had to be impeccable, too: no legal or moral problems, including sexual misbehavior. Early on, entry requirements had been lower, but this was rectified by expelling many thousands of SS men who seemed to fall short of the new, higher criteria, such as alcoholics, homosexuals, self-seeking people, those who were not of pure Aryan descent, and some ordinary ruffians. The slogan "SS man, loyalty is your honor" was inscribed on their uniforms. In his influential book about the SS, Heinz Höhne describes them as "an Imperial Guard of strict puritans."[30] The quest to be a superior class of people was fairly successful in many ways. In 1946, after the war, the Catholic archbishop of Freiburg acknowledged that he and others had generally considered the SS to be "the most respectable of the Party organizations."[31] Yet the SS were precisely the ones who manned the concentration camps and death squads.

And that is the key point about the SS: The people designated to carry out the most brutal and wicked actions were the ones who had been chosen and taught to be an elite force, superior in character and virtue to everyone else. It was not the dregs and thugs, but the finest flower, who committed the most horrible deeds.[32] In a strange way, the SS have some resemblance to the comment that it is the good men who do the most harm in the world. In their own view and in the view of their colleague organizations, they were the best, the noblest. They were therefore the logical ones to use for making sure that mass murder was carried out in the most decent and morally proper fashion, in the official view.

Beyond Individuals

One far-reaching difference between idealistic evil and other forms of evil is that idealistic evil is nearly always fostered by groups, as opposed to individuals. When someone kills for the sake of promoting a higher good, he may find support and encouragement if he is acting as part of a group of people who share that belief. If he acts as a lone individual, the same act is likely to brand him as a dangerous nut.

One reason for the importance of groups in idealistic evil is the power of the group to support its high, broad ideals. Abstract conceptions of how things ought to be gain social reality from the mere fact of being shared by a group. Without that group context, they are merely the whims of individuals, and as such they do not justify the use of violent means. To put this more bluntly: It is apparently necessary to have someone else tell you that violent means are justified by high ends. If no one of importance agrees with you, you will probably stop short of resorting to them. But if you belong to a group that shares your passionate convictions and concurs in the belief that force is necessary, you will be much more likely to resort to force. People seem to need others to validate their beliefs and opinions before they put them into practice, especially in a violent and confrontational way.

This is one of the less recognized aspects of the much-discussed experiments done by Stanley Milgram. In those studies, an experimenter instructed an ordinary person (a volunteer) to deliver strong electric shocks to another person, who was actually a confederate posing as an unsuspecting fellow subject. These ordinary people complied with instructions and delivered many severe shocks to the victim, far beyond the predictions and expectations of any of the researchers involved in the project.

As Milgram noted, many of the participants were upset about what they were doing. They showed signs of stress and inner conflict while they were pressing buttons that (supposedly) gave painful and even potentially harmful or lethal shocks to another person. As we will see in the next chapter, such distress is the normal reaction to hurting others.

Despite their inner distress, however, the vast majority of participants delivered increasingly severe shocks, up to the maximum level possible. A crucial factor was the presence of a fellow human being assuring them that their actions were justified and, indeed, were their duty. They had nothing to gain by inflicting harm, nor did they get any prestige or other advantage from hurting the victim, but their actions did presumably serve the commendable goal of advancing scientific progress. The presence of the experimenter to represent the community of scientific researchers was a central aspect of this experiment. By pressing the button, the subject participated in the group's worthy enterprise.

The importance of the interpersonal dimension was indicated by the effect of physical distance. In later replications of the study, Milgram varied how close the subject sat to the experimenter as opposed to the victim. Being closer to the victim made the subject less willing to deliver hurtful shocks. Being closer to the experimenter (the authority figure) made subjects more willing.

In most cases, of course, such extreme acts are committed by devoted members of the group, rather than by temporary recruits. Thus, they share the group's beliefs and ideals and are presumably willing to do what will further the positive goals of the group. The group is an important source of moral authority. Individual acts may be questioned, which usually means questioning them in terms of how well they fit into the recognized goals and procedures of the group. But the group itself is above question.

This pattern of deferring to the group's moral authority is seen over and over again in violent groups. Consider again the Khmer Rouge. Like many Communist parties, it was a firm believer in the practice of self-criticism by individual members. But this meant examining one's own acts (and thoughts or feelings) to see whether they corresponded to the proper party line. Criticism of the party itself was strictly off-limits.[33]

Criticism sessions in Western Communist groups showed the same pattern. Individuals sat around and scrutinized themselves to see how they fit or failed to fit the official party line, but they never questioned the party line.[34] When the party adopted a new position, individual members scrambled to agree with it and to convince themselves that they had believed this all along. Arthur Koestler cynically described the process from his days as a Communist: "We groped painfully in our minds not only to find justifications for the line laid down, but also to find traces of former thoughts which would prove to ourselves that we had always held the required opinion. In this operation we mostly succeeded."[35] Whether one looks at religious warriors, members of Fascist or Communist groups, or modern members of street gangs, one finds the same pattern: The group is regarded as above reproach. The members of the group may sometimes think rather poorly of one another, but the group as a whole is seen as supremely good.

Why do groups seem to have this effect? Although several factors contribute, it is necessary to begin with the fundamental appeal of groups. Probably this appeal is deeply rooted in human nature. The human tendency to seek a few close social bonds to other people is universal, and nearly everyone belongs to some sort of group, whether a family or a mass movement. People who lack close social ties are generally unhappy, unhealthy, and more vulnerable than other people to stress and other problems. Some theorists have argued that the tendency to form small groups is the most important adaptation in human evolution, ranking even above intelligence, and so natural selection has shaped human nature to need to belong to groups.[36]

The need to belong may be universal, but it is not always equally strong. One factor that seems especially to intensify the need is competition with other groups. Thus, one could debate the evolutionary benefits of belonging to a group, noting that the advantages of sharing others' resources could be offset by the pressure to share one's own resources with them. There is no doubt, however, about the competitive disadvantage of not belonging to a group when there are other groups. If there is some scarce resource such as food that a group wants and a lone individual also wants, the group is almost sure to get it. Thus, the need to bond with other people may be stimulated by the presence of a rival or enemy group.

This tendency toward intergroup competition fits well with what we have already seen. The words *Devil* and *Satan* are derived from words meaning "adversary" and "opponent," which fits the view that rivalry or antagonism is central to the basic, original understanding of evil.[37] Evil is located in the group that opposes one's own group. The survival of one's own group is seen as the ultimate good, and it may require violent acts against the enemy group.

Are Groups Nastier than Individuals?

The tendency toward intergroup competition sheds light on one aspect of what some researchers have called the *discontinuity effect*; that is, the pattern by which a group tends to be more extreme than the sum of its individual members. In particular, higher levels of aggression and violence are associated with group encounters than with individual encounters. People generally expect that a meeting between two individuals will be amiable, and that even if they have different goals or backgrounds they may find some way to compromise and agree. In contrast, people expect that a meeting between two groups will be less amiable and less likely to proceed smoothly to compromise. Laboratory studies support these expectations and indicate that groups tend to be more antagonistic, competitive, and mutually exploitive than individuals. In fact, the crucial factor seems to be the perception that the other side is a group. An individual will adopt a more antagonistic stance when dealing with a group than when dealing with another individual.[38]

Probably the easiest way to understand this difference is to try a simple thought experiment. Imagine a white man and a black man encountering each other across a table in a meeting room, one on one, to discuss some area of disagreement. Despite the racial antagonism that is widely recognized in the United States today, the meeting is likely to proceed in a reasonably friendly fashion, with both men looking for some way to resolve the dispute. Now imagine a group of four white men meeting a group of four black men in the same room. Intuition confirms the research findings: The group dispute will be harder to resolve.

There is nothing sinister or wrong with wanting to belong to a group, of course. Groups may perpetrate evil, but they can also accomplish considerable good (and without doing any harm in the process). Groups can accomplish positive, virtuous things that go beyond what individuals can do. Groups do provide a moral authority, however, that can give individuals sufficient justification to perform wicked actions. Moreover, when groups confront each other, it is common for the confrontation to degenerate into an antagonistic and potentially hostile encounter. In these ways, the existence of a group can promote evil and violence.

Yet that is not the whole story. We will now consider how groups can be strengthened by their own violent actions. Evil can make a group draw closer together, which in turn increases the potential for further evil.

The Group Itself as an End

So far, we have considered groups that see themselves as pursuing high ideals and goals. But sometimes the group becomes an end, a positive value, in itself.

Part of the emphasis on keeping the group together comes from the awareness of outside, opposing forces. But having an enemy is not a full explanation. Idealistic groups tend to place a heavy stigma on people who leave the group. Ex-members or apostates are seen as especially dangerous, and it is common for groups to regard them as the worst and most dangerous people in the world. Arthur Koestler recalled how the Communists regarded those who quit the party as "lost souls, fallen out of grace." As long as he belonged to the party, to talk to such a person or listen to him, even just to argue with someone who had left the party, was forbidden: "trafficking with the Powers of Evil."[39]

A similar pattern can be seen in the French Terror. Preserving the unity and integrity of the new Republic and its government became an end in itself, and the worst hostility was directed toward traitors among the leaders. Historian R. R. Palmer pointed out that many leaders of the Revolution had strong personal and ideological hatreds of the upper classes or various other groups, but they did not usually direct murder campaigns against these enemies. Instead, the guillotine was reserved for traitors, or at least those who came to be seen as traitors. The Terror was "primarily a weapon for enforcing political allegiance," in Palmer's summary.[40]

A moving account of how an idealistic group closes up against anyone who leaves was provided by writer Richard Wright, a black American writer who joined the Communist party and then left it (thereby unintentionally joining the "Powers of Evil," as Koestler called them) in the 1930s. He joined because he shared the values and goals of the Communists, who seemed intent on standing up for the oppressed and disadvantaged workers of the world against the system that beat them down and took advantage of them. Gradually, however, Wright began to feel uncomfortable about belonging to the group. He was shaken when one of the new members rose quickly to power in the group and led a purge of some members who had seemed to Wright quite sincere in their loyalty. Then, by accident, it was discovered that this new leader was a mental patient who had escaped from an institution. Wright thought, "What kind of club did we run that a lunatic could step into it and help run it? Were we all so mad that we could not detect a madman when we saw one?"[41]

Wright found that his own ambitions to write about the experiences of American Negroes were not approved by the party, which began to tell him where to travel, what to work on, and whom to have as friends. Gradually, he came to feel that belonging to the Communist party was too stifling. His objections to the party were all linked to its procedures and rules; he agreed with its values and objectives. Finally, one day at a meeting, he got up and said that although he agreed with the party on ideological grounds, he wished to be dropped from the rolls of active members, so that he would not be bound by the party's decisions and commands. He said that he hoped he could continue to find ways to help the party in its efforts.

He sat down amid silence. One of the group leaders moved that discussion of Comrade Wright's statement be postponed, and the others went along. Wright walked out feeling that a great weight had been lifted from him and feeling happy that he had been able to leave in a friendly, reasonable, decent manner, without bitterness, accusations, or recriminations.

A few days later, however, he spoke with some other members of the group (who had missed the meeting where he asked to be dropped from the rolls), and they said the official story in the group was that Wright was in league with a Trotskyite clique and was trying to get other members to leave and betray the party. Wright was shocked to hear this. He offered to resign officially from the party, as opposed to being merely dropped from the rolls of active membership, but the others in the group said no: "No one can resign from the Communist Party!"[42]

Over the following weeks and months, he was amazed and saddened by the way that all his friends in the group shut him out of their lives. Some refused to speak with him; others insulted him to his face, calling him a traitor and a renegade Trotskyite. Because he felt he shared their beliefs and values, he expected that they would remain friendly, but this was apparently out of the question. Wright recalled lying in bed at night, sadly telling himself that "I'll be for them, even though they are not for me."[43]

The low point came on May Day of 1936. May Day is a major Communist holiday, and it was to be celebrated in Chicago by a parade in which many of the workers' unions, including Wright's own, took part. He arrived too late for his own group, but an old friend and Communist comrade saw him and invited him to march with them. Gratefully, he fell in and began to march along, enjoying the solidarity with the Communists who shared so many of his values and beliefs. Abruptly, however, other marchers recognized him and began to shout abuse at him as a traitor to the cause. He protested that he wanted to march, but the others insisted that he leave the ranks. Finally, they picked him up and literally pitched him headlong out of the ranks of marchers. He had to use his hands to break his fall, or else his head would have smashed against the curb.

Similar attitudes can be found in many groups. In most, presumably, the rejection of apostates does not reach the point of physically throwing them through the air, but the rejection is still severe and often painful to the person leaving the group. Sometimes, indeed, the treatment is even more severe. David Rapoport's account of the Islamic terrorist group Al-Jihad quoted its writings to the effect that permanent, lethal hostility toward apostates is obligatory: "An apostate *has* to be killed."[44]

Hostility toward apostates is hardly a modern phenomenon. In Dante's *Inferno*, the very lowest pit of Hell is reserved for traitors, which suggests that in Dante's time the sin of betraying one's group was regarded as the ultimate wickedness. Satan himself lived there as the original traitor: He had betrayed God, heaven, and all the forces of good.[45]

Thus, it seems fair to say that an idealistic group typically regards the people who quit the group as the extremity of evil. Although one might think that the group would reserve its strongest hostility for its clear enemies, instead it directs it toward those who leave the group even if they claim to remain sympathetic to its values and goals and wish to remain friends with its members. The implication is that people who leave the group represent an even greater threat than its enemies. If other members were to interact with them, perhaps they would leave too, and the solidarity of the group would be undermined. Keeping the group together with a strong sense of separateness and commitment is in many cases a more fundamental and urgent goal than accomplishing its stated purposes or defeating its actual external enemies.

What happens is that the group evolves from being a means to being an end. The group may start off as a method of advancing several high ideals and valued goals. Gradually, however, the group itself seems to take on the value that was initially attached to those goals. What is good for the group becomes right, almost regardless of whether it has any clear positive link to the group's original goals. The transition may occur without anyone noticing it very much, if only because the group members probably believe that the group is essential for the idealized goals to be achieved. But if we wish to understand how a new ruling party that is devoted to liberation and equality can turn to repression, terror, and inequality, we must recognize that people often begin to transfer their adoration of the ideals to the group itself. Once the preservation and advancement of the group becomes accepted as a valued end in and of itself, the restrictions on violent means and measures will often diminish.

Can Evil Serve Good?

This chapter has looked at how evil means can be adopted to serve good ends. It is clear that many people with lofty ideals and good intentions have perpetrated enormous cruelty, crime, and suffering on others. Yet it is worth pausing once more to ask whether these evil means can ever succeed in bringing about the positive, idealistic goals that they are supposedly serving.

Certainly there have been some spectacular failures. One can debate whether the utopian dreams of the Khmer Rouge or the Nazis were themselves good ends, but there is no doubt about the failure of their violent means to create their "paradise." Moreover, the evil means they adopted played an important role in causing their failure. The Khmer Rouge and the Nazis gained national power for a brief time by virtue of their violent means. It was their continued and escalating violence that gradually brought outside powers to intervene against them, thereby dooming any chance for them to set up the society they wanted.

The French Revolution provides a more compelling and fascinating case, in part because so many of its ideals are ones we continue to espouse today. The famous trio of goals in their revolutionary slogan— liberty, equality, and fraternity (that is, community)—are above reproach, and indeed it would be a peculiar and unappealing utopia that rejected these ideals.

However impeccable the ideals of the French Revolution were, one must conclude that the violent means the new regime adopted were by and large a failure, at least if one judges them in terms of the desired effects sought by the people who resorted to them. The Terror failed to bring an end to political dissent. True, many dissenters were killed, but there were always more, and in any case those who remained alive simply fell into hostile factions once their common enemies were eliminated. As historian R. R Palmer wrote, each purge was supposed to be the final one, after which peace and harmony were expected; but inevitably, new enemies were found and new purges seemed necessary.[46] He adds that the year of terror left France more divided than ever, even though all that suffering was supposed to bring about unity.

The Terror certainly failed to cement the power of the people who implemented it; indeed, many of them became its victims. Even Robespierre, the fanatical idealist who presided over many extreme measures that he hoped would safeguard the Revolution, ended up on the guillotine himself. Like so many others, he was executed in the hope that, since he had supposedly been the tyrant responsible for the Terror, finally the ideals of the Revolution could be implemented. Although the Terror came to an end, the Revolution did not succeed. Indeed, that is the broader failure of the entire Terror: The Republic it was supposed to protect was soon utterly gone. The monarchy was restored a few years later. The very idea of the Republic was discredited in France for more than a century afterward, being ironically associated in the minds of the people with repression, violence, persecution, and other evils.[47] The means ended up tainting and corrupting the ideals they had been intended to promote and protect.

Likewise, the original idealism of the Crusades is undeniable, but so is the deplorable outcome. What had begun as service to religion and God gradually evolved into the self-serving pursuit of wealth and power. The Western church, centered in Rome, gradually came to see the Crusades as an opportunity to break the power of its great Christian rival, the Eastern church and empire centered in Constantinople (Byzantium). According to the historian Steven Runciman, this policy shift can be documented barely 10 years after the first Crusade set out, which is very early in the history of the Crusades.[48] A century later, the extremity was reached in the Fourth Crusade, "the Crusade against Christians,"[49] which early on abandoned any pretense of fighting against the infidels. The Crusaders sailed to Constantinople, which had been a friendly stopover on the way to the Holy Land for earlier Crusades. This time, however, the Crusaders took over the city and nearly destroyed it in an orgy of pillage and destruction. They carried many of its treasures back to Europe, and even today tourists visiting Venice and other centers admire some of the great works looted from Constantinople by that evil expedition.

I have emphasized the major developments and important outcomes of the Crusades, but there is a minor story that is also worth considering. When the First Crusade approached Jerusalem, the city prepared to defend itself, and one precaution taken by the Muslim governor was to ask all the Christians living in Jerusalem to leave. Most of them, of course, belonged to the Eastern Orthodox church, and they complied with the order. Their priests took along the holiest relic of the Jerusalem Christian church, a large piece of wood that supposedly had been part of the True Cross (the cross upon which Jesus was crucified).

After the city fell, the local Christians began to return to their homes. The Crusaders owed allegiance to the Roman church and were intolerant of the beliefs and practices of the Eastern Christians, and they set about suppressing them. The local Christians quickly began to realize that they had been better off and enjoyed more religious freedom under Muslim rule than they would under the new regime of supposedly fellow Christians.

The newly elected Roman Catholic head of the Jerusalem church, Arnulf, wanted the sacred relic that the departing Orthodox priests had taken. But the Orthodox priests had already begun to recognize that the new Christian regime was hostile to their faith and their rights, and so they refused to give it up. Arnulf had several of the priests tortured, until finally they revealed where they had hidden the piece of the True Cross.[50]

This small event is noteworthy for several reasons. In the first place, it is troubling that a spiritual leader, sort of a junior pope, would subject other Christian priests to torture. Even more remarkable is the reason: to get them to reveal the whereabouts of a sacred relic. Today, of course, we know that most of the alleged relics of the True Cross were frauds. But setting aside these modern insights, it still seems amazing to think that a leader of the church would expect to benefit from a holy relic obtained by means of torture. One must assume that Arnulf believed his religion, and one can hardly avoid the conclusion that he thought his God would let him reap the rewards or enjoy the powers that the pieces of the True Cross would provide, rather than punish him for having profaned it by torturing the priests to whom God had entrusted it. In short, one must conclude that Arnulf thought God would think that Arnulf's ends justified his means. Even when torturing Christians was the means.

One could go on listing examples, but the main ones covered in this chapter are sufficient to illustrate the general conclusion that evil means do not reliably promote good ends—in fact, they often seem to corrupt and undermine the ideals they were intended to serve. In the long run, the ends often fail to justify the means, and instead the means tend to contaminate the ends. Resorting to oppressive violence is thus a doubtful and self-defeating way to promote ideals or utopian dreams.

Still, the question remains: Can evil ever serve good? The general pattern may be that evil means fail to promote and often seem to thwart the ends they serve. But are there some cases in which good ends can result from wicked means?

Undoubtedly, it is sometimes necessary to resort to violence to protect oneself against wicked enemies. Despite reluctance to shed American blood in Europe, America and its allies found it necessary to fight two world wars to keep liberty and democracy alive. Still, most people would not regard those as evil means. Fighting to protect oneself from a vicious attack is hardly a resort to evil.

It certainly does appear that evil actions can sometimes promote good causes. Europe did benefit from the Crusades, at least in terms of cultural stimulation and increased trade. By the same token, the present United States exists partly as a result of the cruel conquest and destruction of the people who lived here before the European settlers arrived and took over. Yet such benefits are indirect; they are not what the wicked means were used to create. The Crusades were not undertaken to increase trade with the Middle East or to gain exposure to other cultures that might end up stimulating the cultural traditions of Europe. They were undertaken to make the Holy Land a safer place for Christian pilgrims and, more broadly, to promote the reign of Christianity in the world, and in this they largely failed.

As this book was being written, the United States celebrated the 50-year anniversary of the end of World War II, and the celebration was somewhat diminished by the 50-year anniversary of the atomic bombings of Hiroshima and Nagasaki. Those bombings, like the involvement of the American labor movement with organized crime, may be good prototypes of the benefits of evil for good causes. The two bombings killed around 200,000 people, mostly noncombatants, yet they helped to end the war and bring victory to the side of freedom and democracy. In retrospect, the war's outcome seems beneficial to both the United States and Japan, which today is a prosperous and well-respected country. Yet the resort to such extremely violent means tainted the victory and left the victors with some guilt and doubts. The American diplomatic policy of advocating nuclear arms control has always been weakened by the bombings. American insistence on the evils of nuclear weapons is diminished by the fact that America remains the only country ever to have used such weapons in war.

The American labor movement was weak and vulnerable in its early days, and the brutal tactics of management and strikebreakers put it in jeopardy. Forming a covert partnership with organized crime enabled some unions to prevail in their street battles and, indeed, to succeed earlier and better than they otherwise would have in the broad campaign to improve the lot of the American worker. Yet there was also a significant cost. Various union leaders were jailed or killed, and it was difficult to keep organized crime from gaining ever greater control over some unions. Indeed, the unions lost some of their respect and prestige by virtue of their links to criminal organizations. It is clear that the labor movement has achieved positive ends, and the evil means may have helped. But the cost was substantial.

That brings us to the bottom line. Evil means can sometimes be adopted in defense of good causes that are under attack by others—but that scenario is most commonly the rationalization by which good causes generate evil. Moreover, evil means tend to have unforeseen consequences, side effects, and backlashes that often end up weakening or undermining the very idealistic goals they have been employed to promote. And it also appears that evil means tend to contaminate and discredit the noble causes that resort to them.

The resort to evil means in service of noble ends is a Faustian bargain that often does far more harm than good. It may seem that one puts oneself at an unfair disadvantage not to adopt the most destructive and seemingly effective means at one's disposal, and leaders are often faced with the tragic possibility that their noble cause will be defeated because they were unwilling to use the strongest means available. Yet such evil means carry less obvious dangers, and leaders who resist them deserve an extra measure of respect.

One such leader was Abraham Lincoln. During the Civil War, the Southern army insisted that arming black soldiers was illegal and that they would execute white officers who led black troops. They did in fact carry out a few executions of officers they captured, and the Northern military command requested permission to execute some captured Rebel officers in what seemed to them a fair reprisal. Lincoln said no, because he foresaw a downward spiral that would lead to ever more killing of prisoners.[51] By unilaterally refraining from such a reprisal, he prevented that downward spiral, and he also saved his cause from the moral damage that would have resulted from such measures.

But leaders like Abraham Lincoln are exceptional. The temptation to resort to violent means in the service of a good cause is common, and many a good cause has suffered contamination and worse by yielding to it.

Can Evil Be Fun? The Joy of Hurting

In 1941, a young German journalist was stationed as a naval correspondent in Liepaja, one of the territories overrun by the Germans. One day the journalist received a pass that enabled him to witness the shooting of Jewish civilians. Writing about the event later, he passed over the plight of the Jews and the killing procedures, because he said those had already been sufficiently described elsewhere.

What interested him was the behavior of the killers, or as he more delicately put it, "the people who had to carry out such an action." He said there was no single pattern of response, but a broad range. At one extreme, some of the security policemen were crying during the killings because they could not cope with the horrible reality. These later spoke to him of suicidal despair and the hopeless feeling of being unable either to disobey the orders or to carry them out. Others, however, seemed to have a more positive attitude, to the point that they kept a score sheet with the number of people they had shot. The journalist reflected that it was hard to tell the two extremes apart in any other way than their actions at the time. "Who today can determine which were those who wept as they carried out their duties and which the ones who kept a score-sheet?"[1]

Certainly one must think that those who made a game out of killing people are the clearest examples of evil. Victims' accounts sometimes even refer to the perpetrators laughing and enjoying themselves as they beat and shoot helpless people. The perpetrators themselves, at least the ones who later write about the experience, tend to emphasize the disgust, guilt, and depression that attend it.

Enjoyment of hurting others is one of the central features of the myth of pure evil. It is repeated in countless movies and other entertainments. Indeed, the James Bond novels and movies depend on it, for most of them include a sequence in which Bond is captured by the villain, who devises some clever and entertaining way to kill him, except that Bond manages to escape. The James Bond fan cannot help but reflect that if Bond were ever to fall into the hands of a less sadistic and more practical villain, who would shoot him on the spot, the series would end abruptly. Yet somehow writers (and presumably audiences) continue to find it plausible that each new villain ends up being thwarted by his own sadism.

If people could widely and commonly derive pleasure from hurting others, there might be little need for the rest of this book. The myth of pure evil would be essentially correct in its notion that bad people hurt others for the sheer pleasure of doing so. Why look further for explanations? Some people are violent and cruel for the fun of it. End of story.

This explanation is plausible. In fact, it has ardent supporters. The idea that human nature includes an aggressive instinct, or the similar idea that aggressive impulses are based on an innate genetic factor, is essentially an assertion that people are programmed by nature to want to inflict harm. That presumably implies that they get some kind of pleasure or satisfaction out of doing so, just as satisfying any of the other innate appetites (such as for food, drink, and sex) brings good feelings. These views have been asserted by some of the finest minds of the twentieth century, including Sigmund Freud and Konrad Lorenz.

Yet do people really enjoy killing? We know that it is not safe to rely solely on either victim accounts or fictional depictions for insight into the minds of evildoers. It will be necessary to consider the perpetrators' perspectives and accounts and to look very closely at the evidence before concluding that people enjoy inflicting pain on others. Of course, the perpetrators' accounts are also unreliable, especially when they are trying to rationalize their actions or reduce their blame after the fact. Perpetrators know the myth of pure evil, too, and they know that to admit to having enjoyed torturing or killing someone will put them in a very bad light. Most of them know that they'd better say they were reluctant and upset and that they didn't believe in it and are sorry they were forced to participate.

Still, there are some who will speak frankly and describe what it was like at the time, even to the point of whether it was fun. At this point, another problem emerges: Victims and bystanders will seize on such accounts and emphasize them, possibly overgeneralizing or overinterpreting what is said. Even the journalist's quotation that started this chapter deserves a second look. He didn't say the men actually enjoyed the killings, only that they kept a score sheet. It could be that they were simply keeping track of the chore or had become inured to such duties and were trying to enliven a dull, slightly distasteful task.

The question of whether people enjoy harming others—and, if they do, the question of how much evil can be explained by this pleasure—is the single most elusive and vexing problem in the entire topic of evil. This chapter will take a hard but open-minded look at the evidence. Probably the best sign of open-mindedness is frequent revision of one's opinion. The conflicting, inconsistent evidence has gradually led me to conclude that sadistic pleasure is genuine, unusual, acquired only gradually, and responsible for only a minority of evil. When it does come into play, however, it can make the victim's plight immensely worse.

For want of a better term, *sadism* can be used to describe getting enjoyment or pleasure from hurting others, as well as the desire for that pleasure. Unfortunately, the term *sadism* is also sometimes used to describe a pattern of sexual behavior involving dominance over others, and that narrower, more precise and specialized usage is not what is meant here.[2] Moreover, I particularly do not wish to claim that true sadistic pleasure is inherently sexual or indeed is related to the pleasures that accompany such sexual transactions. The present question is the more far-reaching and urgent one of whether human evil is driven by the pleasure of harming others.

What It Feels Like to Hurt Someone

Most people have some experience with hurting others. It is not usually a pleasant experience, contrary to the sadism theory. Back when parents used to use corporal punishment to discipline their children, one common line was, "This hurts me more than it hurts you." We (the children) didn't really believe it, but in retrospect at least there can be little doubt but that well-meaning, loving parents suffer when they hurt their children, even for a good cause.

More broadly, it seems safe to say that most people find it deeply upsetting to inflict harm, pain, or death on another person. The cheerful sadism that is often found in victim accounts and in the movies, where enemy soldiers laugh with pleasure while shooting, pillaging, raping, and torturing helpless victims, almost vanishes when one looks at the perpetrators' own stories and experiences.

One of the biggest surprises to emerge from World War II was the reluctance of American soldiers to shoot at the enemy. That war was marked by an unprecedented involvement of social scientists and other mental health professionals who sought to learn about the reactions and coping mechanisms of soldiers in combat. To their surprise, they found that about one in every four American soldiers could not bring himself to aim and shoot his gun at enemy soldiers during a battle. Such reluctance is especially remarkable because there is no apparent moral issue. In battle, a soldier's job is to fight the enemy, and he is bound by duty and obligation to do so. Hardly anyone maintains that it is immoral for a soldier to try to kill the enemy in battle, and of course soldiers are aware that the enemy is trying to kill them, too. Yet many soldiers could not pull the trigger. It seems there is some deeply rooted gut reaction that inhibits many people from shooting someone even when it is appropriate or possibly vital to do so.

A famous instance of this reluctance was documented during the Spanish Civil War in the 1930s.[3] George Orwell, who like many Western writers and intellectuals volunteered to fight against the Fascists, was dug in across from the enemy trenches, but the rifles were not effective at long range and so the men had to hide in no-man's-land and snipe at the enemy. On one occasion, Orwell's group fired upon small group of Fascists who were out of their trenches. Orwell took careful aim at a soldier who had been relieving himself when the shooting started and had turned to run off, holding up his pants with his hands. Orwell could not bring himself to shoot him. "A man who is holding up his trousers is not a 'fascist.' He is visibly a fellow creature," said Orwell. Of course, he did not have time to think through such reasoning in the split second in which he had the chance to fire. His comment was probably made later as an articulation or rationalization of the sudden, unexpected gut reaction that made him unwilling to shoot.

Our own generation is more familiar with the sufferings of Vietnam veterans, such as the widely recognized posttraumatic stress syndrome. To be sure, some of the stress and suffering of these soldiers is a result of having been exposed to severe dangers, distressing losses of comrades, and feelingly helpless, at the mercy of unseen but deadly enemies. Other Vietnam veterans, however, suffer from the stress of having been perpetrators rather than victims. After the war, they were tormented by nightmares and anxieties about the things they did, rather than the things done to them. In one study of Vietnam veterans who sought therapy for posttraumatic stress disorder and related problems, 30 percent of them were found to be motivated by problems connected with their own violent actions.[4]

In March 1968, American soldiers massacred the inhabitants of the village of My Lai, in what is almost certainly the most discussed American atrocity of the Vietnam War. Considerable information is available about the incident, and although it seems that some of the American boys acted callously or vindictively, many were deeply upset during and after the incident. One private was guarding a group of about 40 villagers when Lt. Calley told him "you know what to do" with them. When Calley returned about 15 minutes later, he was angry to see the private still guarding them, and he asked him why they weren't dead yet. The private said, "I didn't know we were supposed to kill them." Calley helped line the villagers up, and the two GIs shot them with their automatic weapons. The private and other witnesses later testified that he had been crying while he fired at the people. He said he felt "all broke up" by the act of killing the civilian prisoners.[5] Some other soldiers were unable to bring themselves to shoot, and they either directly refused the orders or contrived ways to avoid them. Reportedly, one man deliberately shot himself in the foot as a way of getting excused from the killing duties.[6]

Another relevant group is police, because police officers sometimes must shoot someone in the line of duty. Unlike soldiers, who are often drafted into service, most police officers have voluntarily sought that career and worked hard to gain that job. Sometimes they find themselves in situations in which dangerous, armed criminals must be shot, both for self-protection and to protect the public. Such shootings are thus eminently justified by professional duty, the need to protect the public, and self-preservation. Yet these officers too often find themselves having nightmares or other disturbances afterward. In recent years, most police departments have instituted mandatory counseling for all officers who have shot someone, as a way of helping these men and women cope with the stresses that arise from such an act.

Moral scruples should also be irrelevant when the victim desires to be hurt. Such cases are presumably rare, but that makes them all the more interesting. The anthropologist Gini Graham Scott spent several years studying people who desire sadomasochistic sex play. According to her research, one common problem is that a person desires a submissive, masochistic experience but is unable to persuade the spouse or romantic partner to take the dominant role.[7] (Most people start off desiring submissive experiences, and so the desire to be spanked is far more common than the desire to spank someone.) Again, a deeply rooted reluctance to hurt someone seems to be operating in such cases. If your spouse desires to be tied up and spanked by you, why should you refuse? Even if you do not have a strong personal desire to do those things, you should be willing to do them if only to give your partner the sexual enjoyment that he or she anticipates. But many people refuse. Or they cannot bring themselves to go through with it even if they want to consent.

To turn from the safe and consensual back to the horrific, the Holocaust has provided probably the most extensive evidence about how otherwise normal people respond to sudden demands to perform horrible deeds. Systematic killing of civilians began during the eastward thrust of the German troops, when special units were detailed to execute certain categories of people living in the captured areas. The killing procedures were still evolving at this point and were subject to local variations, but the broad pattern was roughly as follows. The unfortunate civilians were notified to be in the town square at a certain time. They were marched off in a group to a place near the execution site. Some were detailed to dig a pit. Then they were led to the killing site in small groups. They were ordered (perpetrators prefer the word *instructed*) to undress and stand in line. Soldiers with machine guns then mowed them down. Those who were not killed instantly had to be dispatched with a pistol shot to the head or other vital organ or stabbed to death. When one group was completely dead, the next one was brought along, and the procedure was repeated.

Apparently, many of the soldiers were very distressed by this duty. From a soldier's point of view, it might be regarded as fairly easy work: It is far safer than combat and spares them from the helpless vulnerability of the modern battlefield. Yet the military psychiatrists found themselves called upon to treat a broad range of psychological disorders, comparable to those resulting from the stresses of combat. Anxiety and depression were common, as well as nightmares and other sleep disorders.[8] There were also physical problems similar to those produced by stress in general, especially vomiting, diarrhea, and other gastrointestinal disturbances. One psychiatrist who treated many of these problems estimated that about 20 percent of the soldiers assigned to kill prisoners suffered some of these psychiatric problems.[9] Presumably, many more felt some suffering but did not seek treatment. Although the basis for such an estimate is far from clear, the figure of 20 percent does suggest that the suffering was very common and yet certainly not universal. One must wonder how many of the other soldiers felt no qualms, as opposed to how many merely kept their problems to themselves.

The massacre of Jews at the small town of Jozefow, Poland, is vividly described through the perpetrators' eyes in Christopher Browning's book, *Ordinary Men.*[10] These perpetrators were older reserve policemen who had been called up for active duty to maintain order in the occupied country. They didn't expect to be shooting at civilians, except maybe occasionally during a mutual shoot-out with resistance partisans or bank robbers. One morning they were roused very early and assembled in the dark to be given the day's orders by the old major, "Papa" Trapp, who was visibly upset. He meandered through some explanations of duty and wartime necessities and the obligation to follow orders even if they were unpleasant. And then he told them that the day's job would be to kill all the Jews in the nearby village, except for a few able-bodied males who would be sent to a work camp.

The procedure used for this killing operation turned out to be especially hard on the perpetrators, and substantial changes were made in later operations of the same type, as the police group became experienced in this kind of unpleasant duty. The first time, though, the victims were marched off to a waiting area. Each policeman then had to select one person from the group, march him or her (more were women) off to the killing site, instruct the victim to lie face down on the ground, aim his gun right up close at the back of the victim's neck, and shoot. The extremely close contact with the victim—individual selection, walking together as a pair, and then shooting from close proximity—undoubtedly increased the horror of the act. Like the troops at My Lai, the policemen at Jozefow found ways to resist and evade the duty. Some refused outright or politely asked to be reassigned. Others sneaked away or managed to avoid both refusal and participation.

Despite the point-blank range, the killing operation was greatly delayed because many of the men repeatedly missed their targets. The Germans developed a special word for the problem, calling it "shooting-past." The technical obstacle of shooting-past seems to represent the same kind of inner inhibition that blocked the American soldiers from shooting at their enemies on the battlefield. At the moment of truth, one simply could not bring oneself to kill this person. The poor woman is lying face down on the ground, your gun is aimed right at the back of her head, inches away, and when you force yourself to pull the trigger somehow your hand jerks the gun away and you fire into the ground near her head, missing her completely. You'll have to shoot at her again, unfortunately; the job doesn't go away just because you're weak. No doubt she makes some unnerving sound at this point, too. All of this would be extremely upsetting.

After the killing was completed, the men returned to their barracks for the night. This had been their first experience with such grisly duty. Many could not eat, but most of them drank alcohol very heavily. There was little conversation. Many men had nightmares, and the barracks atmosphere was further disturbed in the night when one man woke up from a bad dream firing his gun into the ceiling.

From the safe vantage point of a half century and a continent away, one may think that of course the policemen should have suffered severe moral qualms about what they had done. They were, after all, participating in a genocidal crime that has defined the cultural conception of evil ever since. But Browning reports that when the policemen testified about the incident years later, they did not generally cast their personal struggles in terms of ethical principles or moral scruples. Even those who managed to escape the horrible duty failed to claim that some personal trait of character or ethics motivated them. Instead, he said, these men "overwhelmingly cited sheer physical revulsion against what they were doing as the prime motive."[11] The perpetrators' accounts of the massacre, even the ones that condemned it most thoroughly, tended not to express the horror in the moral terms in which we now discuss the

Holocaust and similar events. They emphasized instead the disgusting, gruesome nature of the task, such as the sound of the screams, the feeling of being splattered with a victim's brains, or just the horrible gut feeling of killing a person. The first day of mass murder did not prompt them to engage in spiritual soul-searching so much as it made them literally want to vomit.

Similar evidence comes from observations of other perpetrators. Normal American citizens who participated in Stanley Milgram's famous experiment were instructed (ordered) to press buttons that they (falsely) believed were delivering painful electric shocks to another person, and although the subjects complied with their instructions, they showed many signs of stress and distress. At the other extreme, serial killers cannot be assumed to be normal or healthy at all, but they, too, often show negative reactions to their killings (especially their first ones). They report finding the experience disappointing and upsetting, and the long gaps between their early killings are due to the fact that they decided not to repeat the horrible experience (although they changed their minds later). The famous serial killer Ted Bundy said he never really achieved the satisfaction he expected from killing, and in fact his murders usually left him feeling empty, depressed, forlorn, and hopeless of ever finding emotional satisfaction. Other serial killers have reported the same feelings of emptiness and depression afterward.[12]

Last, professional torturers hurt others as a job, but they, too, often find it stressful. In one of the few studies of such professionals, researchers found that after the Greek military regime fell, many former torturers came forward to describe their own problems and sufferings. These resembled the posttraumatic stress patterns we have already seen in other groups: nightmares, depression, severe irritability.[13]

Thus, there is a convergence of evidence from many sources. Hurting someone is generally unpleasant, and it often evokes severely negative reactions. This is not to diminish the sympathy that the victim deserves, nor does it diminish the culpability of people who do bad things. The present question, however, is concerned with what it feels like to inflict harm on another human being, and the answer appears to be that it is quite upsetting. At least, that is how most people react the first time or first few times. As we will see, it does become easier with repetition.

Moreover, the distress associated with hurting or killing seems to be different from the moral or spiritual objection that might be expected. It is not that people feel that their principles have been violated, although some may indeed have such objections. Rather, it seems to be more of a gut reaction.

Why Do They Laugh?

Satan laughs when human beings suffer. By the same token, it is a standard pattern in movies and other entertainments to depict the villains laughing with pleasure at the pain and suffering of their victims. We have seen that reactions to hurting others often involve disgust, depression, and sympathy, which seem the very opposite of amused enjoyment. How can these views be reconciled?

The problem is all the more acute because victim reports do sometimes claim that their tormentors were laughing. For example, Mevludin Oric is a Muslim villager who accidentally survived a massacre by Serb soldiers in July 1995 when his cousin and best friend, who stood next to him, was shot and fell on top of him. Mevludin passed out from terror, lying soaked in his friend's blood under the pile of corpses, and therefore the Serbs did not finish him off. He recalls the actions of the Serbian soldiers: "They were laughing like crazy men—they must have been on drugs, that's all I can think."[14] He said that right up until they opened fire, he could not believe the soldiers would shoot him and his unarmed, innocent friends.

Undoubtedly, one major reason to emphasize the laughter is the myth of pure evil. Victims can quickly and effectively make their point about the evilness of their captors by reporting this laughter. (In Mevludin Oric's account, the myth is also invoked in the seeming incomprehensibility of the action, as well as in his ascribing their wicked acts to the alien power of drugs.) Yet it would stretch credibility to suggest that victims entirely invented the notion that their captors were laughing. Presumably, there must be some truth to the matter. Does laughter prove the existence of evil sadism? And if not, why would people laugh in the presence of others who are suffering and dying?

My own conclusion is that laughter is not very conclusive proof of sadistic pleasure, although it is revealing of how the perpetrator is feeling. People may laugh for a variety of reasons. Indeed, humor is one defense against a shocking or disgusting task. Thus, for example, an important part of medical training is growing accustomed to seeing injured bodies, and medical students are renowned for pranks and jokes featuring body parts from cadavers, such as hiding a severed hand in a lunch box. Such humor helps to overcome the normal reactions of shock and disgust that a physician cannot afford.

Nor are these reactions confined to medical students. An experiment by Bella DePaulo and Matthew Ainsville videotaped people's facial reactions to a series of slides, and one of the slides involved a repulsive photograph of an accident victim.[15] Males often responded to the disgusting slide with a smile (although females hardly ever did). It was not a smile of pleasure, but rather one that suggested embarrassment and an effort to distance oneself from the shocked or offended reaction. Still, something similar may be at work among people who find themselves working in a place where torture or execution is occurring.

Laughter may also arise from nervousness or uncertainty about how to react. In Milgram's experiments, some of the participants laughed when they followed instructions to deliver painful electric shocks (or so they believed) to another person who was banging on the wall and shouting for them to stop. Milgram reported "the regular occurrence of nervous laughing fits" that "seemed entirely out of place, even bizarre." And he was not just talking about the occasional nervous giggle. For three participants, the laughter reached the point of "full-blown, uncontrollable seizures." In the postexperimental debriefing conversation, many of the subjects were embarrassed by their laughter and loss of control. They "took pains to point out that they were not sadistic types, and the laughter did not mean that they enjoyed shocking the victim."[16] Milgram concurred that this laughter was not a sign of pleasure or amusement but rather reflected some effort to cope with one's distress at a pressure-filled, upsetting situation in which one was hurting someone. A similar reaction may be evident in the way people sometimes laugh to break the tension, during a moment of anxiety or uncertainty or even during a frightening movie. But victims may not make such fine distinctions between different kinds of laughter, especially when the mere fact of laughter will strengthen their account by indicating that their tormentors are evil.

Laughter may also occur out of sheer pleasure over doing a job well. Jerome Kagan's book on self-awareness in two-year-olds included the observation that many young children spontaneously smile when they succeed in mastering a new skill or task, indicating a presumably natural or innate source of pleasure.[17] It may be true that most acts of harming a defenseless victim would not involve much skill. But some would.

Torture, in particular, is a craft involving particular procedures and goals. The journalist Elizabeth Becker found the notes of a young Khmer Rouge cadre who had worked as a torturer in the infamous Tuol Sleng prison. These were private notes and were probably not intended for the outside world, so they may have been more candid than usual. He quoted his instructors as saying that "the purpose of torturing is to get answers. It's not something we do for the fun of it." The instructor went on to talk about the danger of losing control and lashing out at a prisoner in a blind rage, such as when frustrated. But then he made a remarkable statement: On some occasions, the enemy prisoner will "respond in a way that fits with the desires of our questions, [and] we get so happy we laugh and have a good time."[18]

Is that a rationalization? It seems unlikely. An instructor speaking to trainees about torture would probably want to provide accurate guidance about what to expect, and his comments were never intended to be published for the broader world to see. He was not trying to make torture look good.

And it is certainly plausible that groups of men (and perhaps women) would sometimes laugh with pleasure when they are succeeding at a difficult task. Thus, there is nothing inherently funny about football or basketball, and in fact these are difficult, strenuous games that require exhausting exertion and hold the risk of serious injury. Yet near the end of an important contest, one can often see the players on the winning team smiling and laughing. Although it seems a grotesque stretch to propose that a group of torturers would experience the same sort of pleasure, it is actually quite plausible, provided that they managed not to be too distressed over the suffering of their victims. And as we will see in the next chapter, that numbness or lack of empathy is often sought and cultivated in such work. Thus, torturers might end up laughing or seeming to enjoy themselves in a way that their victims could easily misinterpret as sadistic pleasure. They would be laughing in spite of the violence, rather than about it.

The analogy to a sports game brings us back to the quotation at the start of this chapter, in which the journalist noted that some of the German soldiers assigned to shoot civilians kept a score sheet to record their kills. This report is not unique. Other sources have documented that Nazi killers occasionally made games out of the activity. Some required the naked prisoners to run across a field while the troops shot at them, thereby increasing the marksmanship challenge. One of the police battalions guarding the Warsaw ghetto was encouraged by the captain to take pot shots at Jews near the wall of the ghetto. Scores were kept, top shooters were rewarded, and "victory celebrations" were held whenever a high score was reached.[19]

Yet making a game of killing does not prove that the killing itself was pleasant. Rather, it suggests a shockingly callous attitude toward the deaths. A callous develops for a purpose, however, which is to reduce sensitivity. If the killing were especially unpleasant, people might try to make it into a game to make it more bearable. Focusing on the game and the score would detract attention from the moral worries and the disgusting unpleasantness of the duty. Many people seek to enliven tedious, unpleasant jobs by elaborating them into games.[20] We certainly have every right to disapprove of killers who treat the killing as a sport, but we cannot infer that they did so out of love of killing. The reason may have been the opposite.

A final reason to laugh is the humiliation of another person. Humiliating, degrading experiences are sometimes funny to watch, and indeed a great deal of comedy is based on just that principle. Stand-up comedians tell stories about embarrassing things that happened to them, and televised comedy shows often get laughs by depicting events that make fools of their protagonists. Undoubtedly, many victims of oppression or torture are degraded, and their oppressors might at some point begin to find these scenes funny. Thus, to see a dignified, powerful adult man reduced to naked, fearful helplessness might possibly have an element of amusement in it, especially if he urinates involuntarily or begs to be released or unexpectedly makes an odd squeaking noise in response to pain. Sympathy for the victims would preclude seeing any humor, but one must recall that the attitude of the captors often precludes such sympathy. Imagine, for example, that Adolf Hitler were captured alive and pissed his pants in fear. It might be funny.

Powerful people sometimes do enjoy the humiliations they inflict deliberately on their victims. For example, sometimes perpetrators require their captives to sing, which has no instrumental or material benefit to the captors but does embarrass the victims. During the Stanford Prison experiment, in which college students were randomly assigned to work as either guards or prisoners in a simulated prison, the guards at one point required a prisoner to sing "Amazing Grace" by himself while the other prisoners did push-ups.[21] Likewise, in a recent television documentary, gang members described one of their capers in which they forced a robbery victim who was riding with them as a prisoner to sing several songs for their amusement. In such circumstances, the singer knows that he or she is being deliberately humiliated, which affects the singing and makes it more difficult to hold the tune—thereby intensifying the amusement of the captors who can play at being music critics and comment on the false notes or resolute style of the singer.

There are plenty of reasons that people may laugh during the victimization of others without indicating that they are deriving direct amusement and pleasure from hurting someone. Probably, most group tasks contain some occasions for laughter, if only to break the tension, and these occasions may arise even when the group task involves oppressing or hurting a detested enemy who is now safely cowed and in one's power. Still, victims probably attend specifically to such laughter and accommodate it to the myth of pure evil. To them, it provides welcome proof that their oppressors are sadistic, wicked individuals.

And so I don't doubt that killers and torturers and other people sometimes laugh when inflicting harm. But that doesn't prove that they enjoy the harm. There's plenty of evidence that most people don't.

Then again, maybe some of them do.

The Fascinating Spectacle of Violence

Now let us look for positive indications that people sometimes get pleasure directly from harm or violence done to others. A first and very clear set of evidence concerns the interest in viewing violence. People seem to enjoy the spectacle of other people being hurt or killed, when they are not taking part.

The conclusion seems indisputable. If nothing else, it is clear that people enjoy entertainments based on harm and violence. The majority of movies by Eastwood or Stallone or Schwarzenegger have some humor, some plot devices, some acting, but people don't see them for those reasons; rather, they go for the violence. They enjoy the humor and all that as extras. Many films have little to offer except violence, but they draw millions of viewers, and indeed slasher films such as *Halloween*, *Nightmare on Elm Street*, and *Friday the 13th* have often managed to beget multiple sequels. Nor is this appetite confined to North America: Many of Hollywood's blood-and-guts films are popular around the world.

The ongoing national debate about violence in movies and television is over the tough question of whether media violence is a cause of real violence. What is all too easily overlooked is the fact that media violence is essentially an effect, a consequence. People *want* to see violent movies. Movies are made to make money, and so the moviemakers film what people want to see. If people did not want to see violence, there would be very few such movies, because no one would pay to see them. But people do want to see them. Apparently, lots and lots of them.

Movies are hardly the only source of violent entertainment. The more literate segment of the public reads books, and many of these books deal with violence. Over the past decade, a new genre of "true crime" books has become big business. These books take actual violent events and describe them in detail. An early instance of this genre was Truman Capote's *In Cold Blood*, a slightly embellished account of a true story in which a pair of convicts broke into a midwestern family's house to rob them and, finding nothing much to steal, slaughtered the entire family. At the time, the book created quite a sensation, but by now one can routinely expect such a book on nearly every gruesome crime.

The fascination with the spectacle of human suffering goes beyond any interest in crime or violence itself. Almost invariably, people stop to look whenever there is a chance to see an injured human being or some other serious suffering. Many traffic jams could be avoided if people did not all slow down to look when driving by an accident: It is the slowing down for the sake of rubbernecking that causes the cars behind to have to wait. Likewise, when there is a fire, neighbors and strangers gather to watch.

This fascination with violence should not be attributed to any special depravity of modern society, because it is not limited to modern times. The violent entertainments of the Roman Colosseum are well known but not usually appreciated in context. Today, people tend to condemn them for their anti-Christian violence or exploitive operation, but such criticisms (although legitimate) miss the point from the perpetrator's perspective. The Romans did not have cable television movies with Steven Seagall wreaking havoc on dozens of enemies. To see a spectacle of violence, they had to put real violence on stage. Hence the gladiators, the wild animals, and the rest. The lions were not introduced to the Colosseum to provide a special punishment for the hated Christians. Rather, the Christians were put there for the sake of the lions. The audience wanted to see somebody (anybody) being mauled and eaten by lions, and so suitable categories of criminals were used to furnish the victims. The Christians were simply one of these unfortunate categories of criminals.

Indeed, public executions have always been an important spectacle. Once again, the modern sensitivity tends to side with the victims and condemn such practices, but these modern attitudes differ from how people at the time regarded them. Criminals were evil, and seeing a criminal put to death was probably comparable to seeing a villain in a modern movie killed by the hero. It signified a morally good, correct act of justice, and some enjoyment of the scene was appropriate.

Popular historian Barbara Tuchman recorded a story in which a medieval French village purchased a condemned criminal from another village so that they could stage the execution in their own town.[22] Tax money and public funds were as tight then as now, and it is surprising that one municipality would expend some of its budget on punishing a criminal who was under the jurisdiction of another. Yet the purchase makes sense if one understands that the execution was a major public entertainment, like a concert or play. Such rural villages had few entertainments to offer the citizens: no televisions, radios, stereos, video games, board games, or other amusements. To see a criminal put to death might be the most interesting and exciting thing to see all year, and possibly the only such thing. If the village had money, why should they be deprived of such a stimulating event, simply because they had no criminal of their own to execute?

Some of the greatest spectacles were provided by the major religious persecutions such as the Spanish Inquisition. From the public's perspective, the high point of each phase of the Inquisition was the auto-da-fé,[23] in which the convicted heretics were put to death. These were treated as great events and were sometimes timed to coincide with major celebrations, such as the one in 1632 held in honor of the Spanish queen's giving birth to a baby princess. Typically, the auto-da-fé was announced well in advance, and people would come from many miles to the city to see it. Getting a room the night before an auto-da-fé was more difficult than finding one in South Bend the night before the Notre Dame homecoming football game is today. The festivities included a parade of the guilty, the collective recital of Christian vows by all the audience (comparable perhaps to the singing of the national anthem at modern sports events), the pronouncing of sentences, the individual responses to the sentences, and then the executions. The actual executions sometimes occurred at a different place, requiring yet another procession.

The worst condemned heretics were burned alive. Others who repented at the last minute gained the mercy of being garrotted (strangled with a rope) before their corpses were thrown on the flames. To be burned alive, of course, is an especially nasty way to die, and it was common for the condemned to recant when facing that fate. Still, garrotting was not popular with the audience, and some crowds jeered and booed if too few heretics remained alive for the actual burning.[24]

Thus, people do enjoy the pleasure of watching other people suffer and die. The spectacle of violence holds a fascination that seems to transcend time and culture. This does not prove that people can enjoy inflicting the harm themselves, but it is difficult to dispute the fact that they can get some pleasure out of seeing others hurt. At the very least, one can say that inflicting harm on others would be a way of bestowing on oneself the well-tested pleasures of being able to observe someone suffering.

Empathy, Children, and Psychopaths

One day at the beach near our home, a group of schoolgirls found that a big fish had swum into the small space between the pier and a cement beach wall and had trapped itself. The fish was in a pool of water, but in front of it the water ended, it could neither turn around nor back up. As it happened, a woman came by walking her dog, and the four girls appealed to her to help them save the fish. When she described the incident later, the woman said that her normal response in such a situation would be to fetch her husband to perform such a gross task as picking up a big fish. But on this occasion, she felt some pressure to be a role model to the girls, and that ruled out the option of running off to get a man to do the icky part.

She also had to cope with her dog, which was part wolf and quite ruthless in such situations. In the dog's checkered past, she had killed many squirrels, groundhogs, and other small creatures, and she had not refrained from biting the occasional human either, usually without bothering to alert them by barking first. This monster dog had the preposterous name of Lucy. Lucy did not like the big fish, not at all. Whenever the woman managed to get the fish freed up a little, it would move forward a couple inches, and then Lucy would start forward herself as if to kill the fish, and the woman had to tell Lucy to keep back. The big fish and Lucy remained in constant, unsmiling eye contact, while the woman tried to find a way to get the fish turned around, to save its life as the girls wanted.

Finally she succeeded in picking up the fish and turning it around. As she recalled, the fish was big and heavy and scaly and slimy and flopping, each of which increased the difficulty of lifting it. The girls cheered. Lucy was disappointed. The woman went home to shower and change her clothes.

One response to this story is to reflect that the big fish was very lucky to have been discovered by a group of girls rather than a group of boys, who probably would not have settled on saving it as the most appealing response. In fact, though, the woman recalled that it had been a somewhat close call even with the girls, because a couple of them expressed interest in throwing stones at the fish and poking it with sticks. But somehow the spirit of helping it prevailed. The point, though, was that it would not have taken much for the children to have killed the fish. Doing something was the key; whether they saved it or killed it was not such a big deal. The fish presented a problem and a potential adventure, and tormenting or killing it would have been one very feasible response.

Are children sadistic? Certainly, killing a big fish would be in character. Children do plenty of things that harm or kill other creatures. They pull the wings off flies or moths. When a couple of boys discover an anthill, they may spend the better part of an hour stomping all the scurrying black or red critters to death. Some children throw frogs into the air to see them go splat on the pavement. Some fire slingshots or BB guns at birds, rabbits, or squirrels. A recent news story reported that a group of 11 boys and girls, from 8 to 14 years old, chased a small horse into a barbed wire fence where it broke its leg, then beat the animal with sticks until it died.[25] Children also pick on one another, and although this does not usually reach the point of maiming or killing, it is acutely unpleasant to the child being tormented or humiliated, even just by malicious teasing.

Yet all of this does not seem to add up to pure sadistic pleasure, as normally understood. Curiosity and a spirit of play tend to guide these activities, not a fully emerged enjoyment in the suffering of others. Indeed, what generally brings these activities to a halt is the intervention of adults, who tell the child to imagine how that would feel if someone did that to you: Put yourself in the other's place. As the child develops some empathy with the victim, the cruelty subsides.

Empathy is an important inhibitor. The capacity for empathic response emerges quite early in life, but it takes years for empathy to be developed and refined into a common response—and to be strong enough to keep people from inflicting harm.

Because empathy has to be developed, there are wide variations in how much people have. Young children may have only a rudimentary version. Sensitive, fully socialized adults, in contrast, may be able to feel sharp empathic pain simply by reading about the suffering of total strangers in distant parts of the world.

Other adults are less sensitive. At the low extreme are the psychopaths, who seem in many respects to be utterly lacking in empathy. Indeed, the disregard for other people's rights is regarded as one of the defining features of the antisocial personality disorder (the new name for psychopathy in clinical diagnosis). Research psychologist Robert Hare, who has specialized in studying psychopaths, defines such individuals in the following terms: They are superficial, impulsive, egocentric, grandiose, and deceitful. Compared to other people, they lack remorse, empathy, guilt, responsibility, emotional depth, and self-control.[26]

As children, psychopaths often take the lead in petty cruelties to animals and bugs and seem to be more fascinated and less troubled by the sufferings of the tiny creatures than their friends are. Later, as adults, they treat other people with almost the same indifference. "Do I feel bad if I have to hurt someone? Yeah, sometimes," said one psychopath who was in prison for kidnapping, rape, and extortion, when interviewed by Hare, "But mostly it's like . . . uh . . . [laughs] . . . how did you feel the last time you squashed a bug?"[27] Moreover, it looks like such answers are sincere, not just bravado. They really just don't feel much about it.

Psychopaths do get some amusement from the sufferings of their victims, although this does not seem to be a driving force. One man in Hare's study had been imprisoned after a burglary. He broke into a house and was searching for valuables when an older man came downstairs and began "yelling and having a fucking fit," as the psychopath recalled it callously. He struck a few hard blows to the old man's head and throat, "and he like staggers back and falls on the floor. He's gurgling and making sounds like a stuck pig,"[28] he said, with a laugh. In response, he kicked the man in the head repeatedly until the old guy fell silent. Another man described a fight in which his opponent pulled a knife on him, but he got the knife away and "rammed" it into the opponent's eye. He recalled the opponent's response with amusement: "He ran around screaming like a baby. What a jerk!"[29]

Normal human beings (as opposed to psychopaths) seem at least able to accept harm to animals without feeling much regret or empathic pain. Hunting and fishing represent popular pastimes that revolve around the killing of animals. Of course, there is room to question how much of the enjoyment is based on killing, and hunters are often rather testy about this topic, but it is clear that the killing at least fails to detract from a pleasant experience.

Several years ago, legal restrictions on hunting caused the moose population in the northeastern United States to expand dramatically. To control the overpopulation, a few states passed emergency measures allowing hunters to shoot them freely. The usual challenge of hunting was mostly absent, because after years of legal protection, the moose had lost most of their fear of humans. They were tame enough to stand right next to you. Yet many hunters still found enjoyment in shooting them. Newspapers had photos in which a hunter would walk right up to a moose, aim his rifle point blank at the unsuspecting, tame moose's head, and shoot it. Such incidents suggest that the killing itself furnished some pleasure, because there was little need for the stalking and other skills that many hunters cite as the central focus of the pleasure.

Taken together, the evidence does indicate that some people can inflict harm without great suffering. The implication may be that people only learn to be deterred by empathy. Many children start off being able to inflict harm without suffering a great deal of remorse, and psychopaths never seem to acquire the empathy and other factors that make one adverse to cruelty. This is not to say that they enjoy cruelty, but they do not necessarily find it to be objectionable and upsetting, either.

How can these observations be reconciled with the earlier evidence that people are often distressed and disgusted by their first experiences of inflicting harm on other human beings? There are two possible answers. One is that people are different. Only some people are upset, while others have no inner regrets or problems. The other is that the capacity for empathy does not always come into play.

There is some evidence for both answers. Let's begin with the psychopaths. Psychopaths do not seem to feel much regret over the suffering of others. "How did you feel the last time you squashed a bug?" as the one said. Such individuals seem to be incapable of feeling sympathy with people who suffer, including their own victims. (They may become fairly adept at pretending to have sympathy, however, to manipulate people into trusting or forgiving them.)

Now to the second explanation. It appears that most people develop a capacity for empathy, and this capacity deters cruelty. The fact that it appears between childhood and adulthood does not necessarily mean that it depends entirely on socialization, because it may have to wait until natural processes of maturation make certain abilities available. Empathy depends heavily on the ability to take on another person's perspective and imagine what that person is thinking and feeling. Such mental gymnastics develop only gradually. Thus, it is likely that empathy increases slowly with age, through both cognitive development and the influence of teaching and socialization.

Still, it seems that many people can disconnect their empathic responses and the inhibitions they bring. Some people become woefully upset at cruelty to animals, to the point of becoming vegetarians, protesting against hunting, shouting at people who wear fur, or demonstrating against research that involves the death of laboratory rats. Other people have no problem with these types of harm to animals. The difference is not a matter of the presence versus the absence of empathic sensitivity in general. Indeed, Adolf Hitler was a vegetarian and abhorred hunting and other forms of cruelty to animals, yet he initiated and presided over one of the greatest mass murder campaigns in history, and he remained coolly detached even from the sufferings of his own most loyal soldiers and followers.

The key point is that this empathic sensitivity seems to be selective. People may feel a great deal in some situations and toward some targets, but they seem to lack it utterly in others. And people are surprisingly flexible in their capacity to feel sensitive and empathic toward some and not toward others.

Can People Really Enjoy Hurting?

Now we turn to the heart of the matter: what perpetrators say about getting enjoyment from hurting people. Most perpetrator accounts do not include such statements, and far more perpetrators describe how their fellows or colleagues enjoyed hurting than say that they themselves got pleasure from it. Still, references to pleasure from hurting are too common in perpetrator accounts to be dismissed or ignored.

One of the classic, definitive works on violence was Hans Toch's detailed study of violent offenders and violent policemen. He sorted the men in his sample into several categories based on their motives and patterns of behavior. He labeled some men "bullies" based on the fact that they found pleasure in the suffering of others. Such a man would "go out of his way to be unfair, unmerciful, and inhumane in his violence."[30] When the victim shows signs of weakness or suffering—the point at which most violent predators regard their victory as secure and cease their violence—the bully intensifies his attack, as if the fun were just beginning. Such individuals seem to be rare—only a small minority (6 percent) of Toch's sample fell into this category—but they do exist. Moreover, some of Toch's observations suggest that bullies are made, not born, at least to the extent that violent patterns increase over time. "Violence is habit-forming," he concluded.[31]

Some American soldiers in Vietnam appear to have learned to enjoy inflicting pain and harm on their enemies. Interrogation of captured Vietnamese typically included some physical coercion, at least to the extent of hitting or slapping them. The American captors would generally start out treating this procedure as just another routine duty, but some would begin to discover a sensual pleasure in the work. Indeed, one scholar has proposed that "unless one sets out to do so, it is actually difficult to avoid the development of an involving esthetic in the sounds and rhythms of repeatedly slapping another person."[32] In some cases, the interrogation developed into a frenzy that caused the prisoner's death. Torturers from other cultures and other parts of the world report the same kind of problem. The premature death of prisoners due to overzealous torture is considered a common cause of unsuccessful interrogation all over the world. Thus, it is apparent that people can get carried away to the point of enjoying beating a helpless enemy prisoner.

Killing itself is sometimes pleasurable. In the words of one American veteran of Vietnam, "There is incredible, just this incredible sense of power in killing five people. . . . The only way I can equate it is to ejaculation. Just an incredible sense of relief, you know, that I did this. I was very powerful."[33] He said he felt like a successful hunter.

Indeed, it appears that several serial killers got their start in Vietnam. The notorious murderer Arthur Shawcross described his tour of duty in Vietnam as one of the best times of his life. He had free rein to kill men, women, and children, and he not only killed them but tortured and mutilated his victims, sometimes even dismembering them or in a few cases roasting and eating parts of the carcasses (there is some question about whether the last actually happened, although he admitted it). Years later, he said, "I was never happier."[34] Another serial killer, Joe Fischer, got his start in World War II and was pleased to learn that killing brought medals and other rewards. He found that "killing felt too good to stop,"[35] and so he continued to murder after returning home from the war.

Obviously, serial killers are far from typical, and most people would like to believe that they are genetically twisted in some way and should not even be considered in the same breath as the rest of the human race. But the deeds of serial killers cannot be reduced to explanations based on extraordinary genetic configurations. Some cultures and eras produce far more serial killers than others, and in particular something about modern culture seems to bring out such acts. At best, one may suppose that there are certain (genetic or other) predisposing factors that are activated by experiences that help one discover the pleasure in killing. Modern warfare provides one such place to learn that killing can be satisfying.

There are similar reports from other wars. In the Spanish Civil War, good-natured and idealistic young men who volunteered to fight for freedom against the Fascist menace sometimes succumbed to an "emerging taste for blood"[36] in the phrase of one journalist. In a revealing incident, a man encountered someone he had known for years as "a cheerful fellow fond of youngsters" sitting in a bar drinking coffee one morning. The fellow said he had been up all night and boasted that he had "accounted for" eleven Fascists himself, and indeed his group of "lads" had killed more than 100 prisoners that night. The man asked him why he was participating in such killings. "Well, someone has to," the younger fellow replied, almost automatically providing the standard justification, but then he added in a more thoughtful tone, "The worst of it is, you know, that I'm beginning to like it."[37] Of course, the fact that this story was told indicates that someone thought it was unusual, perhaps rare. But was it rare in its frank honesty, or in its enjoyment of killing?

During the nineteenth-century colonial wars fought for control over Africa, the brutal violence led some men to discover pleasure in it. The Europeans had substantial advantages over the African natives in weaponry and tactics, and so some of them came to feel relatively safe. The campaigns of Carl Peters, in particular, show ample evidence of violent treachery (such as killing African rulers with whom he had signed a peace treaty), and he openly confessed that he found "intoxication" in killing Africans.[38] On the other side of the planet, one scholar summarized his research on the conquest of the Americas by saying that the early European conquerors "never ceased to take delight in killing just for fun," as indicated by numerous reports of gratuitous sadism against the native peoples.[39]

The twentieth century has seen more of the same. A British House of Commons select committee recorded that natives were being cruelly treated on the notorious rubber plantations of Argentina. Some of the cruelties represented punishments that, although excessive, seemed at least to have some practical intention behind them. Others, apparently, were merely for sport. The committee reported that company officials would "amuse themselves" by shooting at Indians. To celebrate Easter Sunday or other holidays, they would douse Indians with kerosene and set them on fire "to enjoy their agony."[40] Such reports do not prove that these sadistic practices were the norm, let alone universal or even widespread. But they did occur, at least occasionally.

It is doubtful that the committee's evidence proved that enjoyment was the motive. Still, the gratuitous cruelty suggests an element of sadistic pleasure. The inference from gratuitous cruelty is important, because it allows us to see proof of sadism without having direct assertions of pleasure and enjoyment. Consider the serial murderers, for example. Some of these individuals frankly admit to having gotten pleasure from the experience, such as David Bulock, who told a New York state judge that "killing makes me happy,"[41] or Charles Schmid, who said it made him "feel good" to murder young girls and bury their bodies in the desert.[42] Even such remarks cannot be taken without a little skepticism, however, especially insofar as once one is a prisoner of the legal system, one may recognize the impossibility of providing a viable explanation for these horrendous crimes. In front of the judge, these killers may begin to realize how monstrously evil their acts appear to an outsider, and so they may claim enjoyment as a way of expressing defiance to conventional morality and its judgments on them.

Hence, signs of gratuitous cruelty are helpful as converging evidence. To be sure, it seems already gratuitously cruel to kidnap a stranger and kill him or her, and so the mere fact of serial murder could be taken as proof of the existence of sadism. Then again, these perpetrators might conceivably have some motive or reason for the acts according to their own twisted logic, by which the killings are seen as necessary or rational. But when the cruelty involves torture or other acts beyond the killing, then sadism is difficult to dismiss.

Henry Lee Lucas was one of the most notorious and sadistic serial killers, and his acts seem hard to explain without invoking sadism.

Squeamish readers may wish to skip ahead. At the height of his murderous career, Lucas was not satisfied with merely killing his victim or even with destroying the corpse. He liked to mutilate the bound and struggling victim before killing her and before he even made it clear to her that she would die. He would use a chain saw or other cutting tool to chop off her fingers and toes, forcing her to watch her body being destroyed piece by piece.[43] She would presumably realize that even if this horrible nightmare were to end and she were to escape or be saved, she would already have suffered permanent physical damage and would be a cripple for the rest of her life. Plus, of course, the pain of having one's fingers sawed off would be intense. If Lucas was going to kill her anyway, there was no need to go through the additional steps of carving her limbs off—unless he enjoyed it.

Another serial killer, Arthur Shawcross, likewise recounted actions that go so far beyond killing that one can only assume he enjoyed them (as is confirmed by the way he boasted about the events later). One of these occurred (supposedly; it is difficult to verify) when he was fighting in Vietnam, and he captured a young woman and a teenage girl who had hidden some ammunition. He could have killed them both right away, but instead he wanted to prolong the experience. He tied up the girl and forced her to watch while he killed the woman, cut off her head, carved her body up like a steer, roasted parts of the body over the fire, and ate some. After the girl had miserably watched the fate of her unfortunate friend, he did the same to her.[44]

Less extreme criminals also show some signs of getting pleasure and enjoyment from tormenting their victims. There was a telling moment in a recent public television special about teen violence. A sad-faced young woman was being interviewed in the youth prison facility where she was serving a multiyear sentence. She now felt remorse for her crime and victim, and she described the incident in a voice that occasionally showed danger of breaking with emotion, and with a hint of moisture in her eyes. She and her friends had abducted a man at gunpoint, planning to rob him. They discovered he only had $20, which disappointed them, but they had decided in advance that they would have to kill him to prevent his being a witness. He had begged them to let him take them to where his elderly parents lived so that they could rob the parents. They had kept him begging for his life for several hours, had tortured and humiliated him, and had finally indeed robbed his parents, too, although they had not killed him. She added that they had done similar things previously without getting caught. When the interviewer asked her why, she shrugged and said it was mainly for the fun of it. Fun? asked the interviewer immediately. The girl's face lit up and a wistful look of pleasure came into her eyes. Oh yes, she said, seeming surprised that he did not understand this. With a marked tone of nostalgia for lost pleasures that one now knows must never be repeated, she spoke of driving around, robbing ("jumping") people with guns. It was fun. But she knew that such pleasures were now forbidden and unwanted, and she fell silent.

Similar comments emerge in other interviews with teen gang members, although more commonly the interviewees say that it was mainly others who found pleasure in violence. In a typical comment, one person said of other young gang members, "They like the feeling of firing randomly at people who have nothing to do with the gang. It becomes a high."[45]

Gratuitous harm can also be invoked in cases of youth violence to suggest that people get pleasure from it. Thus, for example, the desire for cash might be enough to explain why a young man would break into people's homes and steal their valuable possessions, and so burglary alone would certainly not be proof of sadistic pleasure. But some burglars like to inflict gratuitous damage on the houses they invade. Thus, some of them urinate or defecate in the home, or they break items that they cannot steal.[46] Such practices suggest that people enjoy inflicting the damage, because there is no other benefit to them other than the intrinsic pleasure that they get from the act.

Gratuitous harm is not confined to furniture and appliances, either. The following story was quoted in Leon Bing's book on teen gangs, *Do or Die*.[47] A young man was talking to a girl when the girl's brother, nicknamed Sidewinder, came by. Sidewinder asked the young man where he was from, and when he heard the answer he realized that the young man was part of a rival gang. There existed the usual set of vendetta grievances—in the future, after telling this story, Sidewinder added that one of that gang had killed a member of his own gang, and he suspected that this young man "was probably there when that happened"[48]—but he had nothing personal against this individual. Still, he did belong to the enemy, and that was enough.

Sidewinder slipped away and collected three of his friends. They returned, and the young couple were still talking. The four jumped the young couple and began beating up the man. So far, perhaps, one could attribute these actions to the standing enmity between the groups. But then Sidewinder and his friends turned more sadistic. First they put him in the trunk of a car and drove to an empty field. There they took him out and tied him by a rope to the car's trailer hitch. Then they dragged him around the field behind the car. "He got skinned up all bad, tore his scalp half off. Got all dirt and like gravel and stuff stuck in the blood,"[49] Sidewinder recalled. Next they drove to one of the other fellows' houses and threw him into the yard where there were two pit bulls, who attacked him viciously. "Man, they chewed him up—big ole chunks of meat comin' off his arms and legs, blood pourin' out, and [the victim] just screamin' and cryin' for us to take him on outta there."[50]

Sidewinder recalled that the young man had at first tried to act tough and stand up to the torture, but by this point he had broken down. The group rounded out the afternoon with a series of humiliations. They made the victim kneel and recite various demeaning statements, such as saying he wanted to perform fellatio on each of them, or "fuck my dead homeboys" (which was contemporary gang slang to express disgraceful insult to the memory of one's own fellow gang members who had died, often regarded as the ultimate insult and provocation). By this time the fellow had been "almost killed," presumably including severe bleeding from various cuts and some broken bones, so they "dropped him in the riverbed" and left him there. The pursuit of pleasure is evident in Sidewinder's final generalization about such escapades, which seem quite restrained to him because the victims are not killed: "When we tired of lookin' at 'em, we let 'em go."[51]

Still, it is important not to overgeneralize. Not all youth gang members claim to enjoy fighting, and many say they do not. Most often they merely point to a couple of individuals who seem to get such pleasure. One of the most thorough research projects on teen gangs was conducted by sociologist Jankowski, who lived with various gangs for a decade. He acknowledged that some do enjoy the violence, but they are a minority: "Only a small number of gang members enjoy fighting. . . . Most do not enjoy fighting at all and try to avoid it."[52]

Works on the Nazi Holocaust often include allusions to a callous, brutal, or laughing attitude while the perpetrators were doing their work, but as we have seen, such responses might be understood as practical strategies and coping methods. Such explanations fail in the rare but clear instances of obviously gratuitous violence, as in the following story. A German police lieutenant, heavily drunk early in the day, was waiting for the assigned Jews to finish digging the mass grave in which the village's Jews would be buried after execution. He personally selected about two dozen men from the Jews waiting for execution. These men were ordered to strip naked and crawl on the ground. The lieutenant then instructed his noncommissioned officers to get their billy clubs and beat the Jews vigorously as they crawled.[53]

Compared to the mass murder that was going on all around, inflicting a few nasty bruises or even broken bones may seem like a relatively trivial matter, but it is psychologically instructive. The victims were going to be shot that afternoon, and their deaths should have satisfied any pragmatic or idealistic purpose. To beat them before shooting them was pointless and gratuitous. The purpose of that gratuitous brutality must therefore have been in the act itself, which suggests that the lieutenant got pleasure out of inflicting harm. Again, this incident is not typical, and one should not conclude from it that sadism was the norm—but it is rather unambiguous in suggesting that sadism was genuine.

One might think that Mafia killers would maintain a more professional attitude and not get carried away with pleasure. But some, apparently, begin to find enjoyment in such work. In Chapter 5, I quoted one example, in which the mob chief is said to have exclaimed "I love this" when bundling up a victim's body to dispose of it, and he later expressed the wish that he could bring the despised victim back to life so that he could kill him again.

A more thorough and thoughtful set of observations was furnished by Antonino Calderone, the Sicilian Mafia informant interviewed at length by criminologist Pino Arlacchi. Although every member of a Mafia family must be capable of murder and many will do the job eagerly because such acts often lead to career advancement, there is a norm that prizes remaining cool and detached. The Mafia does not respect gratuitous cruelty, and it admires the killer who remains calm and businesslike while taking a life.

That norm does not conceal the fact, however, that some men come to enjoy killing. Calderone observed that some men took to killing better than others, and he said that certain "sick" people found pleasure in it. When they first kill, something "springs loose" inside them, which they cannot understand or explain. "And in time murder begins to be pleasing; it becomes a vice, an illness."[54] His description resembles the process of becoming addicted to a drug, and we will return to this analogy when we try to explain the enjoyment of killing. For now, the important point is simply that even some professionals find themselves gradually succumbing to enjoyment that emerges, perhaps surprisingly, from killing.

Next, let us consider rape. A small minority of rapes include gratuitous sadism that seems based on getting direct enjoyment from the victim's suffering. Researcher Nicholas Groth characterized these cases as involving men who plan and calculate how to torment a woman and who become excited through the process of inflicting pain on her. In some cases, the man does not even seek direct sexual gratification for himself; he may use a stick or bottle or some other object to penetrate the woman. In such cases, there is little basis for speaking of rape as a sex crime in the sense of the illicit taking of sexual gratification. His pleasure lies in hurting the woman, not in his own orgasm.

Groth concluded that about 5 percent of rapes fall into this category. The number is close to Toch's finding that about 6 percent of the violent men in his sample were bullies who engaged in violent acts for the sadistic enjoyment of hurting another person.

Marital rape also can contain signs of sadistic pleasure, although it is likely that some twisted urge for revenge over real, exaggerated, or imagined grievances lies behind many such domestic cruelties. In one well-known study of marital rape, several cases fit a pattern of sadism. One husband was attracted to detective magazines and other accounts in which women were treated brutally, and he would sometimes read these aloud to his wife. He hid in the closet one day and then jumped out to surprise her, forcing her down on the bed and raping her anally. He was angry afterward that she had resisted so hard. (She said she had not known at first that the attacker was her husband.) On another night, she went outside into the yard to see what some noise was, and he grabbed her from behind, tied her arms together, bent her over the stack of firewood, and raped her anally. He began to tie her up and take pictures of her with various objects, such as a banana, inserted into her vagina, and although sometimes she went along with these requests, she was very upset to learn that he showed these pictures to his buddies.

Finally he moved out rather than accede to her demand that they begin marriage counseling. After he left, she was going through her things and made a very distressing discovery. He had kept a card file of the forced-sex episodes between the two of them. Each card contained the date of the incident, a coded description of what he had done to her, and a rating of the episode on a zero-to-ten scale. This discovery made her realize that he was far more systematic and calculating in his marital brutality than she had thought. She had assumed that the attacks were merely spontaneous outbursts, but that assumption did not square with his keeping a file with codes and ratings.[55]

A very different form of sexually tinged domination occurs in sadomasochism, and indeed the most precise and specific meaning of the term *sadism* refers to a sexual activity. Sexual sadism is therefore worth considering briefly as another possible source of insight into whether people get pleasure from inflicting pain. Although sexual sadism is not fully understood, enough is known to confirm the broad outlines of what we have already seen.

Sexual sadism is rare. Only a small proportion of adults engage in sadomasochism at all, and the overwhelming majority of those are primarily or exclusively interested in the submissive side (masochism). It is a common complaint in S&M communities that there are not enough people willing to take the dominant role. Everybody wants to be spanked; no one wants to do the spanking. In S&M clubs, for example, there are typically three or four times as many submissives as dominants.[56]

Moreover, most people who do enjoy the dominant or sadistic role seem to have acquired this preference after a long initial phase of being submissive and masochistic. I once met such a man when I was testifying as an expert witness at a pornography trial. He had been locally famous in the San Francisco scene as a submissive, but lately he had taken the dominant role. He spoke of "discovering your dark side" as a very gradual process of learning to embrace the dominant role. He had several women who were his slaves, and he was slowly finding more and more pleasure in spanking them and dominating them in other ways. Thus, the pleasure was real, but it had taken him years to discover it, and he said it was the same for every other sexually dominant person he knew.

A Natural Basis for Sadism

Three clear conclusions emerge from our survey of evidence about getting sadistic enjoyment from inflicting harm or pain on others. First, there are too many such incidents, spread across too many different times and places, to ignore, and so one must conclude that sadistic pleasure is genuine. Second, it is nearly always a small minority of perpetrators who derive such pleasure—something perhaps on the order of 5 percent, or one out of twenty people, who are actively involved in inflicting harm. Third, it seems that sadistic enjoyment is something that is gradually discovered over a period of time involving multiple episodes of dominating or hurting others.

In those respects, sadistic cruelty seems to resemble addiction. Few people get much enjoyment out of their first glass of beer, cigarette, cup of coffee, or even their first drug experiences. Moreover, most beer drinkers and drug users are not addicts, and there is even evidence that many tobacco users are not addicted.[57] Addiction thus afflicts only some of the users, just as only some perpetrators are sadists. And addiction, like sadism, is typically a process that develops gradually and escalates over time.

There are some signs that sadistic pleasure may be experienced as an addiction, in the sense that the person comes to crave that pleasure and to want ever stronger doses of it. We already quoted several men who said that killing became a habit, or "a vice," as one of them put it (thus making the parallel to addictive pleasures like tobacco especially clear). The same goes for rape. One researcher found that some rapists described it as habit-forming, saying "Rape is like smoking. You can't stop once you start."[58]

Similar remarks are made by torturers. It is fairly clear that in most cases torture is officially supposed to be a routine part of police work, aimed at securing information. Moreover, it appears that most torturers start out that way. Instructors emphasize that the goal is to gain a confession of relevant crimes and to obtain useful military intelligence that might help save the lives of comrades who may be in danger from enemy plots and attacks. As one continues to torture, however, one begins to discover sadistic pleasure in it. As a Uruguayan lieutenant reported in an interview with Amnesty International: "Subsequently the idea [of torture as merely a means to a legitimate end] began to lose its force and changed into the application of torture for its own sake . . . and also as an act of vengeance against the detainee."[59] One might have expected the converse, that the young, new torturers would tend to get carried away and go wild, while the older and more experienced ones would keep their cool and be more professional about it. But apparently torturers grow meaner and wilder over time.

Addiction Processes

To understand sadism, it may be useful to apply what is known about addictions. One of the most important theories about addiction, called opponent process theory, was proposed in the 1970s by Richard L. Solomon and John D. Corbit.[60] Their theory begins with the body's natural tendency to maintain a stable, peaceful state of equilibrium (called homeostasis). To maintain this state, the body must have processes to restore homeostasis whenever it is disturbed. Running a race, for example, will get the body excited; by the end of the race, one's heart will be beating hard and one will be breathing heavily. When the race is over, the heart can't continue to beat so fast forever, so there must be inner processes to slow it back down. Thus, the body operates on the basis of opponent processes: one process moves away from equilibrium (speeding up) and another has the opposite effect (slowing back down).

A very important point of opponent process theory is that the second, restoring process tends to get stronger over time. It is as if the body learns and becomes more efficient at counteracting the unusual state. Run a mile after not exercising for a year, and you'll gasp for air a long time afterward; but run a mile every day for a year, and by then you'll catch your breath very quickly afterward. Moreover, you probably won't even lose your breath as badly. Just as the second, restoring process grows stronger, the first process gets weaker. Together, these two trends may be nature's way of keeping us from being repeatedly pulled out of equilibrium. In running, this is called getting in shape: The same run puts less of a strain on your body, and you catch your breath faster afterward, than when you first started running.

Now consider alcohol use. Alcohol produces various pleasant feelings, such as euphoria and relaxation. These take the body away from its normal state. The body then has its own inner mechanisms for sobering itself up. Just as the intoxicated state may be very pleasant and easygoing, the hangover state is unpleasant and irritable. As one continues to drink on many occasions, one develops a tolerance for alcohol, so that the same dose produces less and less of a kick. Meanwhile, the hangovers get longer or more severe.

By the same token, drug addicts often find that the phase of withdrawal and depression becomes longer and more unpleasant as the months go by and they continue taking the drug, even if the amount of drug they take does not change. Addiction is spurred because the person thinks that taking another dose is the only way to feel good again quickly, instead of waiting for the body to regain its original state.

With alcohol and other drugs, the pleasure is all in the initial, departure phase (the A phase), and the restorative process (the B phase) is unpleasant. Being drunk feels good; having a hangover feels bad. But there is no reason to assume that the initial phase is always the pleasant one. Some opponent processes show the opposite pattern: The A phase may be unpleasant and the B phase pleasant.

For example, consider the recent fad of bungee jumping (or hang-gliding, mountain climbing, parachuting, and the like). The fear of falling is deeply rooted in human nature, and almost everybody responds to a free fall with panic. Thus, the initial (A) phase reaction is an extremely unpleasant one: terror. But of course the body is not going to remain in a state of terror indefinitely, especially once the fall is completed and the danger is past. To restore homeostasis, the body goes through some process of making itself feel better, such as releasing some inner chemicals that will calm the panic and compensate by giving pleasure. Sure enough, people find that the terror of falling is immediately replaced by a wave of euphoria and relaxation. On the face of it, it seems absurdly stupid to seek pleasure by jumping off a bungee pole or out of an airplane, because that seems a sure way to produce bad feelings; but the intense feeling of pleasure that follows may be quite desirable. People do seem to like it, after all.

Moreover, the tendency for the B process to grow stronger and the A process to grow weaker means that over repeated trials the person will get more and more of the pleasant part. A first bungee jump or parachute experience may be so frightening that the pleasure afterward may not seem entirely worth it. After a dozen such experiences, however, the fear has diminished and the pleasure is stronger than ever. Anyone who reaches that point is likely to find that the experience is compelling, and he or she may begin to crave to repeat it more often. One may also seek out even stronger or more extreme versions, such as jumping from yet higher places.

Sadism: Pleasure in the Backwash

Let us now apply the opponent process theory to sadism. We have seen that the initial reaction to hurting someone is typically very unpleasant. People are shocked, dismayed, disgusted, upset. But they do not remain in that state forever; the body finds a way to return to normal. Because the initial reaction is unpleasant, the offsetting (opponent) reaction must be pleasant and positive. Thus, the first time they hurt or kill someone, they will feel bad, but the body will also create subtle good feelings in order to recover and get back to normal. The first time, probably, the bad feelings will be quite vivid and salient, while the good feelings of the B process will remain muted.

If the person inflicts harm on subsequent occasions, however, the balance between good and bad may shift, according to the pattern of opponent processes. The shock and disgust will grow weaker. The enjoyment will grow stronger and more obvious. (It will also start sooner, in keeping with the gradual rise in efficiency that one sees in opponent processes; like the parachutist or bungee jumper who begins to feel pleasure earlier and earlier in the process, instead of having to wait until the danger is entirely past.) In this way, sadistic acts of cruelty may start to bring pleasure.

In this view, the pleasure that one gets from hurting or killing is all in the B process, not the A process. It is somewhat misleading, therefore, to compare rape to smoking tobacco, as the rapist quoted earlier in this chapter did. The thrill of killing may be closer to the thrill of parachute jumping than to the thrill of taking drugs: The pleasure is in the backwash.

This theory seems to fit with the all the observations about sadistic pleasure we have quoted. The initial reaction to committing a violent act is unpleasant, and it predominates the first time. Over time, one begins to find more pleasure in the aftermath, while the unpleasant part becomes weaker. Gradually, one may start to crave the experience. One may also seek stronger experiences, as the initial reaction becomes muted. Thus, sadists should become crueler over time, in the search for ever stronger highs.[61]

Consider the following account provided by psychologist Ervin Staub.[62] An American soldier in Vietnam was on helicopter duty. When he flew over a group of civilians, his commanding officer ordered him to fire his machine gun at them. He did not obey. The helicopter circled the area, and when it passed the civilians again, the same command was given, and again he refused. The officer in charge threatened to court-martial him for disobedience. The third time, he did shoot at the people on the ground. This experience shook him up to the extent that he vomited and felt very upset for a time afterward.

On later missions, however, the soldier complied more readily with such orders, and in a fairly short time he said he began to enjoy shooting civilians. He compared it to shooting at targets in a gallery. (Today's young people would presumably use the analogy of playing a video game.) Thus, the same act that had initially produced severe distress in him was soon converted into fun. He went from having to vomit to actually liking it.

There is one major problem with this theory: Why doesn't everyone become a sadist, once exposed to the thrill of inflicting harm? Because opponent processes are natural reactions, they should be roughly similar for everyone. Yet we have seen that typically only a small proportion of perpetrators develop into sadists. What prevents this evolution in everyone else?

A Vaccine against Sadism?

The most likely answer is guilt. Guilt is a learned, acquired reaction that makes people feel bad when they hurt other people.[63] So guilt would tend to stand strongly in the way of the opponent process pattern of becoming addicted to the pleasure of harming people.

Guilt may be unable to prevent the opponent process entirely, however. One can only become a full-blown sadist by recognizing that one likes to hurt others, as demonstrated by the comments from sadists quoted earlier in this chapter. Guilt may prevent this recognition. A well-developed conscience would not allow one to admit (even to oneself) having enjoyed the infliction of harm. Just as in sexual repression, guilt does not actually prevent the body's positive response—instead, it makes one refuse to acknowledge it. Guilt makes one disown and disavow the pleasure.

Guilt may even retard the initial emergence of sadistic pleasure. After the first killing, the killer may be full of distress and disgust, and even after recovering from that may feel bad because of guilt. Any pleasure that accompanies the body's recovery (the B process) would be concealed by the guilt. (As a highly socialized, acquired reaction, guilt would not be likely to set off opponent processes of its own.) This would explain why people might learn to enjoy watching violence, as in violent movies, more readily than they would learn to enjoy performing violent acts themselves. The opponent process may begin to grow faster and be accepted more easily when guilt is not present, such as when one is merely watching a film.

If this analysis is correct, then there is a potential sadist inside everyone, but our capacity for guilt—the conscience—keeps it hidden. Once we begin to gain experience with inflicting harm on others, the capacity for sadistic pleasure will emerge, but guilt can thwart it. A person prone to a guilty conscience would be unlikely to allow himself or herself to learn to enjoy hurting others. Without the inner restraint of guilt, however, someone might well discover—gradually—that genuine pleasure could be found by tormenting and killing people.

Having a Little Fun

Now let's look at another very different link between pleasure and harm-doing. Sometimes people take up certain activities because of the fun involved in them. Inflicting harm or damage may be a minor, tangential aspect of what they are doing, at least at first.

The word *fun* can encompass an impressively broad array of activities. Some of them are probably so thoroughly harmless that there is no way to link them to evil. Others may involve crimes and even violence.

Fun can be defined in terms of two broad properties. First, it is arousing or exciting. The word *fun* would not usually be used to describe calm, placid, serene activities. Second, it brings pleasure. Pleasure and excitement come in many forms, and they are not necessarily incompatible with causing some harm or damage, unless the harm is severe enough to elicit the distress reactions we just discussed.

It is clear that many people find enjoyment in the simple act of breaking rules. Doing something naughty is almost inevitably exciting, and if one succeeds at it, there is the pleasure of success. Thus, the simple recipe for fun is satisfied.

Shoplifting provides a good example. We saw in Chapter 4 that shoplifting generally brings fairly minimal benefits. Indeed, Jack Katz's research on shoplifting found that the items people stole were typically stored away, lost, or otherwise forgotten. The corollary is that people shoplift for the fun of it. Katz called these pleasures "sneaky thrills,"[64] because the accounts people gave him of shoplifting focused on the excitement of taking the item and getting out of the store without being caught. "I think the reason I steal is the adventure," as one teenager put it, after saying that he would shoplift items and then deliberately break them or throw them away. "You know, the fact that when you get out of the store and you've gotten away with it, your heart's pounding, you know; whaaa!"[65] He said the same applied to stealing cars. The appeal was the thrill of driving around in someone else's car. You didn't particularly want to keep the thing you stole.

It may seem discordant to speak of fun in connection with the Nazi Holocaust, but if one can get past the initial shock the notion is plausible, especially with regard to the early stages of the movement. The photos in the Holocaust Museum in Washington show activities that might easily seem like fun to young people who did not anticipate that large-scale mass murder was to be the eventual outcome. The beginnings of the public Nazi movement involved torchlight parades, marching in uniforms, chanting, and other group activities that might well bring pleasure. On Kristallnacht and other occasions, there was an accepted license to break windows and smash the furniture in Jewish shops and homes. Such acts of vandalism can certainly be fun, especially when there is official permission to break the normal rules of respect for property. Indeed, people have told me about church groups here in the United States that would include "car smashing" as part of their youth group holiday celebrations. The church would purchase an old used car and put it in the parking lot. The young people were then given a pair of sledgehammers and free rein to demolish it. Even normally quiet, religious, well-mannered boys—somehow, the girls did not seem to see the point of this fun—would become wildly aggressive and clamor for extra turns in reducing the car to an unrecognizable pile of twisted fragments.

Likewise, many young people like bonfires and dislike the school discipline symbolized by books, and so a bonfire of books might fall into the same category of naughty fun. In my own youth, we sometimes would celebrate the end of the school year by burning a couple of our notebooks, in a sort of ritual celebration of summer. Again, if one did not see the horrors that lay ahead, the Nazi book-burnings might have appealed to people on the basis of fun. The legitimacy of the act is difficult to appreciate, but it may help to simply reverse the politics. If a giant trove of neo-Nazi hate propaganda were discovered in your neighborhood and the authorities decided to burn it in a big public bonfire, you probably would walk over to see the event, and by the time you stood around watching the fire and talking with your neighbors it might well end up being fun.

As we will see in the next chapter, the Ku Klux Klan started out specifically as a club devoted to fun, with no political or racial purpose. At first they played jokes on one another and then on members of the public in general, and then gradually they began to aim their pranks at black people. The violence didn't start until later. Even then, though, one can understand that the organization may have had appeal as a source of fun. Members of the Ku Klux Klan in later decades would often reject the notion that racist politics were central. To them, it was a society devoted to good family fun: picnics, bonfires, parades, fireworks, baby shows, and pie-eating contests, mixed together with the costumes, rituals, and secret words.

The contrast is evident in Kathleen Blee's book, *Women of the Klan.* The researcher herself focused on the hate propaganda and racist cruelty that have become associated with the Klan, and as a feminist scholar she wanted to understand how women could come to participate in evil, violent behavior. She thought such behavior would normally be associated with men, and the idea of studying Klan women to gain insight into a feminine version of hatred and oppression was very promising. Unfortunately, the women Blee interviewed were no help. They kept turning the conversation away from racist hatred, which they seemed to regard as a minor and unfortunate aspect of the Klan. Instead they wanted to speak of being with friends, having parties, doing good deeds for the community, sewing quilts together, supporting churches, and so forth.

It is also necessary to consider that the exuberance of defying convention may enable fun-seeking people to do things that cause more severe harm than they might have intended. I recall reading a magazine letter when I was a teenager. The letter writer said he had belonged to a "shit club" in high school. The group would rove up and down the streets looking for parked cars that had been left unlocked. When they found one, they would get in. The two girls would climb in the back seat, lower their trousers, and defecate, and the three boys would urinate all over the front seat. I recall wondering whether that would be fun: defacing the car, breaking the rules, the excitement of not getting caught, plus the somewhat shocking intimacy of boys and girls sharing activities that were normally confined to separate bathrooms. Focusing on these thoughts, I was brought up short when the editors' response pointed out how this kind of fun would have to ruin someone else's good times. Like me, the young club members probably focused their attention on the excitement and mere naughtiness of what they were doing, without giving realistic consideration to their victims.

Similar logic applies to more extreme activities. Recent news coverage depicted a dramatic crime in which five young friends knifed a man to death in a robbery that brought them only a single dollar.[66] The news coverage emphasized the single dollar, as if to imply that a human life was worth so little to these young men that they would kill for a dollar. The facts of the case suggested a different picture, however. The young men had intended to beat up a victim at random, as their form of fun. The robbery was not part of their plan, nor was the killing. The victim was on his way to a pay phone to call his girlfriend, because he had no phone in his home. The group accosted him and held a knife on him. One of them stabbed him, and the others took his wallet and ran. They had nothing against him and no reason to want to kill him. It was just supposed to be a random physical assault, for fun.

The one-dollar murder brings us back to the magnitude gap, which is essential to keep in mind when trying to understand sadistic pleasure. It is shocking to think that someone might enjoy hurting or killing someone, because the suffering of the victim is so very terrible. But to understand the perpetrator's enjoyment, one must appreciate that to the perpetrator the whole episode is a small thing, not a big thing. To judge the perpetrator's acts by the victim's loss may make moral and legal sense, but psychologically it is misleading. The five young men who killed someone and stole a dollar were not out to end a human life, with a full sense of the magnitude of such an act. They were only seeking a little excitement. If they had not been caught, they would have begun the next day just about exactly where they had begun the previous one, regardless of whether they had killed someone or not. To the victim's family and loved ones, life may never be the same, but to the killer it is only a small difference. The enjoyment is small. The whole experience is small.

Thus, the search for fun may bring people to activities that can lead to serious crimes and violence later on. To escape from boredom, people want activities that offer pleasure and excitement. Young people in particular tend to suffer from boredom, and they often find that violating rules creates excitement. Their initial acts may stop far short of violence. But as Chapter 9 will show, once people get started, the steps toward greater violence and evil are deceptively easy to take.

Power

The novels written by the Marquis de Sade give literary expression to a remarkable (and remarkably unappealing) assortment of sexual practices, perversions, and deviations. One of de Sade's goals was to record in literature every known perversion, as well as perhaps inventing a few new ones. His ambitions went beyond producing an encyclopedia of pornography, however; he also aspired to be a philosopher. In his novels, the characters have long philosophical discourses in between the carnal acts. The result was a body of philosophical work that is, if somewhat less systematic and elegant than what Kant or Hegel produced, much livelier than theirs.

Along the way, de Sade's characters give a wide assortment of philosophical justifications for and reflections on their deviant sexual practices. One memorable point that he proposed on several occasions concerns why it is more satisfying to whip or flagellate a partner than to have simple intercourse with her.[67] With flagellation, one is more certain that her responses are sincere. The most fervent caresses may elicit a moan of pleasure that is faked, but the moans elicited by a fervent whipping are presumably sincere and believable.

This explanation for the supposed superiority of whipping over intercourse is based on an assumption that one's main goal is to elicit a sincere emotional response. If this is not the goal, then the argument becomes irrelevant. Still, there is something to it, at least to the extent that people do desire genuine emotion from their sexual partners. Indeed, even today, some people who have presumably never read de Sade use a version of the same argument in articulating their preference for certain types of pornography. In spanking films, one can believe that the moans are sincere, whereas the expressions of sexual pleasure in ordinary pornography are often merely acted (and sometimes not very convincingly).

One important pattern of sadistic pleasure, therefore, may be based on the wish to elicit sincere, believable emotional responses from another person. Is there such a wish? It might seem that eliciting emotion would not be much of an end in itself. There is one category of people for whom such responses are extremely important and desirable, however: those with a high need for power.

The need for power is essentially the motivation to have an impact on other people.[68] Power, intimacy, and achievement were the three main motives that garnered the attention of researchers during the glory days of motive psychology. Achievement involves the wish to do better and succeed at tasks. Intimacy involves forming close emotional connections with other people, based on mutual understanding and caring. Power refers to having an impact on other people, for better or worse. Each motive has its own hell. The achievement seeker is miserable when he or she fails at a task. The intimacy seeker is miserable when he or she is unable to form a close, positive connection with one or two other people. The power seeker is miserable when he or she fails to have a strong effect on people. To be ignored, to be treated as irrelevant, to believe that one's own presence and actions make hardly any difference in what others do—these are the experiences that upset and frustrate people who have a high need for power.

Thus, power is a matter of eliciting responses from others. Of course, power may be sought as a means to an end, such as if someone wants to be elected president to carry out some reform or change. But power is also sought as an end in itself. Powerful people find validation in seeing others change their actions because of them. Power may be used to help or to hurt others, but the goal is to produce an effect. To be powerless is to live among people who go on about their business exactly as they would if you were not there. Rape, sexual harassment, and even children's teasing can also be understood in terms of power motivation.

Power is thus an interpersonal motive, not a solitary pursuit. As the political scientist Hans Morgenthau argued in a famous essay, power and love may spring from the same root of loneliness.[69] Love seeks to unite people by dissolving the boundary between them, so that they merge into one. Power likewise merges two into one, but it does so by imposing the will of one on the other. The power seeker wants to connect with others, but the connection is sought in order to have an impact on those people so that they change their actions.

Power is not inherently bad. Indeed, someone might find a very satisfying exercise of power in giving money to people, because the money will make a big difference in their lives. The leaders of large philanthropical organizations, for example, probably do not get much satisfaction of either their achievement or their intimacy needs in their work, because giving money to needy people neither creates close and lasting bonds nor produces direct successes. Such individuals probably do get immense satisfaction in power terms, however, because the money they give makes a huge difference in the recipients' lives. The distribution of charity is a very positive, beneficial, and socially desirable way of exercising power.

Our concern is with the other extreme, in which the lust for power leads to sadism. Here de Sade's theory becomes central. You can be very certain that you are having an impact on someone if you are hurting or harming that person. The groans and tears you elicit are palpable, unmistakable signs that you are having an impact, that that person's life at this moment is quite different from what it would be if you were not there. Through the victim's cries, the power seeker gains validation of his own being, his importance, and his power.

The urge to cause suffering in order to establish one's power over others may well be one of the factors that affect torturers. Although they may start out performing torture as a job, and they often do seem to have achievement goals typical of work in general, they may come to enjoy the victim's suffering because it proves that they are succeeding in having an impact on others. Some torturers speak of how they react to the occasional victim who refuses to scream or cry or confess. These "tough ones" represent a challenge to the torturers, who may set aside their goals of getting information to pursue instead the goal of eliciting a reaction. As one French torturer said, "When we're dealing with those tough ones, the first thing we do is to make them squeal; and sooner or later we manage it." In a revealing comment, he added, "That's already a victory."[70] He said that he and his colleagues gained some satisfaction simply from eliciting a "squeal" of pain from the victim, even if no information was obtained. To them, the victim's tough resistance is a denial of their power, a way of refusing to acknowledge that they are in full control. Silence is a rebuke, a way of denying that one has been affected. The squeal is the victim's admission that the torturers have had an impact on him or her. It proves their power and control.

Another torturer told the following story, as a way of complaining about the effect that the job was having on him.[71] One day he went down to the street to buy a newspaper, but there was a line of people at the kiosk. He was in a bad mood and became annoyed at having to wait. He knew the man at the newsstand, so he cut in front of others and took his paper. One of the other patrons made an angry protest, wanting him to wait his turn. The torturer felt an immediate urge to beat him up. He said nothing, but he thought to himself, "If I had you for a few hours, my fine fellow, you wouldn't look so clever afterwards." Thus, in this incident, his wish to torture the other man was not a mere part of a plan to get his newspaper faster. Rather, he wanted to change the other's attitude toward him, to make the other realize that he was no one to be trifled with.

When Empathy Serves Cruelty

There is one final twist to our analysis of sadism. As we have seen, there is reason to believe that empathy is generally a deterrent to cruelty. Empathy involves knowing what someone else is feeling. It is easy to see why people might be cruel, even unintentionally, if they did not fully appreciate what the victim must feel like.

Yet the most extreme cruelty makes use of empathy. To be seriously, thoroughly cruel, it is necessary to know what the victim is feeling, in order to maximize the suffering. Such knowledge may not correspond to the standard, somewhat careless way that psychologists use the term *empathy*, but it is literally correct. Perhaps it is most precise to say that maximum cruelty makes use of empathy without sympathy. To hurt someone, you must know what that person's sensitivities and vulnerabilities are, without having compassion or pity for the person's suffering. This is perhaps most obvious in the emotional abuse of intimates or family members. Intimates can say the most hurtful things because they know the other person's areas of vulnerability. The empathic bond to the other person becomes an instrument to facilitate cruelty.

Return for a moment to the torturer confronted with one of the "tough ones," a victim who refuses to succumb and submit. No matter how the torturer threatens and beats him, the victim remains silent and refuses to answer any questions. Torturers find such people aggravating.[72] The frustration goes beyond mere personal offense and encompasses the torturer's professional reputation and ambition. He doesn't want to fail to get the confession. Indeed, after he's been beating someone for hours, he may sense that the victim is close to yielding. If the torturer takes a break and lets someone else take over, the new person may get the glory of finally eliciting the confession, even though the way was prepared by the previous torturer's hours of work. So the torturer becomes desperate to break the victim's will before he has to stop, before his shift comes to an end.

Under such pressures, the torturer wants to find some extra measure with which to break the victim's resistance, to make him "squeal" with pain and provide the confession. To be effective, this extra measure must find the prisoner's most vulnerable area and cause exceptional pain there. And to do that, one needs empathy: One needs to understand the prisoner's feelings.

And so it seems that the most fiendishly cruel acts that people inflict on one another derive from an empathic understanding of the other. Empathy, especially when unmixed with sympathy, can be a dangerous tool in the hands of someone who wants to hurt. Of course, it is plausible that any very successful form of torture may be adopted by others simply for pragmatic reasons. The original invention, however, is aided by empathy.

One of the saddest and cruelest forms of torture involves making the main prisoner observe his or her family members being tortured. For example, S. V. Kossior was one of the original Bolshevists, having joined up in 1907. He served the Communist party faithfully through the Revolution, and in 1927 he became a member of the Politburo, the top group of powerful men in the Soviet Union. In the 1930s, however, Stalin wanted to eliminate any potential rivals, including completely loyal people who had never differed with him, and he began to have the Old Guard members arrested. They were pressured to confess to nonexistent crimes against the party and country they had served faithfully all their lives. Some complied, yielding to party discipline or won over by the false promises of leniency that the authorities held out in exchange for confessions. Others, however, refused to make false confessions.

Kossior was in the latter group. Torture was applied, in the form of severe beatings with fists and wooden sticks (usually the legs of a chair), as well as wearing down the prisoner's resistance by preventing sleep and withholding food. Kossior stood up under all of it and refused to sign the false confession. Finally, though, the authorities found a way to break him. They brought in his 16-year-old daughter and beat her up and raped her right in front of him. Kossior broke down and confessed to all sorts of untrue things, such as having been a Polish spy and having taken part in terrorist acts against the Soviet people.[73]

Such indirect forms of cruelty are not limited to professional torturers, of course. They surface occasionally even in modern American households. In an important book on domestic violence, Richard Gelles and Murray Straus[74] related an incident in which an abusive father became angry at his young daughter. To punish her, he grabbed the pet rabbit that she loved and got out a big knife. The little girl sat in the kitchen watching silently while her father methodically killed her rabbit and gutted it. Similar incidents involve killing other pets, destroying favorite toys, or attacking special possessions of the child.

Emotional abuse can be exceptionally cruel, and yet victims find it hard to gain sympathy because they do not have scars or bruises. The success of emotional abuse relies on the abuser's knowing just what to say or do to cause the victim distress. Hence, there may be considerable cruelty in a family without violence, as long as the abuser has enough empathy to know how to hurt the victim. One approach is to know what the victim especially loves or enjoys and then spoil it. Some people wait all week to watch a favorite television program, for example, and may look forward to it with great anticipation. To be mean, all one has to do is wait until the program starts and then insist on watching something else (assuming there is only one television set). Yet even though such an event can produce intense disappointment and unhappiness, especially if it is part of a pattern in which one sees one's partner systematically trying to ruin all one's joys, it will seem trivial to outsiders. Claire Renzetti quoted one such case in her study of domestic cruelty in lesbian relationships. The unhappy woman said that if her lover had beaten her up, her friends would have come forward to support her and help her escape. But not for such minor events: "You can't say, 'My God, she makes me change the channel.' They just don't believe that could be such an awful thing."[75]

Of course, subtlety is not essential to emotional abuse. Such abuse may take the form of a man telling his wife she is stupid, fat, ugly, worthless, or bad. He may criticize her endlessly, saying that she is a poor cook, a lousy lover, a terrible housekeeper, an incompetent mother. He may accuse her of flirting with other men or having affairs, even though at other times he will say she is so unattractive and overweight that she is lucky to have him because no other man would ever want her. Women who abuse their husbands will often demean the man's earning power and virility. In general, such abusers seem to find the special sensitivities of their victims and then make cruel remarks in that area.[76]

Thus, empathy may prevent cruelty in some cases, but it can also serve it. The true sadist is not lacking in empathy—on the contrary, empathy helps the sadist to derive maximum pleasure and inflict the greatest pain.

The discussion of empathy leads back to one of the most basic questions about evil: Are human beings basically good or evil, or some of each, or neither? The phenomenon of sadism points strongly toward the view that some people are basically evil, because they seem to prove that human nature contains the capacity to hurt others for the sheer pleasure of it. Yet, as we have seen, the enjoyment in hurting others is probably not one of the main causes of evil. Rather, sadism seems to enter the picture after evil is already in progress. The fact that empathy can be used to increase cruelty should not diminish the high value of empathy, which after all is responsible for some of humankind's most socially beneficial sentiments and noblest acts. The study of sadism does not justify the conclusion that human beings are basically or partly evil. It would be more accurate to say that human nature contains some built-in mechanisms that can be (and all too often are) adapted and recruited into the service of evil.

PART 3

How They Do It

CHAPTER

8

Crossing the Line: How Evil Starts

The Ku Klux Klan is recognized as one of the most evil organizations ever to flourish in the United States. And flourish it did: At various times, it boasted of having millions of members. Harry Truman joined the Klan (although he soon quit) before he become president. Warren Harding became a member while he was president, and his initiation ceremony was performed right in the White House. As for being evil, the Klan's record speaks for itself. Although the Klan supported some good works and community service, it committed many violent acts, including lynching, whipping, raping, maiming, and murdering people it classified as enemies (such as blacks, carpetbaggers, and Republicans). It damaged or ruined the businesses, reputations, and careers of many others (such as Catholics).[1]

Yet the Klan did not begin as a violent organization. According to Wyn Craig Wade's history of the Klan, it was founded in 1866 by a group of young men who had fought on the losing side in the Civil War and who were simply bored and lonely now that the war was over. Jobs were scarce and there was very little in the way of action or opportunity, given the military occupation of their region and the economic collapse of the Confederacy. Most people were sitting at home with nothing to do, trying to survive. These six young men started a club to pass the time. They came up with the idea of wearing ghostly costumes, made from bedsheets decorated with meaningless occult symbols and conical hats, as a lark. The club had no purpose beyond self-entertaining. Like many other clubs of young men, the organization was designed only to "have fun, make mischief, and play pranks on the public."[2]

Like a fraternity, the Klan put new members through elaborate hazing rituals and enjoyed some good laughs at their expense. These amusements were not enough to keep the organization going, however, possibly because there were not enough initiation ceremonies to take up all their time. And so the young men hit upon the idea of playing their pranks on outsiders, especially black people, most of whom were recently freed slaves with little education and little familiarity with such humor. Early Klan stories described with great hilarity how the members would pretend to be ghosts or spooks and thereby frighten the gullible, unsuspecting black citizens. For example, a member might wear his white sheet over his head and put a phony head on top. At night he would approach a former slave and then pretend to remove his own head, handing it to the black man and asking him to hold it for a while. Later, the club members would sit around over drinks and laugh about how that silly black man ran off in fright from a ghost who could detach his own head.

In retrospect, we can see a malicious aspect to such pranks, and perhaps this maliciousness was even apparent at the time to thoughtful, sensitive individuals. Yet these pranks may have seemed quite harmless to the less morally sensitive fun-lovers. Practical jokers are not Satans. Even today, there are plenty of innocent and friendly pranks that are based on throwing a scare into someone, and what these first Klansmen did was not so different from the modern rituals of Halloween and April Fool's Day, at least in their own estimate and among their friends.

How did the Klan progress from a group of pranksters to perpetrators of murder, rape, and violent assault? Playing pranks was neither illegal nor immoral; some line was crossed when the pranks turned harmful and violent.

The transition probably occurred something like this. The freed slaves may have been superstitious and lacking in formal education, but they were not stupid, and they probably soon came to know that such nocturnal encounters with these apparent ghosts were actually pranks by living people. Soon the pranksters would find that their intended targets failed to provide a satisfactory amusement. Instead of running off into the woods shrieking in fright, a mark might simply say he did not want to play their games. To elicit the fear they had sought, they might then do something more threatening.

One can well imagine a group of late-adolescent white males dressing up in goblin costumes and anticipating how much fun it would be to scare some ignorant blacks—and then finding out that the blacks were not scared, that they had learned about these pranks, and that they told the young men to grow up and quit these childish games. The fun was spoiled, and the hoped-for pleasure of frightening their intended victims was lost. They themselves had been made to look foolish (in other words, their egos suffered a blow), instead of their intended victims. To recapture this pleasure, they did something violent, which did finally frighten the victims. Perhaps they merely brandished a gun or knife. The point is, they did what was necessary to cause fear in their targets. Probably they knew at this point that violence is morally more objectionable than playing pranks, but then they were provoked by the insulting tone the blacks took in response to their pranks when they were just pursuing innocent fun. If a morally sensitive person were to reproach them, they could honestly say that it was all harmless fun. But they had actually threatened violence: a line had been crossed.

Alternatively, maybe that decisive line was crossed when they chose a target for some particular reason. Threatened egotism, which we have seen is a powerful cause of violence, could well have helped motivate such young men to strike out at black citizens. There is little denying that the former Confederate soldiers felt that their privileged place in the world was in jeopardy. Their army had been defeated, their would-be nation dissolved and occupied, their honor lost, their social status undermined. A black man who seemed to them too eager to assert his new legal equality to whites might be chosen as a target of a prank; the Klansmen might think that scaring him would be a good way to intimidate him. Imagine having your former slaves suddenly be your equals! It is difficult to appreciate today how unsettling that was, because today we believe that slavery is wrong. The new equality of former slaves was probably close to unthinkable to many members of the old southern ruling class.

The Klansmen might approach such an ambitious fellow some night and try to frighten him, if not with their ghostly costumes, then by their weapons and menacing attitude. In such a situation, if his response failed to satisfy their expectations, someone might well strike him to drive the lesson home. Even if no one was seriously hurt, the seeds of later Klan violence would already be apparent: A victim was targeted for political reasons, and force was used to intimidate him.

These scenes are speculations and reconstructions, not proven facts, but they do offer a possible bridge between the two well-documented versions of the Klan that have been established: the harmless club of young men looking for amusement, and the organization that used brutal violence to prevent black citizens from enjoying their legal and moral rights. The first founders of the Klan were not working from some vision of a large organization of white people who would terrorize, injure, and kill innocent black (and white) victims throughout the South and Midwest; in fact, I suspect those first few young men would have been aghast at such an idea. They just wanted to make mischief and ease that ubiquitous curse of youth: boredom. Somehow, though, the pranks subtly began to turn mean. From that point, the step to systematic cruelty was perhaps just a matter of degree.

The question "What causes evil?" has to have at least a three-part answer. First, it is necessary to describe the root causes. Second, one must explain the immediate, precipitating causes. Third, it is vital to understand what escalates the initial deed into cruelty or oppression. The previous four chapters examined the root causes. This chapter will examine how perpetrators get started, and the next will examine the processes of escalation.

Evil can be compared to a plant or tree that requires both the planting of a seed and a set of favorable conditions for growth. If either the seed or the conducive environment is lacking, there will be no tree. As we will see in Chapter 9, the factors that help evil to grow are quite powerful, which implies that the initial seed does not have to be anything spectacular. Great evil can come from small, unremarkable, seemingly innocent beginnings. Contrary to the myth of pure evil, one does not have to be at all evil to cross the line. Once one has done so, there are powerful forces that sweep one along into greater acts of cruelty, violence, or oppression.

Blurring the Line: Ambiguity, Uncertainty, Misinformation

Henry II of England was irritated when he heard from others (in distorted versions) how his former friend and helper, Thomas à Becket, now Archbishop of Canterbury, was defying the king's will and excommunicating the archbishop's own personal enemies (including some of the king's men). Henry is said to have remarked, "The man ate my bread and mocks my favors. He trampled on the whole royal family. What disloyal cowards do I have in my court, that not one will free me of this lowborn priest?"[3] Several of the king's barons took this as a sign of a royal wish for them to murder the archbishop, and they did.

After the fact, King Henry did penance, condemned the murder, and began to praise the memory of "the irreplaceable Saint Thomas."[4] Thus, he acted as if he had not intended for his men to murder the archbishop. Whether *he* had intended the murder is much harder to say. The point is that the ambiguity of his remarks left ample room for sinister interpretations by others, and so some of his men acted on those interpretations.

If evil begins when someone crosses a moral line, then it may be promoted by anything that tends to make the line fuzzy or unclear, including ambiguity and misinformation. When the line between right and wrong is clear, most people will consistently do what is right. They cross the line into doing wrong most readily when they cannot even see for certain that the line is there.

The role of ambiguity does not end with the initial action; indeed, as we will see shortly, it is centrally involved in the escalation of evil and violence. Still, ambiguity is often a decisive factor in getting someone started in immoral or cruel acts. This fact is recognized by powerful people who want others to carry out their own malicious wishes. It is easier for people in power to give commands that lead to harm if they are ambiguous, because the authorities can later deny that they intended those outcomes. They can repudiate the evil that their words have caused, as Henry did. It is hard to know for certain whether Henry really intended to bring about the murder of the archbishop, but if he did, he certainly went about it very effectively. He was able to maintain his own apparent innocence and even bemoan the violent act, all the while benefiting from it.

Ambiguous, uncertain commands have continued to play a role in evil down to our own time. It is apparent that Lieutenant Calley and the men who directed the famous massacre at My Lai in Vietnam believed they were following orders, although their superiors have consistently denied that they issued any such commands. The initial commands from Lieutenant Colonel Barker apparently implied but did not specifically say that the villages in the area were to be obliterated. The initial ambiguity was retained and passed along as the orders were transmitted down through the chain of command, although at some point a literal and drastic interpretation was made to the effect that the mission involved shooting the villagers en masse.[5]

One crucial aspect of ambiguity is that it enables people to justify and rationalize their actions. Many laboratory experiments have been done to study aggression, but rarely has it been made clear to the individual participant that he (or, less often, she) is being aggressive. A subject might be asked to deliver painful electric shocks to someone else, for example, but usually these shocks are described by the researchers as being part of a procedure to help someone else learn (such as by punishing mistakes), as a way of distracting people from another task, or as a way of furnishing helpful data for scientific progress. Subjects in such studies can behave aggressively without facing up to the fact that that is what they are doing, because the situation offers them ready-made alternative ways of thinking about their actions. Chapter 10 will look much more closely at how people rationalize and justify their violent actions. For now, the important point is that ambiguity can make such rationalizations easier and thereby weaken some of the inner restraints against aggression.

No doubt, part of what made John Dean's memoir *Blind Ambition* a bestseller was its portrayal of how easy it was to cross fuzzy moral boundaries on the path that led to complicity in the Watergate scandal and the fall of the Nixon presidency. As Dean tells it, he started out as merely another bright, ambitious young lawyer who was thrilled to get the job as White House counsel. One of his first assignments was to target a magazine, *Scanlan's Monthly*, that had printed something embarrassing about Vice President Agnew, including the absurd charge that Agnew was scheming to cancel the upcoming presidential election and repeal the Bill of Rights. Dean was told that Nixon was furious at the magazine and wanted to strike back at it. Dean advised against the lawsuit that the president wanted, but the president's second plan (after the lawsuit idea was abandoned) was to get the Internal Revenue Service to investigate the magazine.

Dean was not certain whether it was legal or ethical to do that. The IRS has an official job to do: collecting and correcting tax returns. It is not supposed to be a weapon for the president to use to harass people or groups whom he dislikes. Dean consulted a friend, who was a lawyer as well as one of the president's advisors. The friend told him bluntly, "If the President wants you to turn the IRS loose, then you turn the IRS loose. It's that simple." When Dean said it wasn't necessary, his friend corrected him again: "I'll tell you this, if Richard Nixon thinks it's necessary, you'd better think it's necessary. If you don't, he'll find someone who does."[6] When Dean asked about the legality of such a tactic, his friend said it was legal as far as he was concerned. He said Lyndon Johnson had used such tactics against Nixon's people when he was in power, and it was only fair that Nixon be allowed to do the same. "It's the way the game is played," he said, possibly suggesting that moral scruples such as Dean's were naive and out of place at this high level of power politics.

Dean had a former police detective (now an administrative investigator) working with his office. He mentioned the problem to him, and the man cheerfully said he'd take care of it. He reported back that the magazine was only a few months old and so the IRS had nothing on them, but he had suggested that the IRS investigate the people who produced the magazine: owners, editors, publishers. Nothing came of these investigations, and the magazine went out of business a few months later for reasons that had nothing to do with its enemies in the White House. Still, Dean was able to report that he had checked into the possibility of an IRS investigation, as he had been instructed to do, and that it had yielded little; but on his own initiative, he had taken the further step of having the private citizens who produced the magazine investigated, too. Thus, he had performed his duties perfectly well. And yet, "Within a month of coming to the White House, I had crossed an ethical line."[7] His objections to using the IRS to harass the president's enemies had all been technical and pragmatic, and he now took credit for an operation that had been an easy success—but had compromised him both legally and morally.

Another way of helping people cross the line into committing violence is to keep them in ignorance of what they are doing for as long as possible. When people do not know what they are doing, they have no basis for objecting to it. This tactic can work even if the deeds themselves will be clearly objectionable. If the instructions become clear only moments before the deed is to be done, then there is minimal time or opportunity for protest.

One of the best examples of this tactic was provided in Browning's account of how German policemen became participants in the mass murders of Polish Jews during World War II. The Germans involved were mostly middle-aged, working-class policemen who were conscripted and sent into action in Poland as "Order Police" (as in "law and order"), officially just to perform standard police duties in the conquered territory. They were not given specific instructions until the last minute. There had been occasional, vague comments about "special actions" and such things, but nothing was said that clearly indicated committing atrocities.

The naked truth of the matter—that their duty was going to include rounding up and shooting civilians—was not revealed until one day at 6 A.M., when the major assembled the battalion and explained that those were the regrettable orders to be carried out at once. Had they been told a month in advance that they would be shooting innocent, helpless civilians, they might perhaps have objected, but it is hard to leap onto a moral high horse in response to a blind surprise at six in the morning when everybody is preparing to do a tough job. Of course, and ironically, the victims were kept in the dark in the same way. Apparently, the men who ran the show had learned that the most effective way to get one group of people to kill another, in an orderly and cooperative fashion, was to avoid giving either side any advance notice.

Keeping people in the dark is thus one form of the more general pattern of manipulating ambiguity and misunderstanding to promote evil. An example of how simple misunderstandings can lead to violence (although in this case, fortunately, no one was hurt) was provided in another recent history of the Ku Klux Klan.[8] At one of the Klan rallies in Indiana in the heyday of the organization there (the 1920s), one of the men was making a speech about the dangers of Catholicism, and he repeated the fairly standard assertion that the Pope was plotting to take over the United States. To drive home the point, he added the presumably hypothetical suggestion that the Pope might be on the train from Manchester (Indiana) tomorrow, the implication being that the dastardly pontiff was surveying the lands he expected soon to rule. Unfortunately, the speaker made his point so vividly that it was much repeated by the audience, and it quickly lost its hypothetical character.

The next day, about a thousand people were there to meet the train from Manchester. As it turned out, it was mostly a freight train, having only one passenger car with a single occupant. That unfortunate man, actually a carpet salesman headed for Chicago, was pulled off the train and found himself urgently trying to convince the potential mob that he was not the Pope. Once proved innocent, perhaps aided by his suitcase full of carpet samples, he escaped unscathed and was permitted to resume his journey on a later train.

In the absence of reliable information, people often resort to rumor and guesswork—and the chance for false information to dictate events increases. Suppose, for example, that Henry II had not really intended to have Thomas Becket killed. His remarks might have been misquoted, and the murder would have been basically a mistake. Today, with effective communications and news media, it is hard to appreciate fully how uncertain and misinformed people can be. One contemporary example is violent youth gangs, because the information about events that concern them does not come fully reported on television or documented with computer printouts. Jankowski's book on such gangs contained plenty of incidents in which rumors about other gangs led to violent reprisals that were misdirected or wholly inappropriate. Some of these were simple cases of mistaken identity, in which a crime or offense had been committed and the wrong person was identified and targeted, usually without having the chance to prove his innocence. These actions often led to disasters for the gang, because to go around attacking innocent people is a sure way to make enemies and get into trouble with one's own community, the police, and rival gangs.

Once You've Accepted the Premise . . .

People often enjoy the exercise of asking "What would I do in that situation?" with regard to moral dilemmas. They ask themselves whether they would go along with orders to torture a dangerous enemy, shoot prisoners, or the like. As I have said, people tend to conclude that they would not commit such acts, but when the circumstance actually arises, most people do go along. Something is wrong with the way people play these hypothetical games.

One factor is that the luxury of reflection allows people to contemplate details and to see the choice framed in stark moral terms, on a high level of moral principle. In reality, however, people often find themselves unexpectedly thrust into situations that require them to make these highly consequential decisions. Moreover, they do not always recognize the issue as a great moral test of character at that crucial moment. Other factors and concerns are often present. If you were an American soldier in the Vietnam War, would you shoot civilians on mere suspicion that they were aiding the enemy? Probably you would say, of course not—from the vantage point of time and distance, with leisure to reflect, and with a clear perception that a moral dilemma is involved. Many soldiers might have to face the same decision under circumstances that were far less ideal. They might have been tired, under stress, hung over, disoriented by drugs, afraid for their lives, and badly upset about having seen a close friend killed by villagers recently. The moral issue of respecting civilian innocence until guilt is proved may have been obscured by other factors, such as a pragmatic concern with one's own survival or a desire for revenge.

Even when people do object, however, they often avoid phrasing their objection in moral terms. Instead, they focus on a lower level objection. Such an objection can trap the person into subsequent compliance. To fail to make the objection on the highest level the first time is often to implicitly accept the broad assumptions. Thus, in Dean's account of the Nixon White House, the president wanted to use the apparatus of government to harass and punish a magazine he detested. Dean phrased his objections in practical terms: A lawsuit was too risky, and the magazine was too new to have a record at the IRS. He did not tell the president or even the superiors who passed him the president's orders that what was being proposed was illegal and immoral. This pragmatic approach worked for him at first but gradually got him implicated in the crimes of the Watergate cover-up, which ultimately cost him his job and landed him in prison.

Several writers have made this point about the vexing question of why the victims of the Holocaust cooperated so extensively and fatally in their own destruction. From our enlightened perspective today, we can see that the victims should have refused very early in the process. Had no Jews cooperated with the authorities, such as by showing up at the train station ready for deportation or by walking in an orderly fashion to the killing sites, the killings would have been much more difficult to carry out and would not have resulted in anywhere near the same body count. When faced with the demands to comply, however, people sought to find an objection that would be accepted as valid by the perpetrators. Instead of saying, "No, it is wrong to deport me to a camp, because it is wrong to deport anyone, and I refuse to comply," they said, "I cannot go now because I am working on such-and-such a job that is important to the war effort," or "I am caring for an aging mother." Such objections seem safe because they do not offend the authorities in the same way as saying "What you are doing is criminal and wrong" would do. They seem to be phrased in the way most likely to persuade the authorities to agree with your position. To get the authorities to agree, you have to communicate on the basis of *their* assumptions.

Yet such excuses implicitly accept the premise. You say you cannot go to the camps because you need to care for your mother; the authorities respond by arranging for your mother to go to the camps, too. At this point, you cannot easily say, "The entire enterprise is wrong," because if you really believed that, you would presumably have said that at first and not wasted time on specific excuses. The excuse about caring for your mother implicitly acknowledges that some people can legitimately be sent to the camps, and you are merely seeking an exception from the rules that you otherwise accept. As a result, once the objection was handled, the victims tended to go along, hoping to find another valid excuse or exemption at a later stage. When they were standing in line for death, naked and shorn of hair and helpless, it was too late to raise broad philosophical objections to the entire enterprise. One should have brought them up long ago.

Similar processes operate on perpetrators. The sergeant tells you to shoot the Vietnamese prisoners. You know it is generally against the rules of war to kill prisoners, but obviously this war is different, and these prisoners may have killed some of your buddies. Maybe they committed some other crimes that your superiors know about and you do not. In any case, as a nineteen-year-old high school graduate, you are not about to enter into a moral debate with your superiors. Instead, you think frantically of the best excuse you can find: You do not have the right kind of weapon or ammunition, or you have been temporarily assigned another duty. These excuses try to appeal to the person giving the order by invoking some principle that he will accept.

In seeking to make such excuses, however, you implicitly accept the common assumptions behind his order. You do not say that it is absolutely wrong to shoot prisoners. Instead, you merely say that you cannot perform that duty right now. But this form of excuse-making traps you. Obviously, if you thought it was always wrong to shoot prisoners, you would not bother with making a specific excuse. If you would never shoot prisoners under any circumstances, it doesn't matter whether you have the right kind of weapon or not. By making the excuse, you imply that you would shoot the prisoners if only you had the correct ammunition. You use the excuse because you think it will get you off the hook at the moment and at least buy time, but in the long run it ropes you into accepting the evil assumption. Next week, when the sergeant gives you the same order and brings you the right weapon, you have no basis for objecting again.

There seems to be a sort of social trap at work in these situations. When confronted with the demand to do something that is possibly immoral, people usually look for a reason to object. And for obvious reasons, they don't tend to object by saying that the entire authority structure (and its uniformed troops with all those guns) is doing something horribly, morally repugnant. They look for objections that will not require such a radical breach, or they simply look for the reason they think will work best. In either case, the eventual effect is to get them caught up in discussing and considering the problem on the terms of the authorities who are initiating the evil, which is likely to be a low level of practical procedures rather than a high level of moral principle. And once one has abandoned the high level of moral principle and thus implicitly accepted the authorities' broad assumptions, one's latitude for returning to it later is reduced. Even if one's excuse is accepted this time, one will probably have to go along next time.

Why Isn't There *More* Evil?

Before going any further, let us consider a serious problem that plagues most theories about evil or violence: Why isn't there more of it? In Part I, I explained that—contrary to the myth of pure evil—very few violent people think of their actions as evil or are deliberately devoted to inflicting harm as an end in itself. This raised the question of why there is so much violence in the world. Part II sought to answer that question by explaining the root causes of evil, which include greed, lust, ambition, egotism, idealism, and perhaps a touch of sadism. There are plenty of reasons for evil to exist.

Yet maybe these explanations were too effective. After all, greed, lust, ambition, and egotism are extremely common, and idealism is fairly widespread, too. If all these cause evil, why isn't there more evil?

Many theories about evil suffer from this problem: They point to some cause that is so common that it seems as though there should be a great deal more violence or oppression than there is. For example, it is almost a truism that poverty breeds crime, and poor people are certainly more likely than rich people to commit crimes. But most poor people do not commit crimes. So there is a serious flaw in the theory that poverty causes crime: Usually poverty doesn't cause crime. Likewise, it is now well established that abused children are more likely than others to grow up and become abusive parents themselves, so one might easily conclude that victimization causes abuse—but most abused children do not become abusers. Why not?

Violence Starts When Self-Control Stops

Evil or violent tendencies are usually met with strong restraining forces, most of which can be conveniently categorized as self-control. Greed, ambition, egotism, and the rest may be powerful factors that promote evil, but they can be met with equally powerful inner restraints.

The immediate, proximal cause of violence is the collapse of these inner restraining forces. This point is crucial, because it means that many of our efforts to understand violence are looking at the question the wrong way. To produce violence, it is not necessary to promote it actively. All that is necessary is to stop restraining or preventing it. Once the restraints are removed, there are plenty of reasons for people to strike out at each other.

Some experts have begun to recognize this fact. In 1990, *A General Theory of Crime*, by Gottfredson and Hirschi, two eminent criminologists, appeared.[9] The general theory that they proposed was essentially one of low self-control: Most crimes are the result of a lack of inner discipline and restraint.

To flesh out their theory, Gottfredson and Hirschi noted that criminal acts are quick and easy ways of getting what one wants. The best way to get economic security is probably by pursuing a long and thorough education and then working steadily at some professional job for years. But that takes a great deal of patience, hard work, acquisition of skills, and other forms of self-control. In contrast, it takes no skills and minimal time to point a gun at someone on the street and demand his or her cash. Crime is marked by the short-term focus and simplicity that are common to people who lack self-control. It also furnishes excitement and thrills, which is another feature that appeals to such people.

In support of their theory, Gottfredson and Hirschi presented a great deal of evidence about people who commit crimes. One of the most compelling facts is that criminals do not tend to be ordinary citizens who resemble everyone else in most respects except for having an illegal specialization. Rather, they show a lack of self-control in many other areas of their lives, both legal and illegal. Criminals are more likely than other people to smoke and drink (to excess), to abuse drugs, to have impulsive sex, to become involved in unwanted pregnancies, to have unstable marriages, to get into petty fights, to be involved in automobile accidents, and so on. When they do make a large sum of money from some crime, they tend to blow it in short order, as opposed to, say, investing it in interest-bearing mutual funds. Moreover, criminals usually do not specialize in one type of crime. Instead, they tend to commit many different kinds of crimes, depending on whatever opportunity presents itself. There is a whole criminal life-style, marked by the search for quick, easy gains and the easy yielding to temptations.

Thus, people whose inner restraints are relatively weak are the ones most likely to commit crimes. It is not that criminals' desires differ greatly from everyone else's: money, sex, pleasure, and a feeling of superiority. Good citizens want those things and know that violent or illegal means might bring them, at least in the short run, but they have inner restraints that prevent them from resorting to criminal means to get them. For someone who lacks self-control, however, violent and illegal means may seem like the most attractive way to get them.

Conflicting Obligations

Why, then, does self-control sometimes fail to prevent violence? One common problem arises when there are conflicting, inconsistent, or ambiguous obligations. Even someone with an exceptionally strong capacity for self-discipline will find it difficult to exercise that capacity in a situation marked by such a conflict. When the rules contradict each other, it is hard to do the right thing, and so it becomes far easier to do something that may turn out in the long run to have been wrong.[10]

Moral dilemmas based on conflicting obligations have been debated for hundreds, probably even thousands, of years. During the Middle Ages, such a dilemma concerned the vassal's obligation to join his lord in military action. This duty was widely recognized and very strongly supported. When the lord went to war, it was the sacred duty of his vassals to help him out. But what was the vassal to do when the lord initiated an unjust or wrongful war? Disobedience and disloyalty were crimes (and sins); but then again, it was surely wrong to hurt or kill innocent people. People in the medieval times believed strongly that only one side in a war (at most) could be in the right, and so all actions by the other side were wrong and sinful.

A dramatic illustration of such a dilemma involved Richard the Lion-Hearted, the famous crusading king of England who was immortalized by his portrayal in the Robin Hood stories. Before he was king, however, he actually fought in a war against England (and against his own father, who was king at the time). Richard happened to be the lord of some lands in southern France, and he lived there as a vassal of the French king. When France and England went to war, his duty to his French lord superseded any obligation to his father (or to the nation whose ruler he was to become), and so he brought his troops into battle on the French side.

Another form of this dilemma is the difficult choice faced by a soldier who is given orders to commit actions that may be evil. I say "may be evil" because if the commanded actions are clearly, definitely evil, then perhaps the dilemma is resolved: One should not perform evil actions. But things are not usually so clear. It is wrong to hurt or kill people, and indeed the Ten Commandments specifically prohibit killing, but all wars involve killing, of necessity. Soldiers learn early on that ethical principles are generally limited by situations. They also learn that people in their position do not always have all the relevant information. Thus, a command to shoot a prisoner may seem morally wrong; but what if the prisoner can inform the enemy of your position and thus bring death to your entire unit? What if the prisoner is a terrorist who has illegally killed dozens of innocent people or committed other capital crimes? What if the enemy is killing prisoners, including one of your buddies who had saved your life? No doubt, many people would argue that killing prisoners is still wrong despite such circumstances; but these and similar circumstances have sometimes made the injunction against killing prisoners a little less certain.

The great Christian thinker St. Augustine concluded that soldiers do have an ultimate obligation to carry out all commands, wicked or not. Augustine recognized the moral dilemma of the soldier who receives unjust commands as an especially difficult one, but he finally concluded that the obligation to obey orders given by proper authorities overrides other obligations. He decided that soldiers could not be held responsible for their actions, as long as those actions were carried out under orders. Later medieval thought upheld Augustine's conclusion.[11] Your Christian duty was to carry out your orders even if they seemed wrong or evil to you.

It is difficult for modern Americans to appreciate this view, for our society has largely come to the opposite conclusion. To say "I was only following orders" has become almost the prototype of an inadequate excuse. But this view resulted from the retrospective outcry against the Holocaust, the My Lai massacre, and similar events, which forced modern citizens to recognize how important it is to reject any justifications for participating in such acts, including following orders. Earlier eras came to the opposite conclusion. No doubt St. Augustine would have been shocked by the actions of Calley or Eichmann, but he might well have accepted their self-justifications based on the need to obey commands. St. Augustine would have voted to acquit them.

The point is not to exonerate the perpetrators of atrocities but rather to emphasize the difficulty of doing the right thing when there are conflicting obligations. Obedience has long been recognized as an important and far-reaching obligation. Our modern American attitude toward obedience and authority is probably at the far extreme of skepticism, and even so the injunction to obey orders is compelling. Again, I am not arguing that people ought to obey illegal or immoral commands. The point is that the obligation to obey may come into conflict with other obligations, and there is no clear or universal conclusion about which obligation should prevail. Conflicting moral obligations pose a fundamentally unsolvable dilemma.

Moral conflict was another of the neglected aspects of Stanley Milgram's obedience studies, in which ordinary people complied with instructions to deliver severe electric shocks to another person. Those who hesitated or objected were told that they must continue giving shocks, and most of them did so, even up to levels that could have proved fatal to the victim.

The people who took part in those experiments were typically neither sadistic nor indifferent. Many of them exhibited severe signs of inner conflict, including distress and agitation. Their hands shook, they began to sweat, and their voices became shaky. Often Milgram's studies are cited as evidence that people will willingly perform immoral actions out of mindless respect for authority; but if that were the case, one would not have expected so many signs of inner struggle. In my view, such interpretations ignore the moral obligation of obedience. To follow the clear instructions of a legitimate authority figure is an obligation that is learned along with the very first moral lessons about right and wrong that parents teach their children. From the thoughtful standpoint of sophisticated ethical philosophy, one might conclude that the moral obligation to show concern for the welfare of others should take precedence over obedience to authority, but ordinary people caught in a moral conflict may not have the time for such reflections. The automatic response is to do what you're told.

There are several other factors that contribute to the obedience pattern. First, most people probably learn very early in life that obedience should take precedence over one's own doubts. Doubt and reluctance are nearly always bound up with obedience; after all, if you wanted to do something anyway, there would be no need for somebody to command you to do it. Parents teach children that the obligation to obey takes precedence over what they may want to do. Again, upon reflection, one should conclude that there is a fine distinction between reluctance based on selfish inclinations and reluctance based on a principled moral objection; but this is not a distinction that usually occupies the attention of an ordinary person caught in a moral dilemma. The habit of setting aside one's reluctance to follow orders is instilled early (and more strongly in most other cultures in the history of the world than in our own).

Second, even if the person can think through the decision according to abstract moral principles, the choice is often between a possible wrong and a definite wrong—in which case, it may seem rational and sensible to do the possible wrong rather than the definite wrong. Children, soldiers, and other subordinates often do not have enough information to make a fully informed evaluation of all the moral niceties surrounding an order they have been given. The order may seen immoral, but perhaps there are factors they do not understand or appreciate. Thus, although it may seem wrong to carry out a particular order, it is hard to be certain.

In contrast, disobedience is clearly and definitely wrong, per se. The moral obligation to obey is implicit in the very concept of command. When the colonel commands you to sweep the floor or make your bed or stand over there, you are supposed to obey, which is why a command alone is sufficient (as opposed to requiring the colonel to try to persuade or induce you to sweep the floor). If you disobey, you can be charged and punished, and the court-martial is not likely to investigate whether the floor needed sweeping or whether you were satisfied with the colonel's reason for giving the order. Every child whose parent has answered "Because I said so, that's why!" will recognize the same moral premise: Disobeying the commands of legitimate, recognized authority figures is wrong.

Hence, a soldier who might be moved to question a command on moral grounds faces a dilemma, because both obeying and not obeying carry moral risks. Either course of action may be wrong, but one course is more surely wrong than the other. Moreover, disobeying the command puts the moral burden of proof squarely on you. Obeying might turn out to be wrong, but the burden of proof (and seemingly of responsibility) is not on you, at least not just then.

A third and related factor is the wrongness of second-guessing one's superiors. This factor is also difficult for modern Americans to appreciate. Those of us who grew up in the 1960s and 1970s learned to challenge and question authority as a matter of course. From iconoclastic theories to the impeachment of a president, there was a strong pattern of attacking established authority. In the history of the world, however, it has been far more common to hold the attitude that the people in authority have superior knowledge, understanding, and virtue, and that it would be absurd and pretentious—not to mention insulting and treasonous—for a lesser person to question them.

Here and Now

Another factor that reduces self-control and fosters the crossing of moral boundaries is a certain kind of mental state. This state is marked by a very concrete, narrow, rigid way of thinking, with the focus on the here and now, on the details of what one is doing. It is the state that characterizes someone who is fully absorbed in working with tools or playing a video game. One does not pause to reflect on broader implications or grand principles or events far removed in time (past or future).

I will have more to say about this mental state in Chapter 10 (Dealing with Guilt), because people do seek out this state to avoid emotions. For now, the relevant point is that this state may blind people to the crossing of a moral line. It may seem ironic to suggest that people can pay so much attention to what they are doing that they do not fully comprehend what their actions mean, but that is precisely what happens. By attending to the *how*, they may fail to think about the *why*—and especially the *why not*. To perceive that one is crossing a moral boundary into something that may be wrong, it is necessary to step back from what one is doing and think about one's actions in the context of broad moral principles. Actions do not come labeled right and wrong, and they only acquire those moral qualities when evaluated from the perspective of meaningful principles. If one remains focused on the acts themselves, one may scarcely notice their moral aspect.

Put another way, self-control requires the person to see beyond the immediate situation. The term *transcendence* is commonly used to refer to this mental activity of perceiving the broader implications of current events. Thus, if you are hungry and you are offered some tasty food, you eat it. Self-control requires stopping this natural response and saying to yourself that eating this food would violate your diet and thwart your attempts to look appealing in a swim suit next summer. Or, as another example, it is normal and natural to take a rest when one is tired of working, but self-discipline can override that response if one needs to meet a deadline or prepare for a test.

There is a tendency for people to shift to low levels of meaningful thought while carrying out morally problematic, dangerous acts. In the words of John Douglas, one of the FBI experts on serial killers, "Crime is a moral problem. It can only be resolved on a moral level."[12] The other side of that coin is that low-level thinking is amoral.

A smattering of evidence suggests that such concrete, here-and-now mental states facilitate crime and violence. One relevant sign is that when participants in major killing actions speak about what they did, they generally focus on techniques. This is true even when they are not trying to evade moral responsibility or defend themselves. It was probably the way they thought about their activities while they were doing them. Focusing attention on how to do something forces the mind to stay at a low level of meaningful thought, concerned with practical details rather than broad implications.[13] Thus, Nazis who discuss their actions during the Holocaust tend to emphasize the practical and logistical problems, which were often quite formidable. Likewise, a recent television special by Oprah Winfrey on child abuse showed several men describing the sexual molestation of children, and again their explanations focused on just how one carries it out: first gaining the child's trust, then intimidating the child into remaining silent, and so forth.

We have seen previously that the notebooks of self-criticism kept by Khmer Rouge torturers in the notorious Tuol Sleng prison focused on technique.[14] Self-criticism is an important part of Communist practice. It obviously holds the potential for making people face up to their misdeeds and acknowledge the need to change themselves to become better citizens. Yet what these torturers criticized themselves for was ineffective torture techniques: sloppiness, deviating from standard procedures, failing to keep pencils sharpened, or causing the prisoner to die before a full confession was obtained.

Was this a defense? A disingenuous practice of criticizing minor faults to shift attention away from heinous actions? Possibly. But it is also necessary to recognize that these individuals were not encouraged by the Communist authorities to develop serious moral objections to the goals of the regime. Had they said, "Torturing someone is inhumane and unethical," it is doubtful that their self-criticism would have been approved. Focusing on the technical failures and shortcomings in their job performance enabled them to perform more effectively.

Emotional Distress

Another factor that may make it easier to cross the line is emotional distress. Emotion by itself does not produce evil, but in combination with several of the factors we have already noted, it can help to facilitate evil. In particular, it is well established that emotional distress breaks down self-control in many spheres. When people are upset, they say or do things that they would ordinarily hold back from saying or doing and that they may regret later.

Emotional distress is unpleasant, and people want to escape from it. Few people like to wallow in unpleasant feelings indefinitely; most will exert themselves to find some way to feel better. These efforts may even involve taking some chances or trying various activities that might hold the chance of improving one's mood. All of this exertion is draining, and it weakens the capacity for self-control. When there is a violent impulse, the person is less able to restrain it.

Also, emotions can cause something akin to the here-and-now mental state I just described. When in an emotional state, people are often thoroughly wrapped up in what they are doing and feeling, and so they do not see beyond the immediate situation to broader issues, principles, and implications. There is a fair amount of evidence that when people are upset—that is, during an emotional state marked by unpleasantness and high arousal—they do not think things through adequately before acting. Instead, they seem to act on the first impulse or option that strikes them in a positive way.[15] The emotion seems to narrow their focus to their own immediate concerns, and they do not consider all the alternatives or other outcomes. Thus, one experiment showed that when people are under stress, they do not look at all the answers on a multiple-choice test; they simply take the first one that looks right. In other studies, people who were emotionally distressed tended to take stupid, costly risks because they were drawn to the potential for gaining something good—and they ignored the risk of having something bad happen.

Thus, emotion weakens one's self-control and other defenses. Does it also increase aggressive impulses? Undoubtedly, some emotions do. Anger and frustration seem to give rise to the urge to hit someone or something, or to lash out in some other way. Indeed, it seems likely that the natural emotional response of rage was instilled in the human psyche by evolution as a way of prompting people to fight when necessary. True, not all anger or frustration leads to aggression, but aggressive responses are far more common when people are in such emotional states. In a sense, that is what the emotion of anger is: The feeling of an aggressive impulse. Emotions predispose people toward action, and anger involves the potential action of attacking or defending.[16]

Alcohol and Evil

Alcohol may also contribute to violence in a variety of ways. It is well established that many, perhaps most, violent crimes are committed by people who are under the influence of alcohol. Some other drugs (such as crack cocaine) may have similar effects, although research with such drugs is sparse, vague, and inconclusive compared to the large body of evidence about alcohol.[17]

Does alcohol lead to aggressive impulses? The answer appears to be no. A well-known compilation of the research on alcohol concluded that alcohol by itself does not produce wild behavior.[18] Instead, alcohol produces wild behavior only when the person under its influence has some sort of inner conflict. If you feel like insulting your boss but normally hold back because doing so would be bad for your career, alcohol may make you more willing to express the insult. But if you like your boss and have no desire to insult him, alcohol will not cause you to do so. Alcohol seems to reduce self-control and thereby free impulses that are already there. It does not create new impulses or desires.

The effect of alcohol on aggression has been confirmed by laboratory studies. In one, college students took turns delivering electric shocks to one another. Some of them had been given alcohol to drink before the experiment, while others remained sober. Alcohol did not uniformly increase the level or severity of shocks that people gave. It did, however, increase the severity of retaliation. That is, if the other person was nice to you, you held back on shocking him, regardless of whether you had had any alcohol or not. If the other person gave you a nasty shock, though, you were more inclined to retaliate by giving him a hefty zap in return—and if you had been drinking, your response was even more extreme and aggressive. Thus, alcohol did not produce aggressive tendencies, but it increased them if they were prompted by the situation.[19]

Alcohol weakens self-control, and this effect is abundantly documented. Alcohol seems to contribute to almost every form of self-control failure, from aggression to gambling, from smoking to emotional outbursts. Like people who are emotionally upset, people who drink cease to think through the implications of their actions. They stop keeping track of what they are doing (indeed, sometimes they cannot remember the next day what they did). They lose the ability to transcend the situation and instead respond to immediate pressures, impulses, or temptations.

The implications for understanding violence are important. It is incorrect to blame violence or aggression on alcohol. Intoxication is at best a contributing factor. Drinking is neither necessary nor sufficient to cause aggression, but it does reduce the inner restraints that normally prevent violence. Alcohol does not create violent impulses; it merely removes the inner blocks that normally stop someone from carrying them out. Alcohol will make violent people act more violently than they would normally.

A Culture of Violence?

Until now, I have emphasized individual factors and causes of violence, but cultures and subcultures undoubtedly shape the actions of individuals, too. There is no question that some cultures have higher levels of violence than others. Indeed, by most measures, modern America is one of the world's most violent cultures. A bad weekend in New York or Washington will produce as many murders as many as an entire country will have in a full year. Faced with such variations, one has to suspect that the values, attitudes, and norms of a community can help determine its level of violence.

Yet the matter is not so simple, and the links between culture and violence are currently a focus of hot debate by experts. The current controversy is partly a result of the gradual collapse of the theory of "subcultures of violence." The notion that there are violent subcultures was proposed in the 1960s as a possible explanation for the fact that certain groups, such as poor people living in the inner city, have higher levels of violence than others. This theory proposed that such groups must have more positive attitudes about violence than others, and so people who grow up in such cultures learn that violent activity is a proper way to gain respect and prestige (and possibly other benefits). Although the argument was aimed at subcultures within the United States, it could readily be extended to entire cultures, such as the Yanomano tribe, which has been identified as especially violent.

The Fruitless Search for Subcultures that Endorse Violence

Initially, researchers embraced the theory that violence was learned as a positive value in certain subcultures, but the theory gradually lost favor and was discredited. One of the most decisive reasons the theory was dropped was that it proved impossible to find groups or subcultures that held positive or favorable attitudes toward violence. In particular, surveys found that inner-city black people did not endorse violence or report favorable attitudes about violent actions any more than suburban whites or other comparison groups. (Even if only some of the members of any particular group were favorably disposed toward violence, that still should have shown up in the overall averages, but there was no sign of it.) Although certain groups did have higher levels of violence, they did not seem to hold positive attitudes about it.

The theory of the subculture of violence also lost ground as studies showed that people who behaved violently did not seem to regard these actions as a means of gaining prestige or making a positive impression on others.[20] If the subculture were somehow encouraging violence, then presumably people would do violent things to gain approval, but this did not seem to be the case.

More recently, there has been a little evidence to the effect that in violent youth gangs and other groups who live violently, certain individuals do cultivate reputations for being dangerous and aggressive.[21] Possibly these findings could support the theory of a subculture of violence. Still, it is not clear that even these individuals seek such reputations because of a positive value placed on violence. The reputations may be sought strictly for pragmatic reasons. They may even be sought because of a generally *negative* attitude toward violence. Jankowski concluded that members of youth gangs who wish to avoid fighting can do so best by building a reputation for extremely dangerous, unpredictable aggressiveness, because such a reputation causes others to leave one alone. If you are known for an odd propensity to do remarkably nasty and cruel things unpredictably, people will become reluctant to trifle with you. In contrast, the individual or group that is perceived as reluctant to fight may become a target for the violence and exploitation of others. Thus, Jankowski cited several instances of gang members who, ironically, were known as exceptionally violent and who therefore hardly ever fought. No one dared provoke them.

As a result of these and other findings, researchers largely gave up on the notion of a subculture of violence. Today it is not among the major or prominent theories about aggression.[22]

Subcultures, Irresistible Impulses, and Self-Control

In my view, however, the notion of a subculture of violence deserves another look—but with a few changes. The idea that certain groups place positive value on violent behavior may be wrong, but that does not mean that cultural and subcultural values are irrelevant. The most important relevant values may be those concerned with maintaining versus losing self-control.

Thus, modern America may be violent not because it approves of violence (which it clearly doesn't) but because it supports the belief that people will inevitably lose control on many occasions. Our culture has lately become increasingly fond of notions of "irresistible impulses" and genetic causes of addiction. But in research on self-control, one conclusion stands out over and over again: People *acquiesce* in losing control. In other words, they let themselves lose control, and they become active participants. Whether it is a matter of breaking a diet, going on a drinking binge, or abandoning an unpleasant task, usually the person somehow allows it to happen. The same applies to violence. The concept of an irresistible impulse is somewhat misleading, because most violent behavior is not truly the result of irresistible impulses. People allow themselves to lose control. And they do so in part because they learn to regard certain impulses as irresistible.

Often the person's acquiescence in losing control is cleverly disguised. For example, people speak as if an eating or drinking binge were simply a matter of being overwhelmed by strong impulses that rendered them passive and helpless. Yet during these binges, they continue to procure food or drink, prepare it for consumption, put it in their mouths, and swallow it. These are active, not passive actions. Resisting the impulse may have been too difficult for them, but they have not simply quit resisting, they have become active accomplices in indulging their desires.

The same is often true of violence. Many people speak as if certain provocations produce an unstoppable rage that make violent action impossible to stop. Since the legal system has often given lighter penalties to people who commit crimes in the heat of passion, it is hardly surprising that people often claim that their actions were provoked. The point is not that they are lying; rather, they know in advance that certain provocations produce acceptable reasons for becoming so passionate that one can lose control and commit violent acts. Most of the time, they do actually retain some degree of control. For example, an angry husband may say that he was so provoked by his wife that he could not stop himself from beating her severely, but in fact he does usually stop himself before he permanently injures or kills her. Whatever his heat of passion, he usually does know when to stop.

A vivid illustration of the hidden operation of self-control was provided by a young man interviewed in a study of violent offenders in a British prison.[23] This man described meeting his wife's lover in a bar and attacking him in a wild rage. At one point he took a bottle and broke off the end to create a dangerous weapon with sharp points of broken glass. But then, as he recalled, he realized that if he were to use that weapon he would probably kill the other man, which would send him to prison for a long time. And so he put down the bottle. Then he resumed attacking the other man with his fists, beating him quite severely. The man ended up in prison after all, but of course with a sentence that was much lighter than he would have received had he used the broken bottle to kill the man. Even in the heat of rage and violent combat, the man could and did resist a very violent impulse.

The irresistible impulse notion was likewise rejected by FBI expert John Douglas. After spending his career studying hundreds of serial murderers and other killers, he said there was no way to believe that they were temporarily insane and out of control. For one thing, he noted that none of these killers had ever murdered someone in the presence of a uniformed police officer. Such a murder would be foolish, of course, but if the impulse were truly irresistible, it would not be deterred by the threat of arrest.[24] For another, he described several cases in which a serial killer would choose a victim and then cancel the abduction because circumstances did not seem favorable (for instance, witnesses might be nearby). Finally, he said, it is simply implausible that someone who was out of control and temporarily insane could get away with 10 murders without getting caught. Avoiding capture takes too much careful planning and caution for a psychotic or even for an uncontrolled person to manage.

Nor are these arguments limited to individuals. Mobs, too, seem to be able to know when to stop. At the beginning of 1993, Rwanda, Africa, was in the grip of escalating violence against the Tutsi minority. The number of victims was small in comparison with what came later, but there were deaths, burnings, and refugees. On January 7, an International Commission on Human Rights arrived to investigate claims of abuses. The violence stopped abruptly. The commission left two weeks later, and immediately a "murder rampage" killed several hundred people and inflicted many lesser atrocities over the next six days.[25]

In such cases, it is hard to avoid the conclusion that people know just how much they can allow themselves to lose control. Yet that point is not firmly determined by natural law; rather, it is influenced by cultural beliefs. This is where the theory of a subculture of violence needs to be revised. It is not that cultures place a positive value on violence but that culture dictates when and where (and how much) it is appropriate to lose control.

The provocations that make people angry do not vary all that much from one person or culture to another, but the degree of violence in the response may vary quite a bit. Is it appropriate to punch someone who insults you? What about running him through with a sword? Is it reasonable to kill someone you catch in bed with your spouse? Should a man strike his wife or child who willfully disobeys him? (And if so, should he use the palm of his hand, his fist, or a small stick?) If someone attacks you, can you fight back, and if so can you use other weapons than the ones he used? May a woman stab, maim, or kill a man who tries to rape her? Must you challenge someone to a duel if he insults your mother (or does it depend on the degree of insult)? Different cultures have varied widely in the answers they have given to these and similar questions.

Thus, violence occurs when people allow themselves to lose control of angry, violent impulses. A culture of violence does not have to place a positive value on violence. It can encourage violence merely by making it appropriate to let oneself go in response to a broad range of provocations. Culture does not have to encourage violent behavior in order to produce it (and this may be where the previous theories about subcultures of violence went wrong). People will have violent tendencies or impulses without needing a culture to instill them. All the culture has to do is stop restraining them, and these tendencies will emerge.

Indeed, the very notion of an "irresistible impulse" seems to me to be a cultural construction and one that is highly questionable on psychological grounds. There is such a thing as an irresistible impulse, but usually such impulses are limited to biological necessities. If you require someone to stand up for an indefinite period of time, eventually the urge to sit or lie down will become irresistible. Likewise, the urge to urinate can eventually become irresistible. To me, "irresistible" means that you would do it even if someone were aiming a gun at you and forbidding you to do it; and indeed people will eventually lie down or urinate despite such a threat. But such cases are rare and exceptional. There are very few other impulses that are truly irresistible.

There are, however, plenty of impulses that people can learn to treat *as if* they were irresistible. Resisting impulses is hard work, and if people have a readily available excuse for not doing that work, they will often be only too happy to give in. If your culture tells you that a normal and reasonable person would not resist a certain impulse, you may feel free to act it out. This can mean gambling large sums of money, eating too much, drinking to excess—or hitting or shooting someone at whom you are angry.

How Cultures Exert Influence

There are many ways in which cultures can teach people that it is appropriate to lose control and become violent under particular situations. We have already touched on the role of laws and courts. In some countries, for example, it was not considered a crime for a man to kill his wife's lover or the wife herself, as long as he had certain proof of their indiscretion. In our culture, such an act would be illegal, but defense attorneys are steadily expanding the scope of irresistible impulses to excuse an ever broader range of crimes.

There are two other major ways that the culture can exert influence over individual decisions. The first, most fundamental and most universal, is through social learning. One sees what other people do, and one learns to do the same. Children learn a great deal about managing anger and violence right in their own families. Some children grow up in families where they never see either parent raise his or her voice, and the notion of physically striking a family member would be appalling. Other children are exposed to shouting and slapping almost daily. It is hard to imagine how children could emerge from such widely different backgrounds and hold identical views about the self-control of anger.

Indeed, this sort of learning is probably the most potent factor in the intergenerational transmission of domestic violence. In recent years, a great deal of discussion has been devoted to the research findings that people who were abused as children are more likely than others to become child abusers themselves. Research has also found that children who saw their parents fight with each other physically are more likely than others to engage in physical violence in their own marriages.[26] Rather than postulate a genetic cause or a Freudian unconscious compulsion to explain this violence, I would say it seems likely that the main cause is learning. The child simply learns that this is how one treats family members.

Again, I doubt that children who observe their parents fighting come to the conclusion that beating one's spouse or other family member is good. Some researchers have suggested such conclusions, but I have not seen evidence to support it. Indeed, the evidence seems to indicate that most children think violence between their parents (or other family members) is frightening and upsetting. But it is not necessary to encourage violence in order to produce it; it is merely necessary to stop discouraging it. When children see their parents fight, they learn that hitting is one way to resolve a conflict or win an argument, and they may learn that love does not end and families do not break up simply because of a few blows. They saw their parents lose control in response to certain provocations, and they may allow themselves to lose control when similarly provoked.

The second way in which culture can influence individuals is through the mass media. The topic of violence in the media has been debated (with good reason) for several decades. At present, the main conclusions are as follows. Media violence can have a small but genuine effect on aggressive behavior: Specifically, people who are exposed to media violence are sometimes more violent in their own subsequent actions. These effects appear to be short-term and depend on cues to connect the film violence with one's own situation—such as if you are angry at someone who reminds you of the villain in the film.

Television and movies also provide people with evidence about what life is like and how people deal with problems. This information may be inaccurate, but it is nonetheless influential. Heavy television viewers are prone to various misconceptions about the world. For example, they tend to believe that there are many more physicians and lawyers than there actually are, because such characters are common on television. Also, and more to the point, people who watch a great deal of television gradually come to develop a greater fear of crime than other people, because there is so much crime on television. Still, the spread of television through the United States has not seemed to lead to any direct increase in violent crime; instead, it has produced an increase in property crimes, such as auto theft. Apparently, television does not have its effects by producing copycat criminals who perform the deeds they see on the tube. Instead, it makes people desire material things and suggests to them that many people might turn to crime to satisfy such desires.[27]

The copycat phenomenon deserves further study, however. Probably only a few people are inspired to commit violent deeds that they see in the mass media, but these few can be quite important. This aspect is missing from much of the debate about media violence. The debate is usually phrased in terms of whether watching violent entertainment will inspire violent behavior in the average person. Although there are a few such effects, they seem to be weak, limited, and temporary, and on that basis, one cannot blame the media for society's violence. But a few people who may be inclined toward violent action may find that the mass media affect them and inspire them to commit crimes.

One FBI expert on mass murderers and serial killers believes that the media do play a role. Robert Ressler[28] notes that the spread of serial killing in the United States coincided with a historical shift in the film industry. Up through the 1950s, most horror movies featured supernatural villains such as Dracula and Frankenstein. Beginning in the 1960s, however, films began to depict ordinary people committing monstrous crimes. Alfred Hitchcock's *Psycho* was famous in this regard, because the bloodthirsty killer was the apparently quiet and friendly clerk in a motel. Ressler thinks that lonely, violently inclined individuals scattered around the United States may not have been inspired to identify with Dracula, and so watching the earlier horror films had little effect on them. But when they began to see ordinary people killing victims in the movies, something clicked. These films planted something in their imagination and made them begin to think about how they might do similar things.

Ressler's argument does not mean that movies planted the urge to kill. Instead, he thinks that these people may have had vague violent urges that remained shapeless and ambiguous for a long time. Movies enabled these people to imagine themselves tormenting and killing victims. Imagining something is an important step toward actually doing it. For that reason, Ressler thinks that the modern epidemic of serial murder coincided with the rising popularity of horror films that feature violent acts by seemingly ordinary people.

Recent experimental work paints the same picture. The serious effects of media violence are found only in a small minority of highly aggressive individuals. To be sure, there is a short and temporary effect of watching a violent film that may make almost anyone a little more aggressive if provoked soon after in a way that is reminiscent of the film.[29] But nonaggressive people are only slightly affected.

So media violence seems to affect people who are inclined toward aggression anyway. The effects are multiple, as shown in recent work by Brad Bushman.[30] First, aggressive people are more likely to seek out violent films. Second, such films have a more arousing and anger-producing effect on aggressive people than on others. Third, such individuals are more spurred to violent or aggressive actions by such films than are other people.

One way to understand these effects is to imagine a lonely, unhappy man with an abusive childhood behind him and a vague anger against other people, or against some particular category of other people (such as women who remind him of his mother). Without television or movies, his anger might smolder for a long time, but it does not get formed into clear impulses for particular attacks and tortures. Yet if the man begins to see violent films, he may start to flesh out his vague angers into specific and vivid fantasies. He finds himself drawn to watch such movies more than other people, and he finds them very arousing. He begins to imagine himself capturing a woman and doing particular things to her. Over time, these acts become more and more cruel. It may be a long time before he acts on them, but the day of action has moved much nearer.

Robert Ressler's long-time colleague and friend John Douglas, another FBI expert on serial killers, made a telling comment in a recent discussion of his work. He was describing a very brutal murder on which he had been called to consult. The victim, Francine Elveson, was a 26-year-old teacher. She was shy and lived with her parents in an apartment building. One day she went out to work and apparently disappeared. Her wallet was found in the stairwell, and when her mother called the center where she worked, she was told that Francine had never shown up. A search of the area found her body on the roof landing at the top of the stairwell. She was nude and had been severely beaten with some blunt object. Her nose, jaw, and cheeks had been fractured and her teeth had been loosened. She had been tied in a spread-eagled position with her own garments, apparently after she was already dead. Her nipples had been cut off and placed on her chest. Her underpants had been cut off and put over her face. There were small knife wounds all over her body, and there were bite marks on her thighs. She had not been raped per se, but traces of semen were found on her body, which suggested that the killer had masturbated, presumably onto the corpse. Her vagina had been penetrated with her umbrella and her pen. Her comb was left on her pubic hair, and her earrings were arranged symmetrically on the floor by her head. Douglas's comment: "This advanced a sexual fantasy would take years to develop."[31]

Douglas concluded (correctly) that Francine Elveson had been this particular killer's first victim. But he had obviously been thinking about it for a long time. The exorbitant attention to detail, including all the things he did with the corpse, reflected the working of a twisted imagination over a long period of time. By labeling this fantasy "advanced," Douglas was acknowledging that the path from vague hostility to ritualistic murder is a long and slow one. Unfortunately, though, the media can help bring people along this path. The media are, after all, tools to help the imagination. Normally this is a wonderful gift and a marvelous advantage to living in the modern era. When the imagination turns to evil, however, the media's influence can be just as harmful.

How Evil Grows and Spreads

"First we will kill all the subversives; then we will kill their collaborators; then . . . their sympathizers, then . . . those who remain indifferent; and finally we will kill the timid."[1] These words were spoken by one of the governors in Argentina in the mid-1970s. He was referring to the coming phase of government repression and terror. The ruling class in Argentina believed that their way of life and their culture were under attack, and when the military took over they decided to enforce discipline by getting rid of these internal enemies. It is not surprising that the governor was able to foresee that imprisonment, torture, and murder were in store for the suspected enemies of the regime. What is remarkable, though, was that he was able to foresee the gradual escalation of repression. Large-scale evil is probably most often the end of a long road that no one foresaw at the start. People become caught up in the process gradually, and things become more and more extreme. The punishments become more severe and the categories of victims become broader. Only the most far-sighted individual (such as this governor) would be able to predict in advance, however, that what starts out as suppressing people who are actively subversive will end with murdering people whose only crime is that they do not show sufficient enthusiasm in their support for the government.

In the last chapter, we examined what might bring someone to cross over the line and do something immoral or cruel. In most cases, these first acts are small and minor. If such acts stayed at that level, the world would be a much kinder and gentler place. The great crimes and atrocities of history did not generally appear abruptly and full-blown. Rather, they were the result of a period of escalation, often one that occurred very gradually.

Once the line has been crossed, other factors start coming into play to produce gradual increases in the severity of the actions. The violence or brutality of the final result may be far beyond what anyone imagined at first. On the other hand, if these factors don't fan the flames of evil, then the initial misdeed may remain trivial and harmless. It is these secondary causes that bear central responsibility for the triumphs and excesses of evil in the world.

Escalation: Growing Nastier over Time

Because severe violence is typically the product of a process of escalation, it is essential to understand what contributes to such escalation. The fact that many violent patterns grow worse and more extreme over time cannot be disputed. Once evil gains a foothold, it seems very capable of growing and flourishing. For example, marital violence does not start off all at once. Recent studies indicate that the usual sequence is an escalation from verbal to physical aggression. People typically start off insulting each other or saying cruel things, and then perhaps they shout and scream at each other, and from there they proceed to hit each other.[2] They do not start off hitting but arrive at that level of violence only after passing through lesser stages of aggression. Similar patterns are found in disputes among strangers.[3]

Moreover, escalation of domestic violence proceeds not just in a single episode but through a series of episodes. The major studies of marital violence by Gelles and Straus concluded that there is a general pattern of domestic violence growing more severe over time (as well as showing escalation within each incident). The first time a couple becomes physically violent, their violence is typically limited to minor acts. He shoves her angrily; she slaps him. After a few such incidents, however, there is a punch thrown, and later there may be more severe beatings.

As I wrote this, the nation was fascinated by the trial of O.J. Simpson, a former football star and celebrity whose wife was murdered along with a male friend. Simpson was eventually acquitted of murder, although the acquittal was based more on uncertainties and weaknesses in the prosecution's case than on any resounding proof of his innocence, and many observers continued to suspect after the trial that Simpson was guilty. In any case, if Simpson did commit the murders, they came at the end of a long series of increasingly violent episodes. Los Angeles police records showed that his wife had often called to complain about his rages and his attacks on her, and the news media featured one old tape of an incident in which he came to her dwelling while they were separated. He broke down the door and threatened her with severe violence, all while she was on the telephone to the police.

It is rare that a gentle, peaceful person will abruptly kill his or her spouse. Spousal murder typically occurs at the end of a long sequence of increasingly violent disputes and acts.

The interpersonal exchange contributes to escalation. As we saw earlier, much violence is reciprocal, and revenge tends to be poorly calibrated so that the retaliation often exceeds the provocation. A young gang member articulated this pattern succinctly: "It's like this. If you slap me, I'm gonna hit you with my closed fist. If you stab me, I'm gonna shoot you. An eye for an eye doesn't exist—it's one-up. One-up is what it is in gang life."[4] As each side strikes back harder than it was struck, a vicious circle of escalating violence results.

Even one-sided violence escalates, however. Studies of the Holocaust suggest that large-scale mass murder came only after a long and slow progression of lesser actions against its victims. The German Jews were at first stigmatized, discriminated against, deprived of various legal rights, subjected to special taxes, and in other ways mistreated for years before there was any systematic plan to kill them.[5] Even sending them to concentration camps was not necessarily done with an intention to kill large numbers of them. Hannah Arendt has pointed out that most European countries between the two world wars had concentration camps where they detained people whom they wished to deprive of citizenship and other privileges and, ideally, to deport to other countries. (The United States also interned many U.S. citizens of Japanese descent in similar camps.) Sometimes, the police units in neighboring countries sustained low-level border wars with each other based on their respective efforts to dump these unwanted people across the border. One local police department of a large city would take a couple of truckloads of these people across the border and turn them loose. Returning afterward, they would occasionally have to cover their retreat in an exchange of pistol fire, not very deadly, with police from the other side. Opinions about how early Hitler intended to kill the Jews differ widely, but there is plenty of evidence to suggest that many Germans who participated in the relocation process thought only of deporting people who did not fit in. The final solution of mass killing was implemented after it became apparent that there was no place to which the unwanted Jews could be permanently deported.

Historical examples are often subject to controversy, counterexample, and reinterpretation, and so laboratory studies are useful. Such studies confirm the conclusion that aggression tends to escalate. When subjects are put in the position of delivering electric shocks to another person, and they can freely choose how severe the shocks will be, they escalate the shocks gradually over time. By the end of the experiment, they are choosing to administer much more intense and presumably painful shocks than they chose earlier in the procedure. These patterns are not limited to reciprocal, tit-for-tat exchanges, although such patterns of retaliation do show plenty of escalation. But even when the subject in an experiment thought that he or she was simply performing the role of a teacher and punishing an alleged learner for getting wrong answers, the punishments tended to become more severe over time.[6]

Getting Used to It

One of the first factors that leads to the escalation of aggression is *desensitization*. In plain terms, desensitization is essentially a matter of getting accustomed to something and ceasing to react strongly to it. Desensitization is not necessarily bad, and indeed it is often used for constructive or therapeutic ends. In treating phobias, such as a fear of flying, for example, many therapists will carefully expose people briefly to the things that frighten them, and they gradually become less and less frightened, until eventually they can, for example, take long airplane trips without succumbing to a paralyzing panic attack.

As we have already seen, most people become very upset when they kill or hurt another human being. The theory of desensitization holds that if they keep killing people, they will suffer less and less distress each time. Killing, torturing, or raping someone may be a shock the first time. The second time, it is less of a shock. By the fiftieth time, it may be no shock at all. Just as is the case with eating the same foods or seeing the same person naked or jumping over and over into very cold water, the body and the psychological system grow accustomed to events that initially produce a strong reaction. Eventually, the reaction is minimal.

A recent critique by James Tedeschi and Richard Felson[7] concluded that research has failed to prove that desensitization affects violence. In my view, their critique is valid in suggesting that the evidence in support of desensitization has not met the very highest standards of methodological rigor. On the other hand, I think there is so much evidence (however imperfect) in favor of desensitization, from both inside and outside the psychological laboratory, that it is appropriate to assume it is true unless some contrary evidence can be marshaled. There are indeed questions about the extent and scope of desensitization effects; for example, does watching violence on television make people indifferent to the actual harming of others? But the core of the theory appears to be true.

We have previously considered Browning's account of the German policemen who were assigned duties, including mass killings, in occupied Poland during World War II. The reactions of those men seemed to show strong patterns of desensitization. Their accounts of the first massacre indicated that most of the men were profoundly shocked and upset by what they had done. The evening after those first killings, the men sat quietly, shaken, unable to talk about what had happened or about anything else. They ate little and drank a great deal of alcohol. Some had nightmares.

But as they participated in further massacres, they showed fewer signs of distress. Although killing people may have remained an unpleasant duty, it became far less upsetting. After a day's work, the men would sit together at meals, talk, laugh, play cards, and do other normal activities. The later killings were apparently not a moral and psychological shock to their systems the way the first ones were. Part of the explanation was that they devised ways of performing those duties that made them easier, but it also appears that they were less shocked and upset by shooting people. The involvement in killings, like the rest of the job, had faded into an ordinary routine.

Vividness of memory is one sign of sensitivity, and vividness fits the pattern of desensitization. Several months after the first massacre, the police battalion was given orders for a similar mission: Round up all the people in a certain Jewish village and shoot them. This time the battalion was badly understaffed, apparently because a large part of the group was on another assignment elsewhere. As a result, many new men were pressed into the murderous duty. Browning says that there was a striking contrast years later in the accounts of this day. The old hands who had participated in multiple killing actions did not have clear or distinct memories of this particular one. In contrast, the men who were killing for the first time had stark and vivid recollections of it, full of details.[8] They remembered it as distinctly as the old hands had remembered their first action. Apparently, then, taking part in a mass killing made a much deeper impression on people who were doing it for the first time than on people who had done it before, consistent with the desensitization view.

Many similar patterns can be found in Nathan McCall's gripping account of his career as a youthful criminal and gang member in urban Virginia. He provides a very moving report of his first participation in gang rape. He knew that the older boys did such things, but the first time his friends found an opportunity, he was nervous and reluctant. He described the victim, Vanessa, a 13-year-old "black beauty," as naive and a virgin; he had seen her in school and thought about dating her, although he quickly abandoned those thoughts once the prospect of raping her existed, because he thought that someone who had been subjected to a multiple rape would be permanently beneath his dignity to have as a girlfriend. He said he felt sorry for her as he watched her argue and struggle and slowly resign herself to what seemed inevitable. He described his feelings of embarrassment, worry, and disgust; after he took his brief turn between her legs, he "felt sick and unclean" (p. 46). He said he sensed that some of his fellow rapists felt sorry for her and suffered pangs of guilt, too.

Following this moving description, however, McCall notes that the guilt was short-lived, and indeed after the girl left they had a "victory celebration." He ended the story by saying that soon after this event he and his friends began conducting similar gang rapes on a fairly regular basis, perfecting the art of luring girls into the trap, sometimes using the guys' homes while their parents were at work, and so forth. The matter-of-fact summary of these later activities contrasts sharply with the reluctant, vivid, ambivalent account of the first time, again consistent with the desensitization view.

In all the reading I did for this book, the most unforgettable story of desensitization was one that was not even told by a perpetrator. (At most, one could say he was a peripheral and involuntary accomplice.) It was told to journalist Gitta Sereny by a man named Richard, who had been a Czech Jew deported to Treblinka.[9]

Treblinka was not a concentration camp; it was simply a death camp. Trains full of people arrived there each day, and almost all of the passengers were immediately killed. The only people who lived there were the handful of SS guards, their Ukrainian helpers, and a small contingent of Jews who performed menial labor. Richard was selected for menial labor. Remarkably, he arrived there early in the killings and remained there almost to the end and still survived.

Richard's job was to collect and sort the belongings of the victims. Trains from the east brought mostly dirt-poor peasants who had only the clothes on their back, and these were usually full of lice, so they were collected and destroyed. But the trains from western Europe carried reasonably well-to-do Jews (and a few others) who had brought along their most important possessions, including fine clothes, good food, and valuables. In a few hours, these unfortunates were marching naked to the gas chamber, while Richard and his colleagues were frantically gathering up their clothes and going through their suitcases. Many trains arrived every day, and it was a rush to get everything from one group of victims sorted and stored away before the next group arrived.

Although Richard's group was vulnerable to being shot by the SS or Ukrainian guards almost at whim, it gradually reached a working harmony with these men and the danger of execution subsided (as long as the Jews were careful never to give offense). Their special job also gave them an advantage over most inhabitants of concentration camps, who had to survive on a starvation diet of the lowest quality bread and soup. Richard and his colleagues were allowed to feed and clothe themselves from the victims' booty. The food was good and plentiful, and they kept their health.

Then, in March 1943, things changed. The trains stopped coming every day. Only a few trains arrived, and those were full of poor gypsies who brought little with them. And then the trains stopped altogether. For six weeks there were none. Of course, Richard and his men had not been given any explanations or indeed any information at all. They knew only that there were no trains.

Richard recalled those six weeks as miserable, for several reasons that are important to appreciate. First, and most obviously, the lack of trains meant that their food (and clothing) supply was cut off. They had to eat the regular camp food, which was unhealthy and inadequate. Like starving people everywhere, they lost weight, felt depressed and lethargic, and began to grow weak and fall ill. Some died.

Second, the lack of trains contained a deeper threat. The Jews knew they had been kept alive simply to handle the possessions of the victims. No trains, no victims—and no possessions. Each day, they wondered whether someone would decide that their work was no longer needed and they would take their own turn in the gas chambers. Richard said that he had always seen the storage bins just bursting with clothes and other possessions, but now these had all been shipped off. He said they felt indescribably depressed and afraid when they looked at those huge bins, now standing empty. When full, those bins had been their reason for being allowed to live.

A third cause of concern was the behavior of the Germans. Richard said that the Germans started to seem as panic-stricken as he and his fellows, and so he was constantly afraid that one of those nervous blond men would just shoot him. In retrospect, the Germans' fear was probably parallel to Richard's: If there were no more trains, the camp would be shut down, and instead of working there as guards they would be sent, not to the gas chambers, but to the Russian front, which was not a vastly superior prospect.

Finally, one day when Richard and his friends were sitting together in their barracks, doing nothing, one of the Germans walked in with a big smile and announced, with a flourish, that as of tomorrow the trains would be rolling in again. Richard says that he and all the other Jews immediately stood up and cheered.

Years later, he said it made him sick to recall that moment. He and his friends had essentially celebrated the fact that other innocent Jews were being brought to their deaths. He said in retrospect it seemed impossible, but it was the truth: That was the point they had reached. Moreover, it was not just a single outburst of relief. He said they spent that evening "in an excited, expectant mood."[10] They talked about where the train might be coming from—they hoped it was a rich country "like Holland," whose citizens would have good food and fine clothes. For Richard, it meant a new lease on life. "The fact that it was their death, whoever they were, which meant our life, was no longer relevant; we had been through this over and over and over."[11] That last line expresses the desensitization he and his fellows had been through. They had simply grown accustomed to the deaths of others, even though they had no reason to rationalize or justify it. He and his fellows reacted to the prospect of a resumption of the killings solely in terms of what it meant for their own work and well-being.

I do not wish to overstate the case for desensitization; it does not always happen. There may even be occasional trends in the opposite direction. Sometimes people are bothered by what they are doing and cannot put aside their scruples, which seem to accumulate and eventually interfere with further acts. These individuals seem to become sensitized rather than desensitized. But they appear to be the exceptions. Generally, people react less strongly each time they inflict or witness harm.

How does desensitization contribute to escalation? There are several likely answers. First, one must assume that people's normal repugnance at inflicting severe harm on others holds them back from being as extreme as they could be. Like the shooters who ended up missing their targets at point-blank range (discussed in Chapter 7), people's inhibitions sometimes prevent them from carrying out violent intentions. With desensitization, these internal blocks are weakened.

It is important to recognize that the contribution of desensitization will most likely be limited. In a first act of violence, internal emotional objections will tend to ameliorate the violence, but as the person becomes less and less sensitive to the suffering of others, he or she will be less hampered by these emotions. This desensitization will not necessarily produce ever more extreme acts of violence; it merely means that the same level of violence can be carried out more efficiently and with fewer failures, delays, and problems.

Among the sadistic few who enjoy hurting others, however, desensitization will have a quite different effect. As they grow less sensitive, they will find their pleasurable reactions diminishing (as opposed to finding merely their reluctance and repugnance diminishing). One might hope that this tendency would cause them to abandon violence as the yield of pleasure diminishes; but more likely, it will prompt them to become ever more cruel in order to recapture the degree of pleasure they found before they became desensitized. Instead of merely killing their victims, sadists may find that they must first torture and humiliate them to get the same degree of satisfaction.

Getting Away with It

For many people, the idea of committing some violent or harmful act is surrounded with strong inhibitions. From early in life, we learn that such actions lead to disastrous consequences, possibly because in a small child's frame of reference, disastrous consequences can be easily arranged. Participating in torture or murder will seem immensely consequential to an adult, and as a result most people will be effectively inhibited from doing such things.

But what happens if, by some remarkable series of events, someone comes to engage in one of those acts after all? Very likely, the disastrous consequences will not ensue. The world does not end, sirens do not go off, people do not immediately see that you are an entirely different person. Things may go on pretty much as before. Such a discovery may be a profound shock and may cause the person to have doubts about all those scruples, worries, and inhibitions. In plain terms, one is surprised to find how easily one gets away with such an act, and so one concludes that the reluctance was overblown. What was I so afraid of?

It helps to consider some mundane examples. In graduate school, one of my married friends experienced a mutual attraction to a female student, and he agonized over whether to violate his pledge of marital fidelity. Finally, temptation won out over conscience, and with some trepidation and inner struggle he walked across the campus to the young woman's dormitory room. They soon undressed and got into bed. By coincidence, the moment they began having intercourse, the dormitory fire alarm went off. Actually, the alarm was prone to go off rather frequently, but he did not know this (he lived off campus with his wife), nor did he even know that it was the fire alarm; all he knew was that as soon as he had crossed the line into forbidden pleasures, there was this horribly loud buzzing sound all around him.

Having such a signal from the environment at the moment one begins to do something wrong is a parody of what people imagine will happen. Far more often, of course, nothing out of the ordinary happens, and the person is surprised by the absence of condemnatory reaction. This issue is revived periodically in connection with the national antidrug propaganda campaigns. My generation was brought up hearing alarming stories about the catastrophic dangers of drugs, and many of us simply accepted that if one were ever to use illegal drugs, one's entire life would instantly be turned upside down, one's health ruined, and one's career destroyed. It was a shock to me, and I assume to many others, to arrive at college and meet many young men and women who seemed to use drugs constantly while still coping well with life and even earning top grades. Some of my friends experimented with marijuana themselves and were surprised at how trivial and temporary the effects were; they concluded that all the antidrug warnings were simply lies, and they began experimenting with considerably stronger (and more dangerous) drugs. Thus, when they crossed the line, they were surprised that nothing happened, and that lack of catastrophe encouraged them to go further.

Undoubtedly, similar processes can produce escalation of violence. Ervin Staub has emphasized that the silence of bystanders is often a crucial contribution to evil, even though they may think that being silent is not any form of encouragement or action. Like most scholars, Staub says that the first major modern genocide was the Turkish massacre of the Armenians. The path leading up to this episode is revealing. Late in the nineteenth century, the Turks committed several massacres in suppressing a revolt in Bulgaria. These so-called Bulgarian atrocities were widely reported and protested throughout Europe, although officially the great powers did not censure Turkey or initiate sanctions (mainly because they were caught up in the more pressing concerns of the power politics of the time). Thus, there was bad publicity but nothing more.

The next step involved killing Armenians inside Turkey. A small local uprising of Armenians was ended when the insurgents surrendered after receiving a promise of pardon and safe conduct. The promise was immediately broken, and the rebels were killed. Then, in 1895, more than 200,000 Armenians were killed, but the international protest was minimal. The ruling Turks may well have learned from these incidents that killing European subjects bought only a few protests and killing Turkish Armenians not even that. In 1915, they initiated a more thorough genocide, in which roughly one and a half million Armenians were killed.[12]

The Turks were not the only ones to be impressed with how easily they got away with large-scale murder. Indeed, one of Hitler's most famous lines, spoken just before the invasion of Poland, was "Who, after all, speaks today of the extermination of the Armenians?"

The Armenians were only the first victims of our genocidal century. In the subsequent mass killings around the world, similar patterns of gradual escalation can be seen. One perennial reason (although not the only one) for these gradual steps is that the perpetrators wait to see whether there will be some outcry, some protest, some international intervention. When the rest of the world does nothing, they go further.

It is not even necessary to assume that they start out with the intention of going all the way to genocide if no one stops them. The first measures often simply restrict the civil rights and benefits of the victim group, perhaps as a way of punishing or getting revenge against them. However, when the perpetrators are surprised at how little protest there is, they may grow willing to inflict more severe sanctions the next time they feel they have a cause.

The pattern of growing more violent when one's first acts elicit no retaliation or sanctions can be found among individuals just as well as among repressive governments. Experts on domestic abuse believe that one reason for escalation in family violence is that abusers learn how easy it is to get away with hitting.[13] To strike one's husband or wife in the face would go against a great deal of conditioning for most people, and they would worry about severe consequences—loss of love, dissolution of marriage, even arrest and imprisonment. Instead, however, one typically finds that the person one has struck is willing to continue the marriage, accepts one's apology and pledges love in return, and in many cases will even actively conceal one's misdeed (such as when a woman wears sunglasses to hide a black eye). You crossed the line, you actually struck your wife (or husband or parent) and, surprisingly, there was no penalty. Hence, it is easier to do it again next time, because there is less reason to worry or hold back. Indeed, if one is really angry next time, one may easily go further, because what one did last time turned out to be so trivial.

Discovering the Pleasure

The last two sections have covered the two main factors that produce escalation, namely, desensitization and the discovery that one can get away with it. There are additional factors, however, including some that have been anticipated in previous chapters. One of them is the discovery that hurting people can be a direct source of pleasure. People may learn to enjoy committing harm.

The issue of sadism has already been covered, and there is no need to recross that ground here. Nevertheless, one aspect that was fairly peripheral to our discussion in Chapter 7 is important now, which is that the pleasure in hurting is typically something that people discover gradually. Sadism is rarely the original or driving force that initiates violence; it is not one of the major or common roots of evil. Instead, violence usually begins for some other reason, and sadism may emerge as a factor over time, if the person continues to commit violent acts. This implies that sadism can become a factor that contributes to escalation.

Sadism is especially important as a late-emerging factor because it provides a new, additional reason to inflict harm. Thus, people may first get involved in hurting others because it is their job, or because they believe they are furthering their idealistic cause, or for instrumental reasons—but then they discover that it becomes gratifying to inflict harm. They discover that they enjoy it. Henceforth, their violent acts spring from both the original cause and the additional motive of enjoyment.

Tit for Tat and Vicious Circles

The chapter on revenge (Chapter 5) showed yet another process that can lead to escalation, and indeed in history, many group conflicts or vendettas have escalated in violence over long periods of time. Most people believe they are justified in striking back at someone who has attacked them. As we saw, there is a tendency for these reciprocal and retaliatory acts of aggression to grow more severe, and so the initial antagonism may spiral into worse violence.

A major reason for this escalation is the magnitude gap between perpetrators and victims. The magnitude gap makes it very difficult to settle a vendetta or other grievance in a way that both sides will see as fair. Perpetrators see what they do as smaller in scope, importance, and severity than victims see it, and so the victim's notion of a fair retaliation will be more drastic and extreme than what the original perpetrator thinks is fair. Just when one side thinks things are even, the other side thinks it has been the victim of an outrage that cries out for retaliation. This leads to a continuing escalation of the violence.

The Ambiguous, Expanding Mandate

We have seen that ambiguity sometimes contributes to stepping across the line into wrongful or hurtful actions. Ambiguity plays at least as large a role in escalation. Ambiguity permits a steady expansion of the categories of victims and in the scope of actions that can be taken against them.

Part of the effect of ambiguity has to do with the fact that evil is in the eye of the beholder. I have pointed out throughout this book that perpetrators often do not regard their actions as evil, and so evil flourishes in the gap between the perspectives of actor and observer (or between those of perpetrator and victim). When the rules and meanings are all precisely clear, there is less chance for such divergent interpretations, and hence less room for one person to do something he thinks is right but that someone else will judge as radically wrong.

The connotation of the word *ambiguity* is somewhat misleading here, because many people think of ambiguity as involving a lack of meaning, such as when it is unclear how something should be understood or interpreted. It is better, however, to understand ambiguity as involving multiple possible meanings, so that the person is uncertain about which of these meanings is the correct one. Ambiguity is a surplus of meaning, not a shortage. Some foreign languages make this clearer than English. In German, for example, the word for ambiguous is *zweideutig*, which is made from the words for "two" and "meaningful"; thus, something is ambiguous insofar as it has at least two meanings.

Ambiguity breeds evil because many actions can be viewed in widely different ways from different perspectives. An act may seem cruel or violent from one perspective but correct and even morally obligatory from another. The other side has done something that may be acceptable—or may be a direct attack on your group or its goals. A certain act of retaliation may be appropriate—or it may be excessive. There may be a rule against a certain kind of violent reprisal—or the current case may be an exception to such general rules, for some general rules don't apply during times of emergency.

When the perpetrator is a group rather than a single person, the opportunities for dangerous ambiguities to arise increase dramatically. We have already seen that sometimes the members of a violent group privately think one thing but say something quite different aloud to one another, and so the group communication is distorted. In particular, these distortions tend to breed greater violence, because the group members' open comments tend to insist on strict adherence to the party line even if they privately have qualms and moral doubts about the whole enterprise. The gap between private meanings and public meanings—between what is thought and what is said—tends to foster greater violence.

The great Russian writer Alexander Solzhenitsyn once remarked on how Americans could not really understand what it must have been like to fall into the clutches of the Soviet penal system, because in America we take our Constitution and laws for granted. He said we cannot imagine how terrible it is when judges must operate without clear or explicit laws. In the United States, when the laws do not explicitly condemn some act, then it is permitted. In the Soviet Union, he said, there was no clear set of written rules that the judges could consult, and it was considered important to punish people who acted wrongly, despite the absence of a constitution. Indeed, some of the most important offenses were quite imprecisely defined, such as counterrevolutionary comments or actions. There is a substantial capacity for such a system to produce repressive, evil patterns of judgments. How can you prove you are not an enemy of the people? And if you are therefore judged guilty, how could a judge dare be lenient in punishing an enemy of the people? Giving a lenient sentence might even be grounds for someone else in the future to prove that the judge was himself an enemy of the people. One never knew. It happened.

One of the saddest predicaments described by Robert Conquest in his history of the Soviet purges was the one faced by women who were arrested for being "wives of enemies of the people."[14] At some level, to the perpetrators' way of thinking, the crackdown seemed plausible. After all, if someone marries a major traitor to your country and continues to love and support him while he is betraying it, then probably she is herself dangerous or at least inimical to the decent people of the land. Something should be done with her, lest she carry on her husband's treasonous activities while he is in prison.

In practice, however, many wholly innocent women found themselves accused of something vaguely terrible but nonspecific and hence impossible to defend against. After all, if your husband has been convicted for whatever vague reasons of being an enemy of the people, and you are unambiguously his wife, then you must belong to the guilty category of "wives of enemies of the people" and hence are destined for punishment yourself. Most of these women had committed no specific crime or other wrong act, and often they did not know what their husbands were supposed to have done. (Nor had the husbands actually done anything, in most cases.) There is almost no reasonable basis for deciding on an appropriate punishment for such a noncrime; the judges tended to sentence the women to prison labor camps for 25 years, which often meant the rest of their lives.

The sort of instruction that is most likely to produce violent, oppressive, evil measures consists of harsh but vague rules. Injunctions to root out and punish "enemies of the people" are a perfect example; clearly it is important to take severe measures with such enemies, but it is far from clear just who those enemies are, and it is also often unclear just how severe the severe measures should be. Should enemies of the people be fired from their jobs? Fined? Imprisoned for 3 years, or for 25 years? Permanently deprived of all civil rights? Executed? Along with their families? Tortured until they reveal names of accomplices, who are then also imprisoned and perhaps shot?

Harsh but vague laws were a centerpiece of the French Terror,[15] which in many ways was the first modern episode of murderous governmental repression. More recent atrocities have kept the same pattern. Elizabeth Becker's account of the Khmer Rouge terror emphasized the absence of specific rules. Indeed, she says that there were no formal laws at all after the Khmer Rouge took over.[16] Local authorities answered no questions about who had been arrested or why. The people gradually realized they were utterly at the mercy of the authorities. They lived in fear that they might unknowingly say or do the wrong thing and be executed.

At one point, the Khmer decided to intensify their nationalistic campaign by outlawing any identification with other ethnic groups or nations. The vagueness of this law can be seen in the wide differences in its result. In some parts of the country, ethnic minorities were forbidden to practice their customs and religions, wear their preferred clothes, or speak their own languages, but otherwise they went on as before. In other parts of the country, there were wholesale massacres of such minorities.[17]

The power of ambiguity can be seen in lesser crimes by individuals, too. The Soviet practice of sending political dissidents to mental hospitals provided a good example of this.[18] Psychiatric diagnosis is far from an exact science even today in the United States, where all political views are officially tolerated and where psychological research is most advanced. One Soviet psychiatrist who later settled in the United States spoke about this Soviet practice. He asserted that many of the top Soviet psychiatrists actually believed that political dissidents, almost by definition, must be insane. Communists believed in the objective truth of their account of the world, and any fellow citizen who refused to go along with the party line was in an important sense out of touch with reality. Other psychiatrists, however, were presumably more cynical about the accuracy of their diagnoses. They told the state what it wanted to hear in order to get on with their jobs as required and hence perhaps advance their careers. They signed the forms that condemned sane, healthy individuals to long-term incarceration under the guise of psychiatric treatment for their nonexistent illnesses.

Yet it is unlikely that they were so cynical that they honestly recognized these victims as fully sane, for under the expert gaze of a psychiatrist there are precious few people who can get a totally clean bill of mental health. In the United States, a famous experiment was conducted in which a group of normal, healthy individuals went to various mental hospitals and asked for treatment, initially claiming symptoms that were actually bogus and nonexistent. They had been instructed that if they were admitted, they were to drop all pretense of illness and act normally, to see how long it took for a sane person to get out of a mental hospital. Not a single one was ever recognized as healthy. They were diagnosed as having various mental disorders, and eventually they were discharged as being in remission—which meant that they were presumably still insane but temporarily free enough of symptoms to be released from the hospitals.[19]

Thus, the criteria for recognizing mental illness tend to be loose and slippery, even today, and they were certainly much more ambiguous during the heyday of Soviet power. There was some basis for thinking that anyone who failed to recognize the officially sanctioned truth of Communist doctrine must be mentally ill, just as the sanity of a modern American who believes that the earth is flat or that the government plants mind-control drugs in the municipal water supply would be suspect. A determined inspection of almost anyone's life and mind can find evidence of abnormality, neurosis, and other pathology. This ambiguity has made psychological diagnosis a useful tool for the repression of political dissent.

Trust and Responsibility

Another important way in which ambiguity contributes to evil among idealistic groups is the shuffling and hence eclipsing of personal responsibility. When people act alone, it is obvious who made the decisions and who is to blame. In large and complex groups, however, responsibility can sometimes be divided up into such small parts and pieces that no one seems to be to blame even if there are utterly horrific results. Several broad principles combine to make groups better able than lone individuals to produce evil.

Diffusion of Responsibility: All in This Together

The principle of diffusion of responsibility was introduced in 1968 by John Darley and Bibb Latané to explain why bystanders might fail to help a victim in need. Their work was stimulated by a sensational news event, the murder of Kitty Genovese in New York in 1963 by an assailant who beat and stabbed her for nearly an hour. More than 40 people saw or heard what was going on, but no one came to her aid or even called the police. Commentators said that the alienation, indifference, or moral bankruptcy of urban dwellers was to blame for the fact that people could watch someone be killed without doing anything to help. Darley and Latane proposed, however, that the mere fact that there were so many people made each of them feel that someone else would probably act. In carefully constructed laboratory studies, they showed that lone bystanders will often come forward to help a victim, whereas bystanders who believe they are part of a large group will not. The reason is that the responsibility for taking action is divided up among members of the group. The larger the group, the less responsible any individual person feels.[20]

The concept of diffusion of responsibility was used later to explain why people do not work as hard in groups as they do as individuals, a phenomenon called social loafing.[21] The idea can also be applied to group violence. No one person feels the pressure to say that a certain action is wrong. Indeed, the very fact that "everyone else is doing it" (in the standard phrase that people offer in moral defense of their questionable actions) seems to indicate that it is correct, or at least acceptable.

Division of Labor

A second principle is the division of labor. Groups can work far more efficiently and effectively than individuals if the task is divided up so that everyone does what he or she does best. The evolution of modern manufacturing shows this process at work. The original factories, or "manufactories," were simply places where groups of very skilled technicians made things—but each individual worked on his own project. Because these technicians had to have a wide range of skills, their labor was quite expensive. Imagine, for example, how much one would have to know to build an entire car, cabinet, or clock all by oneself. And they had to be paid the cost of their expensive labor even when they were just sweeping the floor after the job was done. It was much more efficient and hence much cheaper to hire such experts only for the most difficult tasks and to have other people with lesser, cheaper skills do the rest of the tasks. Critics of the task division of labor have pointed out that the new arrangement reduced everyone's feeling of identification with the product. If you made an entire cabinet yourself, you would look upon it with pride as something of yours; if all you did was tighten the screws on the doors of 50 cabinets, you would probably feel much less pride. The division of labor reduces feelings of responsibility, too.[22]

When large governments or other organizations embark on a campaign of killing people, a careful division of labor can help conceal any individual's responsibility for the killings. In particular, many groups have found it effective to separate the people who decide whether to kill and whom to kill from the people who carry out the executions. Each individual may see that there is a huge bureaucratic organization, with thousands of people doing thousands of jobs, and his or her own part is quite small. By refusing, one would accomplish little of value, and in particular no one would be saved. Refusing would alienate all one's friends and colleagues, for one would be implicitly accusing them of doing something terrible. Well, they are doing something terrible, but people are always reluctant to point that out to their friends, if only because accusing a friend of immorality is a good way to lose that friend. In contrast, to go along and do one's own little part may seem like a fairly innocent and safe choice.

Trust and Loyalty

A key aspect of the nature of groups is trust. This trust is related to what I have already described in terms of separating the decision-makers from those who carry out the cruel decisions. In most groups where there is a hierarchy of authority, there is almost necessarily a liberal dose of moral trust involved. Specifically, the people at the bottom trust the decision-makers at the top to do the right thing.

It is perhaps unusually difficult for modern American citizens to recognize this trust. We live in a society in which the news media have free rein to investigate the morality of the top authorities, including both the morality of their national policy decisions and the morality of their private lives. The tradition of moral trust of top authorities is undoubtedly weaker in the United States than in most other cultures, and recent historical events have provided ample lessons to Americans of the importance of questioning authority.

Yet even in the United States one can see the pervasiveness of moral trust. In large corporations, whistle-blowers are rare and are often condemned. Robert Jackall's landmark study of corporate ethics[23] found that most managers believe that it is fundamentally wrong to go against your boss unless he or she is undeniably engaged in something atrocious, which normally never happens. Even when some kind of abuse comes to light, one should try to remain loyal. Most of the time, it is considered safe to assume that the boss knows more than you do and that you should do what you are told without question. You certainly do not go about trying to prove that your company's top bosses are morally bankrupt.

Such patterns are not confined to executives. Investigations of police departments or military units often encounter difficulties when the officers refuse to implicate their colleagues. These officers feel that their first moral obligation is loyalty to their fellows, and so they deny having knowledge about misdeeds. Such problems have come to be expected as almost routine in such investigations. For example, in the 1990s, a widespread corruption scandal led eventually to the firing or disciplining of many of New York City's Harlem precinct police, but the investigation stalled and dragged for months because nobody would talk. The media labeled the hostile silence "the Blue Wall."

The issue of moral trust was a central one for physicians during the Nazi era, too, as shown in Robert Jay Lifton's fascinating account, *The Nazi Doctors*.[24] Before the killing of the Jews began, even before the war began, Germany had begun a policy by which certain hopeless cases were put to death. The euthanasia program under the Nazis was aimed at people who had profound and incurable handicaps, such as severe mental retardation or illness. The paradox was that doctors who had sworn to protect human life were put in the position of killing people if it was determined that their lives were no longer worth living. In this early killing program, one could already recognize some of the features that were so successful in the later mass murders of Jews and other victims. Decisions were supposedly made by committees and distant authorities and then carried out by others, so no one felt individually responsible. In the case of the euthanasia program, each of the physicians involved was encouraged to believe that someone else made the final decision, thereby diffusing and concealing any responsibility. The oversight committees made recommendations and thought that the administering physicians would have the final say. Meanwhile, the administering physicians thought that the expert committee had made the decision and they were merely carrying out what everyone else had determined was the right and proper thing to do.

As Lifton records, the procedure followed in the euthanasia program was for older, highly respected senior physicians to make policy and render individual decisions, while younger doctors were assigned the actual duty of making the lethal injections. When young, inexperienced doctors were thus put into contact with very senior members of their profession, they felt honored and flattered, and they were quite willing to cooperate in their assigned tasks (including killing), partly because they turned over feelings of responsibility to their senior colleagues. In effect, they had been chosen for a special honor that brought more rapid career advancement than they otherwise would have had, and contact with a famous person in one's own field is usually a flattering and intimidating experience. It was highly unlikely that a young physician who had a chance to work with such an eminent older physician would throw away this opportunity by telling the older man that his actions were disgracefully immoral.

The system greased the wheels for such cooperation by choosing the younger physicians carefully. They were selected for their idealism, their political enthusiasm, and their lack of experience. They were the ones most likely to go along, and the system was set up to take away any feelings of personal responsibility they had. Indeed, one of them recalled his reaction when he was first told, by a famous older man in his field, that the duties would involve putting certain patients to death. "I told [the senior colleague] I could not take on any responsibility at all because I knew I was not qualified medically," he said. The older physician replied, "All right, you will not have responsibility." He emphasized that the decisions would be made by a panel of professors and specialists who would make careful evaluations of each case. The young physician had only to do his duty, which would be a valuable service to the profession and the society at large. It might be disagreeable, but soldiers at the front had to perform disagreeable duties, too.[25]

The crucial element of trust was articulated by another physician who had been one of the young doctors in this program. Like many people in Germany, he had reserved the absolute highest level of respect for professors, and it had been a professor who had recruited him into the euthanasia program. "It never would have occurred to me that a professor, in no matter what field, would expect a student or a young colleague to do something that would step over the boundaries of human ethics."[26] The older man was for him the person he would regard as being the highest moral authority. If this person said it was all right, then it must be all right.

Groups Suppress Private Doubts

A final way in which groups contribute to the escalation of violence emerges from the discrepancy between what the members of the group say and what they privately believe. The group seems to operate based on what the members of the group say to one another. It may often happen that the members harbor private doubts about what the group is doing, but they refuse to say them, and the group proceeds on its course of action as if the doubts did not exist.

Social psychologists have known for several decades that a group is more than the sum or average of its members. Influential early research showed that groups sometimes make decisions that are riskier than what the average private opinion of the group members favor.[27] More relevant recent work has shown that groups tend to communicate and make decisions based on what the members have in common,[28] which may differ substantially from what the individual members think. In a remarkable series of studies, psychologists Garold Stasser and William Titus showed that groups sometimes make poor decisions even when they have sufficient information to do better. In one study, each group was supposed to decide which of two job candidates to hire. Each member of the group came to the meeting armed with preliminary information about the candidates. The researchers provided more information favoring one candidate, Anderson, but they scattered it through the group. In contrast, the smaller amount of information favoring the other candidate, Baker, was concentrated so everyone knew it. Had the group really pooled their information, they would have discovered that the totality pointed clearly toward hiring Anderson. But instead of doing this, group after group merely talked about what they all knew in common, which was the information favorable to Baker. As a result, group after group chose Baker.[29]

We have already seen how groups involved in evil will suppress doubts and dissent. Chapter 6 quoted some of the people who worked in the

Stalinist terror. These individuals said they privately doubted the propriety of what they were doing, but whenever anyone would begin to speak about such doubts, the others would silence him by insisting on the party line.

The Terror following the French Revolution showed how cruelty can escalate as a result of the pattern in which private doubts are kept secret and public statements express zeal and fervor. The Terror was directed mainly at the apparent enemies of the Revolution, and the Revolutionary government was constantly obsessed with internal enemies who presumably sought to betray it. Hence, those at the center of the government were paradoxically its most likely victims. To criticize the Revolution or even to question its repressive measures was to invite suspicion of oneself. Accordingly, the members of the tribunal and others began to try to outdo each other in making strong statements about the need for harsh measures, because only such statements could keep them safe from the potential accusation of lacking the proper attitudes. The discussions and decisions featured mainly the most violent and extreme views, and the degree of brutality escalated steadily.[30] Ironically, the leaders' fear of one another caused them to become ever more violent, even draconian, with the result that they all really did have more and more to fear. And one by one, most of them were killed by the Revolution over which they were presiding.

Many people will sympathize with victims or question whether their own side's most violent actions are morally right, but they will also feel ashamed of these doubts. What is said in the group, and what is likely to dictate the group's actions, will be the most extreme and virulent sentiments. Whatever their private feelings, the members may express only the politically correct views of strong hatred of the enemy. In such an environment, the group's actions may reflect a hatred that is more intense than any of its members actually feel. The group will be more violent than the individual people in it. Given all the other processes that foster escalation, it may not even be necessary for groups to have this effect forever. Once the members of the group are waist-deep in blood, it is too late for them to question the group's project as a whole, and so they are all the more likely to wade in even deeper.

CHAPTER 10

Dealing with Guilt

"Guilt? It's this mechanism we use to control people. It's an illusion. It's a kind of social control mechanism—and it's *very* unhealthy. It does terrible things to our bodies. And there are much better ways to control our behavior than . . . guilt."[1] These remarks illustrate a common opinion about guilt, that it is a wasteful and self-destructive emotion that does far more harm than good.

Then again, perhaps guilt has been unfairly stereotyped in our culture, which for historical and ideological reasons, may be reluctant to see any positive value in guilt. The statement just quoted was spoken by the notorious murderer Ted Bundy, who killed a number of pretty young women across the United States. If he had had a stronger sense of guilt, perhaps some of those women would be alive today.

Evil is the inflicting of harm or suffering on other human beings. Guilt is the distress that comes from hurting other human beings. Guilt is thus an inherent, perennial problem for evildoers. Those who perpetrate harm must find some way to free themselves of guilt, lest they end up feeling bad. Although there may be a few perpetrators who by some quirk are immune to guilt, most people are not. Most people would feel guilty about killing, harming, torturing, exploiting, or abusing someone.

It works best to deal with guilt in advance. Some people make the mistake of thinking that guilt is something that arises only *after* a person has committed a misdeed. Guilt is backward-looking in many cases because it focuses on what one has done wrong in the past. But guilt also has a strong anticipatory element. People often know well in advance what actions will make them feel guilty, and they try to avoid those actions. If you set out to rob, rape, cheat, or murder someone, you may well anticipate the possibility of feeling guilty. You will probably be looking for excuses and rationalizations to escape the guilt before you commit the act. If you cannot find any, you may refrain from causing harm. This is the valuable social function of guilt. It makes people avoid doing things that are wrong and that harm others. If guilt did not change behavior but merely made people miserable after the fact, it would be nothing more than a senseless form of self-torture.

The threat of guilt will often change the way people perform evil acts. Harm-doers take definite steps (or follow certain guidelines) to prevent guilt. Guilt thus shapes the reality of evil. Guilt may prompt evildoers to avoid certain kinds of harm even while inflicting other kinds. It may drive them to take certain precautions or perform certain rituals. It may shape the way they think about what they are doing, or it may prompt them to get drunk so they can't think about what they are doing.

The broad view of evil presented in this book portrays a range of violent and oppressive impulses springing from several common and powerful roots and held back, most of the time, by such internal restraints as self-control. Guilt is one of the key emotional forces that drives self-control. People refrain from hurting others because they want to avoid feeling guilty. When guilty feelings are thwarted or submerged, harm can be done more easily.

Lame Rationalizations and Loopholes

Before taking a systematic look at guilt and people's strategies for dealing with it, it is instructive to consider some of the more extreme strategies. There are ways people rationalize guilt that seem so preposterous that one wonders how anyone could have believed them. Their very implausibility shows how hard people have to try to bring themselves to believe them.

The explanation for these bizarre rationalizations is probably twofold. First, the perpetrator wants very strongly to believe them. Second, they are superficially plausible enough that the person can accept them as long as he or she doesn't think about them very carefully. The combination of some kernels of truth and an intense will to believe enables some perpetrators to get by with dubious justifications.

Such a combination is apparently necessary for biased thinking or self-deception in general. The research evidence shows that people cannot simply believe anything they want, and they cannot even draw preferred conclusions from any sort of evidence.[2] The scope for distortion is limited. But when there is some evidence that supports a preferred conclusion, people are willing to overlook its flaws and find ways to dismiss contrary evidence. The combination of desire and minimally plausible evidence is a powerful recipe for distorted conclusions.

The Crusades relied on several peculiar rationalizations.[3] At several points, the Christians in the Holy Land found themselves fighting a desperate war—and losing it. Despite the supposedly firm belief that the one true God could only be supporting the Christian side, the Christians lost battles, and many individuals surrendered to save their skins. Sometimes, even top Christian leaders became captives of the Muslims.

The Arabs, however, did not have enough places to put these captives. It was wrong to kill prisoners of war, but they could not feed and house them indefinitely. As a result, the Christians were able to persuade the Arabs to fall back on a traditional way of dealing with this problem: The prisoners would be released after swearing a sacred vow never to fight against the Arabs again. Over and over, Christians took the vow.

And over and over, they broke it. These Christian soldiers typically returned to their camp or city to find that the military situation was still desperate and their help was needed. They could not stand idly by while their comrades were defeated, their women and children enslaved, their new homes conquered, and their religion humiliated by the enemy. So despite their vows, they fought again.

How did they rationalize this? After all, the requirement to keep one's vows is one of the Ten Commandments and had been repeatedly reaffirmed by medieval theologians who dealt with the Christian ethics of war.[4] The Christians developed a new principle: Vows made to heathens were not binding. It was not a sin to do the opposite of what one had sworn if the person to whom one had sworn was not a Christian. This rationalization does not really bear close examination. How can one swear an oath in the first place if it is not really an oath? But the principle was superficially satisfactory, and so people could use it as long as they did not examine it carefully. (Of course, if the same enemy captured you a second time and inquired about your oath, you might abruptly find yourself giving the matter some hard thinking!)

Skipping ahead to the twentieth century, one can find some remarkable somersaults of justification. The major genocides produced several of these, in part because many ordinary and well-meaning citizens found themselves obliged to perform horrendous actions. The "most astonishing" of the rationalizations for shooting Jews given by the members of Reserve Police Battalion 101, according to scholar Christopher Browning, was that of a 35-year-old metalworker who said he got through the day by specializing in shooting children "because I reasoned with myself that after all without its mother the child could not live any longer. It was supposed to be, so to speak, soothing to my conscience to release children unable to live without their mothers."[5] Browning pointed out that the policeman used the unusual word *release* (*erlösen*), which in German is also the religious word for redemption and salvation, which gave his act of shooting children the connotation of an act of grace.

Such a remark might be dismissed as a unique way of thinking peculiar to one bizarre man, but an almost identical sentiment was quoted in an Associated Press news story about the Rwandan genocide more than half a century later and half a world away. The perpetrator in this case was a woman named Jualiana Mukankwaya, herself a mother of six children. During the well-orchestrated killings of Tutsis, Jualiana and a group of other women rounded up children in their neighborhood. In the explicit language of the Associated Press, "With gruesome resolve, she said, they bludgeoned the stunned youngsters to death with large sticks." She herself killed the son and daughter of people she had known for most of her life. Her explanation was given with a blank face and in a flat voice. "She was doing the children a favor, because they were orphans who faced a hard life. Their fathers had been butchered with machetes and their mothers had been taken away to be raped and killed, she said."[6]

Killing children is one of the most difficult and gut-wrenching things for adult men and women to do. Some readers might easily dismiss such rationalizing statements as the feebly absurd and hypocritical comments of thoroughly evil individuals, but that view is probably not correct.

Whether the metalworker and the village woman thoroughly believed that they were doing children a favor by killing them is far from certain, but they were probably trying hard to believe it. The two key components of rationalization were both present: There was at least a vestige of plausibility in the argument that the children were doomed anyway, so that a quick death spared them further suffering, and the perpetrator had a powerful desire to believe that there was something good about what he or she was doing. A dispassionate observer would probably not agree that the killers were doing the children a favor, but the perpetrators themselves could hardly afford to be dispassionate, and if they tried hard enough to believe it, they could.

Thus, rationalizations that seem preposterous at first can be accepted gradually by people who are sufficiently motivated to accept them. Further examples of this pattern can be seen among the comments made by modern street gangs with regard to their violent actions. In general, these groups believe that their kind of people have been attacked and exploited by enemies, and so they are justified in fighting back.[7] In many cases there is a clear and direct basis for such beliefs, and the attacks are actually happening. More interesting, however, are cases in which the victim is irrelevant to the attack, so that people must convince themselves that they are justified in harming someone who has not wronged them.

In recent years, the most discussed instance of that pattern concerns black-on-black violence. It is quite clear that the white-run government of the United States has helped the white majority oppress and exploit black people, especially in the past. The argument that white people have exploited black people might conceivably justify violence against the exploiters, but how would it justify the most common crimes committed by black street criminals, whose victims are other black people?

Attempts at just such rationalization are not uncommon. Researcher Leon Bing described an interview with a south central Los Angeles gang member in his home. Bing specifically asked about the violence against other blacks, and the gang member explained, "The government plays a big part in why we kill our own kind."[8] He went on to say that the government oppressed black people with job discrimination, making them want to attack each other for money. Another gang member Bing interviewed was just as blunt yet also just as vague about how the white establishment was responsible for the deadly gang war between the Crips and Bloods, the two giant networks of gangs who dominated

Los Angeles. "My real enemy—the United States government. That's who controls the Crips, the Bloods, and me."[9]

Black intellectuals have commented on the same pattern. Milton Morris, the vice president for research at the Joint Center for Political and Economic Studies, was quoted in *Newsweek* as saying, "When black young people slaughter other black young people on the street . . . they all come back to 'Look what the white people make us do.'"[10] More broadly, the attitude that prevails in such groups was summarized by black author Ellis Cose as "a no-fault attitude, a conviction that 'nothing I do is my fault, since the white man created the awful conditions in which I live.'"[11] Cose's own appraisal of that attitude identified the same two components we have already seen in the other rationalizations: It has kernels of truth (Cose blamed white people for conditions in black ghettos), but it requires a strong will to believe to become usable as a justification for specific acts of violence against innocent black victims.

There seem to be two main ways that these criminals rationalize their exploitive violence against their fellows as being the fault of their racial enemies. One is to say that criminal violence is an affirmation of black nationalism, or at least a tool of black survival outside the white society, even if its victims are black. Nathan McCall described this rationalization in a poignant passage in his memoirs. He noted that he and his friends were robbing and hurting other black men and women, including some of the most vulnerable and victimized people in the entire country. He clearly recognized the possibility of feeling guilty over the fact that he, as a black man, would cause suffering to other black men and especially black women. (Actually, he was unwilling to use the word *guilt*, but at several points he said that brutalizing innocent people sometimes made him feel "weird," and it seems reasonable to assume that the weird feeling was guilt.) Yet he said this was the only way that he and his friends could avoid having to get legitimate jobs, and it was essential to avoid that at all costs. To take such jobs would essentially mean supporting the society run by and for white people, who were the enemy. Anything that enabled him and his friends to survive without capitulating to the establishment was acceptable.

The other rationalization was even vaguer but corresponded even better to the everyday reality of these young men's lives. This belief was that the enemy white society had somehow conspired to force black people to fight against each other. Although this internal war among blacks might be deplorable, there was nothing that could be done about it at the moment, because the mortal danger from the enemy blacks was so urgent that it consumed all one's efforts. Sister Souljah, a black celebrity and musician, created a minor national stir recently when she proposed that blacks should stop killing one another and kill white people instead. But to most black street criminals and gang members, this was not a feasible solution, because their most dangerous and familiar enemies were other blacks.

The result of this second rationalization is that these young black people can go on killing and robbing other blacks while simply blaming all their own actions (as well as those of their enemies, perhaps) on the white society. These rationalizations are appealing and plausible enough that if you want to believe them you can, as long as you do not question them too deeply.

There are plenty of other, similar rationalizations that perpetrators use, but these examples are sufficient to illustrate the point. People will settle for any vaguely plausible argument when they want badly enough to believe that their hurtful actions are justified. Before taking a more systematic look at how evildoers maintain their justifications, it is necessary to explain the nature of guilt, because guilt is what the justifications are designed to prevent.

The Nature of Guilt

On the surface, guilt is nothing more than an unpleasant emotion that comes from doing things that are wrong. This simple understanding is somewhat misleading, however, and it also conceals some complexities in the way guilt originates and is felt. There are several key points to understand about guilt.[12]

Guilt is primarily a result of harming other people. Guilt does not attach equally to all actions that might be regarded as wrong; it is most commonly felt when one is responsible for interpersonal harm, such as causing someone to suffer. Because evil is a matter of causing people to suffer, guilt and evil will show up in many of the same places. Or, more precisely, the same circumstances may result in *either* evil or guilt, because guilt prevents evil.

Guilt is linked to relationships. Not all acts of harm cause equal guilt; the degree of guilt is often proportional to how much you care for the victim. Failing to return a phone call to your mother brings more guilt than failing to return a phone call to a stranger or an insurance agent.

Cheating on your spouse causes more guilt than cheating on the IRS. People do sometimes feel guilty toward strangers, but they feel much stronger guilt when people they care about are involved. When people are asked to describe something that made them feel guilty, for example, the vast majority of their responses involve family, romantic partners, and close friends.[13] Guilt seems to grow amid the strong emotional bonds between people who care about one another.

The interpersonal nature of guilt brings up the issue of its roots. Guilt seems to originate in two basic emotional patterns. The first is empathy. People feel upset when they have empathy with someone who is suffering, and this empathic distress forms a basis for feeling guilty. He or she feels bad, so you feel bad to see his or her suffering. The other root of guilt is fear of losing a relationship. When people hurt those who care about them, they increase the risk that the victim will withdraw from the relationship. People inherently want to maintain and prolong their social attachments, and so they become upset at the prospect of someone withdrawing from them.[14]

These considerations point to the crucial interpersonal functions of guilt. Guilt makes people treat their relationship partners better. Guilt motivates people to be kind and attentive to others who care about them, to live up to their expectations, to refrain from harming them, and so forth. Guilt is thus fundamentally prosocial: It helps to strengthen the bonds between people.

Although guilt begins with emotional responses such as fear of being abandoned and distress upon seeing someone suffer, it evolves into something more complex and sophisticated. Adults have elaborate notions of personal responsibility, intentions, mitigating circumstances, and other factors that determine whether they ought to feel guilty or not. Thus, the best way to understand guilt is as a gut reaction that gets filtered through an elaborate conceptual system about rules and responsibility.

The system is far from perfect. Sometimes people feel guilty when they presumably should not. For example, some people who made it through the concentration camps or the atomic bombings ended up feeling guilty for having survived when their family members died.[15] In a modern parallel, when corporations go through mass layoffs, some of those who keep their jobs feel guilty toward those who were fired. Meanwhile, some people seem to be free of guilt even when inflicting serious harm or death on others.[16] Still, these imperfections should not be enough to condemn a system that by and large works quite well. Guilt deters people from committing evil, criminal acts and makes them treat those they care about well.

Guilt is unfairly stigmatized and despised in our society, yet there is a method to the unfairness. Guilt does have costs to the self, in that it makes us feel bad. Its costs are obvious, whereas its benefits are harder to see. Each person's guilt brings benefits to everyone else except that person. Psychopaths, in particular, seem almost entirely free of guilt feelings, and they do not seem to be greatly handicapped by this (except when they are caught and imprisoned for committing crimes). In contrast, everyone associated with a psychopath has to pay the price for the psychopath's lack of guilt. Psychopaths see no point in contributing to the general good or in refraining from taking advantage of somebody who cares about them.

Viewed in this way, guilt is the opposite of self-esteem. High self-esteem brings advantages to the self, particularly in that it makes us feel good, but its costs (such as violence) are borne by those around us. In other words, high self-esteem benefits the individual at the expense of the group, including relationship partners. Guilt, in contrast, benefits the group at the expense of the individual. It makes us feel bad, but to avoid these feelings we do things that are better for our relationship partners and fellow group members.

The relationships of guilt and self-esteem to evil fit this analysis. As we have seen, high self-esteem is an important cause of evil. People who think highly of themselves will exploit others and will attack someone who does not show them the respect they think they deserve. In contrast, guilt is a counterforce that restrains evil, violent, aggressive impulses. Guilt prevents people from just doing whatever they might like to do or might benefit them, if it would involve hurting someone else.

The individualism of modern American society leads directly to worship of self-esteem and contempt for guilt. For better or worse, Americans place more importance on the individual than on the group or community. Self-esteem is better for the individual and worse for the community, and so Americans prize self-esteem. Guilt is better for the community and worse for the individual, and so they detest guilt. The American attitude that values the rights of the individual above the community's best interest apparently contributes to high levels of happiness.[17] It contributes to individual freedom and deters tyranny.[18] But it also promotes violence, along with oppression and individual forms of evil.

In any case, guilt is a crucial emotion for restraining violence. Indeed, in Chapter 7, I proposed that the path to sadism is available to almost everyone, but most people are kept off it by guilt. Guilt prevents people from discovering or admitting to themselves that they can get pleasure out of hurting others. More generally, people avoid a broad assortment of acts that would harm others because they want to avoid feeling guilty. Perpetrators want to minimize guilt.

Not One of Us

One strategy for avoiding guilt feelings is based on the interpersonal nature of guilt. People feel guilty when they hurt people with whom they share some kind of social bond. Therefore, to hurt people without guilt, make sure that your victims do not share any bond with you. The lower the fellow-feeling, the less guilt.

The strategy of distancing oneself from one's victims is implicit in the common device of labeling them as subhuman creatures. One shares a community with all other human beings and should feel guilty about hurting any of them, and so one can avoid guilt by ejecting the victims from this broad human community. To kill a human being is wrong; to kill a fly or a rat is acceptable and perhaps even praiseworthy. Perpetrators often denounce their victims as vermin, as slime or filth, as a disease or the carriers of a disease, and so forth. Such remarks are insulting, of course, but they are more than mere insults. They are important devices for securing legitimacy. They justify killing and reduce guilt, because they rule out any human connection between perpetrator and victim.

Another version of this strategy is to see the victims as utterly foreign enemies who deserve their fate. It is not surprising that so much bitter violence arises between groups that regard each other as different. Many racial, ethnic, and religious groups see themselves as close, important communities—and see anyone who is different as outside that community.

We have seen that otherness is a core aspect of the myth of pure evil. There is a certain validity to the myth, in the sense that people feel less empathy toward those who belong to other groups. No empathy, no guilt.[19] The lack of empathy makes violence toward outsiders easier, because it undermines the restraining power of guilt.

A defining statement of this guilt-avoidance strategy was spoken by a minor official in Stalin's purges. In central Russia, men had been sent to a labor camp where the conditions were brutal and frequently lethal: working outdoors in freezing weather with inadequate food and clothing. At great risk to himself, a local man went to protest at the camp, but the camp administrators were unmoved. Finally, after trying more diplomatic ways of phrasing things, the local man pointed to the conditions under which the unfortunates were working and bluntly said, "These people might die!" The camp administrator replied, "What people? These are *enemies* of the people."[20]

That response precisely articulates the key point. The victims are not like us and do not belong to our community, even our very broad community of "the people." There is no need to feel sympathy for their suffering or even to feel guilty about causing them to die.

Although I have emphasized perpetrators and victims, evil can also arise when an empathic connection between leaders and followers is absent. An important and fascinating study by John Mayer has analyzed the characteristics of dangerous leaders, and foremost among them is the lack of an empathic bond with their followers.[21] Leaders who lack such an emotional bond can be cold and cynical about using their followers to further their ends, and any suffering that ensues is merely a means to an end.

The modern era has furnished plenty of examples of leaders who felt no guilt about causing their followers to suffer. Napoleon's march into historical greatness required many small and not-so-small sacrifices by the men who fought for him, but he took their suffering in stride. "Soldiers are meant to be killed," he said, in one of the classic statements of leaderly detachment. Hitler and Stalin repeatedly sacrificed great numbers of their loyal followers, even condemning them to death out of hand, without any apparent signs of guilt. Not only were these millions of deaths unhelpful to the country, they were positively harmful. Stalin nearly destroyed the Red Army with his purges and vendettas, which left his country almost defenseless for a time. Hitler's final orders before his suicide entailed the destruction of the country's remaining infrastructure and would have made Germany uninhabitable. When he saw that the war was lost, he commanded people to destroy all the power and water plants, which would have left the wartime survivors even more at the mercy of the elements than they were.

In our own time, Saddam Hussein provides another vivid example of a leader whose lack of empathic bond with his own Iraqi people causes them to suffer. He has not hesitated to involve them in ruinous wars for the sake of his own territorial ambitions, first a long and bloody war against Iran, and then the invasion of Kuwait that resulted in the spectacular defeat by the United Nations. Later, during the international boycott, he refused deals that would have brought much-needed food and medicine to his people, because he was using the suffering of his people as a bargaining chip for his own ends.[22]

Two of the roots of evil are especially relevant to this strategy of denying guilt. One is egotism. There is a strong sense of superiority implicit in the pattern of categorizing one's enemies as subhuman vermin. It is all right to kill them, because they are so low and worthless in comparison with the needs and wants of the perpetrators.

The other is idealism. Idealists can best avoid guilt if they are convinced that they are fighting against evil, and they feel the least guilty when their enemies resemble the myth of pure evil. Two prominent features of that myth are the fundamental otherness and innate wickedness of the enemy. Evil people commit bad actions for their own sake and therefore initiate many conflicts and problems. If we are fighting against such people, there is no reason to feel guilty about hurting or killing them. Being evil, they must have started the battle, and we are doing good by defeating them. Moreover, they are fundamentally different from us and belong to a totally different category of being, so we need feel no empathy with them.

Language as Smoke Screen

Language exists to express and communicate, but perpetrators reluctant to face up to their guilt often find ways to use language to conceal, confuse, and mislead. Often this process begins with the words themselves. Perpetrators play endless games with words, and one point of these games is to present the shocking and horrific as mundane and ordinary. Institutional campaigns of oppression and murder have used such seemingly innocent terms as *ethnic cleansing* (Bosnia), *final solution* and *special handling* (Nazi Holocaust), *relax* (Spanish Inquisition), and *bush clearing* (Rwanda) to disguise their brutality.[23] Studies of torturers have revealed a highly specialized vocabulary built of euphemisms referring to methods of torture, such as *tea party, dance, birthday party, the telephone, the submarine, the swallow, the airplane,* and so forth.[24] Even the list of ordinary slang terms for killing reveals by its length the importance of concealing the blunt meanings of violence: *to waste* or *off someone; to order a hit; to have someone whacked; to rub him out; to push the button on him; to wipe them out; to take care of somebody; to snuff out* or *pop someone; to liquidate, exterminate,* or *terminate someone; to knock him off.*

Two sets of metaphors for killing deserve special mention because many different groups have found them appealing. The first involves extermination. To say that the enemy must be exterminated is to reduce the enemy to the status of subhuman vermin and to present killing as a matter of getting rid of worthless, troublesome pests.

The second common metaphor is a medical one. Medical metaphors have been generally popular in the twentieth century, which is perhaps not surprising given the high prestige of the medical profession and the great advances that link modernity and technology with medical interventions. The analogy of amputation was popular with leaders of the Terror following the French Revolution, the Nazis, the Stalinist cadres in the Soviet Union, the Argentinean military oppressors, the Colombian death squads, and many others. By cutting off a diseased limb, amputation saves the rest of the body, and this metaphor has proved appealing to executioners everywhere.

The medical metaphor also helps to depict the victims as deserving of their fate. They are the carriers of disease who pose the risk of infecting the rest of the societal body. They may look like ordinary human beings, but in fact they are dangerous.

Although innocuous terms may be the most obvious means of concealing evil, styles of phrasing do just as well. A linguistically skilled perpetrator or apologist can mold a few grains of truth into a solid wall of justification, enough to keep guilt and accusations at bay.

A compelling illustration of this technique was provided in Ryszard Kapuscinski's interviews with the ministers and other leading figures in Ethiopia during the student protests that eventually culminated in the revolution. These ministers remained loyal to the emperor even after he had been dethroned, and from long habit they spoke in ways that constantly praised his wisdom and goodness while blaming troubles on outsiders and others. The manner of speech is very revealing of the patterns of thought in the former, doomed government, which was badly out of touch with the people.

At one point during the emperor's rule, the government was shocked by a local uprising. After it was forcibly suppressed, the government wanted to stage a student demonstration to show support for the emperor. The minister described how the government's plan failed: "When the march of [the emperor's] supporters, composed of policemen disguised as students, started, a great and rebellious mass of real students joined in, this ominous rabble started rolling toward the Palace, and there was no other solution but to bring out the army..."[25] The minister went on to regret the "irony" that several policemen were killed during the army crackdown, "And yet were they not completely innocent?"[26] He passed over the fact that no real students could be found to demonstrate in support of the emperor and that the government was seeking legitimacy by staging a fraud, with policemen pretending to be students. He thought it inappropriate that the "ominous rabble" of real students joined the mock demonstration. He felt sorry for the "completely innocent" policemen who were killed along with the students. This seemed to him an unfortunate accident, and in a sense it was, but then one must consider the fact that the government first sent the policemen there (as bogus students) and then sent the troops in to shoot them. Still, the minister saw no fault in the government's actions.

The next day, a public funeral was held for the real students who had been killed, including their leader, and not surprisingly a new demonstration erupted spontaneously at the funeral. The emperor again called in the army, including tanks, and called for order to be restored. "As a result more than twenty students perished and countless others were wounded and arrested." The end of the story is the most remarkably phrased part: "His Highness ordered that the university be closed for a year, thus saving the lives of many young people. Because if they had been studying, demonstrating, and storming the Palace, the Emperor would have had to respond again by clubbing, shooting, and spilling blood."[27]

To be sure, the students were being troublesome, but the government repression seems brutal and excessive. To the minister, though, the fault lay entirely with the students. The government had no choice but to send in the army. "There was no other solution," he said. Instead of saying that orders were given to shoot the students and quell the demonstration forcefully, he says only that the emperor commanded that order be restored, and "as a result" some students "perished" while others "were wounded and arrested." The passive voice thus hides any active role taken by the government and presents the students' sufferings as a misfortune that came upon them as an inevitable result of their own actions. Finally, and most bizarrely, the emperor's closing of the university is described as an act of kindness to the students instead of a punitive strike to silence dissent. In the end, the minister's way of speaking transforms the emperor into the student's savior instead of the one who gave the orders to kill them.

Do euphemisms and other innocuous phrasings succeed in concealing crimes or deflecting guilt? Undoubtedly, most large-scale evils have involved some degree of concealment, and the manipulation of language is part of it. For example, reading through Kapuscinski's interviews with Ethiopian officials, one is repeatedly struck with how sincere and thorough their belief was in the basic, innocent goodness of the emperor and his fallen government. Yet mostly they were describing events in which they did not actually participate; their speech may have reflected the way these events were discussed at court rather than their personal experience. It is difficult to believe that someone who actually rapes and kills people would be misled by the harmlessness of such terms as *ethnic cleansing*.

One possibility is that such terms are used as flagrant hypocrisy. Even as perpetrators knowingly inflict harm on someone, they may use misleading words to conceal their guilt or deny the extent of their actions.

A more likely possibility, though, is that perpetrators simply find it unpleasant to speak frankly of their deeds. To use the literal, blunt, ugly terms for their actions would be upsetting and stressful. It is necessary to appreciate that group perpetrators of atrocities have the same need to discuss their tasks as any other sort of work group. Almost no team, crew, or other group doing any sort of work can perform its task without talking about it. Groups of evildoers are thus presented with the problem of how to talk about what they are doing among themselves. To use strongly evocative language might well be counterproductive, because it would upset the members of the group or distract them from their tasks. There is also the possibility that blunt speech might evoke enough guilt to cause members of the group to refuse to do their tasks. Of course, this is what victims and humanitarian bystanders hope will happen, but the leaders of the group do not want a dissenter or objector popping up unexpectedly while the group is trying to get its job done.

Imagine the chief administrator of any of our century's death camps saying to a member of his staff, "I'm putting you in charge of mass murder group #2. We're having lots of innocent victims coming in this week, so I need you to slaughter them as fast as possible. And don't leave any bloody corpses lying all over the place, because that stench is sickening." It seems wildly implausible that two people who are actually engaged in mass executions would speak in those terms, if only because it would make the job harder on them both. Yet the conversation must be held and the assignment must be made, at least within the context of the operation of the camp.

And so the chief is more likely to say something like this: "I'm putting you in charge of operations group #2. We have an unusually large number of units coming this week, so you'll need to process them as efficiently as possible. But be sure that the workers follow through on proper cleaning and disposal procedures afterward, so the work area remains presentable." The message would be the same, but it sounds more like a normal workplace discussion of administrative procedures and less like a plan for evil—and, in the perpetrators' views, it is an administrative matter that they are discussing. Hence, such language is likely to facilitate the smooth and effective operation of the camp. The immediate problem being discussed is a pragmatic one, and talking about it as such (instead of in the morally evocative terms of the previous paragraph) makes it easier to address.

There is one additional reason that perpetrators use more innocuous words than victims or dispassionate bystanders would use: the magnitude gap. Of course it is shocking to the victims that the people who are killing them one after another would speak of them as "units" to be "processed." But that is because so incredibly much is at stake for the victim. Being killed means the end of everything: no more waking up on a sunny morning, falling in love, having successes and failures at work, enjoying a fine meal or good glass of wine, talking and laughing with a friend, having sex, helping others, sitting spellbound through a great performance, going shopping.

For the perpetrator, in contrast, very little is at stake. Whether he kills 35 or 40 people on a particular day will make little difference in his own life and feelings and what he will experience in the coming weeks. Even if he is later caught and prosecuted for crimes against humanity, the difference between 35 and 40 victims on a particular day will probably not matter much. Although perpetrators sometimes do use minimizing language to conceal their guilt, they may also use such language because ultimately the acts are relatively trivial (to the perpetrators, at least).

I Had No Choice: Justification through Necessity

The Ethiopian official's account of the violent suppression of the student demonstration contained several phrases that are worth a second look because they exemplify one of the most popular justifications of evil: the appeal to necessity. The government staged a phony student demonstration, and real students joined in and changed the tone of it, at which point "there was no other solution but to bring out the army to enforce the restoration of order."[28] The important implication of this statement is the necessity of responding in this way because of a lack of alternatives. The official does not say that the government reviewed various options, such as ignoring the demonstration, negotiating with the students, or setting up an investigation to hear complaints. Instead, he says that there were no options except violence.

The potential logical power of such a claim is enormous. We have understood guilt as a gut feeling that gradually becomes enmeshed in a web of complex meanings. Foremost among these meanings is responsibility. Guilt is supposed to occur only when the person recognizes that he or she is responsible for the misdeed. Responsibility is typically understood as involving freely chosen behavior. But if there were no options to choose among, then there was no choice, and hence no responsibility. Even if the perpetrator still feels a few nagging guilt pangs, these can be put aside if he or she can say with certainty that there was no other possible response.

Pointing to external necessity is therefore a popular strategy of perpetrators. "I couldn't help it," they say, "I had no choice." To the extent that this is true, their responsibility is eliminated.

We saw early in this book that pointing to external necessity is part of the way perpetrators think in general. In the study that compared victim and perpetrator accounts of minor interpersonal conflicts, perpetrators were much more likely to describe external factors that caused their actions. Furthermore, it is probably wrong to propose that perpetrators only start thinking that way after the fact, when they are trying to make excuses for their heinous actions. More likely, they embrace such beliefs while they are doing their evil deeds or even beforehand. Moral doubts or scruples might inhibit them from inflicting harm in the first place, but if they can persuade themselves that they have no choice, then they can put such doubts aside and perform their tasks more efficiently and with less distress.

The most famous and familiar version of the "I can't help it" defense involves following orders. As we noted, St. Augustine and many other thinkers have believed that followers have a moral obligation to obey commands of legitimate authorities. This means that one cannot refuse an order without questioning the entire legitimacy of the authority figure, which in many cases would be unthinkable, and which certainly is something that one would do only after careful thought and consideration. To say that one is following orders is to say that one had no choice.

Milgram's studies of obedience likewise used the phrase "You have no choice" in order to pressure doubtful individuals to continue giving (supposedly) painful electric shocks to a confederate.[29] Thus, the procedure for the study involved the initial instructions to deliver a higher shock every time the other fellow made a mistake, and if at any point the subject hesitated or refused, the experimenter responded with a standard series of comments. The comment "You have no choice" was literally and patently absurd, because the subject obviously did have a choice, and indeed the whole point of the experiment was to learn about what choices people made in that situation. But hearing the authority figure say that you have no choice was enough to conceal the fact of choice and to get people to continue giving shocks. The reason, presumably, is that the subjects in the experiment did not want to believe they had a choice. They wanted to complete their assigned tasks without getting into an argument with the experimenter who was supervising them. To believe that they were responsible for their own decisions would have forced them to make moral calculations and difficult decisions on very short notice. It was better to accept the authority figure's word that they had no choice.

Part of the reason for this finding is the way that people understand nearly all their actions. One of social psychology's most influential theories of the 1970s held that observers think that other people do things because of the kind of people they are and for other internal reasons, but that they see their own actions as responding to the situation.[30] The actor-observer discrepancy arises in part because of what people pay attention to. Observers pay attention to actors, whereas actors pay attention to their surroundings. In this respect, perpetrators follow the same pattern in understanding their behavior that everyone does: "I was only responding to the situation."

The actor-observer effect is likely to be much stronger in perpetrators of harm and other morally questionable actions, because they want to avoid blame. To see oneself as responding to external circumstances is to reduce one's responsibility.

The "I was only following orders" justification became a cliché of Nazis and other Germans who were implicated in killing Jews. The U.S. military now has an explicit policy that soldiers should not follow illegal or immoral orders. But how valid was this justification when used by the Germans?

Nearly all works on the Holocaust deal with the question of moral responsibility or justification based on following orders. Many Germans who used this excuse elaborated on it by saying that they would have been shot themselves if they refused orders, including orders to shoot Jews. As they often put it, they did not want to kill civilians, but they were compelled to by military duty and by the mortal danger of immediate execution if they refused.

My reading of the literature points to several conclusions. First, some Germans did refuse to take part in killing Jews, and these Germans were not shot. I found only one alleged exception, a story in which a group of soldiers was preparing to shoot and one of them raised his hand to say he could not, so he moved over to line up with the victims and was shot by his former comrades.[31] The story is anonymous and quite possibly apocryphal; it may have been nothing more than a false rumor. For the most part, those who refused were simply transferred elsewhere or assigned to other duties. They did seem to be penalized by a lack of career advancement afterward. Still, such a penalty is obviously a much weaker justification than execution.

Hence, most scholars have rejected the soldiers' claim that they had to take part in killings of Jewish civilians, because the evidence does not show that soldiers who did refuse were executed. On the other hand, as we have seen in this chapter, many justifications do not depend primarily on factual reality. All that is required is a will to believe and some kernels of truth. And the kernels of truth were quite adequate in those cases. Instead of asking, "Were those who refused executed?" we should ask "Could soldiers have believed that they would have been executed for refusing?" The answer appears to be yes.

Thus, although those who refused to shoot civilians were not executed themselves, they were often threatened with execution. Many an officer's first response to the men who asked to be excused from shooting civilians was to deny their request with the comment that if they could not do their duty they should take their place among the victims.[32] The rumor quoted above may not have been true, but it may well have circulated through the German forces because it buttressed the belief that one had to comply with orders. More generally, the entire code of the German military, and especially the SS, emphasized complete, unquestioning obedience. In fact the Germans did execute their own soldiers during World War II at an exceptionally high rate, more than a thousand times the rate of executions by Germany's military in World War I.[33] Apparently, the commanders quietly kept a distinction between disobeying normal orders and disobeying orders to shoot civilians, but this distinction would not have been widely publicized, especially to the troops.

Judged by objective criteria, the excuse of following orders was probably not a valid justification for participating in shooting civilians. But subjectively it was plausible. There were enough kernels of truth that those who wanted to believe it could do so. And the will to believe it was undoubtedly strong once one had crossed the line and participated in the killing of civilians. As we have seen, the situational pressures to go along at the first moment were probably strong, because it was difficult to refuse the order on moral principle immediately. Once one has started killing, then, one might well want to rationalize one's actions by believing that refusal would lead to one's own death, and there were enough cues available to support this belief, even though it was false.

The "I couldn't help it" defense has added a new dimension lately, which is based on the notion of irresistible impulses. In a highly publicized trial, Lorena Bobbitt recently managed to persuade a jury that she couldn't stop herself from going to the kitchen to get a knife and then using it to mutilate her husband. Alcoholic husbands often assert that they cannot keep themselves from beating their wives when they get angry. Contrary to such assertions, the weight of the research evidence suggests that irresistible impulses are in fact few and far between.[34] The belief in irresistible impulses, despite evidence to the contrary, is probably due to the appeal of the notion: It enables perpetrators to escape responsibility for their actions. They can believe they had no choice.

The notion of following orders brings up the issue of how groups can facilitate evil by shifting responsibility around. Let us turn now to consider some of these group strategies for spreading guilt around until it seems to disappear.

Group Evil and Individual Guilt

We have already seen that operating as part of a group facilitates evil, particularly because people lose a strong sense of individual responsibility for their actions. The loss of responsibility reduces the power of guilt and self-control to prevent harmful actions. Let us briefly reconsider the four main ways that groups accomplish this effect.

The first is the principle of *diffusion of responsibility*.[35] The responsibility for the group's actions is divided up among all the members of the group. Even when one person acts, he (or she) may regard his own actions as being done for the group, so that other members of the group share the responsibility. The sharing of responsibility probably increases confidence that the actions are right and proper, because surely it seems that the entire group could not be making a major moral blunder. Moreover, there is less apparent need for any one person to feel guilty, because the individual's responsibility is greatly reduced.

The second principle is *deindividuation*.[36] One effect of being part of a group is that people lose awareness of themselves as individuals and cease to evaluate their own actions thoughtfully. Because self-awareness and self-scrutiny constitute a central, integral aspect of self-control,[37] the normal restraints and inhibitions tend to be reduced when people blend into a group, and the group may end up doing wilder or more harmful things than the sum of individual members would lead one to expect.

The third principle is *division of labor*, which has been one of the essential functional advantages of groups throughout history. This was the aspect of the Nazi killing system that so impressed many commentators. The death of one person was the result of dozens of individual actions by different people, no one of whom felt anything more than a slight responsibility for the lethal outcome. Each person could say something like "I just drove the train, I didn't kill anybody." Even the one who did administer the poison gas knew it was hardly his fault. The people had been selected, brought here, stripped naked, and lined up in the bogus showers for death, without any doing of his. His own role was that of a technician, and his responsibility was a mere formality.

The fourth principle is *separation of the decision-makers from those who carry out the acts*. If people are to be killed, then someone must eventually flip the switch or pull the trigger. That person is the one most likely to have moral qualms or to feel potentially responsible (and hence not to want to kill until the moral questions have been resolved with high certainty). To minimize such doubts (and hence to facilitate evil), it is most effective to make that person believe that full responsibility rests elsewhere. By the same token, those who must decide to send people to their deaths will find their job easier if they are far removed from the actual victims and killings. To single a person out from a group and then shoot her would be stressful and difficult. It is much easier to select a stranger's name from a list while sitting in an office and never expecting to meet the person or hear about the actual death.

The gulf between decision-maker and executioner is often very wide in successful evil. For example, the Spanish Inquisition institutionalized the split by having the Church decide who would die, and then turning the victim over to the secular authorities. The Church could debate someone's faith and fate in relatively abstract terms, without having to involve clergymen in actual bloodshed. And the secular authorities could carry out the executions without any moral qualms or questions, because the supreme moral authority had marked these people for death.

Once responsible authority is effectively separated from carrying out the acts, it becomes very difficult to thwart a group's evil project. If someone balks at carrying out harmful actions, another can say straight out that the decision and responsibility lie elsewhere and so it is wrong to question or hesitate. The Nazi doctors interviewed by Lifton could often cite specific conversations in which they were told bluntly that the decisions were not their responsibility and that the absent, higher-up decision-makers would be fully responsible.[38] The soldiers who carried out the killings of civilians were often told precisely the same thing.

The same blunt response can be found in corporate America. The notorious Dalkon Shield intrauterine contraceptive device is known to have resulted in the deaths of at least 18 American women and caused serious infections, often resulting in permanent infertility, in tens of thousands of women around the world.[39] Before the calamity, at one of the factories that was producing the devices, the quality control supervisor became concerned about potential safety and conducted a series of tests on his own that showed a serious danger that infectious bacteria would be introduced into women's bodies by wicking along the device's string. When he reported these concerns to his superior, however, the superior told him bluntly that the string was not his responsibility. He was told to do his job and not interfere in areas that were the responsibility of others.[40]

For Their Own Good

If guilt arises from harming others, another possible way to ward off guilt would be to claim that the victims actually benefited from what one did to them. There are relatively few events that have completely one-sided outcomes, and often it is possible to point to some kind of ben-efit that the victim or the victim's group received. Indeed, one of the greatest calamities of European history was the bubonic plague, which killed large segments of the population, yet historians have come to conclude that there were some positive results: increased freedom; a scarcity of labor that enabled the poorest workers to command higher wages and exercise control over their fate; and an increased availability of farms, which allowed some serfs to escape from feudal control. If even the bubonic plague can be seen as producing positive outcomes, we should not be surprised that clever and motivated perpetrators can claim that their victims derived some benefit from the harm the perpetrators caused.

We have already seen a couple of extreme examples of this strategy in the justifications for killing children proposed by the German man and the Rwandese woman who said they regarded killing the children as merciful acts because the youngsters would not be able to survive on their own, now that their parents had been killed. These arguments have the usual grain of truth: It is indeed difficult for a child to get by without its parents, and the odds are that the children would have suffered and eventually died had they been spared on that particular day.

At the opposite extreme, a recent study of minor interpersonal trans-gressions found that some perpetrators sought to excuse themselves by proposing that the victim had derived some benefit. One person pro-mised to take a friend to a concert but then reneged when the chance arose to go with someone more desirable. The first friend was therefore deprived of the concert, but the perpetrator added that the concert turned out to be not very good, which implies that the friend who missed it was actually somewhat better off. A group teased one person and made her very upset, but afterward they reflected that she gained insight into herself from the experience.

Throughout history, similar arguments have been used to justify oppressive and unequal relationships. Early in the nineteenth century, for example, the American South tended to speak of slavery as a "neces-sary evil" and an unfortunate institution, but when the antislavery rhetoric of the abolitionist Northerners became more strident, some Southerners began to speak of slavery as a positive good—even for the slave. Slavery was "a great moral, social, and political blessing—a blessing to the slave, and a blessing to the master," as a senator from Mississippi said.[41] Slaveowners saw themselves as heads of extended families that included both black and white members, and so they idealized their mastery as a parental nurturance of their slaves. Slavery was also credited with bringing religious enlightenment to heathens. On the eve of the Civil War, slavery's apologists insisted that slaves were better off than the unskilled wage-earners of the North, because slaves were fed and housed for life whereas Northern hirelings would be fired for not working and abandoned when too old or sick to produce.[42]

Individual criminals are also sometimes willing to justify their crimes on the basis of supposed benefits to victims. Some burglars and thieves say that they are doing their victims no harm and possibly helping them, because of insurance. One criminal phrased this bluntly: "Sure I stole the stuff. But, hey! Those folks were insured up the kazoo. . . . In fact, I'm doing them a favor by giving them a chance to collect insurance. They'll put in for more than that junk was worth, you know. They always do."[43]

In some cases, there may be enough ambiguity for the perpetrator to believe that the victims' benefits justified the perpetrators' actions. The grain of truth might be large enough to be plausible. But there are also cases that stretch credulity. One researcher quoted a rapist who said his victims benefited because they got their names in the paper![44] An extreme example emerged from the Ethiopian famine, which will be discussed in greater detail in the next chapter. One official sought to justify the government's actions that made the famine worse by saying that the great famine was actually beneficial to many Ethiopians because they needed to lose weight. He was in earnest, and he supported his contention by citing Scripture on the benefits of humility and the spiritual benefits of fasting.[45] The government was helping the common people succeed at their diets.

Robert Hare, an expert on psychopaths, has interviewed hundreds of these remorseless criminals and studied many additional ones indirectly, and in the course of this work he has certainly listened to accounts of many hair-raising acts and preposterous rationalizations. Yet he said that one in particular "dumbfounded" him. A convicted criminal said that his victim had benefited by having learned "a hard lesson about life."[46] I suppose that in many crimes the possibility that the victim learns something would be a final, minimal sort of benefit, although hardly enough to justify the crime. In this case, though, the crime was murder. The experience of being murdered cannot possibly teach one anything worth knowing, because there is no opportunity to use that knowledge.

The benefits of being killed are obviously scarce, but even virtuous men with high principles have occasionally proposed that they exist. The Christian theologians debated at length over some of the crueler aspects of the Crusades, especially the use of apparently unfair tactics by the knights. Yet some theologians argued that such brutality benefited even the victims, because it kept them from living out their lives in sinful opposition to the Christian cause and faith.[47] The argument held that since everything a non-Christian does is sinful, that person is better off dead, because longer life would entail greater sins.

Thus, benefits to the victim have been cited in many contexts as one justification for violence. Most events have both good and bad outcomes, and especially if one includes the broad class of "lessons learned," one can see some positive value in most experiences. The perpetrator can often find a genuine grain of truth upon which to build this justification. Because the victim's benefit usually has little relevance to the perpetrator's actual motive, the argument must be regarded as a rationalization, but by minimizing the victim's suffering while highlighting the victim's benefit, the perpetrator can reduce his or her own blame.

The extremity of some of these defenses and the lameness of others raises the broader issue of whether perpetrators actually believe them. Let us consider that issue directly.

Empty Excuses or Sincere Self-Deceptions?

"In defending myself against the Jews, I am acting for the Lord." Thus spoke Adolf Hitler, and he made similar comments on other occasions to the effect that killing Jews was justified by the highest moral authority in the universe. It is difficult to know whether he really believed this or was merely making hypocritical statements to defend indefensible acts. Actually, it is even difficult to say which would be worse: that he actually believed he was doing the Lord's work, or that he was casually lying.

Are the many self-justifying statements made by perpetrators sincere or disingenuous? This question continues to plague anyone who wades through all the evidence about how people rationalize their evil deeds. Do the people who torture, rape, maim, and kill in the name of some cause really believe that it is their sacred right and duty to do so, or are they merely acting out of baser motives and trying to cover their wickedness with fancy phrases?

The difference affects how these individuals are judged. One may condemn their crimes in either case, but many judges would be inclined to be more lenient with perpetrators who were acting out of a sincere (but presumably misguided) idealism. If their justifications were empty, disingenuous excuses all along, one would judge them more harshly. The difference boils down to whether one views the perpetrators as evil or merely stupid. Are they evil enough to knowingly commit horrible crimes and then lie about it with feeble rationalizations? Or are they gullible enough to believe those justifications?

Undoubtedly, there are cases in which the rationalizations are transparent hypocrisy. Early in this century, anti-Jewish sentiment was inflamed by the publication of the *Protocols of the Elders of Zion*, a book in which Jews purportedly explained their secret plan to conquer the world. The book was a forgery, of course, although many people believed it. Still, those who participated in the forgery or who exploited it for propaganda purposes while knowing it was fake were obviously insincere in using it to justify anti-Jewish actions.

Another famous example of transparent, preposterous rationalization involved Lenin. Soon after the Russian Revolution, national elections were held and a Constituent Assembly was convened. Although the Bolshevists styled themselves the party of the people, in fact the voters elected only a small minority of Bolshevist candidates (amounting to about one-fourth of the Assembly). Lenin had held power since the Revolution and was not about to concede it to an elected assembly that the Bolshevists could not control, and so after a single day he dispersed the assembly. It might seem difficult to justify such a blatant power-grabbing rejection of an assembly that was elected by the people, but Lenin was up to the task. He explained:

> The People wanted to convene the Constituent Assembly, and so we convened it. But the People at once sensed what this notorious assembly represented. So now we have carried out the will of the people.[48]

Of course this was preposterous. No population has ever repudiated its entire elected assembly in a single day, let alone in backward Russia where mass communication media were scarce and the people could hardly have known what the Assembly might have been discussing before it was canceled. The very idea that the will of the people would demand a cancellation of democracy and a rejection of their ballots is absurd. Lenin's comments can hardly be anything except hypocritical rationalization.

Yet such clear-cut cases are rare. Moreover, I think they are rare not just in the clarity of the evidence but also in that the perpetrators seem to be so shamelessly mendacious. It seems far more plausible to conclude that the majority of perpetrators do believe their justifications. They may recognize that they have done wrong, but they emphasize the external causes and mitigating factors and believe sincerely that their actions are not as bad as others, particularly victims, assert.[49]

To understand the perpetrator's point of view, we must recognize one crucial fact: Most perpetrators want very much to believe the justifications. To dismiss them as either blatant hypocrites or deluded fools is to miss the point. A justification for killing may seem feeble in retrospect, but that judgment is made with the benefit of hindsight and dispassionate objectivity that can expose the holes in the argument. The perpetrator does not want to see through the holes in his justifications. To do so would require him to recognize the full evil horror of what he is doing.

Self-deception is an iffy business. People cannot convince themselves of anything that they might want to believe.[50] In fact, the margin for self-deception is often rather small: People can only stretch the facts and the evidence to a limited degree. Groups, however, have several advantages in this regard, because they can support each other's beliefs. When one is surrounded by people who all believe the same thing, any contrary belief gradually seems less and less plausible. It is not hard for us as outsiders to knock holes in the self-justifying reasoning of perpetrators, but such an exercise is misleading. Perpetrators often find themselves in groups where no one would think to raise objections and everyone would agree with even flimsy arguments that support their side.

Great evil can be perpetrated by small groups when the members strive to think alike and support the prevailing views. Unfortunately, power tends to produce just such situations, because the most powerful men (and presumably women) tend to surround themselves with like-minded associates, who become reluctant to challenge the prevailing views. Whether the group is a small religious cult, a set of corporate executives, or a ruling clique in a large country, the justifications expressed by everyone in the group will tend to gain force.

The communication patterns increase this force. Committees and other small groups tend to focus on what everyone believes and knows in common. Private opinions and extraneous facts are kept to oneself. We saw this in the chapter on idealistic evil (Chapter 6). Many individuals might have doubts and qualms but are reluctant to express them, so that everything said publicly in the group conforms to the party line. When the moral acceptability of some violent action is at issue, everyone keeps silent about his reservations and objections, and everyone repeats the overt justifications and rationalizations. As a result, everyone gets the impression that everyone else believes those justifications and that his own doubts are an anomaly. One may even feel guilty about having doubts; everyone else seems so certain.

One of the most remarkable phenomena of the twentieth century is the speed with which countries have abandoned their totalitarian beliefs, despite having advocated them with apparently minimal dissent for long periods of time or at great cost. All the Germans seemed to be behind Hitler, but immediately after the war, the Allies could find hardly anyone who professed to have believed sincerely in the Nazi world view. Likewise, the nations of Eastern Europe apparently supported their Communist governments with little criticism or dissent, and then in 1989 they abruptly abandoned Communism wholesale and embraced an entirely different approach to politics and economics.

Such rapid and radical conversions begin to make sense if one accepts the view of self-deception we have developed here. People want to believe what the government tells them. They want to believe that what their society is doing is the right thing. To help themselves believe, they suspend criticism and questioning, and they go along with others in expressing the preferred views. But when circumstances discredit the ruling view, they suddenly acknowledge all the problems and fallacies they had avoided, and they can say with reasonable honesty that they did not sincerely believe it after all. Their desire to believe makes a great deal of difference when the facts are ambiguous.

Changing the Dance, Not the Tune

Many people think that guilt is something one feels mainly *after* one has done something wrong—especially if the wrong was intentional. The scientific community was therefore quite surprised when a major study of guilt by Kathleen McGraw[51] found that people reported more frequent guilt over unintentional actions than intentional ones.

There is an important reason for these results, as McGraw explained. When people intend to do something that might be wrong, they know well in advance that they might feel guilty. Accordingly, they change their actions to ward off guilt. They start their rationalizations well in advance, and they make certain that the actions themselves remain consistent with these rationalizations. Thus, they do not end up feeling guilty. In contrast, when people hurt someone by accident, they have not had time to marshal their rationalizations or minimize the blameworthy aspects, and so they feel guilty afterward.

A classic example of how harm-doing procedures are adapted to soothe the consciences of the perpetrators is the Requirement, used by the Spanish during the conquest of the New World.[52] The royal court back in Spain was troubled by reports of massacres of natives and other atrocities and wanted to ensure that the activities of the conquistadors remained within the bounds of the Christian faith. The royal lawyers consulted with church officials and eventually came up with a procedure that would satisfy everyone, or at least everyone who had a say.

The procedure was based on the principle that Spanish activities in the New World were guided by the high motive of bringing Christian enlightenment to the benighted peoples there. Violence was acceptable only when it was necessary to further this admirable goal. Accordingly, the Requirement was a document that explained to the natives the importance of converting to Christianity and warned them that if they failed to embrace the true faith right away, they could be subjected to stern treatment, including even being killed or enslaved.

The activities of the conquistadors were modified to include the reading of the Requirement before mounting a devastating attack on a native village. Some scholars believe that the men in the field regarded the Requirement as "bureaucratic nonsense"[53] and few took it seriously, but they did make sure to read it before the intended victims and have the reading witnessed by a notary. Even if the conquistadors themselves treated it as a trivial waste of time, it must be acknowledged that the intentions of the Spanish court were probably earnest and sincerely moral.

The point is that the moral danger was recognized, and the procedures for dealing with the natives were modified to make them fit the justifications. The official justification was that the Spanish were benefiting the natives by bringing them Christianity. It would have belied this justification to shoot and loot innocent victims merely to take their gold and other valuables. But to inform them in advance that they ought to adopt Christianity and would be subject to violent conquest if they refused enabled the Spanish to believe that they were doing morally and religiously valuable work. That way, they only attacked people who had obstinately refused the Lord's truth.

One of the most Kafkaesque stories to emerge from the Holocaust involved the trial and execution of Karl Koch, the commandant of the Lublin and Buchenwald concentration camps, for the murder of two Jews.[54] Thousands of Jews were being killed every day in such places, but when reports of illegal killings came to light by accident, an investigation was initiated.

One must be curious about the thoughts of Konrad Morgen, the man in charge of the investigation that eventually sentenced about 200 concentration camp staff members to various penalties (and Koch to death) for killing Jews in a place where Jews were being killed constantly and in a society whose rulers were pursuing a policy of complete genocide. When a historian asked Morgen about this years later, he explained that there were three types of killing going on. First there were the mass killings of Jews, which were based on official decrees originating in Hitler's Chancellery and about which, therefore, nothing could be done. Second were the euthanasia killings of incurably ill or incapacitated individuals, and this too was official policy and therefore untouchable. Finally, there were arbitrary, capricious, and therefore unauthorized killings of individual prisoners. Only the third kind was illegal, and thus only the third kind came under the authority of his investigation.[55] He was working within the system to stop whatever killings could be stopped according to policy.

The point, though, is that it was crucial to maintain the view that Jews and other victims were being executed only in a legal, orderly fashion according to proper procedures. To kill them casually or recklessly violated the official story that the mass killings were part of lawful, orderly procedures. That official policy meant little to the victims. To the perpetrators, however, it was decisive and powerfully meaningful. If they abandoned it, they would be admitting that they were brutal and evil killers, no better than ordinary murderers. Sacrificing a few of their own to maintain their claim on being agents of the law was presumably worth it.

The twentieth century's most dramatic example of how procedures are sometimes altered to maintain justifications was probably the show trials conducted during Stalin's purges, which were briefly mentioned earlier in this chapter. During the 1930s, the paranoid ruthlessness of the Soviet regime turned from the class enemies (who by then had mostly been exterminated anyway) to the cadres themselves. Even many of the oldest and most distinguished Bolshevists were singled out by Stalin and his group for elimination. Indeed, their very eminence and distinction made them seem all the more dangerous to Stalin, and in his eagerness to eliminate any possible rivals, he executed many of the Soviet regime's best and brightest.[56]

Mass execution of top government officials attracts international attention, and of a most unflattering sort. Although Stalin had been able to have millions of peasants and other ordinary citizens killed with relative impunity, it was more difficult to eliminate top Communists who were internationally known. The solution was to conduct trials that could be covered by the international press. These trials were carefully managed to establish the appearance of perfidy and guilt of the defendants—and of course of the scrupulous legality of the subsequent killings. In most cases, the victims confessed to many acts of treason, and independent evidence of guilt was also supplied. Not all went according to plan, of course. Sometimes the victims recanted their confessions in court, saying that their prior confession had been the result of torture, and so the courts found it necessary to suspend proceedings and send the defendants back for more torture to elicit a more durable confession. In a couple of cases, the legal absurdity and weakness in the prosecution's case would cause a judge to find the defendant not guilty, and then it was necessary to find a new judge (possibly by arresting the previous one as a collaborator in counterrevolutionary activity) and start over, until the requisite guilty verdict could be obtained. Still, for the most part the proceedings went approximately according to script.

The purpose of a trial is normally to establish the guilt or innocence of the defendant. Judged by that purpose, the show trials were a complete waste of time. They were in fact just scripted performances designed to furnish a plausible public pretext for executing men (and occasionally women) whose death had been preordained. The fact that innocent verdicts were systematically thrown out, often with the indignant arrest of the judge, shows that there was no willingness to let the light of truth lead the courts away from their appointed path. What the show trials did prove, however, was that even the most powerful men in the world could not get away with simply killing their enemies and rivals without explanation. It was necessary to furnish a veneer of legality and due process.

A sad story from Castro's Cuba shows the importance of maintaining the legal pretext, however slim. In March 1959, not long after the revolution, a Red military tribunal conducted a trial of 43 pilots and mechanics from the defeated (Batista) air force. These men had not betrayed their country; their only real crime was that they had been in uniform on the losing side. It had not occurred to them to consider themselves traitors, and indeed they had not even tried to flee the country. The Communist tribunal agreed and acquitted them all. Castro, however, was outraged, because he wanted them convicted and punished. Instead of simply ordering that they be killed, however, he changed the constitution to give prosecutors the right of appeal, which had never existed in Cuba (or indeed almost anywhere else). A new trial was duly conducted and the men were all convicted and sentenced to 30 years in prison. "Revolutionary justice is not based on legal precepts, but on moral conviction," explained Castro.[57] Nonetheless, it is obvious that he wanted the legality as well.

Or Just to Escape

So far, we have considered the many ways that people seek to evade guilt by justifying their actions. There is another, very different, strategy for avoiding guilt: One can escape it. One can use mental tricks to keep oneself from recognizing the moral issues surrounding one's actions.

Any reader of the Holocaust literature is sure to find vivid images stamped into his or her memory, and one that lingers for many readers is the image that of the horseback rides of Rudolph Höss. He was the commandant of Auschwitz and presided over the operation of the camp, which killed thousands of men, women, and children every day. He found the work unpleasant, especially the "heartbreaking scenes" such as when a woman would try to push her children out through the closing doors of the gas chambers, shouting and pleading, "At least let my precious children live!"[58] He felt he must not let any doubts or other troubling feelings show, however, because he was the leader and any signs of weakness on his part would spread through the ranks and undermine morale. He knew that everyone watched him, and his frequent doubts and questions had to be concealed.

He tried to keep busy with other aspects of camp administration, such as the building and logistical problems (which were enormous). Still, he could not avoid the killings entirely, and indeed his desire to do his duty as a good Nazi meant that he could not even allow himself to neglect the killing operation. A trooper in the woods might let a victim escape or ask to be excused from shooting civilians, but a camp commander had to supervise the entire operation.

And so he needed some way to cope. He had had a strong affection for animals since childhood. At Auschwitz,

> When something upset me very much and it was impossible for me to go home to my family, I would climb onto my horse and ride until I chased the horrible pictures away. I often went into the horse stables during the night, and there found peace among my beloved animals.[59]

Riding the horse was obviously no source of justification, and it had no logical power to convince him that gassing all those helpless naked civilians was the morally correct thing to do. But it was a response to feelings of guilt, and by his own account it was a reasonably successful one. It did get rid of the feelings.

And so one pictures Rudolph heading off on his horse, early in the evening, his head full of images of the pathetic, humiliated, defenseless strangers whose lives he had helped snuff out that day. From his writings and by all other indications, he was not a man given to strong emotions, and so his upset feelings probably took the form of feeling depressed and sordid, most likely with some unpleasant tension throughout his body, a clenched jaw, an upset stomach. And then one pictures him riding back to the stable later, covered with light sweat, his body tired and relaxed, his mind calm again, ready to spend a quiet evening with his family like any other career man in the world. No more need to think about work until tomorrow morning.

The primary mental trick used to escape guilt feelings can be called *low-level thinking*. The term is based on an influential theory put forward by psychologists Robin Vallacher and Daniel Wegner.[60] They began by borrowing a standard argument of the philosophy of action, which is that most actions can be described in multiple ways that differ in their level of meaning. Thus, one can speak equally well of raising one's arm, throwing a bottle, making a protest, or participating in violent revolution to bring about a new government and social organization. It is not that one level is more correct than the others, because all are accurate descriptions of the same action. They differ, however, in their implications. Raising one's arm carries no emotional or moral weight, whereas performing a symbolic revolutionary act carries extensive and heavy weight.

Hence, if one wants to be free of guilt, including both its emotional side and its aspect of responsibility and principles, it is better to focus one's mind at lower levels. One attends to the details and procedures rather than the broader context and meanings. There is some evidence that this is what criminals typically do.[61] When burglarizing a house, for example, they are not reflecting on how their actions violate the principles of private ownership of property, or will cause distress and anguish to the victims, or will undermine the economic scheme of the broader society. Rather, they focus very narrowly on procedural details: fingerprints, window locks, alarm systems, hiding places, dogs. Not only does this way of thinking help them perform more effectively, but it also prevents any feelings of guilt.

The power of low-level thinking to keep one's mind off guilt is a major reason for the apparent fascination with details that has marked many killing operations. Lenin was constantly looking into minor administrative details. One of his biographers, Dmitri Volkogonov, remarked how ironic it was that the Soviet Union preserved a view of Lenin as a great philosopher, when in fact his writings tended to be quite pedestrian. Most of his papers were more worthy of an accountant than a philosopher, according to Volkogonov. But by focusing on procedures, he could avoid facing up to the enormity of the murder campaign he was setting in motion.

The low-level thinking spread through the entire Communist apparatus. Arthur Koestler recalled two slogans that he heard over and over during his days in the Communist party in Germany. One expressed the inexpediency and inappropriateness of meaningful theorizing in combat: "The front line is no place for discussions." The other defined the appropriate attitude and orientation of each individual Communist: "Wherever a Communist happens to be, he is always in the front line."

In combination, the two slogans required Koestler and his comrades to avoid deep thoughts, abstract principles, and broad questions entirely. The front line is a place for only narrow, concrete, here-and-now thinking.

Similar observations have often been made about the Nazis. Social scientists and other outsiders have routinely professed horror at the way that these men and women seemed to understand their jobs as merely checking lists, driving vehicles, flipping switches, giving instructions, and the like. The horror is that these people seemed to act as if this were ordinary bureaucratic activity—that they failed to see the monstrous evil of mass murder that their jobs involved. But perhaps that was precisely the point. It would be agonizing for any sensitive person to work for a mass murder machine. To become less sensitive it is better to reduce the work to mere red tape. To get up each morning to face a day's work of killing people is probably a crushing, demoralizing way of life. To get up each morning for a day of checking lists is far more manageable. One may know, of course, that the lists have something to do with people being deported and possibly executed, but it is too awful to think about that. Thinking about doing a good job with the lists is far more tolerable.

The low-level focus is also apparent in the self-criticism notes of the Khmer Rouge torturers at the infamous Tuol Sleng prison, which were briefly mentioned earlier. Like Communists everywhere, the torturers were supposed to engage in self-criticism. What did they reproach themselves with, these people who tortured others for months and then killed them? "In these records, the interrogators discuss such mundane problems as lying down on the job while questioning prisoners, not sharpening pencils, smudging papers, and the like."[62] These tasks are certainly low level, as well as trivial. Not sharpening pencils is about as unabstract a problem one can imagine.

Even more revealing, though, was what was said when the topic of the prisoners' fate did intrude into the torturers' self-criticism:

> The major problem discussed in the interrogators' notes, however, was that prisoners were dying under torture ('croaking' is the exact translation, used in the Khmer language to refer to animal rather than human death) before their 'confessions' were complete.[63]

Thus, torturers did occasionally reproach themselves for killing someone, but this was done only as a technical or professional failure, not as a moral problem.

Keeping one's thoughts on the low level of procedures and details is a potentially effective way to avoid guilt. It does not justify one's wrong actions, but it accomplishes the same goal that fancy justifications would, which is to enable one to avoid the feelings of guilt. It conceals the wrongness of the actions. Wrongness is largely a high-level judgment that requires evaluating the higher meaning of actions according to broad, meaningful principles. If one can avoid thinking at that level, the wrongness does not appear.

Erasing Guilt with Alcohol

The drawback of low-level thinking is that it is sometimes difficult to do. The human mind seems naturally inclined to move toward integrative, meaningful thought. This tendency is often helpful, creative, and valuable, but not when one is trying to avoid meaningful thought. Accordingly, people sometimes resort to artificial aids to help keep their minds free from broad principles and deep moral questions. Undoubtedly, the most widely-used of these aids is alcohol.

Alcohol is probably the most universally familiar method of escaping the guilt and other inhibitions that might hold people back from inflicting harm. Although alcohol has certainly brought much pleasure to many human beings, it is also a useful tool for escaping from unwanted emotional states. That makes it a useful tool for performing evil.

No one will be surprised that alcohol is involved in many acts of violence. What is perhaps surprising is how pervasive and even systematic the use of alcohol appears to be. Indeed, in some cases, alcohol use becomes official policy. Before battle, for example, soldiers in many wars and in many countries have been given a strong dose of alcohol to pluck up their courage and reduce their inhibitions about shedding blood.[64]

Alcohol played a central role in the Holocaust. The guards and officers at concentration camps were very often drunk. Some of the physicians interviewed by Lifton mentioned the heavy alcohol use as an occupational hazard or difficulty of concentration camp work, as if it were unthinkable that one might remain sober under those circumstances. And perhaps it was unthinkable: To stand for hours amid frightened, disoriented people, looking closely at their worried faces and haggard bodies to select a few fit ones for work, while the rest were marched off to immediate death—that sort of work is undoubtedly stressful, especially for an idealistic young doctor who had thought that his profession would involve curing the sick and helping people. Apparently, it became a part of the routine that when your turn came to perform selection duty, you got seriously drunk beforehand and brought along a bottle to sustain that state until the task was over.

During the phase of mass shootings of civilians, the German troops likewise tended to become and remain drunk, and in some cases the drunkenness interfered with effective performance. A story in Browning's book[65] on German police would be comical were it not for the horror of mass murder. The Germans had recruited some local volunteers to help execute the local population of Jews and handed over the unpleasant duty of the actual shooting to the locals. The local volunteers arrived late, which was already aggravating to the German police because they were having to stand guard very uncomfortably over a large number of people who were going to be shot, and because Germans in general emphasize punctuality. The reason for the lateness was quickly apparent: The local helpers turned out to be drunk, having taken full advantage of the liquor ration that was provided for shooters.

The Germans had prepared a killing site and an orderly procedure by which the victims would walk in single file to designated positions along a freshly dug pit in order to be shot, but the drunken locals began shooting willy-nilly without allowing the victims to get in proper position. There began to be corpses all over the place.

After a while, the alcohol caught up with the shooters and they began to pass out and sleep it off. The massacre then had to be delayed for a couple of hours. The Germans bickered among themselves as to whether they ought to shoot the Jews themselves. Finally, after a two-hour nap, the drunken shooters began to wake up and the killings resumed.

Other sources from other massacres make similar comments about alcohol. Stories from the Spanish Civil War tell of mass shootings of civilians, in the course of which the shooters often got drunk. This was especially remarkable because the killings were often conducted very early in the morning, so the volunteers had to get themselves out of bed, eat a quick breakfast, and get drunk before dawn. The authorities who supervised the executions were also drawn to drink. One of the most famous was Diaz Criado, a colonel whose job it was to make out the daily lists of political prisoners and others to be executed. He did his work in a cafe and was almost never seen in a sober state.[66]

Torturers are likewise people whose jobs do not lend themselves to deep moral thinking, and the use of alcohol is also common among them. Indeed, some torture victims have noted that their tormentors seemed "almost always drunk."[67]

Alcohol is useful for escaping from guilt because of two related effects. First, it seems to produce low-level thinking. When people get drunk, their thinking becomes narrow, rigid, and concrete, and this focus minimizes thoughts of grand principles (such as morals) and the emotions that accompany them. Second, alcohol tends to deflect thinking away from the self, and so one does not dwell on issues of identity and responsibility.

Getting drunk may seem like one of the feeblest ways to deal with guilt, because alcohol operates directly on one's immediate mental and emotional state rather than allowing one to reframe or justify one's actions. Despite its crudeness, however, alcohol appears to be quite effective (at least for a short period of time). Whether any of the methods of dealing with guilt are really good enough to sustain perpetrators for the rest of their lives is open to question, and probably most perpetrators who have any conscience have uneasy memories for the rest of their lives. But there are plenty of ways, from fancy rationalizations to simple drunkenness, that can suspend guilt long enough to permit people to perform evil acts. That is what is crucial. How the perpetrator deals with guilt after the fact is of little importance to the victims, because the evil has already occurred.

CHAPTER

11

Ambivalence and Fellow Travelers

In 1995, a single father checked into a New York hospital complaining of "bad lungs," and he soon died of lung cancer. His beloved young daughter, Elisa, was returned to the custody of her mother, despite objections that the mother was unemployed, had five other children to feed, and had been accused of beating the girl during weekend visits. The mother became convinced that the child was possessed by the Devil and began punishing and torturing her repeatedly. Finally, one day the mother sent Elisa crashing headfirst into a concrete wall. Two days later, the mother asked a neighbor to call for help. The authorities arrived to find a dead girl with injuries all over her body, some old, some new. The police lieutenant called it "the worst case of child abuse I have ever seen."[1]

One sad feature of little Elisa's story is that there were many complaints of abuse over many years and involving many different social agencies. It seems that the system should have been able to save her. In retrospect, at least, there were ample warning signs, and a number of people who knew the girl had pointed them out very strongly long before she died. Yet the system failed her and left her at the mercy of her mother. "We're all accountable," said New York's mayor, Rudolph

Giuliani.[2] His point was that the community could have and should have prevented this death.

The same sentiment was expressed by the secretary-general of the United Nations, Boutros Ghali, in response to the genocide in Rwanda that claimed about 800,000 lives, more than 10 percent of that nation's population. Referring to the failure of the world to intervene, Boutros Ghali said, "We are all to be held accountable for this failure, all of us, the great powers, African countries, the NGOs [nongovernmental organizations], the international community."[3]

The roles and responsibilities of bystanders is one of the more thorny and vexing aspects of the dilemma of evil. In a simple analysis, one can blame the perpetrators of violence and leave the bystanders out of it. Yet the actions—or inactions—of bystanders often play a crucial role. The New York welfare system did not kill the little girl, but it apparently could have saved her, and in that sense Giuliani's comment is apt. The international community could probably not have saved all 800,000 Rwandese, but it could have saved some of them.

It is appealing but misleading to sort history into perpetrators and victims. Often there are more bystanders present than either perpetrators or victims, and the bystanders have the power to alter the outcome, whether they realize it or not. Furthermore, perpetrators may depend on bystanders in a number of ways, many of which are not directly related to the crime but are nonetheless essential. In the case of Elisa's mother, for example, the system supported her economically because she had no job and her husband was in prison. Taxpayers paid for the apartment where Elisa was killed. In other cases, as we will see, perpetrators of violence depend on others for food, shelter, and other things, without which they could not pursue their violent acts.

People Who Switch Sides

We have seen repeatedly that when individuals do evil, they often harbor some doubts or ambivalence. This ambivalence also occurs in groups. When groups perform violent or evil acts, there are often people who resist or object. Moreover, when one group oppresses another, there are usually members of both groups who work with or for the other side.

Large-scale evil rarely fits the pattern of a united, cooperative group of perpetrators oppressing a united group of victims. First, there are usually people in the perpetrator group who object to what the group is doing and who may work in various ways to prevent it. Second, there are often people in the victim group who collaborate with the enemy and assist in the defeat of their group.

The history of the British Empire in South Africa provides a valuable case study, in part because the defectors on both sides played decisive roles.[4] Viewed from a great distance, it is easy to simplify the history of southern Africa into a simple story of white European invaders defeating and oppressing native black Africans. The familiar story is based on conflict of one group against another, with lines clearly drawn in black and white. And there were plenty of people in that turbulent region who played just those roles. I have already talked about Lord Milner, whose policy of "sacrificing the nigger absolutely" was an overt and explicit plan to bring peace to the white factions (British and Boer) at the expense of the native blacks. And of course the major battles were fought in just those terms: the white British army, armed with rifles and Gatling guns, against the spear-carrying Zulus. Despite one extraordinary Zulu victory, in the end their army was destroyed, their empire conquered, and their emperor taken prisoner.

Let us look at the conflict again, this time focusing not on the obvious participants but on those who deviated from their racially dictated sides. Among the black natives of South Africa were thousands who helped the white British invaders. If the conflict had been a simple matter of white against black, the outcome would almost certainly have been different. Many thousands of black Africans worked directly for the British forces, doing the indispensable menial work that an army requires. Blacks guided the white soldiers around the unknown, mapless country, and they worked as domestic and farm servants in the white settlements. There were even some black soldiers who fought against the Zulus.

The reliance on blacks was apparent to the white people there at the time. After the shocking Zulu victory at the battle of Isandhlwana, there was widespread fear that the white settlements were undefended and at the mercy of the blacks who lived there. If all the blacks had rebelled and attacked the whites, it seems possible that every white person in South Africa might have been killed. The loyalty of many black people to the white cause was decisive in enabling the British to prevail in the end.

Yet there was no greater consensus among the white British than among the black Africans. During the entire episode, there were protests back in England against the oppression of the natives and the attack on the peaceful Zulus. Indeed, the very war that destroyed the Zulu empire had to be created with a dishonest ultimatum and a bogus provocation, because no just or honorable cause existed for the war. There had been some minor territorial disagreements, which some of the British had hoped to fan into a major confrontation. Incredibly, the Zulus agreed to settle the matter in a British court, and just as incredibly, the British judge ruled almost completely in the Zulus' favor. This should have ended the problem and provided a basis for the Zulus and British to live peacefully in neighboring territories for many decades to come. The official who communicated the ruling to the Zulus took it upon himself to add a series of demands and stipulations, deliberately including some that would be impossible for the Zulus to accept. This provided a pretext to report that the Zulus had violated the settlement, and thereby furnished the British with an excuse to invade.

After the defeat at Isandhlwana, the British nation briefly came together to support the war effort, but as the second invasion began to succeed, the protests were again heard. The war was criticized as unjust. The rights of the Zulus to enjoy their own territory peacefully were asserted—again, by white British citizens back in England. The military effort and the protest reached their climax almost together. The great irony of the Zulu war was that England effectively renounced its victory. The Zulu land was left to govern itself with only minimal British authority. The defeated Zulu emperor traveled to England as a royal guest and was treated as a celebrity. British popular sympathy for his people and his lost cause ran high.

The division on the British side was thus just as decisive as the division among the African natives. The British army won the war only with the help of black workers and troops. Then the British protest against their own nation's imperialistic aggression pressured the country into renouncing its victory and giving up any gain from the battles that their soldiers had died to win.

The case of the British in South Africa is hardly unique. In fact, I would regard it as typical. There are some examples that are closer to home and thus are perhaps more difficult for American citizens to appreciate objectively. Most obviously, the Vietnam War showed the same pattern of deep collective ambivalence on both sides. Many Vietnamese regarded the American troops as imperialistic invaders trying to thwart their nation's bid for liberty, but many others worked for and with the Americans and in some cases formed lasting personal friendships.

Meanwhile, the American collective ambivalence about the Vietnam War was overwhelming. Back in the heartland of the United States, people met, marched, campaigned, and otherwise demonstrated on both sides. Some supported the war and the American military; others were passionately opposed to it.

Vietnam may be an excellent example of collective ambivalence, but it is not likely to be convincing because many people regard it as an aberration. The timing of the war was wrong, they say, or it was really based on false premises. Therefore, it is worth looking at other American wars of aggression that had much more of the national interest at stake.

The most important of such wars were those fought against the native American peoples, who were collectively referred to as Indians as a result of a geographical mistake dating back to Christopher Columbus. Most of today's United States had to be conquered from the Indians who lived here before the white Europeans arrived and took over.

Collective ambivalence played a crucial role in the conquest of the Americas right from the start. Indeed, Cortez's conquest of Mexico would almost certainly have been impossible if the natives had united against the invaders. But the huge Aztec empire had made bitter enemies among both the conquered peoples and its neighbors and rivals. In one of the worst misjudgments of all time, many of these groups believed that the Aztecs were a more important and dangerous enemy than the handful of Spanish troops, and they looked upon the Spanish as a minor ally that might be potentially useful to win a brief edge over the Aztecs. They shared their homes and food with the Spanish, helped them understand the local languages, guided them through the utterly foreign and uncharted territory, and fought beside them against the Aztecs. Their help made all the difference in the Spanish victory. Their reward, sadly, was to be decimated by the diseases the Spanish brought and then to be subjugated by force and either massacred or enslaved by the victorious conquistadors.

Up north, the British and other settlers likewise benefited from the Indians. The celebration of Thanksgiving today is partly a recognition that the early settlers owed their very survival to the natives who shared their food with them and taught them how to grow the New World's best crops. Later, during the Indian wars, some Indians again allied themselves with the white invaders against their traditional enemies. Unlike the initial conquests of the Aztecs or the Zulus, the white victory in the Indian wars was probably inevitable, given the eventual mismatch in population and military technology, but it would have been much more difficult if many Indians had not helped the whites.

The division among the Indians lasted until the end of their independence. Indeed, the last great Indian leader, Sitting Bull, was killed by other Indians (specifically, Indian reservation police who had been sent to arrest him).[5] The Indian police were responsible for keeping order and enforcing the laws on the Indian reservations. One can see them as collaborators with the oppressors; they worked for the white government and army. Yet to stigmatize them in that way is not entirely fair. No doubt many Indians felt it was better for Indians to police themselves than to have all weapons and authority vested in white occupation troops. Even the killing of Sitting Bull was most likely the unfortunate act of nervous young men on a dangerous nighttime mission under difficult, ambiguous circumstances.

Meanwhile, the attitude of white settlers toward the Indians was ambivalent, too. "The only good Injun is a dead Injun" was a line presumably spoken by men near the frontier who had suffered at the hands of Indians and fought them. But it was hardly the only view; indeed, the sentence itself suggests that it was said as a response to someone else who was seeking to distinguish "good" Indians from "bad" ones. A moment ago I mentioned that some Indians worked with and befriended whites, and there is no reason to think that these positive bonds were not equally welcome and important to the whites, too.

There was also significant popular outcry against the military conquest of the Indians. People wrote letters protesting their mistreatment; and some individuals went to great lengths to form bonds with the Indians to help them get along better and avoid fatal conflicts with the authorities.[6]

One can go on listing examples. Over and over, victim groups seem to have provided invaluable assistance to their oppressors, without which the oppression could not have succeeded to anywhere near the same degree. The Chinese invasion of Tibet was greatly helped at crucial points by divisions among the Tibetans, who essentially let in the army that was to destroy their culture.[7] Mid-twentieth-century European Jews cooperated with the Nazis, forming small puppet governments that operated the ghettos in accordance with Nazi rules, and, they even organized deportations to the death camps. According to Hannah Arendt, the

Holocaust would have been vastly less successful had the Jews failed to cooperate. (Some dispute her conclusion; my reading supports it.[8]) The Crusaders were aided by Arab allies who sometimes fought alongside them and in other cases allowed them access to cities that had held out successfully against the best sieges the invaders could mount.

Over and over, one finds that many members of the perpetrator group objected, protested, or in some cases actively tried to thwart the efforts of their own side. The Chinese had occasional doubts about the correctness of their oppression of Tibet, and there were periodic efforts to undo the damage and make their policies less destructive. Many Germans objected to the Nazi murder campaign, and some risked their lives to save Jews from death. Some Crusaders protested the atrocities and tried to stop or punish the most brutal offenders. Closer to home, some of Sherman's Union soldiers on the famous march through South Carolina went wild burning and destroying property, but others tried to control them and actively protected Southern homes and civilians from their wilder comrades.

It is sad that the idealistic efforts of those who campaigned to stop wrongdoing by their own group are often forgotten or downplayed by history. Thus, we are familiar with the fact that Jews suffered persecution for many centuries in Europe, but we are less often told of the efforts by other European Christians to protect the Jews. The medieval massacres of Jews were often strongly opposed by the authorities, including both the local aristocracy and the Church officials, and some made vigorous and successful efforts to save Jews from the violent antagonism of the Christian mobs.[9] Liberal protest against unfair treatment of the Jews became "clichés of eighteenth-century rhetoric."[10] Later, the Dreyfus Affair, in which a Jewish officer in the French army was falsely prosecuted for treason, elicited passionate protests and defenses by leading intellectuals from the European mainstream. Indeed, had the protest never occurred, the Dreyfus case would have been simply another lost and forgotten incident among the many imperfect and biased results of military justice. What made the case remarkable was the immense outcry among non-Jewish leaders to support a Jewish victim of discrimination.

One might wonder whether the general principle of collective ambivalence has at least found an exception on the victims' side of slavery. (The perpetrators' side, at least in white antebellum America, was thoroughly divided to the point of civil war.) It is difficult to propose that slaves would ever cooperate to preserve slavery. For a conquered people to go to work with their conquerors may be a matter of realistically accepting the status quo and pursuing their own best chance under the circumstances. But slavery seems to be so complete an oppression that it is difficult to imagine that slaves would condone and aid it.

Slavery may offer less evidence of collective ambivalence than other sources, but there is some. In *Incidents in the Life of a Slave Girl*, author Linda Brent described her efforts to escape from slavery, and she emphasized how vulnerable she was because many other slaves would have willingly turned her in to the slavemasters to gain favor, money, or other advantages.[11] Like downtrodden people everywhere, slaves seemed to divide their loyalties between their fellows and those who had power over them.

The view of slavery as a white oppression against blacks does not entirely fit the historical evidence about Africa, either. Probably there were some cases in which whites landed on the shores of Africa and captured blacks to force them into slavery, but the more common approach was to purchase slaves from African slave traders, many of whom were black. One of the most successful slave traders was Tippu Tip, who made a famous remark about the easy profits to be made by enslaving other black people: "Slaves cost nothing. They only have to be gathered."[12] On another occasion, he is said to have watched a boatload of women and children swept over a waterfall and to have commented, "What a pity! It was a fine canoe."[13] Still, he regarded himself as more sensitive and compassionate than some of the other slave traders he knew.

Indeed, one of the ironies of nineteenth-century history occurred in the Egyptian uprising led by Muhammad Ali (the original leader of that name, not the boxing champion). Ali sought independence from Great Britain, which along with France had ruled Egypt after the Egyptian government had proved itself unable to pay the debts owed to European financiers. Ali recognized that the Egyptian economy was in shambles, and one of his plans to put it on a sounder footing was to revive the slave trade. The British had outlawed slavery throughout their empire and were passionately opposed to any slave trade in Egypt. Thus was fought one of the great interracial wars over African slavery: Black Africans fought to revive slavery, while white Europeans fought to eradicate it.[14]

The civil rights movement during the middle of the twentieth century brought about enormous changes in race relations in the United States, but it, too, proceeded with division on both sides, despite the news reports showing white mobs attacking black demonstrators. The old white men on the Supreme Court and in Congress were crucial to ending segregation and discrimination and increasing the scope of rights and opportunities black citizens enjoyed. Meanwhile, although black people hardly fought against the civil rights movement, some had far less interest than others. For example, many black citizens did not want to take part in the Nashville boycott, and the organizers of the boycott had to form "education committees" to pressure them into participating by administering minor physical harassment.[15]

The Question of Motives

What are the motives that produce such divisions in both oppressor and oppressed groups? The motives of protesters in the oppressor group are relatively easy to fathom. In general, the dissenters are guided by strong ideals that condemn the violent or oppressive acts of their fellows. In addition, they may have vivid personal feelings of empathy toward the victims. The white antislavery movement was marked by both motives. Many people participated in the campaign against slavery out of principle, without having had much personal contact with slaves. (By the same token, most Americans who protested the Vietnam War had never been to Vietnam or met any of its citizens.) Others were moved by personal feelings of empathy and sympathy for the suffering of the slaves.

Even among principled protestors, however, personal self-interest may play a role. For example, it is likely that many young men protested the Vietnam War in part because they themselves could end up risking life and limb in combat.

The motives of collaborators in the oppressed group are more difficult to characterize. One factor might be disaffection with their own group. For example, people who have not done well in their group might well collaborate with a conquering enemy. Another is personal advantage. To collaborate with a victorious enemy brings power and benefits. Many of the Jews who collaborated with the Nazis were motivated by such benefits. The Nazis granted exemptions from deportation to the members of the *Judenrat* (Jewish Council) and their families. Sometimes, council members even got a few extra exemptions, which meant that they had the power to choose a few individuals to keep alive.

The chance to settle old scores or gain power over some particular disliked person is another possible motivation. If the Chinese took over your city, executed all the authorities, and offered you an influential position, you might be tempted if it meant that you could punish your enemies within the city. Indeed, you might be especially tempted if your refusal would enable your local enemies to gain those positions and harass you. If you had no enemies, you would probably be less tempted.

As we've seen, most people reserve their greatest animosities for people they know well. Thus, when a foreign power takes over, they may see an opportunity to punish those they hate. We have seen that animosity toward the ruling Aztecs was a major factor in driving some of their rivals to help the invading Spanish, and similar animosities shaped the reactions of many local Arab and Muslim powers to the invading Crusaders.

One of the most remarkable observations in Rudolf Höss's memoirs concerns a pattern that he claimed to have observed on several occasions while presiding over executions at Auschwitz. He said that occasionally a Jew on his or her way to the gas chamber would give him the address of some other Jews who were presumably hiding from the authorities.[16] At first, one can scarcely believe that Jews would betray fellow Jews to the people who were killing them. But it seems unlikely that Höss would have fabricated this story, especially given his admissions and other observations in his memoirs.

Certainly, he did not claim that such behavior was typical. But if it did happen, what might have motivated it? Possibly, some Jews may have thought they could save themselves by betraying others. Still, Höss said that this explanation was not sufficient, and he spoke of naked Jews shouting out names and addresses from the very gas chambers while the doors were being locked on them. Others thrust slips of paper with such information into his hands while they filed onward toward their death. Thus, the last act of these people was to betray others to a similar fate.

The most likely motivation in these cases was personal animosity. In retrospect, the Nazis were the enemies of the Jews and all Jews should have united against them at every turn. In practice, however, it is inevitable that the personal enmities and antagonisms of most Jews would be directed toward other Jews, because those were the people with whom they had most contact. If you knew you and your family were headed for an unjust death while the person you most despised in the world had evaded capture and might survive, you might just be tempted to reveal his hiding place. Or at least you could understand how one person out of a great many might do so. Among the many thousands of people whom Höss watched on their way to death, it is plausible that a handful of them acted this way.

Those Jews were about to die, but for most people life is going to continue after a conquest, and so collaborating with the victorious enemy may be the only realistic thing to do. The Indian police are a relevant example. One might cling to a romantic notion of heroic resistance until the bitter end, but that would not accomplish anything. The white Europeans and their descendants were going to end up in charge of most of North America. Perhaps the best way for native Americans to have a normal life was to accept that fact and make their own lives within that framework. Throughout history, there has often been a split between those who favored relentless, heroic resistance against superior odds and those who accepted the new terms realistically and went on with their lives. Survivors are disproportionately in the latter group. Indeed, that is the essence of being a survivor: You adapt to the world and proceed on its terms, instead of going down with a lost cause.

Most people want to survive. Although from a distance we imagine that people living in historically interesting times must have been caught up in the grand sweeping events, the majority probably were not. Rather, many people want to live their own lives with as little interference from the grand sociopolitical developments as possible. Getting a job, finding a place to live, falling in love, raising children, and similar concerns continue to dominate the daily lives of most people even during war and revolution. Even if political prisoners are being tortured and killed, young people still want to date one another, parents still need to make sure their sons and daughters do their schoolwork, people still want to get a fair deal when buying or selling or renting a home, and a good meal is better than a bad one. Regardless of one's attitude toward the evil that is going on around you, one has one's own life to live.

Passive Companions

As this book was being written, a brutal civil war raged in the territories carved out of what was once Yugoslavia. The Balkan enmities shocked and stymied the rest of the Western powers. Europe was entering a phase of increased unity, and at first it sent a clear message to the United

States to keep out of the way and let Europe handle its own problems. Soon the Western European powers realized that they could scarcely agree among themselves about what might be done, let alone actually do it, and so the United States was invited to play a role. The Americans were not eager for military involvement in a seemingly unsolvable conflict with no apparent national interests at stake. They had recently elected a new president, Bill Clinton, who lacked much experience with foreign policy and whose appointees were also new to their jobs. The Americans made public statements condemning the violence, sent airplanes flying over the disputed areas, and tried to induce the various parties in the conflict to find a peaceful settlement, but for a long time these efforts led to nothing.

The ironic thing to me was that the various victims in the conflict then began to blame the United States. One day an artillery shell landed in a city street, killing and injuring a dozen civilians, and the bystanders reportedly shouted, "Thank you, Clinton" in bitter sarcasm. Many Americans thought that such blame was absurdly unfair. After all, the Serbs and Croats were killing each other while we were on the other side of the planet, and it was very doubtful that there was anything we could have done to stop them from killing each other. President Clinton had in no way helped fire that artillery shell, and in fact his statements and efforts were all strongly opposed to the violence. Yet they still blamed him.

There is a sense in which the remark is understandable, though. The victims on that street could not stop the violence themselves, nor could they hold much realistic hope that the actual perpetrators—those up in the hills firing the cannons into their neighborhood—could be persuaded to abandon their military advantage and embrace peace. At that point, the European community had proved itself clueless and feckless at peacemaking, and indeed the earlier part of the century had seen several wars start in Europe and end only with American intervention.

Thus, it is quite plausible that the victims believed that American intervention was their only hope. To them, perhaps, their suffering was fated to continue unless and until the United States sent troops to disarm the warring parties and impose peace. It still seems a stretch to blame President Clinton for a particular artillery bombardment, but it is less of a stretch to complain that the lack of American intervention permitted the horrors to continue. The way they saw it, the unfortunate residents of the battered cities of what had been Yugoslavia would continue to endure deprivation, suffering, and death until America finally took action, and so every day of American inaction meant another day of suffering for them.

This incident brings up the moral role of uninvolved bystanders in evil. At first glance, it seems that they have no role, moral or otherwise. If they are uninvolved, then by definition they have no responsibility for what happens. Yet the lack of response by bystanders is often a crucial factor in the promotion of evil, and victims at least can recognize this fact. Whether the bystanders deserve to be blamed is another matter, perhaps, but their action or inaction does have a causal role. The scientific, causal analysis is clearer than the moral one.

I said earlier that violence can be produced without doing anything positive to promote it. All that is necessary is to weaken the internal forces that stop it. In the same way, bystanders do not have to provide active support to the perpetrators of evil and violence. If they merely do nothing, and in particular if they fail to protest or object, then evil and violence are likely to flourish.

Ervin Staub emphasized the role of bystanders in *The Roots of Evil*.[17] His book was devoted to genocide, and he concluded that the lack of international outcry and pressure was a key factor in each of the four major instances of genocide he covered. For example, at each major step in the Nazi Holocaust, Hitler's men would pause to gauge world reaction. Staub says that Hitler's group was encouraged by the lack of international outcry over its incipient persecution of the Jews. The Nazis concluded from the world's silence that everyone else approved and desired the destruction of the Jews but were not brave and resolute enough to pursue it actively themselves.[18]

The century's first genocide was the Turkish massacre of the Armenians, and the response of international bystanders was crucial. There had been one prior incident, a Bulgarian revolt in 1876, which the Turks had suppressed with brutality that extended to multiple massacres. Great Britain had influence with the Turks at that time, but was more concerned with staying on good terms with Turkey (a valued ally in a strategic location near traditional enemy Russia) than with Bulgaria, and no formal protest or sanctions materialized. Around the turn of the century, a few warm-up massacres of Armenians likewise elicited only individual letters of protest rather than any formal diplomatic punishments, and the top Turks began to realize that they could get away with almost anything within their own borders.

The actual genocide was attempted on a large scale in the midst of World War I. By this time, Turkey was at war and allied with Germany, and Germany at least could have exerted considerable influence to stop the killings. Individual Germans wrote and spoke at length in protest against the massacres of Armenians, but the government took no action. Probably it, too, felt that its alliance with the Turkish government was more important than the lives of Armenian citizens. Later, as the world became more sensitized to the issue of genocide, Turkey began to deny officially that the mass killings had taken place, and in 1982 the U.S. State Department—again influenced by the importance of its alliance with Turkey, an important bulwark against the Soviet Union as well as Middle Eastern enemies—declared that the Armenian genocide was not conclusively proved. (After some outcry over this, Congress did reassert that Turkey had indeed attempted genocide against the Armenians.[19])

Thus, the inaction of bystanders implies moral approval even if the bystander could not have stopped the evil. This is particularly important given the many ambiguities and gray areas that characterize evil. If a perpetrator is doing something that he or she knows for certain is evil, then the reactions or nonreactions of bystanders have little importance. But more often perpetrators see themselves ambiguously; perhaps they are using questionable means toward acceptable ends or responding to a prior grievance with an inappropriate measure of violence. In such cases, the perpetrator might be sensitive to the moral judgments of bystanders. If bystanders say nothing, the perpetrator may believe that they did not see anything to criticize. Objectively, one might argue that the silent bystanders did not actually express approval—but perpetrators are hardly objective. They want very much to believe that what they are doing is not evil, and they are willing to take silence as approval.

Research by anthropologist Jill Korbin on child mistreatment [20] provided a chilling illustration of how abusive mothers can manipulate other people into silence, which then can be interpreted as implicit approval. A typical mother in Korbin's sample would beat and torment her child on many occasions, and sometimes this would result in physical injury. The woman would take the child to a hospital and say that the child had had an accident but remain vague and evasive about precisely what had happened. Meanwhile, she waited in great suspense to see whether or not the physician—culturally defined as a godlike figure who knows all and makes wise, profound judgments about people—would condemn her. The woman was probably not fully convinced that she was an evil person who beat her child. Rather, she was a well-meaning mother (in her own mind) who occasionally got carried away in response to exasperating misbehavior by a difficult child.

Usually, the physician would concentrate on treating the child's injuries and not make any accusations. This did not literally signify any direct or true approval of what the woman had done, but often she reacted as if it did. Korbin reported that such a woman said she felt relieved when no one criticized her or reported her to the authorities.

Of course, there are good reasons that the physician did not criticize the woman. Of particular importance was the fact that the woman would typically use a different hospital on each occasion, which prevented any of the physicians from seeing a pattern of repeated injuries to the same child. A single incident could well be an accident, and it makes sense for physicians to concentrate on cases of repeated abuse if they are to suspect and investigate abuse at all. To the woman, the fact of consulting different physicians on different occasions was not seen as a devious ploy she used to fool the system. To her it signified that not just one but several different physicians had seen her child's various injuries and yet not a single one of them had accused her of anything. In her mind, she had passed multiple tests and was still entitled to regard herself as a good mother.

The ambiguity and the relief at the absence of criticism were even more dramatically apparent in the few cases in which one of these abusive mothers would confess to someone what she had done. Typically, the woman would call her own mother or a trusted friend. She would be full of remorse and would manage to say that she had injured her child. The other's response was typically to be sympathetic. Yes, children are difficult at times and it is impossible for any normal human being to live up to the idealized standards of motherly perfection every single minute. The confidante would insist that this must never happen again, but she would not call the woman a child abuser or report her to the authorities. This again was enough to reassure the woman. Of course, at that moment she was convinced that she would never let herself lose control to that degree again. Her future was clear, and her past contained this one sin—but the confidante had told her that such things happen to normal mothers and could be forgiven.

Do such things happen to normal mothers? We can't tell from Korbin's sample, because she was studying women who ended up killing their children, which is an extreme rarity in statistical terms. Each killing had come at the end of a long sequence of escalating abuse. Along the way, however, the woman had managed to forgive herself and escape any recognition of herself as an evil person or chronic child abuser. It is easy to label her that way in retrospect, and with considerable justification, but it was not apparent to the woman herself at the time. After all, she had taken her child to be examined by several responsible, expert physicians, and none had said anything. And then she had even confessed her misdeed and her self-doubts to someone whom she could trust; but even her confession had not elicited a response that she was anything but a normal mother struggling to cope with a difficult child under stressful circumstances.

It is quite apparent that perpetrators are very sensitive to silence by other people and that they often overinterpret such silence as implicit approval. Yet our focus here is not on the perpetrators. How do the bystanders figure into this?

People sometimes just want to live their lives and deal with their own problems, without being called upon to pass judgment upon strangers or take responsibility for the misdeeds of others. Why should Americans have to spend their tax dollars and sacrifice the lives of their sons and daughters to force people on the other side of the planet to stop killing each other? Why should a physician or friend have to take responsibility for stopping a woman from injuring her child?

The system offers plenty of danger, but few rewards, for bystanders who get involved. For example, before the crisis in the former Yugoslavia, America had sent troops to Somalia in "Operation Restore Hope"—an apparent opportunity to do good deeds with little risk. Yet the troops had become stuck amid hostile factions and local warlords. Although some Somalians were grateful for the American help, others protested and resented the interference, and the American soldiers became targets of violent attacks. Eventually, the Americans had to withdraw in embarrassment.

Consider the physician in the emergency room who chooses to treat a child's injuries without reporting the mother to the authorities. Most physicians in emergency rooms are overworked, and strictly speaking their job is to take care of physical injuries, not to investigate suspected crimes. More important, there are considerable legal and financial risks involved in accusing parents of abusing their children. If the physician is wrong, he or she could be subject to lawsuits and official censure, as well as having problems with the hospital authorities.

In some cases, the penalties for taking action are even stronger. During the periods of government terror in Argentina, Chile, Nazi Germany, and Soviet Russia, to speak out carried a mortal risk. Of course one does not always know how serious the risk is. Suppose you see your neighbors being arrested, or you know simply that they have "disappeared" as a result of some apparently official action. Should you complain to the authorities, who arrested them? They might arrest you, too, as a possible accomplice. There is always the possibility that your neighbor really was involved in some kind of spy work or subversive group, and so to stand up for such a person would betray your country. Should you voice objections to the newspapers or to foreigners? Again, the local authorities are likely to find out, and you will be at their mercy. You might disappear, too. At the very least, you would invite suspicion upon yourself by speaking out on behalf of imprisoned traitors.

Among the very few who managed to stage public protests amid government repression were the mothers of some of the victims. In Argentina, a group of women began to gather each Thursday, marching with signs around a small square. They called on the government to release their children who had been arrested. Ironically, the very defenselessness of these women may have made it possible for them to protest, and the strong tie to their children may have made them willing to take the risk. Of course, a military regime can easily break up a protest by a group of older women. Then again, to crack down on mothers who mourn their children is to admit that one has gone to extremes. The mothers clearly pose no security risk, and one would have to be absurdly paranoid to propose that a handful of mothers is working with some kind of international subversive organization. Moreover, who would take responsibility for arresting a group of mothers who miss their children? To do so would require an extreme moral callousness that would not square well with the regime's views of itself as the defender of the good. There were some subtle attempts to deal with the mothers. A couple of them were kidnapped, and some of their relatives as well. But there was no overt crackdown on the group, and the mothers continued to march and protest.

My own sympathies lie very strongly with the inactive bystanders. I recall my student days, during which many students were extremely involved in politics and the effort to promote revolution. I did not share their views, especially during the year of foreign study in which I encountered many radical Marxists among the students at Heidelberg,

Germany. What aggravated me most of all was their insistence that no one could remain neutral. "Not taking a position is still taking a position," they would say, which corresponded roughly to the American student activist slogans of "If you're not part of the solution, then you're part of the problem" or "Whoever is not with us is against us." I was hoping to do well in my classes, possibly learn some interesting ideas, and ideally find a girl with whom to fall in love. Getting involved in the Marxist world revolution looked like a pie-in-the-sky waste of time to me. More generally, I thought politics was a boring, frivolous charade. I deeply resented being told that I was involved in politics one way or another, or that failing to march with the revolutionaries was tantamount to supporting the Establishment.

Despite that bias, however, I must admit that I have been persuaded that it is sometimes indeed morally impossible to remain neutral. Bystanders do have a responsibility to protest evil, because it will grow unchecked if they do not. Whatever the press of one's own concerns or the appeal of minding one's own business, it is nonetheless true that the victims of evil and violence depend on bystanders to bear witness to what is happening and take a stand against it. It is the only way.

The Uninvolved Authorities

In addition to bystanders who are truly uninvolved, there are passive bystanders who have both the authority and the power to prevent evil but fail to use it. The actions and inactions of these bystanders—leaders, governments, police, reporters—can be of paramount importance.

Police are an important example. When the police cease to intervene, victims are suddenly much more helpless and perpetrators have much greater liberty to take violent or oppressive actions. One recent focus of debate in the United States is police intervention in domestic conflicts. Although the evidence about the long-term effects of arresting wife beaters is inconclusive, it does appear that when the police do nothing, the victims feel especially helpless.[21]

Police inaction has also been a source of complaint in some other crimes. Although things may have improved recently, homosexuals have long believed that police would not intervene on their behalf. Groups of young heterosexual men (often athletes) might believe that beating up homosexuals was fair game and good sport, and police would be reluctant to protect the homosexuals against the athletes. Inevitably, the inaction of the police would encourage other young men to regard homosexuals as safe targets for assault. Likewise, in some times and places the police have been slow to intervene in crimes against black people, and all-white juries would refuse to convict white perpetrators for violent crimes against black citizens.

Governments also can play an important role in contributing to evil by simply remaining aloof. Some notable cases of collective brutality occurred when a government tacitly encouraged violent acts by its citizens and showed that it would not intervene on behalf of the victims. The German police did not intervene to help Jews on Kristallnacht, the night on which local roughnecks smashed and damaged Jewish business properties and beat up Jews. The Maoist government sent ambiguous encouragement to teenagers to turn against adults who did not conform to certain Communist ideals and then largely stood by and watched while many innocent people were beaten, robbed, and killed during the Cultural Revolution. The Rwandese authorities likewise showed that they were not about to step in to protect Tutsi victims from their Hutu neighbors during the beatings and massacres that preceded the systematic genocide.

The difference that official passivity makes can be appreciated by considering how victorious armies handle the problem of their soldiers raping women in conquered areas. Indeed, at the end of World War II, Germany was invaded from several sides by different armies, and the girls and women who had survived the bombardments fared very differently depending on which army occupied their town. The American army was strictly opposed to rape, and any American soldiers who were caught raping German girls were subject to prosecution and even the death penalty. In contrast, the Russians did not punish their soldiers for such misdeeds, and the lack of punishment came across to the soldiers as an implicit approval of rape. It is not that the Russian high command issued general orders to rape every female that could be found. Rather, the understanding gradually spread through the Russian ranks that one could do anything one wanted with the women in the occupied towns.

One of the most dramatic cases in which a government's deliberate inaction ended up increasing evil was the Ethiopian government's response to international food donations during the famine of 1973–1974. Ethiopia is a small and poor country, and everyone important tried to remain close to the emperor. The famine in outlying regions did not have much chance of capturing the attention of the royal court. As one official later said, "Death from hunger had existed in our Empire for hundreds of years, an everyday, natural thing, and it never occurred to anyone to make any noise about it. . . . Since this was eternal and normal, none of the dignitaries would dare to bother His Most Exalted Highness with the news that in such and such a province a given person had died of hunger."[22] The emperor did occasionally travel around his country, but he tended not to stop in the poor regions, and in any case wherever he went the people put on a fine show for him rather than complaining about bad conditions. When the foreign press caught wind of the famine by virtue of a British documentary, they asked insistent questions about it, and the minister of information professed to have no knowledge about any famine.

A large contingent of the international press then came to Ethiopia to learn about the famine. The government refused to let them visit the poor areas, because it regarded such press inquiries as intrusive interference into Ethiopia's internal affairs. Thus, the government's egotism—in this case, concern with looking good in the international press—caused them to pretend that the famine did not exist. Ethiopian university students, however, sent people north to get pictures of the famine and passed these along to the foreign reporters. When they waved the photos in front of the government spokesman and asked what was being done, the official was willing to say only that "His Most Supreme Majesty has attached the utmost importance to this matter," and he later thought it an outrage that the "devilish rabble" of journalists were unsatisfied with this answer and demanded to know what specific actions were being taken.[23]

After the journalists left, the Ethiopians debated how to handle the matter. Some favored continuing to deny that there was any famine, but the minister of information had said that the emperor attached utmost importance to it, so it could not be denied. The government then decided to admit that the problem existed and ask for help.

The international community sent aid in the form of food shipments and medical assistants, but the Ethiopian government was not altogether thrilled about all the foreign interference and especially the loss of face that it suffered. "It's never good to let so many foreigners in, since they are amazed at everything and they criticize everything," commented one minister later.[24] He said that the foreigners began to make loud criticisms of the situation they found: "Thousands dying of hunger right next door to markets and stores full of food."[25] The foreigners thought that Ethiopia should simply give their food to the peasants who, because of the smaller harvest, had had nothing left after they had paid the rich landowners. The landowners had raised the price of food in response to the shortage, which is a standard economic response, although in this case a rather heartless one.

To the government, these foreigners' suggestions were absurd, partly because the rich landowners were important people at the royal court who were considered immune from criticism as long as they enjoyed the emperor's favor. It was well understood that a certain amount of corruption was tolerated as one of the perks of the royal court. To accuse "the official representatives of His Well-Beloved Highness"[26] of being speculators who caused the famine would be unacceptable. Indeed, the emperor made a point of bestowing extra favors and promotions on the individuals whose profiteering had caused the famine, "to prove that they were innocent and to curb the foreign gossip and slander."[27]

The next event was most extraordinary and can be appreciated in the actual remarks of another government official:

> Everything seemed to be moving along well, developing favorably and successfully and most loyally; the Empire was growing and even, as His Supreme Highness stressed, blossoming—when suddenly reports came in that those overseas benefactors who had taken upon themselves the trouble of feeding our ever-insatiable people had rebelled and were suspending shipments because our Finance Minister, Mr. Yelma Deresa, wanting to enrich the Imperial Treasury, had ordered the benefactors to pay high customs fees on the aid. "You want to help?" the minister asked. "Please do, but you must pay." And they said, "What do you mean, pay? We give help! And we're supposed to pay?" "Yes," says the minister, "those are the regulations. Do you want to help in such a way that our Empire gains nothing by it?"[28]

Thus, aid was suspended. The Ethiopians put out official statements blaming the West for causing their people to starve by cutting off food shipments, and the members of the court agreed that this response was successful. Yelma Deresa, the finance minister whose customs charges had caused the food shipments to be suspended, was treated very favorably by the emperor, who was relieved to be rid of all that foreign interference and criticism.

The government of Ethiopia did not cause the famine, nor did it particularly wish it to happen or to continue. But its own priorities of egotism, prestige, and greed were much more important to it than the famine, and so the government ended up following a course of action that let people starve (and even prevented aid from reaching them). To the international community, the plight of the victims was paramount, and from that perspective the government's position was morally repugnant. But the Ethiopian government saw matters differently. Issues of threatened egotism were central to its concerns. It could not crack down on the rich landowners whose speculative activities had kept the food from the people and set off the famine, because those landowners were prominent members of the government and representatives of the emperor, and to accuse them would disgrace the government. And the government resented the foreign donations because they came with a large amount of highly unfavorable publicity. The emperor and his group had worked long and hard, in their view, to create an image of their nation as a modern, successful, up-and-coming country deserving of international respect. They hated to see the fruits of their labor destroyed by disloyal students and the noisy rabble of foreign journalists making a big deal out of something that was, in their view, a natural and normal phenomenon: starvation in the poor outer regions of their land.

Indirect Help

There is another, indirect way in which unprotesting bystanders contribute to evil. Satan himself may have the unlimited budget and endless free time necessary to devote himself fully to causing trouble, but actual perpetrators of evil are people (or groups, organizations, or countries) who depend on commerce and social exchange for their very survival. They do not necessarily need the assistance or approval of others for their violent, oppressive acts, but they do need the cooperation of others to go on living and to achieve reasonable levels of security and comfort.

This dependency gives bystanders more leverage than they may assume they have. They may be powerless to stop a particular act of violence, but if they translate their protest into some form of refusal to cooperate in other spheres, the perpetrators may feel the pressure.

International boycotts are based on this principle. Given international law, countries are extremely reluctant to intervene in the internal affairs of other countries, even when they disapprove of them very strongly. Thus, Americans were willing to send troops to fight Iraq when it invaded Kuwait, but when Iraq later waged a brutal war against the

Kurds living in Iraq, the international community did not see any basis for intervening. Disapproval of such acts does sometimes result in a boycott, however, and Iraq was subjected to a severe one for several years. Similar boycotts put pressure on South Africa to end its policies of racial apartheid, and on various other countries that have oppressed minorities or restricted human rights.

Regrettably, boycotts are an imprecise instrument. News reports have consistently indicated that the boycott of Iraq did not have the desired effect. The military rulers responsible for the internal terror campaigns continued to live well because of their wealth and power. In Iraq, as elsewhere, the common people suffered most from the shortages and deprivations caused by the boycott.

Although boycotts and similar forms of pressure do not always produce the intended effects, they are sometimes very influential. Countries are interdependent to some degree, and most countries need many of the goods that come from trading with the broader community. On a smaller scale, the violent youth gangs in the United States need many goods and services that their community provides, and the equivalent of a community boycott could mean the end of many gangs.

The influence of the bystander community was a central point of Martin Sanchez Jankowski's book about urban gangs.[29] Jankowski largely rejected the media stereotype of gangs preying on the community in which they live and keeping neighbors too terrified of reprisals to report criminal acts to the police. On the contrary, he said, most gangs are heavily dependent on the good will of their community. If they are going to perpetrate violence and other crimes, they will generally go to other neighborhoods rather than victimize their own. The gang needs its community. If it loses the support of its community, it is extremely vulnerable. After all, the local community has to provide the gang members with food and shelter (including places to meet and to hang out). If the neighbors start reporting the gang's whereabouts and activities to the police, the gang will find it very difficult to operate effectively.

Why would communities tolerate gangs? Often the gang is seen as a reliable and trustworthy form of neighborhood defense. Many poor communities do not trust the police to protect them, for various reasons including slowness of response, lack of personal ties to police officers, and past history of oppression and discrimination by the police. Indeed, we noted earlier that the United States has a history of police failing to intervene to help black citizens, and it is not surprising that in some places black neighbors might put more trust for their own safety in the neighborhood boys than in the police.

The gang, however, is usually available because the members of the gang live in the neighborhood, too. The boys in the gang are known to the neighbors personally. Moreover, the community often has a substantial need for protection. As researchers have pointed out, a gang will generally go elsewhere to commit its violent crimes, which means that one's neighborhood is subject to periodic invasions and incursions from other neighborhoods' gangs. One's own gang is thus needed to protect the community against the outsiders. Therefore, the relationship may be mutually beneficial. The neighborhood supports the gang and provides it with food and housing, and the gang provides the neighborhood with protection.

Thus, the gang does not need the community to assist it in criminal activity, but it does need the support structure. Jankowski concluded emphatically from his 10 years of living among gangs that when relations between the gang and the community turn sour, the breakup of the gang is imminent. Although individual residents may feel helpless at the mercy of their local gangs, in fact the gang is more dependent on the community than vice versa. The gang needs to stay on good terms with the community to survive.

Even organized crime requires the assistance of people who are not directly involved in crime. As mafioso Nicky Caramandi told author George Anastasia, even the most dangerous and deadly operations of the Mafia involved people who are not in the Mafia themselves. "We borrowed their cars, they held guns for us in their houses, they took all kinds of chances. We made 'em do different things. We would go to a person's house to change clothes after a shooting. See, after you fire a gun, you have to wash down with vinegar and take a shower so the gunpowder doesn't stay on you. And you have to get rid of your clothes." He added that these relationships to people outside the organization "are the strength and backbone of the mob."[30]

Similar factors hold true with terrorists. Again, the stereotype is of vicious, deadly groups of revolutionaries invading the community and committing acts of mayhem against defenseless individuals. In fact, terrorists require a substantial amount of community support. They need safe houses in which to hide. They need money. They need food and shelter. They need places to meet, to store their weapons and other gear.

True, a couple of terrorists can travel to many places in the world rather easily and plant a bomb. But terrorist campaigns of any duration require a strong network of support in the community.

The Irish Republican Army is a good example. Their campaign of bombings and shootings was able to last for years only because they had many supporters in Ireland who wanted to help the cause of Irish independence. Most jobs won't let you take a month off for a bombing mission, and even if you could do the deed in a week, your absence from work would be noticed. Still, somebody has to buy the food and pay the bills, and so somebody has to have a job. If the ordinary working people had all turned their backs on the IRA, they could not have carried on their activities for long.

Keeping Them Happy

So far, we have argued that the perpetrators of long-term evil require at least the passive cooperation of uninvolved bystanders. Apart from the few obvious cases (such as gangs that protect the neighborhood), how do the perpetrators manage to secure this cooperation? Presumably, it must be difficult to induce people to remain silent and cooperative in the face of ongoing evil. Most people undoubtedly prefer to believe that they would take a stand against evil if it were happening in their community. If your state government began arresting and killing innocent members of minority groups, would you protest? Of course I would, say most people. But it is easy to be virtuous in such hypothetical dilemmas. In fact, when such things happen, most people do not protest. How can we understand their silence?

One crucial factor is that repressive governments usually balance their oppression of certain groups with positive accomplishments that the majority will appreciate. Or, at least, they promise to provide major improvements, and people trust them until it is too late. Fascist and military governments often accomplish positive things for their countries. The Nazis restored prosperity, urban peace, and hope to a country that had fallen helplessly into chaos and disaster for a decade. The Argentineans likewise stopped the downward slide that had taken their country from one of the world's richest to a disintegrating chaos.

At the other end of the political spectrum, hopes were even higher, if less thoroughly fulfilled in Russia. The Communists promised that the nation would enjoy land reform (which is nearly always one of the biggest and most controversial issues in a country where most people are impoverished peasant farmers), justice, equality, and national pride. Even the brutal Khmer Rouge was welcomed by many people in Cambodia, not because of any specific promises, but because the current government was so corrupt and ineffective that many people believed the Communist patriots would try to make life better. The reality was apparent by a few days after the takeover, but by then it was too late.

When these governments do deliver, there is a gratitude factor that will sustain support for them even through some questionable actions. Suppose you were out at sea with your family, and your boat sank. Then someone came by and saved all of your lives, fishing you out of the waters and wrapping you in warm blankets for the ride to shore. On the ride, your savior happens to make a few derogatory remarks about people of another ethnic group. You disagree with those sentiments, but do you call him a bigot? Certainly you are unlikely to insist that he stop the boat and put your family back in the water. Probably you say nothing. In fact, when the man makes those bigoted remarks, suppose he acts as if he assumes you agree, by catching your eye and smiling in a knowing way. He has saved your life; you smile back and nod, at least. People who live under some authoritarian governments are in a similar situation. Except that the boat will take years to reach the shore.

Pride is also a contributing factor. Most people want to take pride in their country. Strong governments usually provide a solid basis for national pride, and often they restore a pride that has been damaged or lost. Whatever the shortcomings and failures of Soviet Communism, it at least enabled Russians to feel pride in their great country, with its vast empire, mighty army, and Olympic sports triumphs. The abandonment of Communism in 1989 has been traumatic in part because the Russians had to cope with the diminished prestige and status of being a second-rate power. The loss of pride is one source of nostalgic support for Communism in that country. (These days when I watch the Olympics, I always hope the Russians will do well, because the cause of world peace will probably be best served if the Russians see that they can still achieve symbolic greatness and success under democracy!)

People may also derive individual benefits under oppressive regimes that would discourage them from protesting too strongly when the regimes do something evil. Again, it is necessary to recognize that most oppressive regimes do not oppress everybody, and in most cases they will be bringing benefits to the majority of people or at least the majority of people who count. These benefits go beyond the collective social benefits of a stable economy, law and order, community pride, and the like.

Sometimes these benefits are merely asserted. During the Spanish Inquisition, for example, the authorities promised that everyone who attended an auto-da-fé would gain spiritual benefits.[31] This was one factor that motivated people to attend the great festivals in which heretics were censured and killed. To see the wicked secret enemies of Christendom punished for their false beliefs and subversive acts was supposed to be good for one's soul.

More palpable benefits sometimes attend the purges of modern totalitarian governments. As Hannah Arendt[32] pointed out, a purge is great for a young person's career, as long as he or she is not one of the victims, because it creates job opportunities. If half the top officials at a company or bureau are sent to prison, one result is a large number of job openings. Younger men and women are promoted to positions of prestige, responsibility, and high pay—much more rapidly than they could have expected. Suppose, for example, that you were a young man in such a situation; how would you feel toward the regime? It has brought you occupational success well beyond your dreams. Your family and neighbors all treat you with new respect. Your in-laws, who used to look down on you and think you weren't good enough for their daughter, now look up to you, ask for your opinions or favors, and brag to their friends about their daughter's big-shot husband. It would be hard for you to be critical of the government under those conditions, because it has enabled you to realize your own potential so well. You have flourished under the current system.

From a distance, we can see the flaws in such a response. The young person's advance was not due to his own achievement but to the evil actions by the government toward his former superiors. Moreover, we can anticipate that when another purge comes, many of those who rose so rapidly will find it their turn to be arrested. But it does not look that way to the people who are there at the time. People tend to believe that they deserved their successes. Even if you recognize that the arrest of your former boss was the immediate cause of your promotion, you are likely to focus on the fact that it was the years of good work you had done in your position that brought you the promotion when the opening occurred. Thus, to your mind, you deserved it, and the purge was merely a matter of timing.

Moreover—and this is a crucial point—people generally do not realize how arbitrary and groundless such arrests are until it is their own turn. They may find it hard to believe that there were really so many traitors and saboteurs in their organization, even among people they knew and may have liked, but they typically believe that some of the charges must be true. After all, the government would not just arrest and imprison a large number of innocent people who were loyally serving it, would it?

Later on, the trials and confessions confirm the assumption that something must have been going on. Possibly, the poor achievements of past years were in part a reflection of the sabotage of those former leaders who are now safely in prison or dead. The future looks bright for optimistic up-and-comers like yourself who have now been put in charge and given a chance to realize your dreams. The bubble bursts only when you yourself are arrested later, and even at that point you are shocked and think there must be some huge mistake. You know you are innocent and expect to be cleared. Only gradually do you come to realize that your own innocence will not protect you any more than the innocence of your predecessors protected them. But at this point, it is too late, and in any case the disillusionment of people in prison is hardly an unexpected or serious problem to the regime. There are other young men who have been promoted to replace you, and they feel exactly as you did a few years ago when you were in their place: surprised at your treason and arrest, but grateful to have their talents recognized and optimistic at the opportunity to do important work.

Thus, even a government that is arresting and killing its own loyal citizens can retain considerable support. The ones who are working are doing quite well, and indeed the very purges that will eventually kill them are in the short run increasing their loyalty. The only ones who see through the sham are the innocent ones who fill the prisons, but their opinions are scarcely heard, and in any case they will soon be dead or otherwise out of the way. From the regime's point of view, all it sees in the cities and offices are loyal, grateful, hard-working supporters.

If such benefits fail, then the regime can always fall back on fear and intimidation to silence dissent and secure passive cooperation from the majority. The methods can be combined, of course. The young man who has just been given a tremendous promotion and gained the respect of his in-laws is especially unlikely to put it all at risk by announcing publicly that the purge was illegal and its imprisoned victims were innocent, even if he knows for certain that that is true—and it is highly unlikely that he will have such certainty. And even if he did, he would then also recognize that to speak out would make him a target. Instead of enjoying the shining admiration in his young wife's eyes, the respectful looks from his neighbors, his children's delight in the new things he buys them, or the newly deferential tone in his father-in-law's voice, he would be putting himself and them at risk. He could face prison, torture, and death. His wife and children would be plunged into poverty and have to move in with those very in-laws, who would probably think that his sudden rise had owed more to treasonous conspiracies than to any merit on his part. His neighbors would avoid mentioning that they knew him. And for what? Far better to accept one's good fortune and keep one's mouth shut.

PART 4

Conclusion

CHAPTER 12

Why Is There Evil?

Why, then, is there evil: crime, violence, oppression, cruelty, and the rest? As we have seen, there is no single or simple answer. Evil does not exist in terms of solitary actions by solitary individuals. Perpetrators and victims—and in many cases, bystanders or observers, too—are necessary to the vast majority of evil acts. Evil is socially enacted and constructed. It does not reside in our genes or in our soul, but in the way we relate to other people.

Evil requires the deliberate actions of one person, the suffering of another, and the perception or judgment of either the second person or an observer. Very few people see their own actions as evil, and hardly any acts are regarded as evil if they do not bring harm, pain, or suffering to someone. Occasionally, masturbation, intoxication, or blasphemy may be considered evil even though no one is hurt, but victimless evil is a marginal, derivative category. Victimization is generally essential to evil. Victims are the first persons to spot evil.

Because evil depends so heavily on the perceptions of the victim (along with those of observers who identify with the victim), it is disturbing to the social scientist to realize how many biases and distortions shape the victim's perceptions. I have called these stereotypes collectively the *myth of pure evil*. Social scientists are fully prepared for whitewashing rationalizations on the part of perpetrators, but to recognize the extent to which everyone else's perceptions are also biased discourages one about the prospects of seeing through to the essential nature of evil. People tend to adapt real events to their expectations, based on the myth of pure evil. The result is a scenario involving wholly innocent, well-meaning victims attacked for no valid reason by arrogant, sadistic, out-of-control evildoers who hate peace and beauty and get pleasure from making people suffer.

There are four major root causes of evil, or reasons that people act in ways that others will perceive as evil. Ordinary, well-intentioned people may perform evil acts when under the influence of these factors, singly or in combination. Combinations are harder to defeat.

The first root cause of evil is the simple desire for material gain, such as money or power. These ends are not universally regarded as wrong, although occasionally a religious group or other authority has condemned the desire itself. What distinguishes evil in these cases is not the ends, however, but the means. Everyone wants money, but only criminals use violence to get it. Violent or evil means are chosen because the individual does not think that more legitimate means will be successful. Violent and evil means often do furnish short-term, limited success, but in the long run they do not reliably furnish the material benefits they were intended to bring. At best, violence seems to be an effective tool for creating and sustaining power relationships.

The second root of evil is threatened egotism. Villains, bullies, criminals, killers, and other evildoers have high self-esteem, contrary to the comfortable fiction that has recently spread through American culture. Violence results when a person's favorable image of self is questioned or impugned by someone else. Showing disrespect, attacking someone's honor, insulting or humiliating someone, or in some other way causing a person to lose face will often elicit an aggressive response. The people (or groups or countries) most prone to violence are the ones who are most susceptible to ego threats, especially those who have inflated, exalted opinions of themselves or whose normally high self-esteem does occasionally take a nosedive. Moreover, violence is usually directed toward the source of the ego threat (or occasionally, a meaningful substitute). Such violence may often fall short of providing proof of the disputed self-worth, but it does intimidate, silence, and punish the critic, and it boosts the ego by establishing dominance over the critic.

The third root of evil is idealism. When people believe firmly that they are on the side of the good and are working to make the world a better place, they often feel justified in using strong measures against the seemingly evil forces that oppose them. Noble ends are often seen as justifying violent means. In reality, such means often discredit and contaminate the noble goals, but this outcome is rarely anticipated. Human nature inclines people to align themselves in groups that square off against each other, each group seeing itself as good and the other as bad. Group competition can evolve into brutal conflict in which each side sincerely sees itself as the good guys who need to take strong measures to defeat the forces of evil that oppose them. When the perpetrators are driven by idealism, the victims do not get much mercy.

The fourth root of evil is the pursuit of sadistic pleasure. This root is responsible for a much smaller proportion of the world's evil than the others, and indeed most observations of killers, torturers, rapists, and similar evildoers indicate that only about 5 or 6 percent of perpetrators actually get enjoyment out of inflicting harm. Moreover, sadism appears to be an acquired taste. Possibly, it emerges from the body's natural pattern of compensating for unpleasant emotional reactions with positive feelings, so that people might learn to enjoy torturing or killing in much the same way as they learn to enjoy skydiving despite the innate fear of falling. Still, most people do not seem to learn to enjoy hurting others (possibly because they refuse to let themselves do so, out of guilt or empathy). What looks to victims like sadism, such as when perpetrators laugh among themselves, may be simply insensitivity or camaraderie.

All told, the four root causes of evil are pervasive, which leads one to wonder why violence and oppression are not even more common than they are. The answer is that violent impulses are typically restrained by inner inhibitions; people exercise self-control to avoid lashing out at others every time they might feel like it. The four root causes of evil must therefore be augmented by an understanding of the proximal cause, which is the breakdown of these internal restraints. Self-control may fail because upbringing and socialization have not made it strong enough, because the capacity for self-control is depleted by stress, because being emotionally upset makes people cease to care, or because the culture tells people that it is appropriate to lose self-control under some circumstances. Many instances of profound evil begin with a small, ambiguous act that crosses a fuzzy line and then escalates gradually into ever greater levels of violence. In groups, especially, evil escalates as the group members bring out one another's worst impulses, lose track of individual responsibility, and reinforce one another's wavering faith in the broad justifications for what they are doing.

Harming another person typically makes one feel bad, although this feeling often takes the form of physical disgust rather than pangs of conscience. Many evildoers work out elaborate justifications by which they convince themselves that what they are doing is acceptable and that they should ignore their own unpleasant feelings. Victims and observers often find these justifications to be feeble and absurdly inadequate. But perpetrators make them work by building them around some palpable grains of truth and by refusing to subject them to critical scrutiny. When they want to believe that their actions are justified, they can often manage to do so. The justifications look weak to victims and outsiders because victims and outsiders are far less motivated to accept them.

The myth of pure evil may portray cohesive, dedicated groups of evildoers preying on homogeneous ranks of innocent victims, but in actual cases of evil there tends to be division on both sides. Some members of the victim group collaborate with and accept the perpetrators, and some members of the perpetrator group object to the violence and try to help the victims. In addition, there is often a large group of uninvolved bystanders who may have far more power than they realize.

These are the broad outlines of the structure of evil. It is important to acknowledge that there are many other factors that can make a difference by altering the odds of aggressive action or affecting the degree to which victims will suffer. Researchers on aggression, for example, have identified an impressive assortment of moderator variables, such as hot weather and aggressive cues, and although this book has not devoted much space to them,[1] they are real and important. This book has emphasized the root causes and the subjective processes of evil. There is ample room in this theoretical framework for moderator variables, which are indeed often essential to the success of evil.

Magnitude and Banality

"He seemed like such a nice guy." That line has become a cliché of interviews with neighbors of someone who has just been convicted of some monstrous crime. It means that the neighbors cannot bring themselves to change their perception of this person they have known, to see him as evil. They are surprised that someone who showed no outward sign of being evil—or even of being extraordinary in any way—could do such terrible things.

The neighbors' surprise and their reluctance to believe the awful truth are indicative of the pervasive difficulty of understanding perpetrators of evil. To believe that an apparently normal and decent person from one's own circle—a friend, a neighbor, a colleague—could commit violent atrocities seems to go against one's basic understanding of the world. Some exceptional explanation must be required, because it seems that evil deeds should be done by evil people, and yet many such deeds are committed by people who do not conform to the stereotypes of evil.

Yet these stereotypes are one of the major obstacles to understanding evil. This is ironic, because the myth of pure evil was constructed to help us understand evil—but it ends up hampering that understanding. The myth is a victim's myth, and there is often a wide, almost impassable gap between the viewpoints of victims and perpetrators. As long as our thinking about evil invokes the victim's perspective, our chances of truly understanding the perpetrators are slim.

Nearly all writers about evil have been influenced by Hannah Arendt's famous insight about "the banality of evil," which was based on her observation of the famous Nazi Adolf Eichmann during his trial. Everyone expected a demon in human form, but he was an ordinary person. His ordinariness was profoundly disappointing. When coming into the presence of a high-ranking mass murderer of historical proportions, you expect to feel an electricity, a gut fear even to sit nearby or have his glance fall upon you. Instead, there was a man who looked and acted like just some guy who might have sat next to you on the bus a few times, someone you would scarcely notice or remember.

The essential shock of banality is the disproportion between the person and the crime. The mind reels with the enormity of what this person has done, and so the mind expects to reel with the force of the perpetrator's presence and personality. When it does not, it is surprised. Yet the magnitude gap provides one explanation for the surprise and disappointment at evil's banality. The enormity of the crime is apparent from the victim's perspective, but often to the perpetrator it was far less enormous. It might seem quite fitting and appropriate to be a rather ordinary, banal person, if the crime is viewed from the perpetrator's perspective.

Thus, readers are shocked to hear that "Monster" Kody Scott drove home to watch "The Benny Hill Show" just after he had killed a young acquaintance by shooting him several times in the chest at close range. One thinks he ought to be consumed with feelings of triumph, or guilt, or fear of being caught, or remorse, or sadistic and vengeful satisfaction, after ending someone's life. But that expectation comes from viewing the act on the victim's scale of life-and-death importance. At that point in Scott's life, the killing was not a big deal, and indeed the point of that story was the end of his personal turmoil about his competing obligations and commitments.

Nature and Culture

Many centuries of human thought and religious dogma have explained evil as a supernatural phenomenon, but the present approach of treating evil as a human, interpersonal phenomenon raises the question of whether one should look to nature or culture to explain evil. Psychology has certainly witnessed strong and powerful statements on both sides, with some wise and profound observers proposing that human beings are naturally, instinctively aggressive, while laboratory researchers have scrupulously insisted that learning and socialization explain a great deal and perhaps all of aggression.

The deeper questions here are more than a matter of fashion and parsimony in scientific explanation. The deeper questions are ones that are familiar to most thoughtful people: Are human beings basically good or evil? Are *certain* human beings basically evil? Should parents blame their own mistakes when their children grow up to become killers, rapists, or swindlers? Do genes dictate violent, criminal behavior, and if so, is the liberal ideal of rehabilitation merely a foolish, idle fantasy? Can society be redesigned so that everyone will live together in peace and harmony? Not all these questions can be answered with total confidence based on the currently available research evidence, but the material covered in this book provides a basis for proposing some tentative answers.

We are past the point at which an explanation in terms of either innate nature or socializing culture can completely explain what is known about human aggression. Both extreme views are untenable. Violence and aggression cannot be fully explained by pointing simply to instincts or heredity. It is clear that much aggression is learned and that most is specific to particular situations. Nature does not program most mammals to kill one another, and the awesome carnage of the twentieth century suggests that the process of civilizing the human animal has, if anything, increased rather than decreased the violence.[2] The cultural and historical variation in rates of violent crime and similar indices of evil also suggests that culture plays a powerful role.

A sobering look at some other facts also makes it implausible to chalk up all human violence up to culture and socialization. Social structures can increase or decrease violence and other evils within certain limits, but no one has come close to eliminating it. Contrary to some idealistic fantasies, children do not need to be taught hate and prejudice: They are all too ready to pick on the one kid who is different or to reject the children in the other group. Physiological processes such as testosterone levels have a significant effect on aggressive behavior. And all over the world, regardless of culture or background, the same biological group is responsible for the bulk of the violence: young males from puberty through the prime age of reproductive potency.

Some years ago, at a professional conference, I had the opportunity to speak to a prominent social psychologist whose work I had long admired, and he told me a story that has been for me a lasting image of the disappointment with theories about socialization and aggression. Like many progressive California academics, he and his wife had resolved to bring up their children surrounded only by healthy, socially desirable values, and this meant that their boys would receive no toy guns. The boys did not complain much about not having such playthings. They simply pretended that the toys they did have were guns. The turning point for the parents came when they found one of their boys chasing the other through the house, holding the remains of his peanut-butter-and-jelly sandwich, from which he had taken carefully planned bites to sculpt it into the shape of a pistol. He was pointing the gun-shaped remnant of sandwich at his brother and making loud shooting noises. At this point, his parents were more upset by the peanut butter and jelly that was dripping onto their expensive white carpet than about their dwindling faith in the chances of raising androgynous, pacifist sons by surrounding them with educational playthings, and so they gave in and bought the kids some toy guns.

Those parents were hardly alone in the disappointment they must have felt when they broke down and bought their sons a shooting toy.

Human nature has not generally proved as pliable as the tabula rasa theorists have hoped. Hundreds of experimental utopian communes have broken down amid undone chores and minor bickering or, in some cases, have led to large-scale mass murder. America's ideological shift from the melting pot to multicultural diversity has not eliminated rancor between groups. Shifting control over upbringing from fathers to mothers has not resulted in a more sensitive and pacifist generation of young males; if anything, the statistics say they are worse than ever. Periodic policy changes in the violent content of television programs have not made a noticeable dent in the crime wave.

A satisfactory understanding of human aggression is likely to invoke both culture and nature. It is unlikely that researchers will ever be able to trace specific violent actions directly to specific genes or other inherited physiological properties, but it is clear that nature has programmed people with some tendencies that can lead toward aggressive responses. Rage appears very early in life and is expressed in lashing out at the source of frustration. The tendency to align with one's fellows and feel hostile toward potential opponents and rivals seems almost ineradicable. Yet culture can exert a great deal of influence in teaching people how to express and control their aggressive impulses. Culture also shapes the situations that form the context for those impulses, including the opportunities for response, the importance of proper response, and the norms of what is proper. And culture articulates the beliefs and myths about evil.

The causes of evil have roots that are deep in human nature as well as in human culture, and it does not seem likely that culture can be changed to eliminate them. Culture can make them better or worse, however. Equalizing opportunity can perhaps reduce the tendency to resort to violent means as a way of achieving material gain, although there is no very convincing proof of this. Decreasing the emphasis on pride, self-esteem, and public respect, or providing multiple and clear criteria for proving oneself, may work against the tendency to use violence to maintain one's face. A strong cultural belief in the rights of individuals and in the inability of noble ends to justify violent means can help prevent idealism from fostering brutality.

Individuals have far less control over broad cultural patterns than over one another, however. Individuals can do far less about the root causes of evil than about the immediate causes. The internal restraints that prevent violent impulses from turning into action are probably the most important and promising place for people to make a difference. The question of whether parents should blame themselves because their child grew up to kill someone has a two-part answer. They should probably not blame themselves for the fact that their child had such murderous or violent impulses. But they may blame themselves for failing to teach their child enough self-control to stifle those urges. In some cases, however, they probably had no chance.

The Future of Evil

Is the world getting better or worse? The enlightened intellectuals of the nineteenth century understood history as a gradual evolution toward more perfect societies filled with more perfect individuals. The twentieth century, in contrast, was marked by pessimism about history and a growing sense that the future might be a nasty, evil place. The century's wars and massacres far outclassed anything the less civilized past came up with. By one careful count, the four decades after the end of World War II saw 150 wars and only 26 days of world peace—and that's not even counting internal wars and police actions.[3] The Nazis set the historical standard for efficient mass killing, yet even their records have been broken. Their body count has been surpassed by the Chinese Cultural Revolution of the 1960s. The Cambodians of the 1970s destroyed a larger percentage of the population. The Rwandese genocide of the 1990s killed people at five times the rate of the Nazi death camps, even though the country was much smaller.[4] Meanwhile, even in peaceful countries like the United States, rates of violent crime continue to rise.[5]

Yet toward the end of the century, the totalitarian regimes that kept much of the world's population enslaved changed or were overthrown. Eastern Europe and South America have shifted almost completely to democratic governments in place of the Fascist and Communist ones that ruled for decades. Even Asia and Africa have made huge steps toward freedom and human rights. The progress of democracy is especially welcome because historical surveys suggest that democracies hardly ever choose to go to war against one another. If the world's governments continue to become more democratic, and democracies remain nonviolent toward one another, the world might actually be able to sustain peace.

Thus, both optimists and pessimists can find plenty of current trends to support their predictions of humanity's future. Let us consider the issue from the perspective of what has been covered in this book as the major sources of human evil.

The perceived need to use violence as a means of securing material gain is probably going to diminish, although slowly. The spread of opportunity and freedom gives people more access to legitimate, nonviolent means of getting what they want, and in the long run these work far better than violent ones. On the other hand, the planet's population may be approaching the limit of what the resources can support, in which case wars over arable land or drinking water may arise.

Egotism is unfortunately on the rise, especially now that modern morality has abandoned its religious commitment to humility and the condemnation of selfishness. At the international level, one has to worry about Russia, whose rapid loss of global prominence and prestige is reminiscent of the humiliations that pushed Germany toward World War II. The rising appeal of strong nationalist and Communist parties in Russia does not bode well for international harmony.

In the United States, the push to raise everyone's self-esteem seems ill-advised. Pacifist virtue is found among people such as nuns who cultivate self-control and condemn self-esteem (as pride). The national trend is now in the opposite direction, toward pursuing self-esteem and relaxing self-control. As long as this trend predominates, it seems safe to expect that individual crime and violence in the United States will be high.

Idealistic violence is difficult to forecast. Christianity no longer seems to have the force to set off holy wars, but Islam does. The Soviet Union is no longer actively committed to fostering world socialist revolution, and indeed there is no longer any Soviet Union as such. On the other hand, the main reason that the United States never seriously flirted with Communist revolution was that social reforms improved the lot of the poor and narrowed the gap between the haves and the have-nots, and recent economic commentators seem to agree that this gap is widening again. Extreme differences between wealth and poverty increase the potential for violent political movements that promise leveling in the name of fairness. It is difficult to imagine that the United States would actually have an internal war based on political idealism, but the possibility of such conflicts (especially if one extends the argument to include all countries with vast inequalities of wealth) cannot be dismissed.

I have hardly mentioned China, which is ironic because in my own lifetime China has certainly done more evil than any other country in the world. China's record is remarkable. The body count of the Cultural Revolution, as already mentioned, is currently estimated at around 20 million, which is unsurpassed in world history. China also played a major role in helping the Khmer Rouge, whose mass murder campaign in Cambodia nearly destroyed the country in a few years and showed a ferocity that has rarely been matched. In 1989, when other Communist countries abandoned their repressive ways and let freedom begin, the Chinese brutally put down demonstrators, most famously in the massacre at Tiananmen Square. China has consistently been one of the most unscrupulous members of the international community: They have abused human rights without even pretending remorse, they violate international copyright laws and flagrantly steal the property of other nations, and they show minimal concern for the environment. Worst of all, they destroyed the Tibetan culture, with its priceless knowledge of the human mind and spirituality. China marches on unreformed and unrepentant, and any attempt to make optimistic forecasts about the twenty-first century must reckon with it.

Future generations are likely to look back on people living now as evil, because of the profligate use of the planet's limited and dwindling resources. When future centuries say that the twentieth was the age of supreme evil, they will be referring not only to death camps and world wars, but also to the selfish, reckless consumption of energy and the destructive pollution of the air and water. Projections vary as to how long the planet's precious resources will last, but inevitably they will start to become scarce. Technological advances will probably postpone the crisis—but not forever.

Citizens of the future will look back on us much the way people today look back on the slave traders or warmongers of past eras, with one twist: Future populations will be our victims, whereas relatively little of today's suffering is directly caused by the actions of our nefarious ancestors. When the oil really runs out, or when the water supply is fatally contaminated, or even when the national debt forces a major drop in everyone's standard of living, people will look back on our era as the culprits responsible for their suffering. Moreover, as we have seen, victims' perceptions tend to be especially stark and unforgiving. The future will have its own version of Satan, and it is likely to be you and me (and our governments). But, like most perpetrators, we do not see ourselves as doing evil.

After Understanding, What?

It is customary for psychology or social-science books on evil to insist that understanding does not mean forgiving. Unfortunately, there is ample reason to fear that understanding can promote forgiving. Seeing deeds from the perpetrator's point of view does change things in many ways. To perpetrators, their apparently voluntary acts appear to be driven or mitigated by external circumstances. To perpetrators, starkly evil motives lie in moral gray areas. To perpetrators, the scope and power of events seem much less extensive than to victims. Even when perpetrators recognize that what they did was wrong, it seems much smaller to them than to the victims.

This book has tried to understand violent, cruel, and oppressive actions as an extraordinary human phenomenon. The effort to understand has required some suppression of moral judgment. Few social scientists today really believe that their work can be totally value-free, but still the ideal of being value-free is important because values prevent one from seeing the facts. For students of torture, of rape, of the Holocaust, and of countless other forms of cruelty, the dilemma is unavoidable, because the interest in these topics is driven by values. Mass murder is not just another interesting human phenomenon comparable to wearing blue jeans or forgetting someone's name. Yet one can learn about evil most effectively by studying it as if it were. It is difficult and perhaps impossible to understand any human phenomenon at the same time that one is condemning it. Setting aside one's moral values, however risky that may be, is helpful when one attempts to understand the perpetrators of evil.

Yet, after making a long and strenuous effort to set aside one's values and look objectively and dispassionately at the causes of human violence—a look that itself requires a complex understanding of a daunting mass of information—it is all too easy to stop with that understanding. It is too easy to forget that we had to take a one-sided view of things in order to understand them, and to escape the intuitive tyranny of the victim's view. Understanding how people commit evil acts is one important key to appreciating the human condition, and it may even hold some helpful clues on how to control human violence. But knowledge about evil ultimately can be fully useful only if it is used with the moral sense that had to be silenced for the sake of gaining that knowledge.

I hope that the reader has gained some insight into the causes and processes of human evil from this book. I also hope, however, that the reader will make the effort to resume a moral condemnation of these terrible acts. To do so requires returning to consider the victim's perspective. The victim's perspective had to be suppressed for the sake of this book because it hampers understanding of the perpetrator. But the victim's perspective is essential for making a moral judgment of the perpetrator. It is a mistake to let moral condemnation interfere with trying to understand—but it would be a bigger mistake to let that understanding, once it has been attained, interfere with moral condemnation.

Notes

CHAPTER 1 The Question of Evil, and the Answers

1. See Baumeister, R. F. (1991b). *Meanings of life*. New York: Guilford, chapter 10. See also Bulman, R., & Wortman, C. B. (1977). Attributions of blame and coping in the "real world": Severe accident victims react to their lot. *Journal of Personality and Social Psychology, 35,* 351–363; Hilbert, R. A. (1984). The acultural dimensions of chronic pain: Flawed reality construction and the problem of meaning. *Social Problems, 31,* 365–378; Klinger, E. (1977). *Meaning and void: Inner experience and the incentives in people's lives.* Minneapolis, MN: University of Minnesota Press; Silver, R. L., Boon, C., & Stones, M. H. (1983). Searching for meaning in misfortune: Making sense of incest. *Journal of Social Issues, 39,* 81–102; and especially Taylor, S. E. (1983). Adjustment to threatening events: A theory of cognitive adaptation. *American Psychologist, 38,* 1161–1173.

2. From *Summa Theologica*; see Russell, J. B. (1988). *The Prince of Darkness: Radical evil and the power of good in history.* Ithaca, NY: Cornell University Press.

3. Lerner, M. J. (1980): *The belief in a just world: A fundamental delusion.* New York: Plenum, on a just world. Janoff-Bulman, R. (1985). The aftermath of victimization: Rebuilding shattered assumptions. In C. R. Figley (Ed.), *Trauma and its wake* (pp. 15–35). New York: Brunner/Mazel; Janoff-Bulman, R. (1989). Assumptive worlds and the stress of traumatic events: Applications of the schema construct. *Social Cognition, 7,* 113–136; and Janoff-Bullman, R. (1992). *Shattered assumptions: Towards a new psychology of trauma.* New York: Free Press, on assumptions. Taylor, S. E., & Brown, J. D. (1988). Illusion and well-being: a social psychological perspective on mental health. *Psychological Bulletin, 103,* 193–210, on positive illusions as adaptive.

4. There has been a recent controversy over an apparent exception, and that concerns rape. In the popular view, the statistic that has been in circulation is that one-half of the male college students said they would rape someone if they were sure they could get away with it. The actual study by Neil Malamuth, however, showed no such thing. The finding was that one-third of respondents showed a slight shift away from the extreme end of the scale, such as from "absolutely never" to "probably not." Moreover, this finding was only obtained by tricking the students in a sense: The notion of rape was brought up as a sexual fantasy. Leonard Martin has shown that if rape is presented as a violent crime, which it is after all, then the male college students do not show even that slight shift toward accepting it. Malamuth compares the males' responses to the fantasies of women that involve being

raped—possibly appealing as fantasy but not very revealing about what one wants to do in reality. See also Chethik, N., The distorted reports of rape study lead to faulty conclusion. *Cleveland Plain Dealer*, Dec. 3, 1995, p. 7–F.

5. This has often been quoted. For example, Ellen Goodman, "Children need parents, 'matched' or not'" in *Charlottesville Daily Progress*, Dec. 7, 1993, p. A8.

6. Quoted in "Alienated, marginal, and deadly" (pp. 52–54), in *Newsweek*, Sept. 19, 1994, p. 54

7. Ann Landers, "Readers prove that the world is getting crazier," *The Cleveland Plain Dealer*, Sept. 10, 1995, p. 7–I.

8. S. Nee, "Proposal targets renewal's effect on neighborhoods," *Charlottesville Daily Progress*, Dec. 12, 1993, p. B1.

9. Alain Destexhe, "Genocide and justice," in a letter to *The Economist*, July 23–29, 1994, p. 8.

10. Delbanco, A. (1995). *The death of Satan: How Americans have lost the sense of evil*. New York: Farrar, Straus and Giroux.

11. See Pocock, D. (1985). Unruly evil. In D. Parkin (Ed.), *The anthropology of evil*. New York: Basil Blackwell, p. 42.

12. Original quotation was from *Christian Week* magazine. Both remarks were quoted in *USA Today*, Sept. 28, 1995, p. 3C.

13. Darley, J. M. (1992). Social organization for the production of evil. *Psychological Inquiry*, 3, 199–217, Darley, J. M. (in press). How organizations inflict harm on workers, consumers, and the general public. In D. Messick & A. Tenbrunsel (Eds.), *Behavioral research and business ethics: An introduction*. New York: Russell Sage; Delbanco (1995); also Staub, E. (1989). *The roots of evil: The origins of genocide and other group violence*. New York and Cambridge, England: Cambridge University Press.

14. Thus, for example, Douglas, J. (1995). *Mind hunter: Inside the FBI's elite serial crime unit*. New York: Scribner, notes the implausibility in the argument and the rarity that juries accept it.

15. Stannard, D. E. (1992). *American holocaust: Columbus and the conquest of the New World*. New York: Oxford University Press, p. xi; from Major Scott Anthony, Report on the Conduct of the War, 38th Congress Second Session, 1865, p. 27.

16. The story is from Shakur, S. (1993). *Monster: The autobiography of an L.A. gang member*. New York: Atlantic Monthly Press, pp. 42–46.

17. Recent news reports in *The Economist* indicate that the drug trade has led to a lasting gang truce in Los Angeles, after the Mexican mafia put out the word that the shootings were scaring customers off. We shall return to the issue of drugs and crime in Chapter 3. It deserves to be noted that drugs did, even in Scott's memoir, have an effect of increasing violence, in that the money from drugs enabled the gangs to purchase more deadly weapons.

The net effect of drugs was thus to discourage violent actions but to make such actions more deadly when they did occur.

18. See Daly, M., & Wilson, M. (1994). Evolutionary psychology of male violence. In J. Archer (Ed.), *Male violence* (pp. 253–288). London & New York: Routledge; also Gilbert, P. (1994). Male violence: Towards an integration. In J. Archer (Ed.), *Male violence* (pp. 253–389). London & New York: Routledge.

19. This story is mainly based on Eftimiades, M. (1995). *Sins of the mother.* New York: St. Martins's.

20. More precise statistics on interracial rape patterns will be covered in Chapter 5. According to LaFree, G. D. (1976). Male power and female victimization: Towards a theory of interracial rape. *American Journal of Sociology, 88,* 311–328, prior to 1950, most interracial rapes involved white men raping black victims, and so the black-on-white rape in this incident would have been a relatively rare occurrence.

21. Readers are encouraged to try this for themselves. The special is "Violence: An American Tradition."

22. Hesse, P., & Mack, J. E. (1991). The world is a dangerous place: Images of the enemy on children's television. In R. Rieber (Ed.), *The psychology of war and peace: Images of the enemy.* (pp. 131–153). New York: Plenum.

23. Hovland, C. I., & Sears, R. (1940). Minor studies of aggression: Correlation of lynchings with economic indices. *Journal of Psychology, 9,* 301–310.

24. Hepworth, J. T., & West, S. G. (1988). Lynchings and the economy: A time-series reanalysis of Hofland and Sears (1940). *Journal of Personality and Social Psychology, 55,* 239–247.

25. "The bitter legacy of O.J.," editorial by M. B. Zuckerman, *US News & World Report,* Oct. 16, 1995, p. 100. The figures represent the per capita likelihood of perpetrating hate crimes, as opposed to the proportion of crimes.

26. McCall, N. (1994). *Makes me wanna holler: A young black man in America.* New York: Random House, p. 3.

27. McCall (1994), pp. 3–4.

28. McCall (1994), p. 4.

29. McCall (1994), p. 3.

30. McCall (1994), p. 4.

31. McCall (1994), p. 4.

32. See Baumeister, R. F., Smart, L., & Boden, J. M. (1996). Relation of threatened egotism to violence and aggression: The dark side of high self-esteem. *Psychological Review, 103,* 5–33.

33. This story is from Hee, K. H. (1993). *The tears of my soul.* New York: Morrow.

34. Hee (1993), p. 84 (quotations).

35. Hee (1993), p. 85.

36. Hee (1993), p. 84.

37. Hee (1993), p. 9.

CHAPTER 2 Victims and Perpetrators

1. This is a fairly standard view. Almost all sources agree. For example, Bauman, Z. (1991). *Modernity and the Holocaust*. Ithaca, NY: Cornell University Press; Breitman, R. (1991). *The architect of genocide: Himmler and the Final Solution*. Hanover, NH: Brandeis University Press.

2. Lifton, R. J. (1986). *The Nazi doctors: Medical killing and the psychology of genocide*. New York: Basic Books.

3. In fairness, the Germans at that point had a much longer and more impressive record of intellectual eminence in the world than America had. This has changed somewhat in the past half century. The intellectual superiority of America, although hardly of its average citizen and popular culture, is today well recognized in Germany and elsewhere.

4. Bauman (1991).

5. Prunier, G. (1995). *The Rwanda crisis: History of a genocide*. New York: Columbia University Press.

6. Two centuries earlier, Frederick and the small upstart land of Prussia fought against all the great powers of Europe at once. Frederick's brilliant tactics and strategies and his well-disciplined Prussian troops enabled him to win a remarkable series of battles. Eventually the great powers had accepted a draw. See Koch, H. W. (1978). *A history of Prussia*. New York: Dorset.

7. Keegan, J. (1993). *A history of warfare*. New York: Knopf; Tuchman, B. (1962). *The proud tower*. New York: Macmillan/Bantam.

8. Keegan (1993).

9. Bar-On, D. (1989). *Legacy of silence: Encounters with children of the Third Reich*. Cambridge, MA: Harvard University Press.

10. Baumeister, R. F., Stillwell, A. M., & Wotman, S. R. (1990).

11. Jankowski, M. S. (1991). *Islands in the street: Gangs and American urban society*. Berkeley, CA: University of California Press, p. 171.

12. Scully, D. (1990). *Understanding sexual violence*. Hammersmith, London, England: HarperCollins Academic.

13. Scully (1990), p. 107.

14. Scully (1990), p. 130.

15. Baumeister, Stillwell, & Wotman (1990).

16. Nasby, W., Hayden, B., & DePaulo, B. M. (1980). Attributional bias among aggressive boys to interpret unambiguous social stimuli as displays of hostility. *Journal of Abnormal Psychology, 89*, 459–468.

17. Goldstein, D., & Rosenbaum, A. (1985). An evaluation of the self-esteem of maritally violent men. *Family Relations, 34*, 425–428.

18. Goldstein & Rosenbaum (1985).

19. Toch, H. (1993). *Violent men: An inquiry into the psychology of violence.* Washington, DC: American Psychological Association. Original work published in 1969. These data are not as systematic as the other sources.

20. Katz, J. (1988). *Seductions of crime: Moral and sensual attractions in doing evil.* New York: Basic Books made an especially compelling presentation of this argument.

21. Stillwell, A. M., & Baumeister, R. F. (1995). The construction of victim and perpetrator memories: Accuracy and distortion in role-based accounts. Manuscript submitted for publication; also Stillwell's dissertation, in 1993.

22. Schütz, A., & Baumeister, R. F. (1995). Public and private accounts of harmdoing. Unpublished research findings, University of Virginia/Case Western Reserve University.

23. Sichrovsky, P. (1988). *Born guilty: Children of Nazi families.* New York: Basic Books.

24. Sichrovsky (1988), p. 7.

25. Bar-On (1989).

26. Baumeister, R. F. (1990). Suicide as escape from self. *Psychological Review, 97,* 90–113; Baumeister, R. F. (1991a). *Escaping the self: Alcoholism, spirituality, masochism, and other flights from the burden of selfhood.* New York: Basic Books.

27. Bar-On (1989).

28. Norris, J. (1992). *Walking time bombs.* New York: Bantam; the quotation is from p. 17.

29. Hare, R. D. (1993). *Without conscience: The disturbing world of the psychopaths among us.* New York: Simon & Schuster/Pocket, p. 43.

30. Hare (1993), p. 43.

31. Katz (1988), p. 19.

32. Arriens, J. (1991). *Welcome to Hell: Letters and other writings by prisoners on Death Row in the United States.* Cambridge, England: Faulkner, p. 72.

33. "Serbia: Another country." In *The Economist,* July 23, 1994, pp. 47–49. Quotation is from p. 47.

34. "Serbia: Another country." (1994), p. 49.

35. Peele, S. (1989). *The diseasing of America.* Boston, MA: Houghton Mifflin Co. reviews and critiques this development.

36. Luckenbill, D. (1977). Criminal homicide as a situated transaction. *Social Problems, 25,* 176–186.

37. Gottfredson, M. R., & Hirschi, T. (1990). *A general theory of crime.* Stanford, CA: Stanford University Press, p. 17.

38. Berkowitz, L. (1978). Is criminal violence normative behavior? Hostile and instrumental aggression in violent incidents. *Journal of Research in Crime and Delinquency, 15,* 148–161.

39. Straus, M. (1980). Victims and aggressors in marital violence. *American Behavioral Scientist, 23,* 681–704.

40. Cate, R. M., Henton, J. M., Koval, J., Christopher, F. S., & Lloyd, S. (1982). Premarital abuse: A social psychological perspective. *Journal of Family Issues, 3,* 79–90; Henton, J., Cate, R., Koval, J., Lloyd, S., & Christopher, S. (1983). Romance and violence in dating relationships. *Journal of Family Issues, 4,* 467–482. Stets, J. E. (1991). Psychological aggression in dating relationships: The role of interpersonal control. *Journal of Family Violence, 6,* 97–114.

41. Gondolf, E. W. (1985). *Men who batter.* Holmes Beach, FL: Learning Publications, p. 31.

42. Renzetti, C. M. (1992). *Violent betrayal: Partner abuse in lesbian relationships.* Newbury Park, CA: Sage, p. 110, quoting Hart (1986).

43. Post, J. M. (1990). Terrorist psycho-logic: Terrorist behavior as a product of psychological forces, In W. Reich (Ed.), *Origins of terrorism* (pp. 25–40). Cambridge, England: Cambridge University Press, p. 25; Kellen, K. (1990). Ideology and rebellion: Terrorism in West Germany. In W. Reich (Ed.), *Origins of terrorism* (pp. 43–58). Cambridge, England: Cambridge University Press, p. 55.

44. I am relying on Ford's 1985 account from Ford, F. L. (1985). *Political murder: From tyrannicide to terrorism.* Cambridge, MA: Harvard University Press.

CHAPTER 3 The Myth of Pure Evil

1. Thompson, H. S. (1996). *Hell's angels.* New York: Ballantine Books.

2. Rapoport, D. C. (1990). Sacred terror: A contemporary example from Islam. In W. Reich (Ed.), *Origins of terrorism* (pp. 103–130). Cambridge, England: Cambridge University Press, p. 120.

3. Associated Press story, Feb. 16, 1994; *Charlottesville Daily Progress.*

4. Shakur (1993). He changed his name from Scott and Monster to Shakur when he elected to leave his criminal lifestyle.

5. Twitchell, J. B. (1985). *Dreadful pleasures: An anatomy of modern horror.* New York: Oxford University Press.

6. Trilling, L. (1971). *Sincerity and authenticity.* Cambridge, MA: Harvard University Press.

7. Twitchell (1985), p. 10.

8. Clover, C. J. (1992). *Men, women, and chainsaws: Gender in the modern horror film.* Princeton, NJ: Princeton University Press.

9. Siskel G., & Ebert, R., "At the Movies" television special on villains: aired March 12, 1995.

10. There are so many of these that it is almost silly to offer examples. Indeed, on television the drug dealer became such a popular villain that some cop shows featured them exclusively. In the 1980s, the extremely popular television show *Miami Vice* made heroes of narcotics cops while the drug dealers (and most users) were depicted as the bad guys.

11. Russell (1988), p. 12.

12. Undoubtedly there was some exchange of ideas among some cultures, but Russell thinks this could not explain the broad similarity of evil everywhere. In a sense, though, the question of simultaneous invention vs. dissemination is irrelevant; what matters is the fact that the same idea appealed to people all over the world.

13. Russell (1988), p. 5.

14. Eliade, M. (1982). *A history of religious ideas* (Volume 2). Chicago, IL: University of Chicago Press.

15. See Crossman, R. H. (1987). *The god that failed.* New York: Regnery Gateway, for a compilation of some of the most famous of these writings.

16. Russell (1988), p. 2.

17. Hesse & Mack (1991), p. 143.

18. Gibson, J. W. (1994). *Warrior dreams: Paramilitary culture in post-Vietnam America.* New York: Hill and Wang.

19. Gibson (1994), p. 66.

20. Gibson (1994), p. 69

21. Gibson (1994), p. 78.

22. These first two points were featured in a thoughtful, eloquent essay on evil by Darley (1992).

23. This example is borrowed from Health, L. (1984). Impact of newspaper crime reports on fear of crime: Multimethodological investigation. *Journal of Personality and Social Psychology, 47,* 263–276. The hospital part is

inferred; Heath's account indicated only that the beating was severe but not fatal.

24. Gottfredson & Hirschi (1991).

25. "There are no children here." *The Economist*, Dec. 17, 1994. (Vol. 33, No. 7894). 21–23.

26. Kody Scott's memoir is especially vivid in showing this evolution; see Shakur (1993).

27. "There are no children here." (1994). p. 22.

28. Independent evidence of this point in Tetlock, P. E. (1981). Pre- to post-election shifts in presidential rhetoric: Impression management or cognitive adjustment? *Journal of Personality and Social Psychology, 41*, 207–212; provides research evidence that the speeches of politicians become simplistic and dumbed-down at election time, and then immediately afterwards go back to recognizing the complexity of the world. When politicians want to appeal to people, they know to keep it simple.

29. Some of this is reviewed in Baumeister, R. F., & Placidi, K. S. (1983). A social history and analysis of the LSD controversy. *Journal of Humanistic Psychology, 23* (No. 4), 25–58; see also Blum, R. H. (1969). On the presence of demons. In R. Blum & Associates (Eds.), *Society and drugs* (pp. 323–341). San Francisco, CA: Jossey-Bass.

30. National Research Council (1993). *Understanding and preventing violence.* Washington, DC: National Academy Press; see also Bushman, B. J., & Cooper, H. M. (1990). Effects of alcohol on human aggression: An integrative research review. *Psychological Bulletin, 107*, 341–354.

31. Taylor, S. P., Gammon, C. B., & Capasso, D. R. (1976). Aggression as a function of alcohol and threat. *Journal of Personality and Social Psychology, 34*, 938–941; see also Steele, C. M., & Southwick, L. (1985). Alcohol and social behavior I: The psychology of drunken excess. *Journal of Personality and Social Psychology, 48*, 18–34.

32. Renzetti (1992).

33. Quoted by Rieber, R. W., & Kelly, R. J. (1991). Substance and shadow: Images of the enemy. In R. Rieber (Ed.), *The psychology of war and peace: Images of the enemy.* New York: Plenum. pp. 3–39.

34. Jankowski (1991).

35. Dower, J. W. (1986). *War without mercy: Race and power in the Pacific war.* New York: Pantheon.

36. Dower (1986), p. 64.

37. Cohn, N. (1970). *The pursuit of the millennium.* New York: Oxford University Press; Carmichael, J. (1992). *The Satanizing of the Jews: Origin*

and development of mystical anti-Semitism. New York: Fromm International Publishing.

38. Cohn (1970); Riley-Smith, J. (1987). *The Crusades: A short history.* New Haven, CT: Yale University Press.

39. See Kunda, Z. (1990). The case for motivated reasoning. *Psychological Bulletin, 108,* 480–498, on motivated reasoning; Baumeister, R. F., & Newman, L. S. (1994). Self-regulation of cognitive inference and decision processes. *Personality and Social Psychology Bulletin, 20,* 3–19, on how people direct cognitive processes toward preferred conclusions.

40. Bulman & Wortman (1977).

41. Taylor (1983) is an important source; see also Baumeister (1991b), for review.

42. Jackall, R. (1988). *Moral mazes: The world of corporate managers.* New York: Oxford University Press.

43. Taylor & Brown (1988).

44. Taylor & Brown (1988).

45. Skitka, L. J., & Tetlock, P. E. (1993). Providing public assistance: Cognitive and motivational processes underlying liberal and conservative policy preferences. *Journal of Personality and Social Psychology, 65,* 1205–1223.

46. Janoff-Bulman (1992) has analyzed these implications of self-blame.

47. This reasoning does not, however, apply to uninvolved bystanders who do not take the victim's side. These people would probably prefer to believe that the victims brought their trouble on themselves— such as by provoking the aggressors— because it means that anyone who does not act in such a risky fashion is safe. To such bystanders, the myth of pure evil would tend to be disturbing and frightening (although no less fascinating).

48. Greenwald, A. G. (1980). The totalitarian ego: Fabrication and revision of personal history. *American Psychologist, 35,* 603–618; Taylor & Brown (1988).

49. Toch (1993).

50. Toch (1993), pp. 121–130.

51. Interestingly, Toch noted that most of the aggression was performed by one of the officers; the other's story corresponded somewhat more closely to the young citizen's.

52. Toch (1993), p. 122.

53. Post (1990), p. 25.

54. Kellen (1990), p. 55.

55. Bar-On (1989), (chapter 11) p. 245.

CHAPTER 4 Greed, Lust, Ambition: Evil as a Means to an End

1. Morgan, D. (1986). *The Mongols.* New York: Basil Blackwell.

2. Runciman, S. (1950-1054). *A history of the Crusades* (3 vols.) New York: Cambridge University Press, see volume 3, 1954, p. 241.

3. This account based on Tuchman, B. (1978) *A distant mirror: The calamitous 14th century.* New York: Ballantine.

4. Moreover, for many soldiers, there was not likely to be much available to them even if they did get home.

5. McCall (1994); Shakur (1993).

6. Gottfredson & Hirschi (1990).

7. Scarry, E. (1985) *The body in pain: The making and unmaking of the world.* New York: Oxford University Press.

8. Crenshaw, M. (1990). The logic of terrorism: Terrorism behavior as a product of strategic choice. In W. Reich (Ed.), *Origins of terrorism: Psychologies, ideologies, theologies, states of mind* (pp. 7–24). Cambridge, England: Cambridge University Press; Long, D. E. (1990). *The anatomy of terrorism.* New York: Free Press.

9. Gambetta, D. (1993). *The Sicilian mafia: The business of private protection.* Cambridge, MA: Harvard University Press.

10. Farrell, C. "An anguished cry of 'enough' in America's killing fields." *Business Week*, December 13, 1993, p. 80, reporting on a study by Richard B. Freeman.

11. Gottfredson & Hirschi (1990). These figures were compiled in the early 1980s and should be adjusted slightly for inflation.

12. Katz (1988).

13. Anastasia, G. (1991). *Blood and honor: Inside the Scarfo mob—the Mafia's most violent family.* New York: Morrow; Arlacchi, P. (1992). *Men of dishonor: Inside the Sicilian Mafia.* (M. Romano, trans.). New York: Morrow; Gambetta (1993); Handelman, S. (1995). *Comrade criminal: Russia's new mafia.* New Haven, CT: Yale University Press.

14. Not necessarily worse than the average criminal, though.

15. Mills, J. (1987). *The underground empire: Where crime and governments embrace.* New York: Dell; Currie, E. (1991). *Dope and trouble: Portraits of delinquent youth.* New York: Pantheon.

16. Ford (1985). It must be acknowledged that terrorism or assassination has sometimes succeeded in disrupting a peace negotiation process. Usually that is a short-term end, though, and so it conforms to the general pattern.

17. Ford (1985); also Crenshaw (1990); Gurr, T. R. (1990). Terrorism in democracies: Its social and political bases. In W. Reich (Ed.), *Origins of terrorism: Psychologies, ideologies, theologies, states of mind* (pp. 86–102). Cambridge, England: Cambridge University Press.

18. It is necessary to acknowledge that this particular analysis is complicated by a lack of clear, suitable comparisons. One could say, simply, that no repressive regime has lasted as long as the major democratic regimes such as the United States and England. Then again, perhaps these are unfair comparisons. Internal repressive terror may often only emerge when a government sees its power threatened from within. The U.S. has not faced any real threat of that nature for a long time, and it is noteworthy that the seemingly illusory belief in such an internal threat led to the McCarthyist repressions of the 1950s, not that they approached the severity of repressiveness that has been seen elsewhere. If internal terror is a response to internal threat, then one ought to compare internally threatened governments that do with those that don't engage in violent repressive terror— in which case it may emerge that the violence does prolong the regime's power to some extent.

19. Jonsen, A. R., & Sagan, L. A. (1985). Torture and the ethics of medicine. In E. Stover & E. Nightingale (Eds.), *The breaking of bodies and minds: Torture, psychiatric abuse, and the health professions* (pp. 30–44). New York: W. H. Freeman, p. 40. They quote an Amnesty International report saying, "the majority of torture victims, even in countries beset by widespread civil conflict, have no security information about violent opposition groups to give away."

20. For examples see Becker, E. (1986). *When the war was over: Cambodia's revolution and the voices of its people.* New York: Simon & Schuster, on Cambodia; Roth, C. (1964). *The Spanish Inquisition.* New York: Norton, on the Spanish Inquisition; Scarry (1995).

21. Conquest, R. (1990). *The Great Terror: A reassessment.* New York: Oxford University Press. See pp. 450–451: the Stalinist purge eliminated over half the high command.

22. McPherson, J. M. (1988). *Battle cry of freedom: The Civil War era.* New York: Oxford University Press.

23. Wyden, P. (1983). *The passionate war: The narrative history of the Spanish Civil War.* New York: Simon & Schuster/Touchstone.

24. Morris, D. R. (1965). *The washing of the spears: The rise and fall of the Zulu nation.* New York: Simon & Schuster.

25. Gottfredson & Hirschi (1990).

26. Gottfredson & Hirschi (1990), p. 33.

27. Another personal crime is rape. Rape typically fails to bring much in the way of sexual pleasure, see Groth, A. N. (1979). *Men who rape: The psychology of the offender.* New York: Plenum.

28. Scully (1990); also Groth (1979).
   Rapists report low levels of sexual satisfaction and high frequencies of sexual dysfunction during the rape.

29. Gelles, R. J., & Straus, M. A. (1988). *Intimate violence: The causes and consequences of abuse in the American family.* New York: Simon & Schuster/Touchstone.

30. Katz (1988), especially chapter 3.

31. Baumeister, R. F., & Scher, S. J. (1988). Self-defeating behavior patterns among normal individuals: Review and analysis of common self-destructive tendencies. *Psychological Bulletin, 104,* 3–22; Baumeister (1991a); Berglas, S. C., & Baumeister, R. F. (1993). *Your own worst enemy: Understanding the paradox of self-defeating behavior.* New York: Basic Books.

32. See Platt, J. (1973). Social traps. *American Psychologist, 28,* 641–651; Loewenstein, G., & Elster, J. (Eds.) (1992). *Choice over time.* New York: Russell Sage. 1992.

33. Leith, K. P., & Baumeister, R. F. (in press). Why do bad moods increase self-defeating behavior? Emotion, risk-taking, and self-regulation. *Journal of Personality and Social Psychology.*

34. Gottfredson & Hirschi (1990), noted this as one source of homicide. Katz (1988) paid particular attention to such cases and interpreted them in terms of the identity claims of the perpetrator, who seeks to prove complete control over the situation and who may want to project an image of being dangerous and unpredictable.

CHAPTER 5 Egotism and Revenge

1. Morris (1965).

2. Axson (1994), personal communication.

3. Russell (1988), see p. 103 on St. Augustine and pp. 35–36 on early Jewish and Christian accounts.

4. Brown, B. R. (1968). The effects of need to maintain face on interpersonal bargaining. *Journal of Experimental Social Psychology, 4,* 107–122.

5. Baumeister, Smart, & Boden (1996). Much of this chapter is based on that work, which includes a lengthy literature review. Scholars interested in examining all relevant sources, evidence, and arguments should consult that article.

6. Long (1990).

7. Anderson, E. (1994). The code of the streets. *Atlantic Monthly, 273* (#5: May), 82–94; Renzetti (1992); Gondolf (1985); MacDonald, J. M. (1975). *Armed robbery: Offenders and their victims.* Springfield, IL: Thomas; Kirschner, D. (1992). Understanding adoptees who kill: Dissociation, patri-

cide, and the psychodynamics of adoption. *International Journal of Offender Therapy and Comparative Criminology, 36*, 323–333; Jankowski (1991); Levin, J., & McDevitt, J. (1993). *Hate crimes: The rising tide of bigotry and bloodshed.* New York: Plenum; Wiehe, V. R. (1991). *Perilous rivalry: When siblings become abusive.* Lexington, MA: Heath/Lexington Books; Toch (1993); Schoenfeld, C. G. (1988). Blacks and violent crime: A psychoanalytically oriented analysis. *Journal of Psychiatry and Law, 16*, 269–301; Schoenfeld, C. G. (1993). Crime, punishment, and the criminal law: A psychoanalytic summary and analysis. *Journal of Psychiatry and Law, 21*, 337–361;Oates, R. K., & Forrest, D. (1985). Self-esteem and early background of abusive mothers. *Child Abuse and Neglect, 9*, 89–93; Staub, E. (1985). The psychology of perpetrators and bystanders. *Political Psychology, 6*, 61–85; Staub, E. (1990). The psychology and culture of torture and torturers. In P. Suedfeld (Ed.), *Psychology and torture* (pp. 49–76). New York: Taylor & Francis/Hemisphere.

8. Baumeister, Smart, & Boden (1996) review this research literature.

9. National Research Council (1993).

10. Hare (1993), quotations are from p. 38; see also Meloy, J. R. (1988). *The psychopathic mind: Origins, dynamics, and treatment.* Northvale, NJ: Aranson.

11. Crocker, J., & Major, B. (1989). Social stigma and self-esteem: The self-protective properties of stigma. *Psychological Review, 96*, 608–630.

12. Brearly, H. C. (1932). *Homicide in the United States.* Chapel Hill, NC: University of North Carolina Press; Hoffman, F. L. (1925). *The homicide problem.* Newark, NJ: Prudential Press; Von Hentig, H. (1948). *The criminal and his victim.* New Haven, CT: Yale University Press. It must be noted that bias in the judicial system may have contributed to this difference, at least in the 1800s; white men were more likely to get off easily for killing blacks than the reverse, and so if there is any deterrent effect of punishment it may have contributed to the lesser violence by blacks. Then again, this bias was itself presumably indicative of the sense of superiority, so it fits the argument.

13. Adler, J. "Murder: A week in the death of America." *Newsweek,* August 15, 1994, pp. 24–43.

14. This is a modern judgment. Technically, in many places there was no law against a white man forcing sex on a black female slave, so it did not constitute the crime of rape. My argument concerns forcible sex rather than contemporary legal technicalities.

15. For historical data, see Brownmiller, S. (1975). *Against our will: Men, women, and rape.* New York: Simon & Schuster; on recent patterns, see Scully (1990).

16. LaFree (1976).

17. American Psychiatric Association (1994). *Diagnostic and statistical manual of the mental disorders* (Fourth Edition). Washington, DC: Author.

18. Goodwin & Jamison (1990).

19. National Research Council (1993); see also Gottfredson & Hirschi (1990); Groth (1985).

20. Bushman & Cooper (1990).

21. Banaji, M. R., & Steele, C. M. (1989). Alcohol and self-evaluation: Is a social cognition approach beneficial? *Social Cognition, 7,* 137–151; Diamond, D. L., & Wilsnack, S. C. (1978). Alcohol abuse among lesbians: A descriptive study. *Journal of Homosexuality, 4,* 205–216; Hurley, D. L. (1990). Incest and the development of alcoholism in adult female survivors. *Alcohol Treatment Quarterly, 7,* 41–56; Konovsky, M., & Wilsnack, S. C. (1982). Social drinking and self-esteem in married couples. *Journal of Studies on Alcohol, 43,* 319–333; Orford, J., & Keddie, A. (1985). Gender differences in the functions and effects of moderate and excessive drinking. *British Journal of Clinical Psychology, 24,* 265–279.

22. This analysis is central to Baumeister, Smart, & Boden (1996).

23. For data and examples, see Baumeister, R. F., & Wotman, S. R. (1992). *Breaking hearts: The two sides of unrequited love.* New York: Guilford Press; Baumeister, R. F., Wotman, S. R., & Stillwell, A. M. (1993). Unrequited love: On heartbreak, anger, guilt, scriptlessness, and humiliation. *Journal of Personality and Social Psychology, 64,* 377–394.

24. The eminent aggression research by Berkowitz, L., & Geen, R. G. (1966). Film violence and the cue properties of available targets. *Journal of Personality and Social Psychology, 3,* 525–530, recently proposed a new theory, which is that all of the bad (i.e., unpleasant) emotions lead to aggression, including frustration, anger, sadness, depression, and others. This formulation is clearly too broad: There is not much evidence that sadness leads to aggression, and indeed it may decrease it.

25. Smith, R. H., Parrott, W. G., Ozer, D., & Moniz, A. (1994). Subjective injustice and inferiority as predictors of hostile and depressive feelings in envy. *Personality and Social Psychology Bulletin, 20,* 717–723.

26. Scully (1990).

27. Scully (1990), p. 112; Scully's words, not the rapist's.

28. Walker (1979).

29. See Baumeister, Smart, & Boden (1996) for review.

30. See Gelles & Straus (1988); also especially Hornung, C. A., McCullough, B. C., & Sugimoto, T. (1981). Status relationships in marriage: Risk factors in spouse abuse. *Journal of Marriage and the Family, 43,* 675–692.

31. Hornung, McCullough, & Sugimoto (1981).

32. Peterson, D. (1991). Physically violent husbands of the 1890s and their resources. *Journal of Family Violence, 6,* 1–15.

33. Finkelhor, D., & Yllo, K. (1985). *License to rape: Sexual abuse of wives.* New York: Free Press.

34. Kernis, M. H. (1993). The roles of stability and level of self-esteem in psychological functioning. In R. Baumeister (Ed.), *Self-esteem: The puzzle of low self-regard.* New York: Plenum, pp. 167–182.

35. Kernis, M. H., Grannemann, B. D., & Barclay, L. C. (1989). Stability and level of self-esteem as predictors of anger arousal and hostility. *Journal of Personality and Social Psychology, 56,* 1013–1022; Kernis, M. H., Cornell, D. P., Sun, C. R., Berry, A., & Harlow, T. (1993). There's more to self-esteem than whether it's high or low: The importance of stability of self-esteem. *Journal of Personality and Social Psychology, 65,* 1190–1204.

36. Toch (1993).

37. Berkowitz (1978), p. 158.

38. Renzetti (1992), p. 43.

39. Lewis, H. B. (1971). *Shame and guilt in neurosis.* New York: International Universities Press; Tangney, J. P., Wagner, P. E. Fletcher, C., & Gramzow, R. (1992). Shamed into anger? The relation of shame and guilt to anger and self-reported aggression. *Journal of Personality and Social Psychology, 62,* 669–675.

40. Tangney, Wagner, Fletcher, & Gramzow (1992).

41. Ford (1985), p. 80.

42. Olweus, D. (1994). Bullying at school: Long-term outcomes for the victims and an effective school-based intervention program. In L. R. Huesmann (Ed.), *Aggressive behavior: Current perspectives* (pp. 97–130). New York: Plenum.

43. Jankowski (1991), p. 27.

44. Fitch, G. (1970). Effects of self-esteem, perceived performance, and choice on causal attributions. *Journal of Personality and Social Psychology, 16,* 311–315; Ickes, W., & Layden, M. A. (1978). Attributional styles. In J. Harvey (Ed.), *New directions in attribution research* (Vol. 2, pp. 119–152). Hillsdale, NJ: Erlbaum; Tennen, H., & Herzberger, S. (1987). Depression, self-esteem, and the absence of self-protective attributional biases. *Journal of Personality and Social Psychology, 52,* 72–80; Kernis, M. H., Brockner, J., & Frankel, B. S. (1989). Self-esteem and reactions to failure: The mediating role of overgeneralization. *Journal of Personality and Social Psychology, 57,* 707–714.

45. Becker (1985).

46. Linger, D. T. (1992). *Dangerous encounters: Meanings of violence in a Brazilian city.* Stanford, CA: Stanford University Press, pp. 111–113.

47. Linger (1992), p. 113.

48. Brown (1968).

49. Luckenbill (1977).

50. The term *social reality* was coined by Wicklund, R. A., & Gollwitzer, P. M. (1982). *Symbolic self-completion.* Hillsdale, NJ: Erlbaum. On motivational concern over others' opinions, see Baumeister, R. F. (1982). A self-presentational view of social phenomena. *Psychological Bulletin, 91,* 3–26. Baumeister, R. F. (1982). Self-esteem, self-presentation, and future interaction: A dilemma of reputation. *Journal of Personality, 50,* 29–45; Schlenker, B. R. (1980). *Impression management: The self-concept, social identity, and interpersonal relations.* Monterey, CA: Brooks/Cole; Leary, M. R. (1995) *Self-presentation: Impression management and interpersonal behavior.* Madison, WI: Brown & Benchmark. On selective ignoring of confidential ego threats, see Baumeister, R. F., & Cairns, K. J. (1992). Repression and self-presentation: When audiences interfere with self-deceptive strategies. *Journal of Personality and Social Psychology, 62,* 851–862.

51. Nisbett, R. E. (1993). Violence and U.S. regional culture. *American Psychologist, 48,* 441–449.

52. Anastasia (1991), pp. 125–128.

53. Deuteronomy 32: 41–42.

54. Anastasia (1991).

55. Lawson, A. (1988). *Adultery: An analysis of love and betrayal.* New York: Basic Books.

56. Feather (1994).

57. Scully (1990), p. 134.

58. Groth (1979), p. 14.

59. Scully (1990), p. 127.

60. See Wade, W. C. (1987). *The fiery cross: The Ku Klux Klan in America.* New York: Touchstone/Simon & Schuster; also Brownmiller (1975).

61. On guilt, see Baumeister, R. F., Stillwell, A. M., & Heatherton, T. F. (1994). Guilt: An interpersonal approach. *Psychological Bulletin, 115,* 243–267; also Hoffman, M. L. (1981). Is altruism part of human nature? *Journal of Personality and Social Psychology, 40,* 121–137.

62. Hare (1993), p. 2.

63. Hare (1993), p. 138.

CHAPTER 6 True Believers and Idealists

1. Quoted in the P.B.S. television documentary "The Civil War," aired on February 23, 1992.

2. Armstrong, K. (1993). *A history of God.* New York: Ballantine, p. 18.

3. Eisenhower, D. D. (1948). *Crusade in Europe*. New York: Doubleday.

4. These accounts are from Maalouf, A. (1987). *The Crusades through Arab eyes*. New York: Schocken; see also Runciman (1951–1954).

5. Parker, G. (1987). *The Thirty Years' War*. New York: Military Heritage Press.

6. Runciman (1951–1954).

7. Runciman (1954).

8. I wish to thank Richard Felson for pointing out how many of us act as if ends justify means in our daily lives.

9. He doesn't seem to have lacked for self-esteem, either.

10. Pakenham, T. (1979). *The Boer War*. New York: Random House; quote is from p. 121.

11. Pakenham (1979); Pakenham, T. (1991). *The scramble for Africa: White man's conquest of the dark continent from 1876 to 1912*. New York: Avon/Random House.

12. Pakenham (1979), p. 612.

13. Conquest, R. (1986). *The harvest of sorrow: Soviet collectivization and the terror-famine*. New York: Oxford University Press.

14. Conquest (1986), p. 301.

15. Conquest (1976), p. 230.

16. Conquest (1986), p. 233.

17. Conquest (1986), p. 233.

18. Conquest (1986), p. 234.

19. Conquest (1986), p. 234.

20. Friedan, B. "Beyond gender." *Newsweek*, Sept. 5 1995, pp. 30–32.

21. Russell (1988), p. 131.

22. See Gibson, J. T., & Haritos-Fatouros, M. The education of a torturer. *Psychology Today*, November, 1986, pp. 50–58.

23. Kellen (1990); Post (1990).

24. Carmichael (1992).

25. Becker (1986), p. 186.

26. Wyden (1983), p. 42.

27. Thurston, A. F. (1987). *Enemies of the people: The ordeal of the intellectuals in China's great Cultural Revolution*. New York: Knopf.

28. Blee, K. M. (1991). *Women of the Klan: Racism and gender in the 1920s*. Berkeley, CA: University of California Press, see pp. 19, 26–28, 40.

29. Höhne, H. (1967). *The order of the death's head: The story of Hitler's SS*. New York: Ballantine.

30. Höhne (1969), p. 152.

31. Höhne (1969), p. 151.

32. It must be acknowledged that some concentration camp chiefs complained about the low quality of people who became guards. There is some contention that within the SS, and especially at the concentration camps, the less desirable individuals played a leading role. Alternatively, it may be that the situation brought out sadism and other baser aspects of human nature.

33. Becker (1986).

34. Crossman (1987).

35. Koestler, A. (1987). [Untitled autobiographical chapter.] In R. Crossman (Ed.), *The god that failed* (pp. 15–75). Washington, D.C.: Regnery Gateway, p. 50.

36. For review, see Baumeister, R. F., & Leary, M. R. (1995). The need to belong: Desire for interpersonal attachments as a fundamental human motivation. *Psychological Bulletin, 117*, 497–529.

37. Russell (1988).

38. Hoyle, R. H., Pinkley, R. L., & Insko, C. A. (1989). Perceptions of social behavior: Evidence of differing expectations for interpersonal and intergroup interaction. *Personality and Social Psychology Bulletin, 15*, 365–376.

39. Koestler (1987), p. 34.

40. Palmer, R. R. (1969). *Twelve who ruled: The year of the terror in the French Revolution.* Princeton, NJ: Princeton University Press, p. 160.

41. Wright, R. (1987). [Untitled autobiographical chapter.] In R. Crossman (Ed.), *The god that failed* (pp. 115–162). Washington, D.C.: Regnery Gateway, p. 125.

42. Wright (1987), p. 149.

43. Wright (1987), p. 158.

44. Rapoport (1990), p. 111. Italics in Rapoport's original.

45. Russell (1988), p. 145.

46. Palmer (1969), e.g., p. 367.

47. Palmer (1969), p. 385.

48. Runciman, Vol. II, p. 48.

49. Runciman, Vol. III, p. 107.

50. Runciman, Vol. I, pp. 279–294.

51. For example, McPherson (1988).

CHAPTER 7 Can Evil Be Fun? The Joy of Hurting

1. Klee, E., Dressen, W., & Riess, V. (1991) (Eds.). *"The good old days": The Holocaust as seen by its perpetrators and bystanders* (D. Burnstone, trans.). New York: Free Press, p. 129.

2. I will therefore consider sexual sadism as one possible model for the enjoyment of inflicting harm, at several points in this chapter.

3. Wyden (1983), p. 343.

4. Cited by Gibson & Haritos-Fatouros (1986).

5. Kelman, H. C., & Hamilton, V. L. (1989). *Crimes of obedience: Toward a social psychology of authority and responsibility.* New Haven, CT: Yale University Press, p. 6.

6. Kelman & Hamilton (1989).

7. Scott, G. G. (1983). *Erotic power: An exploration of dominance and submission.* Secaucus, NJ: Citadel Press.

8. For example, Lifton (1986), p. 15, pp. 159–162.

9. Lifton (1986), p. 15.

10. Browning (1992).

11. Browning (1992), p. 74.

12. Norris, J. (1988). *Serial killers: The growing menace.* New York: Doubleday, pp. 32–34.

13. Gibson & Haritos-Fatouros (1986).

14. Nordland, R. "Death of a village." *Newsweek*, April 15, 1996, pp. 52–57. Quotation is from p. 55.

15. Unpublished findings, University of Virginia.

16. Milgram, S. (1963). Behavioral study of obedience. *Journal of Abnormal and Social Psychology, 67*, 371–378. All quotations from p. 375.

17. Kagan, J. (1981). *The second year: The emergence of self-awareness.* Cambridge, MA: Harvard University Press.

18. Becker (1986), p. 295.

19. Browning (1992), p. 41; see also Klee, Dressen, & Riess (1988).

20. See Burawoy, M. (1979). *Manufacturing consent.* Chicago, IL: University of Chicago Press.

21. From the Zimbardo slide show/recording based on the experiment.

22. Tuchman (1978).

23. According to Roth (19654), the *auto-da-fé* was a Portuguese term, which became more common than the Spanish *Auto-de-Fe.*

24. Roth (1964), especially chapter 5.

25. Ann Landers. "Children who killed horse need special counseling." *The Cleveland Plain Dealer,* Dec. 3, 1995, p. 2-F.

26. Hare (1993), p. 34; see also pp. 23–25.

27. Hare (1993), p. 33.

28. Hare (1993), p. 91.

29. Hare (1993), p. 162.

30. Toch (1993), p. 157.

31. Toch (1993), p. 182.

32. Katz (1988), p. 5.

33. Gondolf (1985), p. 47.

34. Norris (1992), pp. 18–19.

35. Norris (1992), p. 63.

36. Wyden (1983), p. 105.

37. Wyden (1983), pp. 104–105.

38. Pakenham (1991), p. 352.

39. Stannard (1992), p. 71. The examples he quotes are mostly references to extremely cruel actions that the writers performed, not explicit statements of having enjoyed them. Still, the tone of such comments seems to suggest that the acts were performed in either a casual or pleasant spirit, which is to say without regret or sympathy or other negative emotions. (To be sure, elsewhere Stannard cites evidence that some participants did feel bad.)

40. Suarez-Orozco, M. (1992). A grammar of terror: Psychocultural responses to state terrorism in dirty war and post-dirty war Argentina. In C. Nordstrom & J. Martin (Eds.), *The paths to domination, resistance, and terror* (pp. 219–259). Berkeley, CA: University of California Press.

41. Norris (1992), p. 53.

42. Norris (1992), p. 47.

43. Norris (1992), p. 32.

44. Norris (1992), pp. 18–20.

45. Olmos, E. "Lives in hazard." NBC television special, aired April 8, 1994.

46. McCall (1994) described how one of his accomplices came to do this routinely.

47. Bing, L. (1991). *Do or die*. New York: HarperCollins, pp. 58–60.

48. Bing (1991), p. 60

49. Bing (1991), p. 61.

50. Bing (1991), p. 61.

51. Bing (1991), p. 62.

52. Jankowski (1991), p. 177.

53 Browning (1992), pp. 82–83.

54. Arlacchi (1992), p. 215.

55. Finkelhor & Yllo (1985), pp. 50–54.

56. See Baumeister, R. F. (1989). *Masochism and the self*. Hillsdale, NJ: Erlbaum; Scott (1983); Samois (1982). *Coming to power*. Boston, MA: Alyson; Weinberg, T., & Kamel, W. L. (Eds.) (1983). *S and M: Studies in sado-masochism*. Buffalo, NY: Prometheus.

57. See Schachter, S., Silverstein, B., Kozlowski, L. T., Perlick, D., Herman, C. P., & Liebling, B. (1977). Studies of the interaction of psychological and pharmacological determinants of smoking. *Journal of Experimental Psychology: General, 106,* 3–40, on addicted vs. nonaddicted smokers.

58. Scully (1990), p. 158.

59. Stover, E., & Nightingale, E. O. (1985) (Eds.). *The breaking of bodies and minds: Torture, psychiatric abuse, and the health professions.* New York: W. H. Freeman, p. 7.

60. Solomon, R. L., & Corbit, J. D. (1974). An opponent process theory of motivation: I. Temporal dynamics of affect. *Psychological Review, 81,* 119–145.

61. One might suppose that this would be unnecessary, but the B process grows stronger over time. But it seems to reach an asymptote; it does not continue to increase indefinitely.

62. Staub (1989), p. 134f.

63. See Baumeister, Stillwell, & Heatherton (1994) on interpersonal benefits of guilt.

64. Katz (1988).

65. Currie (1991), p. 234.

66. Martin, M. (1995). "Teens took life, dollar, police say: Man stabbed to death on street in Lakewood." *The Cleveland Plain Dealer,* July 11, 1995, p. B-1.

67. In principle, the argument could apply to a male partner as well, but I use the female here in part because the issue of faking sexual pleasure is usually discussed in these terms. Females rarely seem to worry whether their male partners are faking orgasms and the like.

68. This goes back to original work by McClelland and others, but this basic point has been well explained by McAdams, D. P. (1985). *Power, intimacy, and the life story.* New York: Guilford.

69. Morgenthau, H. (1962). Love and power. *Commentary, 33,* 247–251.

70. Fanon, F. (1963). *The wretched of the earth.* New York: Grove Press, p. 226. He was not using "squeal" in the recent colloquial sense of confessing, but rather in the literal sound of making a sound of pain.

71. Fanon (1963), p. 267. The quotation is from p. 267.

72. Fanon (1963), p. 265.

73. Conquest (1990).

74. Gelles & Straus (1988), p. 68; see also pp. 119–120.

75. Renzetti (1992), p. 102.

76. Loring, M. T. (1994). *Emotional abuse.* New York: Lexington/Macmillan.

CHAPTER 8 Crossing the Line: How Evil Starts

1. All this material is from Wade (1987).

2. Wade (1987), p. 34.

3. Ford (1985), p. 104.

4. Ford (1985), p. 120.

5. Kelman & Hamilton (1989), p. 3.

6. Dean, J. W. (1977). *Blind ambition: The White House years.* New York: Kangaroo/Pocket, p. 24.

7. Dean (1977), p. 26.

8. Blee (1991).

9. Gottfredson & Hirschi (1990).

10. Baumeister, R. F., Heatherton, T. F., & Tice, D. M. (1994). *Losing control: How and why people fail at self-regulation.* San Diego, CA: Academic Press.

11. Russell, F. H. (1975). *The just war in the Middle Ages.* Cambridge, England: Cambridge University Press.

12. Douglas (1995), p. 374.

13. Carver, C. S., & Scheier, M. F. (1981). *Attention and self-regulation: A control theory approach to human behavior.* New York: Springer-Verlag; Vallacher, R. R., & Wegner, D. M. (1985). *A theory of action identification.* Hillsdale, NJ: Erlbaum; Vallacher, R. R., & Wegner, D. M. (1987). What do people think they're doing: Action identification and human behavior. *Psychological Review, 94,* 3–15.

14. Hawk, D. (1985). The Cambodian way of death: 1975–1979. In E. Stover & E. O. Nightingale (Eds.), *The breaking of bodies and minds: Torture, psychiatric abuse, and the health professions.* New York: W. H. Freeman, p. 39; see also Becker (1986).

15. Keinan, G. (1987). Decision making under stress: Scanning of alternatives under controllable and uncontrollable threats. *Journal of Personality and Social Psychology, 52,* 639–644; also Keith & Baumeister (in press).

16. On emotion and action: Frijda (1986).

17. This is not necessarily because alcohol is more "evil" than other drugs. Alcohol is old, familiar, and legal, all of which have helped scientists compile a large body of research findings. If I wanted to conduct an experimental study on the effects of alcohol, for example, I could arrange that without too much difficulty, but a comparable study on cocaine would be prohibitively difficult to arrange, given the legal complications as well as the pragmatic difficulty of obtaining the drug through legitimate channels. It is no accident that I know quite a few colleagues who have conducted studies with alcohol—but none who have done so with illegal drugs.

18. Steele & Southwick (1985).

19. Taylor, Gammon, & Capasso (1976).

20. For example, Berkowitz (1978).

21. For example, Toch (1993); McCall (1994); Jankowski (1991).

22. Tedeschi, J. T., & Felson, R. B. (1994). *Violence, aggression, and coercive actions.* Washington, DC: American Psychological Association.

23. Berkowitz (1978).

24. Douglas (1995), p. 348.

25. Prunier (1995), pp. 173–174.

26. Gelles & Straus (1988), especially p. 91; also pp. 121–123.

27. Hennigan, K. M., del Rosario, M. L., Heath, L., Cook, T. D., Wharton, J. D., & Calder, B. J. (1982). Impact of the introduction of television on crime in the United States: Empirical findings and theoretical implications. *Journal of Personality and Social Psychology, 42,* 461–477.

28. Ressler, lecture at the University of Virginia, 1993.

29. Berkowitz & Geen (1966).

30. Bushman, B. J. (1995). Moderating role of trait aggressiveness in the effects of violent media on aggression. *Journal of Personality and Social Psychology, 69,* 950–960.

31. Douglas (1995), p. 164; crime scene depiction from p. 160.

CHAPTER 9   How Evil Grows and Spreads

1. Suarez-Orozco, M. (1992). A grammar of terror: Psychocultural responses to state terrorism in dirty war and post-dirty war Argentina. In C. Nordstrom & J. Martin (Eds.), *The paths to domination, resistance, and terror.* Berkeley, CA: University of California Press, pp. 219–259.

2. Stets, J. E. (1990). Verbal and physical aggression in marriage. *Journal of Marriage and the Family, 52,* 501–514.

3. Berkowitz (1979).

4. Bing (1991), p. 257.

5. For example, Davidowicz, L. S. (1975). *The war against the Jews: 1933–1945.* New York: Bantam; according to Zygmunt Bauman (1989), p. 15, the definitive work on this topic was Schleuner, K. A. (1970). *The twisted road to Auschwitz.* Champaign, IL: University of Illinois Press.

6. Buss, A. H. (1966). The effect of harm on subsequent aggression. *Journal of Experimental Research on Personality, 1,* 249–255; Goldstein, J. H., Davis, R. W., & Herman, D. (1975). Escalation of aggression: Experimental studies. *Journal of Personality and Social Psychology, 31,* 162–170.

7. Tedeschi & Felson (1994).

8. Browning (1992), for example, p. 111.

9. Sereny, G. (1983). *Into that darkness: A examination of conscience.* New York: Vintage/Random House, especially pp. 212–213.

10. Sereny (1983), p. 213.

11. Sereny (1983), p. 213.

12. Alexander, E. (1991), *A crime of vengeance: An Armenian struggle for justice.* New York: Free Press; also Staub (1989).

13. Gelles & Straus (1988).

14. Conquest (1990).

15. Palmer (1969), and Schama, S. (1991). *Citizens: A chronicle of the French Revolution.* New York: Vintage/Random House.

16. Becker (1986), p. 45, p. 167.

17. Becker·(1986), p. 253.

18. Block, S., & Reddaway, P. (1985). Psychiatrists and dissenters in the Soviet Union. In E. Stover & E. Nightingale (Eds.), *The breaking of bodies and minds: Torture, psychiatric abuse, and the health professions.* New York: W. H. Freeman, pp. 132–163.

19. Rosenhan, D. L. (1973). On being sane in insane places. *Science, 179,* 250–258.

20. Darley, J. M., & Latané, B. (1968). Bystander intervention in emergencies: Diffusion of responsibility. *Journal of Personality and Social Psychology, 8,* 377–383.

21. Latané, B., Williams, K., & Harkins, S. (1979). Many hands make light the work: The causes and consequences of social loafing. *Journal of Personality and Social Psychology, 37,* 822–832.

22. Braverman, H. (1974). *Labor and monopoly capital: The degradation of work in the twentieth century.* New York: Monthly Review Press.

23. Jackall (1988).

24. Lifton (1986).

25. Lifton (1986), p. 106.

26. Lifton (1986), p. 107.

27. The so-called "risky shift" effect; for example, Wallach, M., Kogan, N., & Bem, D. (1962). Group influence on individual risk-taking. *Journal of Abnormal and Social Psychology, 65,* 75–86.

28. On group polarization, Moscovici, S., & Zavalloni, M. (1969). The group as polarizer of attitudes. *Journal of Personality and Social Psychology, 12,* 124–135, is an eerie and influential source.

29. Stasser, G., & Titus, W. (1985). Pooling of unshared information in group decision making: Biased information sampling during discussion. *Journal of*

Personality and Social Psychology, 48, 1467–1478; further progressin their research program was reported in the same journal in 1987 and 1989. Names of candidates have been added here for illustrative purposes.

30. Palmer (1969), especially p. 103.

CHAPTER 10 Dealing with Guilt

1. Quoted in Hare (1993), p. 41.

2. Kunda (1990); see also Baumeister & Newman (1994).

3. From Runciman (1951–1954).

4. See Russell (1975).

5. Browning (1992). His quotation is on p. 72; the metalworker's is on p. 73.

6. Associated Press story, "Lifelong ties couldn't stop Rwandan slaughter." *Charlottesville Daily Progress,* May 16, 1994, pp. A1 and A6.

7. For example, Jankowski (1991).

8. Bing (1991), p. 194.

9. Bing (1991), p. 262.

10. Cose, E. "Protecting the children." *Newsweek,* August 30, 1993, pp. 28–29, p. 29.

11. Cose (1993), p. 29.

12. For literature review and integration, see Baumeister, Stillwell, & Heatherton (1994); for recent overviews see Tangney, J. P., & Fischer, K. W. (1995). *Self-conscious emotions: The psychology of shame, guilt, embarrassment, and pride.* New York: Guilford Press.

13. Baumeister, R. F., Reis, H. T., & Delespaul, P. A. E. G. (1995). Subjective and experiential correlates of guilt in everyday life. *Personality and Social Psychology Bulletin, 21,* 1256–1268; also Baumeister, R. F. Stillwell, A. M., & Heatherton, T. F. (1995). Personal narratives about guilt: Role in action control and interpersonal relationships. *Basic and Applied Social Psychology, 17,* 173–198.

14. On the need to belong, see Baumeister & Leary (1995); on the roots of guilt, see Baumeister, Stillwell, & Heatherton (1994); on anxiety and social exclusion, see Baumeister, R. F., & Tice, D. M. (1990). Anxiety and social exclusion. *Journal of Social and Clinical Psychology, 9,* 165–195; and Leary, M. R., & Kowalski, R. (1995). *Social anxiety.* New York: Guilford.

15. Survivor guilt reviewed in Baumeister, Stillwell, & Heatherton (1994).

16. This is one defining trait of the psychopath; see Hare (1993).

17. Diener, E., Diener, M., & Diener, C. (1995). Factors predicting the subjective well-being of nations. *Journal of Personality and Social Psychology, 69,* 851–864.

18. Chirot, D. (1994). *Modern tyrants: The power and prevalence of evil in our age.* New York: Free Press.

19. Hoffman, M. L. (1982). Development of prosocial motivation: Empathy and guilt. In N. Eisenberg (Ed.), *The development of prosocial behavior.* New York: Academic Press, pp. 281–313 proposed the theoretical link between empathy and guilt; Tangney, J. P. (1991). Moral affect: The good, the bad, and the ugly. *Journal of Personality and Social Psychology, 61,* 598–607, has provided strong empirical evidence.

20. Conquest (1990), p. 320.

21. Mayer, J. D. (1993). The emotional madness of the dangerous leader. *Journal of Psychohistory, 20,* 331–348.

22. This was repeatedly reported in news magazines in 1995, especially in *The Economist.*

23. For example, Roth (1964); Prunier (1995).

24. Scarry (1985); Conquest (1990); Thurston (1987).

25. Kapuscinski, R. (1984). *The emperor: Downfall of an autocrat.* (W. Brand & K. Mroczkowska-Brand, trans.) New York: Random House/Vintage, p. 102.

26. Kapuscinski (1984), p. 103.

27. Kapuscinski (1984), p. 103.

28. Kapuscinski (1984), p. 102.

29. Milgram (1963).

30. Jones, E. E., & Nisbett, R. (1971). *The actor and the observer: Divergent perceptions of the causes of behavior.* Morristown, NJ: General Learning Press.

31. Walzer, M. (1977). *Just and unjust wars: A moral argument with historical illustrations.* New York: Basic Books, p. 314.

32. Browning (1992), p. 62.

33. Irle, M. (1991). [Keynote address at the annual meeting of the German Social Psychological Association, Mannheim, Germany.]

34. See Baumeister, Heatherton, & Tice (1994); Baumeister, R. F., & Heatherton, T. F. (1996). Self-regulation failure: An overview. *Psychological Inquiry, 7,* 1–15.

35. Darley & Latané (1968).

36. Festinger, L., Pepitone, A., & Newcomb, T. (1952). Some consequences of deindividuation in a group. *Journal of Abnormal and Social Psychology, 47,* 382–389; Diener, E. (1979). Deindividuation, self-awareness, and disinhibition. *Journal of Personality and Social Psychology, 37,* 1160–1171; Dipboye, R. L. (1977). Alternative approaches to deindividuation. *Psychological Bulletin, 84,* 1057–1075.

37. Carver & Scheier (1981).

38. Lifton (1986).

39. Mintz, M. (1985). *At any cost: Corporate greed, women, and the Dalkon Shield.* New York: Pantheon Books.

40. Darley (in press).

41. McPherson (1988), p. 56.

42. McPherson (1988); Patterson, O. (1982). *Slavery and social death.* Cambridge, MA: Harvard University Press.

43. For example, Fagan, B. M. (1984). *Clash of cultures.* New York: W. H. Freeman.

44. Hare (1993), p. 43.

45. Kapuscinski (1984), pp. 112–113.

46. Hare (1993), p. 41.

47. Russell (1975).

48. Volkogonov, D. (1994). *Lenin: A new biography.* (H. Shukman, ed. and trans.). New York: Free Press, p. 72.

49. Baumeister, Stillwell, & Wotman (1990) found that perpetrators did often offer justifications, even acknowledging their wrongdoing. Their accounts thus had shades of gray, in contrast to the black-and-white absolutes of the victims' accounts.

50. Kunda (1990) has made this point effectively.

51. McGraw, K. M. (1987). Guilt following transgression: An attribution of responsibility approach. *Journal of Personality and Social Psychology, 53,* 247–256.

52. Fagan (1984).

53. Fagan (1984), p. 74.

54. Höehne (1979), pp. 434–438.

55. Höehne (1979), p. 437.

56. There are many sources for this, but Conquest (1990) is definitive.

57. Rodriguez, A., & Garcia, G. (1995). *Diary of a survivor: Nineteen years in a women's prison.* St. Martin's Press. Reprinted in *Today's best nonfiction.* Pleasantville, NY: Reader's Digest, p. 300.

58. Höss, R. (1992). *Death dealer: The memoirs of the SS Kommandant at Auschwitz.* S. Paskuly (Ed.). Buffalo, NY: Prometheus, p. 159.

59. Höss (1992), p. 163; translation augmented with Höehne (1994); p. 439.

60. Vallacher, R. R., & Wegner, D. M. (1985). *A theory of action identification.* Hillsdale, NJ: Erlbaum; Vallacher, R. R., & Wegner, D. M. (1987). What do

people think they're doing: Action identification and human behavior. *Psychological review*, *94*, 3–15.

61. Wegner, D. M., & Vallacher, R. R. (1986). Action identification. In R. M. Sorrentino & E. T. Higgins (Eds.), *Handbook of cognition and motivation* . New York: Guilford Press, pp. 550–582.

62. Hawk, D. (1985). The Cambodian way of death: 1975–1979. In E. Stover & E. O. Nightingale (Eds.), *The breaking of bodies and minds: Torture, psychiatric abuse, and the health professions.* New York: W. H. Freeman, p. 39.

63. Hawk (1985), p. 39.

64. Keegan (1976).

65. See Browning (1991), chapter 9.

66. Wyden (1983), p. 110.

67. Kolff, C. A., & Doan, R. N. (1985). Victims of torture: Two testimonies. In E. Stover & E. Nightingale (Eds.), *The breaking of bodies and minds: Torture, psychiatric abuse, and the health professions.* (pp. 45–57). New York: W. H. Freeman, p. 48.

CHAPTER 11 Ambivalence and Fellow Travelers

1. Peyser, M. "The death of little Elisa." *Newsweek*, Dec. 11, 1995, pp. 42–45, p. 42.

2. Peyser (1995), p. 42.

3. Prunier (1995), p. 277. The statistics on Rwanda are from earlier in the same source.

4. This account based on Morris (1965) and Pakenham (1979), (1991).

5. Miller, D. H. (1959). *Ghost dance*. Lincoln, NE: University of Nebraska Press.

6. Miller (1959).

7. Avedon, J. F. (1986). *In exile from the land of snows*. New York: Vintage/Random House.

8. Bauman (1991) addresses this issue. He says that whenever a Jew refused to cooperate, someone else did, so resistance was futile. But I think Arendt's view has to suppose that mass resistance, not individual resistance amid widespread cooperation, would have made a huge difference, and Bauman concedes that that might have been far more powerful. One has to look at it from the perpetrator's point of view; perpetrators need a certain amount of help, and if they get it from some it doesn't matter what the others do.

9. Carmichael (1992), p. 58.

10. Carmichael (1992), p. 102.

11. Brent, L. (1973). *Incidents in the life of a slave girl*. L. M. Child (Ed.). San Diego, CA: Harcourt Brace Jovanovich.

12. Pakenham (1991), p. 30.

13. Pakenham (1991), p. 30.

14. Pakenham (1991).

15. See the P.B.S. television documentary "Eyes on the Prize," vols. 1–3.

16. Höss (1992), p. 160.

17. Staub (1989).

18. Staub (1989), p. 87.

19. Staub (1989), pp. 185–187.

20. Korbin, J. E. (1986). Childhood histories of women imprisoned for fatal child maltreatment. *Child Abuse & Neglect, 10,* 331–338; Korbin, J. E. (1987). Incarcerated mothers' perceptions and interpretations of their fatally maltreated children. *Child Abuse & Neglect, 11,* 397–407; and especially Korbin, J. E. (1989). Fatal maltreatment by mothers: A proposed framework. *Child Abuse & Neglect, 13,* 481–489.

21. Gelles & Straus (1988). On the effects of arrest, see Sherman, L. W., & Berk, R. A. (1984). The specific deterrent effects of arrest for domestic violence. *American Sociological Review, 49,* 261–272; Sherman, L. W., & Smith, D. A. (1992). Crime, punishment and stake in conformity: Milwaukee and Omaha experiments. *American Sociological Review, 57,* 680–690.

22. Kapuscinski (1984), p. 111.

23. Kapuscinski (1984), p. 112.

24. Kapuscinski (1984), p. 114.

25. Kapuscinski (1984), p. 114.

26. Kapuscinski (1984), p. 115.

27. Kapuscinski (1984), p. 117.

28. Kapuscinski (1984), pp. 117–118.

29. Jankowski (1991).

30. Anastasia (19??), p. 226.

31. Roth (1964), p. 226.

32. Arendt, H. (1973). *The origins of totalitarianism.* New York: Harcourt Brace Jovanovich.

CHAPTER 12 Why Is There Evil?

1. Several recent, excellent works on these variables are available, including Tedeschi & Felson (1994); Geen, R. G. (1990). *Human aggression.* Pacific Grove, CA: Brooks/Cole; Baron, R. A., & Richardson, D. (1993). *Human aggression.* New York: Plenum.

2. To some extent, of course, the higher body count of the twentieth century reflects its technological superiority in weapons, as well, perhaps, as better

reporting and larger populations, as compared with prior eras. On the other hand, genocide is a distinctively modern crime (e.g., Bauman, 1991), governmental repression has reached exceptional levels of violence in many places, and with isolated exceptions the policy of waging international war against civilian populations is also quite modern. (Even World War I was mostly a contest between military forces, and did not target civilians.) A third line of argument might examine political forms, based on evidence that democracies do not generally start wars with each other, and so the progress of democracy should eventually pacify the globe; the twentieth century's worst carnage has involved totalitarian, communist, and fascist governments—but these are also modern. In any case, for present purposes it is sufficient to argue that civilization has thus far failed to reduce violence.

3. Sluka, J. A. (1992). The anthropology of conflict. In C. Nordstrom & J. Martin (Eds.), *The paths to domination, resistance, and terror* (pp. 18–36). Berkeley, CA: University of California Press, p. 19.

4. On Cambodia, Becker (1986); on Rwanda, Prunier (1995).

5. The statistics for 1995 suggest a drop in the total number of violent crimes, but this is attributed to a smaller population of young males. On a per capita basis they are more violent than ever, and many experts are predicting a further rise in crime when the large group of today's small boys reach adolescence.

Index

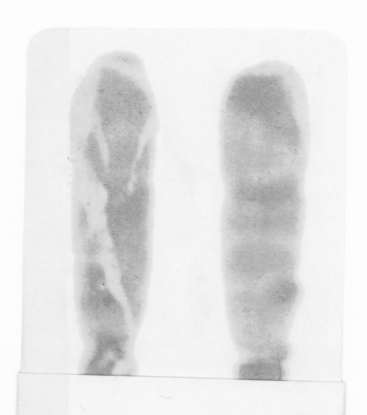